D0079520

FUNDAMENTALISM

Rebecca Joyce Frey

Foreword by Peter L. Berger
Director, Institute on Culture, Religion and World Affairs

GLOBAL ISSUES: FUNDAMENTALISM

Facts On File, Inc.
An imprint of Infobase Publishing
132 West 31st Street
New York NY 10001

ISBN 10: 0-8160-6767-8
ISBN 13: 978-0-8160-6767-1

Library of Congress Cataloging-in-Publication Data
Frey, Rebecca Joyce.
Fundamentalism / Rebecca Joyce Frey; foreword by Peter L. Berger.
p. cm. — (Global issues)
Includes bibliographical references and index.
ISBN 0-8160-6767-8 (alk. paper)
1. Religious fundamentalism. I. Title.
BL238.F75 2007
200.9'04—dc22 2006023364

Text design by Erika K. Arroyo
Cover design by Salvatore Luongo
Diagrams by Dale Williams

Printed in the United States of America

MP FOF 10 9 8 7 6 5 4 3 2 1

This book is printed on acid-free paper.

CONTENTS

Foreword

The term *fundamentalism* is a sort of sponge concept that has been used, usually with pejorative intent, to categorize a great variety of religious phenomena. The term originated within American Protestantism in the early part of the 20th century as a reaction against various modernizing and relativizing developments, both in the general culture and in the churches. Thus the term has a clear meaning in the context of the history of American Protestantism. Because of this, some have been skeptical about its extension to religious phenomena far beyond the boundaries of this particular community. Be this as it may, we are now stuck with this amplified application of the concept. In *Global Issues: Fundamentalism,* Rebecca Joyce Frey does her best to clarify the meaning of *fundamentalism* so that it will be useful for purposes of understanding the real world.

She opens her discussion by repudiating various negative stereotypes. It makes no sense to label every conservative or fervent religious movement as fundamentalist. Frey is probably wise in eschewing a brief, concise definition of her own. Instead, she lists a number of traits commonly ascribed to fundamentalism. The most important trait is described by the (not exactly elegant) term *reactivity:* Fundamentalist movements are always *reactions against* this or that alleged degeneration of a tradition. The other traits follow quite logically from this—such as a dualistic view of the world (either black or white, no shades of gray), an apocalyptic perspective (the world is in crisis, and this will get worse), "chosenness" (the members of the fundamentalist movement are an elect people), and separation from the world and strict behavioral controls (the controls are necessary to safeguard the separation from a wicked environment).

Two important points can be made here: (1) Fundamentalism is defined, not by its doctrinal contents, but by its *cognitive style.* Thus a non-fundamentalist adherent of a religious community can hold the same beliefs as the adherent of a fundamentalist movement emerging from this community, but the two affirm these beliefs in different ways—the latter in an uptight and militant manner that the former does not exhibit. What is more, the cognitive style of fundamentalism also exists in secular movements based on this or that ideology. And (2): There is an important difference between traditional religion and fundamentalism. The difference can be described by saying that traditional religion is one that is taken for granted in a particular social milieu. For that reason, it can be quite relaxed, even tolerant: The "other" is not a threat and may even be a source of entertainment. The belief system affirmed by the fundamentalist movement is, precisely, no longer taken for granted—it is under attack and its inevitability must be forcefully restored. In that case, the "other" is very much a threat, to be dealt with by separation, by conversion, and in the extreme case by physical elimination.

The difference can be illustrated by a piquant episode from the 19th century. Empress Eugénie, wife of Napoleon III, was on a state visit to Britain. She visited Covent Garden Opera in the company of Queen Victoria. Both personages made an impressive entrance to the royal box. Eugénie gracefully waved to the crowd, looked behind her, and sat down. Victoria waved just as gracefully, but she sat down without looking behind her. She knew with certainty that her chair would be under her.

The structure of the book is very coherent. The first three chapters contain Frey's elucidation of the concept, a concise history of fundamentalism in the United States, and a brief presentation of fundamentalist movements (Roman Catholic, Jewish, Muslim, and Hindu) outside the United States. The larger part of the book, then, contains aids for the prospective student of fundamentalism—primary documents, a guide to researching the topic, facts and figures, an extensive bibliography, lists of "key players" and organizations, a chronology, and a glossary.

This is an impressive work. Much erudition and care has produced a balanced account of an exceedingly complex phenomenon. The work is also highly suitable as a textbook, as it contains a wealth of primary texts and guides as to where to go for further information. I can only hope that Frey's massive effort will be rewarded by a wide readership.

— Peter L. Berger
Director, Institute on Culture,
Religion and World Affairs
Boston University

PART I

At Issue

1

Introduction

WHY STUDY FUNDAMENTALISM?

Religious fundamentalism is a phenomenon that must be taken seriously in the early 21st century. Not so long ago, it was regarded by many observers as a curiosity belonging to the past, an episode—or perhaps a series of episodes—in the institutional and intellectual history of American Protestantism, itself an area of limited interest for most academic historians. Anyone who would have predicted in the late 1970s that fundamentalism would become a force to be reckoned with in American politics within the next decade would have been greeted with polite skepticism at best. And anyone who would have concerned themselves with groups or movements in other religions resembling Christian fundamentalism would have had difficulty finding a publisher for his or her research.

In the late 1970s and 1980s, however, fundamentalism became once again a topic of concern as activists belonging to a variety of Christian churches or to new religious movements began to make headlines with their involvement in political matters, protests against "business as usual," or even more extreme behavior. In 1987 and 1988, a group of opponents of abortion formed a movement known as Operation Rescue. Led by a "born-again" evangelical Christian named Randall Terry, members of Operation Rescue sealed off access to abortion clinics, stood or sat down at entrances, and prayed or sang while they waited to be arrested for trespassing.[1] What was even more remarkable about Operation Rescue, however, was the participation of Roman Catholics, including priests and bishops. The Roman Catholic auxiliary bishop of New York, Austin Vaughan, was arrested six times in 1988 and 1989 for participating in Operation Rescue demonstrations; he had the distinction of being the first Roman Catholic bishop to be arrested by police in the history of the United States.[2] Antiabortion protests became even more extreme when such men as Paul Hill, who identified himself as a Presbyterian minister, shot and killed physicians who performed abortions. Hill was eventually executed by lethal injection in September 2003 for the 1994 murder of Dr. John Britton and his bodyguard, James Herman.

With regard to groups outside the mainstream Christian bodies, groups labeled by the media as "fundamentalist cults" emerged as a potentially serious social issue as early as the late 1970s. The tragedy at Jonestown, Guyana, in November 1978 foreshadowed the violent ends of other so-called doomsday cults: Nine hundred thirteen members of Jim Jones's utopian community "People's Temple," as well as a U.S. congressman and members of a United Press International film crew, lost their lives at Jamestown through what has been called mass murder-suicide. Later, such made-for-media events as the Branch Davidian disaster that occurred at Waco, Texas, in 1993 again brought the resurgence of extreme forms of religion to the public's attention. The Branch Davidians were originally an offshoot of the Seventh-Day Adventists, themselves a product of the Millerite movement of the mid-1840s and the failure of William Miller's prediction that Jesus would return to earth on October 22, 1844. Most Adventists are distinguished from other American Protestants chiefly by observing Saturday rather than Sunday as their holy day for worship. The Branch Davidians formed themselves into a communal group living in a compound near Waco known as Ranch Apocalypse and added to the general Adventist belief in the imminence of Christ's return the notion that their leader, David Koresh, was a prophet whose utterances were to be accepted on a level with the Bible. The group bought and sold guns, eventually amassing 11 tons of rifles and other firearms in the compound. When a group of employees of the federal Bureau of Alcohol, Tobacco, and Firearms failed in an initial attempt to arrest Koresh on charges of firearms violations in February 1993, the result was a two-month-long siege that ended in the burning of the compound and the deaths of all but eight of Koresh's followers.

In addition to the Branch Davidians, the acts of mass suicide of the members of the Order of the Solar Temple (who also stockpiled guns) in Switzerland in October 1994 and of the Heaven's Gate group in Rancho Santa Fe, California, in March 1997 also prompted many people to ask questions about the underlying causes and the timing of the formation of these "fundamentalist" groups. One feature writer for the *San Francisco Chronicle* summarized the reaction of large segments of the American public in his headline "The End to Innocent Acceptance of Sects."[3]

Nor were North American or European societies in which Christianity is (at least nominally) the majority religion the only ones affected by religious violence. In India, a mob of angry Hindus stormed and tore down the Babri Masjid, a 16th-century mosque in the town of Ayodhya, in 1992, thus adding another chapter to a long record of conflict between Hindus and Muslims predating the 1947 separation of Pakistan and Bangladesh from India. In

Israel, the massacre of 29 Muslims at prayer in the Cave of the Patriarchs in Hebron in February 1994 and the assassination of Prime Minister Yitzhak Rabin in November 1995 showed that Jewish religious extremists were also capable of violence. Within Israel, the city of Jerusalem was repeatedly troubled by episodes of violence involving the Temple Mount, a site holy to both Jews and Muslims that is under the control of a Muslim administrative body called the Waqf. The Israeli government has granted the Waqf virtually complete autonomy since 1967; the arrangement allows Jews to visit the Temple Mount in small numbers but not to pray there. In fact, an official from the Waqf usually accompanies the visitors to ensure that no Jewish prayers are offered. These limitations have provoked some Jewish fundamentalists and others who believe that the Jews of Israel should be allowed to rebuild a temple on the Temple Mount. On August 21, 1969, an Australian named Michael Dennis Rohan set fire to the al-Aqsa Mosque on the Temple Mount. Although Rohan was not a Jew, he told the police who arrested him that he was acting on divine instructions to destroy the mosque so that the Jews could build a temple in its place. This event would then bring about the second coming of Christ.[4] Twelve years after Rohan's attempted arson, an American-born Israeli Jewish soldier named Alan Goodman went into the al-Aqsa Mosque with an M-16 automatic rifle on April 11, 1981, and began a shooting spree in which he killed the Palestinian guard and wounded four other people. Goodman said that he intended to "liberate" the Temple Mount from Muslim control and start World War III.[5]

In sum, long before the events of September 11, 2001—when four teams of Muslim terrorists identified with one form of fundamentalist Islam hijacked four airplanes and flew three of them into targets in New York City and Washington, D.C.[6]—religious fundamentalism had resurfaced in the closing decades of the 20th century as a source of social division and political unrest. What changed after the 9/11 attacks on the World Trade Center and the Pentagon was not fundamentalism but the number of people who began to take it seriously.

STEREOTYPES OF FUNDAMENTALISTS

It is not easy to study or discuss either beliefs or specific individuals associated with fundamentalism without experiencing strong emotions. Like politics, religion stirs up intense feelings ranging from love and joy in some people to fear, anger, and disgust in others. On the one hand, many regard religion as a positive social good, providing a bond that helps to hold human societies together. The derivation of the English word *religion* from the Latin verb *religare,* which means "to tie" or "to bind fast," is sometimes cited as proof. On the other hand, many persons since the 18th century have held the opinion that religion either underlies or contributes to most of the world's economic and political problems, that it is an insult to the powers of the human mind, and that humanity would be altogether better off without such "superstition."

But it is precisely the need to discriminate between feelings about religion (whether positive, negative, or mixed) and intellectual understanding of the subject that makes a study of fundamentalism so important at this point in human history. In addition to seeking a better understanding of the origins and features of religious fundamentalism, thoughtful readers should learn to identify and challenge some of the misleading stereotypes of fundamentalist beliefs and practices that can still be found in academic communities as well as in the mass media. To give only one recent example, a professor of religious studies at the University of Kansas who had proposed to teach a course on "Special Topics in Religion: Intelligent Design, Creationism and Other Religious Mythologies" decided to cancel the course after he received heavy criticism for having sent a controversial e-mail to members of a student organization for agnostics and atheists. In the e-mail, the professor had referred to religious conservatives as "fundies" and added that his course would be "a nice slap in their big fat face." The chancellor of the university characterized the professor's comments as "repugnant and vile."[7]

This episode is only one of many others that could be mentioned. Another instance is the joking definition of a fundamentalist as "someone firmly committed to religious views I don't like."[8] Both the above news item and the attempt at humor are a useful introduction to the general subject of stereotypes about fundamentalists. A group of psychologists has proposed a list of seven such stereotypes[9]:

- *Fundamentalism is a separate religion.* Whether one regards fundamentalism as a list of doctrinal propositions to be believed or as a mindset and general outlook on life, it crosses over boundaries between the various Christian denominations and between different major religions. This characteristic has been true of fundamentalism since its first emergence within American Protestantism in the post–Civil War period.
- *Fundamentalists are literalists.* Groups resembling American Protestant fundamentalism have arisen within faiths that accord a high value to tradition as well as scripture, such as Roman Catholicism and certain Jewish groups. It is also possible for fundamentalist movements to develop within religions that do not have a clearly defined canon (agreed-upon list) of sacred texts, such as Hinduism.

- *Fundamentalists are militant.* Although many scholars define fundamentalism as a "militant" response to modern life,[10] there exist religious groups that separate themselves from the modern world in most respects and are not politically aggressive. The Old Order Amish of southern Pennsylvania and the Midwest, for example, reject higher education and many of the electronic devices and other conveniences that most Americans take for granted, but their centuries-long emphasis on the virtues of humility (*Demut* in their German dialect) and submission to the will of God and the collective wisdom of the Amish community does not encourage a militant posture toward the rest of American society. Another example is that of certain groups of traditionalist Roman Catholics who emphasize prayer, frequent communion, and similar pious practices as a way of withdrawing from the surrounding culture.
- *Fundamentalism is a complete rejection of modernity.* As will become evident in the sections on the history of fundamentalism in American Christianity and the descriptions of fundamentalist groups in other religions, fundamentalists have shown themselves surprisingly adept in their ability to make use of contemporary advances in technology—particularly travel and telecommunications—and the publicity techniques employed by the mass media to spread their message and maintain a sense of group identity.
- *Fundamentalism is a purely American Protestant phenomenon.* Although scholars disagree about the extent to which religious movements from different parts of the world and different faith traditions can be grouped together as fundamentalist, most would at least agree that there is a "family resemblance"[11] among these groups that justifies the use of the term until a better one can be found. In that sense, it can be said that there are "fundamentalisms" or "fundamentalist-like" movements within Judaism, Islam, and the religions of the East.
- *Fundamentalism is associated with an authoritarian personality structure.* In the years following World War II, such psychologists as Theodor Adorno and Max Horkheimer attempted to explain the rise of fascist and other totalitarian political ideologies by proposing that there is an "authoritarian personality" with identifiable character traits and that this personality structure is commonly found in people with right-wing political views.[12] Later research, however, has shown that there is little or no correlation between personality and political views. In fact, one 1996 study of German men who joined the SS (Nazi security service) between 1932 and 1934, the years of Adolf Hitler's rise to power, found that

these men were less likely to have the psychological underpinnings of an authoritarian personality than were men in the general population.[13] A more recent study of American college students reported that the most commonly used psychological test for measuring authoritarianism itself contains a built-in bias against religious belief.[14] Lastly, studies of people who have converted to fundamentalist faiths have found that the converts did not undergo major changes in personality; only their belief system changed.[15]

- *People who accept fundamentalist beliefs are either stupid, poorly educated, or hypocritical.* This stereotype is quite widespread among American academics, media people, and others who shape public opinion. With regard to fundamentalist clergy in particular, American intellectuals since the 1920s have often depicted these men (and a few women among them) either as knowing and intentional hypocrites—like the title character in Sinclair Lewis's 1927 novel *Elmer Gantry*—or as the intellectually deficient graduates of fifth-rate educational institutions. H. L. Mencken's description of the farmer-turned-preacher is a typical instance of this stereotype:

> *Any literate plowhand, if the Holy Spirit inflames him, is thought to be fit to preach. Is he sent, as preliminary, to a training camp, to college? But what a college! You will find one in every mountain valley of the land, with its single building in its bare pasture lot, and its faculty of half-idiot pedagogues and brokendown preachers. . . . This aspirant comes in from the barnyard, and goes back in a year or two to the village. His body of knowledge is that of a street-car motorman or a vaudeville actor. But he has learned the clichés of his craft . . . and so he has made his escape from the harsh labors of his ancestors, and is set up as a fountain of light and learning.*[16]

CHARACTERISTIC FEATURES OF FUNDAMENTALIST GROUPS

When studying any religious group, it is a good idea to begin with defining terms. In the case of fundamentalism, a discussion of terms and their proper use is doubly necessary because so many of the words associated with American fundamentalist movements have negative overtones. As the professor's reference to "fundies" in the incident mentioned earlier indicates, the word *fundamentalist* has strongly negative connotations for many people, largely on account of the stereotypes just listed. In fact, one network of independent fundamentalist congregations changed its name to a set of initials in order to escape the association of "fundamentalist" with "hatred" and such rituals as snake-handling.[17] That the network's action was not based on imagination is borne out by a series of surveys conducted every four years by a team of political scientists at New York University. The researchers found in 1988, 1992, and 1996 that almost a fifth of the general white non-fundamentalist public felt quite hostile toward fundamentalists, ranking them lower than poor people on welfare in social acceptability. The only group that the survey respondents considered less acceptable than religious fundamentalists was illegal aliens. With regard to highly educated respondents, 37 percent described themselves as "intensely antagonistic" toward fundamentalists.[18]

Following are nine features that characterize fundamentalist groups, as identified by a group of scholars associated with the Fundamentalism Project at the University of Chicago.[19] The first five concern ideology while the remaining four are organizational characteristics. The reader may find it worthwhile and interesting to look for these traits or features in the various movements described in chapters 2 and 3.

Concern about the Decline of Religion

The first characteristic feature of fundamentalism, which underlies all the others, is what the Chicago researchers term *reactivity.* A defensive or protective attitude toward religious belief is necessary, in their opinion, for a group or movement to qualify as fundamentalism.[20] The specific threat perceived by the group may come from general trends in the surrounding culture, from other religions or ethnic groups within the nation, from the state, or from more liberal members within the larger religious tradition.

Examples of such defensiveness are plentiful. In reacting against general secularizing trends in Israeli as well as American society, Haredi, or Ultra-Orthodox, Jews (*haredim*) practice a strategy of withdrawal from the world in which the yeshiva, or religious school, becomes the first line of defense.[21] The *haredim* also tend to cluster in specific neighborhoods of the cities in which they live and often pressure non-Haredi Jews or members of other religions to move elsewhere.[22] The *haredim* are intensely disliked by many secular Israelis for their attempts to force the entire nation to observe their strict regulations about keeping Sabbath. In addition, they are known for frequent protests in which they throw rocks at Sabbath-breakers, Mormon missionaries, Israeli police, or even archaeologists excavating areas the *haredim* consider sacred.[23] Meanwhile, Gush Emunim (GE), another group of activist Jewish fundamentalists involved in the settlement movement, was praised by the larger Israeli society for its opposition to the consumerist mentality that dominated Israel as well as other parts of the developed world in the early

1990s. GE spoke for others who "are troubled by capitalism's gleeful soullessness," as one writer put it.[24]

Defensive opposition to the larger society often produces hostility and violence toward other religious groups. Conflicts between Hindu and Muslim fundamentalists are a major ingredient in the ongoing religious violence in India. In Orissa, a state in eastern India on the Bay of Bengal, political organizations associated with Hindutva, a Hindu nationalist ideology, have begun to harass the Muslim and Christian minorities in the state. In 2002, riots occurred in Gujarat, on the western coast of India, when a group of Muslims set fire to a train carrying Hindu pilgrims. The next day Hindu mobs went into Muslim neighborhoods and torched homes and businesses and killed any Muslim they found. The Hindu groups have also been accused of mistreating Dalits, people outside the caste system formerly called untouchables.[25]

The ultratraditionalist movement within the Roman Catholic Church led by Archbishop Marcel Lefebvre illustrates a type of fundamentalism that develops as a reaction against fellow members of its own communion. Convinced that such documents of the Second Vatican Council as the Declaration on Religious Freedom or the Decree on Ecumenism were contrary to previous Catholic teaching, Lefebvre founded a society for priests that eventually separated from the church.[26] Lefebvre was also opposed to the council's revision of the Latin Mass, referring to the new liturgy as a "bastard" rite. He regarded the council's teaching on ecumenism (a movement that seeks to restore institutional unity among Christians) as equivalent to approving heresy. It is still not unusual in the early 2000s for members of Lefebvre's Society of St. Pius X (SSPX) to call other Roman Catholics "lukewarm" or "half-hearted" believers.[27] Some laypeople who worship in SSPX chapels have disrupted worship services in Catholic churches that they regard as "going too far" in the direction of ecumenical or interfaith conversations. In February 2004, a group from an SSPX chapel forced a group of Buddhist monks who had been invited to the Basilica of St. Adalbert in Grand Rapids, Michigan, to demonstrate traditional Buddhist chanting and prayers, to leave without giving the demonstration. The SSPX members, including several children, had occupied the front pews in the church and recited the rosary in loud voices to drown out the monks' prayers. One of the adults told a reporter, "We can't stand by while this irreligious group uses this beautiful basilica."[28]

Questions to keep in mind:

- What does the group consider evidence for the decline of religion?
- How does it respond to such evidence?
- Are its responses primarily defensive or does it take the offense?

Selective Emphasis

Another important characteristic of fundamentalist groups is their selective emphasis. Just as they pick and choose which features of modernity to accept and which to reject, they also highlight certain doctrines or practices of their religious tradition at the expense of others. They typically focus on certain specific aspects of the modern world as particularly objectionable and deserving of attack.

This selectivity was present in American Protestant fundamentalism from its beginnings in the post–Civil War period. Dwight L. Moody (1837–99), the founder of the Moody Bible Institute, was a famous revival preacher who tended to dwell on a short list of sins in his sermons. Preaching a sermon on the general subject of temptation, he told his listeners that there are "four great temptations that threaten us to-day": attending the theater, failing to keep the Sabbath holy (profaning the Sabbath included using public transportation as well as boating, fishing, or hunting), reading the Sunday newspapers, and teaching atheistic doctrines, including evolution. Other sins that Moody frequently preached against were drunkenness and selling alcohol, "telling vile stories," associating with "fallen women," being disrespectful toward one's parents, and indulging in "worldly amusements" in general.[29] In this he was typical of mainline as well as revivalist preaching of the Victorian era. Harriet Beecher Stowe, the author of *Uncle Tom's Cabin,* published a book in 1868 under the pen name Christopher Crowfield that took issue with churches' selective focus on peripheral issues: ". . . the only thing the Church has done is to forbid and frown. We have abundance of tracts against dancing, whist-playing, ninepins, billiards, operas, theatres,—in short, anything that young people would be apt to like."[30] This narrow focus became even narrower in the temperance crusade that led to Prohibition in 1919. Billy Sunday, an evangelist a generation younger than Moody, was famous for his "Booze sermon," in which he blasted the liquor industry as the cause of all the social and economic problems in the United States.

This selective emphasis is also what distinguishes the term *fundamentalist* from *conservative,* a term that is often used to describe fundamentalists in their attitude toward church doctrine (teaching). However, there are forms of doctrinal conservatism that are not at all fundamentalist, neither in their use of the Bible nor in their understanding of church tradition. For example, the two major confessional traditions, the Lutheran and the Reformed (or Calvinist), follow a doctrinal conservatism sometimes called *confessionalism.* Both churches are products of the Protestant Reformation of the 16th century, and clergy in these traditions are still expected to teach and preach in accordance with their respective confessions as well as the Scriptures. A form of conservatism that is closer to fundamentalism is *extreme traditionalism* or *ultratraditionalism,* which is found in the United States primarily in the Roman Catholic Church. Conservative Catholics generally prefer to draw a distinction between their acceptance of the changes in the church brought about by the Second Vatican Council and the suspicious attitude toward those changes held by ultratraditionalist Catholics. Some writers define extreme traditionalists as those believers who are "more Catholic than the Pope."[31]

One example of selective emphasis in retrieving the traditions of the mainstream religion can be found in contemporary Jewish Zionist fundamentalism. Some members of GE are less interested in the movement's political goals than in preserving the ceremonial aspects of temple worship, particularly ritual purity and offering sacrifices according to Old Testament descriptions. Some, for example, are preparing to serve as priests when the Temple Mount in Jerusalem is returned to Jewish control. Some members of GE even sneak onto the Temple Mount to pray, which is forbidden under the terms of the Israeli government's 1967 agreement with the Muslim religious authorities of Jerusalem. Others made a plan during Passover of 1989 to bring parts of an altar inside the Temple Mount, reassemble the altar, and offer a sacrifice. Still others have engaged in amateur archaeological digging under the Temple Mount in hopes of finding traces of the ancient Temple. In addition to these activists, some GE members weave cloth for the priestly vestments or participate in a research institute dedicated to reproducing the musical instruments and sacred vessels of the Temple. Lastly, a few GE fundamentalists are engaged in a high-technology genetic engineering project to produce a rare red heifer necessary for purifying contemporary Jews before they can go up to the Temple Mount. The purification ritual is described in chapter 19 of the book of Numbers in the Torah. Rabbinical tradition holds that all living Jews require this purification because they are contaminated by the impurity of their dead ancestors in the area of the destroyed Temple. GE gathered a group of rabbis, farmers, and geneticists in order to produce a heifer to fit the traditional specifications.[32]

The search for a ritually acceptable red heifer is a particularly interesting example of selective recovery of tradition because it is also a case study in interfaith convergence among fundamentalists. In 1990, Clyde Lott, a Christian fundamentalist minister in Mississippi, became interested in the red heifer described in Numbers 19 and sent a letter to the Temple Institute in Jerusalem to obtain more information. Rabbi Chaim Richman, a researcher on the staff of the Temple Institute, replied to Lott, and the two men worked together with GE to set up the breeding program cited above. Furthermore, they received some technical assistance as well as livestock from Texas ranchers who are fundamentalist Christians. In 1996, a red heifer was born but proved unacceptable when it reached the age to be sacrificed because several white hairs had appeared on its tail. A second heifer was born in March 2002 and has reawakened fears of a major conflict breaking out in Jerusalem between Jews and Muslims over anticipated fulfillment of biblical prophecies: Fundamentalist Jews may take the appearance of the new calf as a sign that Muslim occupation of the Temple Mount is about to end. As Richard Landes, a professor at Boston University, has been quoted as saying, "It's entirely conceivable that this [heifer] could trigger a new round of attempts to blow up the Dome of the Rock [a Muslim shrine on the Temple Mount]."[33] Fundamentalist Christians identified with Christian Zionism regard the construction of a new (third) temple as a necessary preliminary to Christ's return and the establishment of his millennial kingdom. Landes points out that it is unusual for Jewish and Christian apocalyptic currents to flow together as they have at this point in history. He believes that "This current alliance between Christian and Jewish religious Zionists can last only so long as the hopes remain high and the project does not succeed."[34]

Questions to keep in mind:

- What beliefs or practices does the group emphasize at present?
- Is there a leader or authoritative body who makes decisions about these emphases?
- What other beliefs and practices from the group's past fall into the background?

Dualistic Thinking

Dualistic thinking refers to a black-and-white, either/or approach to life in which people and events are rigidly sorted out and classified as either good or evil, pure or contaminated. This pattern of thought has resurfaced repeatedly in the history of religion. In Christianity, it fits the form of belief that H. Richard Niebuhr identified as the "Christ against culture" position, "the one that uncompromisingly affirms the sole authority of Christ over the Christian and resolutely rejects culture's claims to loyalty."[35] Total rejection of the world outside the church became a theme in the writings of some early Christian bishops and teachers. It accounted for the refusal of the 16th-century Anabaptists—the ancestors of the Amish—to participate in political life, and it motivated generations of monks and nuns to withdraw from worldly concerns into the cloister. Contemporary fundamentalists are in this respect part of a long history of separatist and oppositional groups.

The Church of God of Prophecy (CGP), headquartered in Cleveland, Tennessee, is in many respects typical of the "Christ against culture" position of Christian fundamentalists. It holds that the church was founded by Jesus but then fell away shortly after the death of the last apostle and was not restored until modern times. This belief in the church's corruption or loss of continuity at some point in its history is sometimes referred to as the "Great Apostasy." The CGP maintains that the purity of the church was partially restored by the 16th-century Anabaptist movement and the two Great Awakenings in the United States. The church's purification, however, was completed only in 1903, when Ambrose J. Tomlinson (1865–1943) became the leader of the group. Members of the CGP are committed to a belief in personal holiness maintained by "separation unto God" and abstaining from things of the world in accordance with Tomlinson's "teachings." Teaching 22, for example, strictly prohibits the use of alcohol, while Teaching 23 forbids smoking, and Teaching 26 forbids the wearing of gold jewelry, including wedding rings. Membership in Masonic lodges is forbidden by Teaching 27, and swearing oaths in court, by Teaching 28. Marriage to a "sinner" from the outside is unthinkable. Members who fail to live up to these teachings were once considered hopelessly lost.[36] Although the CGP no longer officially maintains that all Christians outside its own fellowship are necessarily on the fast track to hell, the group still appears to practice shunning of former members and members who attend services in churches of other denominations. Michael J. Ediger, who as a graduate student visited several CGP congregations to collect research, states that some members still believe that the CGP "is the only true church."[37]

Dualistic thinking is also present in such Muslim fundamentalist groups as the Jamaat-e-Islami of Pakistan or the Muslim Brotherhood in Egypt. Bernard Lewis attributes the persistence of such phrases as "the enemies of God" in Muslim fundamentalism to ideas that originated in Iran about the time of Zoroaster (1700 B.C.E.), the founder of a Persian religion. Although dualistic ideas also influenced Judaism and Christianity at various points in their respective histories, in Islam "the notion of the enemies of God assumed a much greater role . . . and could easily acquire political and even military dimensions."[38]

One important difference between Islamic fundamentalists and their Jewish and Christian counterparts, however, is that Muslim fundamentalists regard apostates (people who have fallen away from or renounced Islam) as a greater threat than infidels (people who have never been Muslims). Political murders in Islamic countries from the eighth century onward usually targeted rulers who were considered evil and therefore not true Muslims.

Contemporary Muslim fundamentalists, such as the members of a militant group called the Egyptian Islamic Jihad who assassinated President Anwar Sadat in October 1981, were much less upset by Sadat's making peace with Israel and establishing good relations with the United States than they were by his disestablishment of Islamic law and the introduction of Western customs and practices into Egypt.[39] It did not help matters that Sadat and his half-English wife "had a glitzy Western lifestyle."[40] The group that planned and carried out the assassination compared Sadat to the Mongol rulers of the 14th century, who were considered apostates after their conversion to Islam because they ruled according to their own laws instead of Islamic law.[41] What the fundamentalists wanted to bring about in place of Westernization was the "Islamization" of Egyptian society.[42]

Questions to keep in mind:

- Who or what does the group consider its opposition?
- Does it regard more than one religion, nation, race, or other group as its opposition?
- Does the group regard its opposition as a spiritual enemy, a political enemy, or both?

Absolutist Interpretation of Scripture or Tradition

Another common characteristic of fundamentalist groups is a strict or absolutist reading of the group's holy books or, in some cases, accepted traditions. The term *literalist* is not always appropriate in describing the way that fundamentalists read sacred texts. It is more accurate to say that fundamentalists reject modern methods of interpretation, such as those used by secular philosophers or literary critics, as applicable to their holy books. According to the author of *The Psychology of Religious Fundamentalism,* "The wisdom of fundamentalism is that to lose the objectivity of the sacred text as a revelation from a Divine Being is to lose its authority altogether. . . . It is this objective claim to truth that fundamentalists insist on. It does not demand a consistent literalism for all that is said in a sacred text. In fact, an objective understanding of the text requires an appreciation for when it is and is not appropriate to treat the text 'literally.' . . . the text itself reveals when it is and is not appropriate to take it literally."[43]

An interesting American example of an absolutist interpretation of a text outside mainstream Christianity is the Mormon doctrine of blood atonement. This teaching should not be confused with the classical Christian teaching about Christ's death on the cross. Blood atonement refers to the execution of Mormon apostates, or members of the group who had committed unpardonable sins. There exist at least two sermons preached by Brigham Young (1801–77), the second leader of the Church of Jesus Christ of Latter-day Saints (LDS), in which he stated his view of blood atonement publicly. The first was delivered on September 21, 1856:

> *There are sins that men commit for which they cannot receive forgiveness in this world, or in that which is to come, and if they had their eyes open to see their true condition, they would be perfectly willing to have their blood spilt upon the ground, that the smoke thereof might ascend to heaven as an offering for their sins; and the smoking incense would atone for their sins, whereas, if such is not the case, they will stick to them and remain upon them in the spirit world. . . . And further more, I know that there are transgressors, who, if they knew themselves, and the only condition upon which they can obtain forgiveness, would beg of their brethren to shed their blood, that the smoke thereof might ascend to God as an offering to appease the wrath that is kindled against them, and that the law might have its course. . . . It is true that the blood of the Son of God was shed for sins through the fall and those committed by men, yet men can commit sins which it can never remit.*[44]

In a similar sermon preached on February 8, 1857, Young declared that a devout Mormon was obliged to shed the blood of those who were guilty of unforgivable sins so that they would not lose their chance of salvation: "I could refer you to plenty of instances where men have been righteously slain, in order to atone for their sins. I have seen scores and hundreds of people for whom there would have been a chance . . . if their lives had been taken and their blood spilled on the ground as a smoking incense to the Almighty, but who are now angels to the Devil. . . . This is loving our neighbor as ourselves; if he needs help, help him; and if he wants salvation and it is necessary to spill his blood on the earth in order that he may be saved, spill it."[45] A number of murders have been attributed to a Mormon vigilante group called the Danites. The murders were carried out in obedience to Young's doctrine of blood atonement between 1845, when the Mormons moved westward from Illinois, and the 1870s.

Young's stature as Joseph Smith's successor meant that many of his followers took his words as the equivalent of the Scriptures. Blood atonement was a teaching that some felt should be observed to the letter even in the 20th century. In 1972, a Mormon fundamentalist group leader named Ervil LeBaron began to order the killing of some of his opponents in the name of blood atonement. In July 1984, two brothers who practiced polygamy became angry at their sister-in-law for refusing to allow her husband to take plural wives. They broke into the brother's house one morning after he had gone to work and cut the throats of his wife and 15-month-old daughter.[46]

Even in the mainstream LDS church, the doctrine of blood atonement was accepted by many 20th-century believers. It is thought to explain why Utah was the last state in the Union to allow persons condemned to death the option of execution by firing squad. Some devout Mormons still appear to think that blood atonement is necessary even for members of their own families who are guilty of serious crimes. An example of this persistence is the case of Mark Hofmann, a dealer in rare books and documents who forged a number of letters, certificates, and transcriptions purportedly written by Smith, Young, and other figures in the early history of the Mormon church. Some of these fake documents contained material that, if genuine, would have severely damaged the church because they portrayed Smith as a con artist and dabbler in folk magic. Hofmann sold some of his forgeries to LDS leaders for large sums of money, assuming that they would purchase the documents in order to prevent their falling into the hands of "unbelievers" who would use them to hurt the church's reputation. The tense relationship between the Mormon hierarchy and independent scholars, which is an important part of the story, is described more fully below in the section on behavioral controls.

When Hofmann began to have financial problems in October 1985, he killed two innocent people with pipe bombs in order to keep his creditors from pursuing him. He hoped the bombings would be taken as the work of Mormon fundamentalists out to exact blood atonement from those who had purchased the scandalous papers. In actual fact, the Salt Lake County District Attorney's Office as well as several people in the church hierarchy speculated that the bombs had been planted by a new group of Danites.[47] The most compelling testimony, however, to the faithfulness of contemporary Mormons to Young's words about blood atonement came from Hofmann's father. Bill Hofmann stated that if his son had committed the pipe bomb murders, he must "admit his guilt, request a firing squad, and have his blood spilled to atone for his sin. It was the only way he could be reunited with the family in eternity."[48]

Questions to keep in mind when looking at the teaching of a religious group:

- What are the sources of the group's doctrine? Are they written, unwritten, or both?
- Who are regarded as qualified or competent interpreters of the group's teachings? The leaders? All the members?

Apocalyptic View of History

The word *apocalyptic* derives from a Greek word that means "to uncover" or "to reveal" and refers to a type of literature that is said to contain hidden mysteries, including the secrets of the end of history. These mysteries are usually described as revelations from God to a chosen prophet in a dream or vision or through an angelic messenger. Apocalyptic writings are part of Muslim religious tradition as well as the Hebrew and Christian Scriptures. The book of Daniel in the Old Testament is well known to Christians as well as Jews. Other Jewish apocalyptic writings include the so-called Assumption of Moses, written around the time of Jesus, and the Apocalypse of Baruch, which was originally written in Greek some time after the fall of Jerusalem to the Romans in 70 C.E. In the New Testament, Matthew 24 and the corresponding passages in Mark and Luke, 1 Thessalonians, and the book of Revelation (sometimes simply called "the Apocalypse") are the most commonly cited examples of apocalyptic writings.

The desire of some Jewish fundamentalists in Israel to obtain a red heifer for ritual sacrifice and the assistance given them by some Christian fundamentalists have already been mentioned as an example of interfaith cooperation in the selective use of scripture and religious tradition. The episode can also be studied as an example of a common interest in the apocalyptic, even though the two faiths have different scenarios about the end of history. According to Landes, one reason why the failure of the red heifer project would be a better outcome than its success is that the successful rebuilding of the Temple would bring to the surface the different belief systems of Jewish and Christian fundamentalists: ". . . the messianic Jews [expect that] the Christians will abandon their idol worship of Jesus and become righteous gentiles, [while] the Rapture Christians [expect that] Jews will abandon their blind ways and convert to the worship of Jesus. These apocalyptic expectations are bound to fail."[49]

To turn to the Muslim apocalyptic view, a recent development is its apparent fascination with the United States. This preoccupation is new, because the United States did not exist at the time of the compilation of the hadith, or traditions handed down about the sayings and deeds of Muhammad and his companions. The hadith mention all the other parts of the known world, including Europe. The omission of North (and South) America in the hadith, however, is perceived by Muslims themselves as a problem when it comes to searching sacred texts for revelations about the end of the world. One modern Muslim apocalyptic writer has said, "Why did God not mention America in the Qur'an, and the Prophet not mention it in the prophetic hadith? This is a question which every Muslim has asked himself, and has been confused in finding the answer to it."[50]

According to one scholar, the need to account for a nation not mentioned in the hadith as well as the existence of the modern state of Israel has led to a new style of Qur'anic interpretation that mixes classical Islamic traditions with an anti-Semitic conspiracy theory and apocalyptic imagery ultimately borrowed from Protestant interpretations of the Bible.[51] It is not unusual for contemporary Muslim writers of apocalyptic literature to have strange ideas about the history and government of the United States because of this conspiracy theory. One popular Palestinian writer has stated that the U.S. Constitution as ratified in 1787 already required support for Israel, and the president cannot be legally elected without swearing an oath to abide by the demands of the Israeli government.[52]

Recent Muslim fascination with the year 2000 appears to have been derived from millenarian speculations by evangelical Protestants. One Muslim writer predicted that a great battle would take place in the Mediterranean Sea in 2000, to be followed by a nuclear war between France and the United States in 2001. The waters of the oceans would then rise and "swallow up New York."[53]

Some Muslim apocalyptic writers have decided that the mysterious people of 'Ad, mentioned in the Qur'an about two dozen times, must refer to the United States. This citation of the Qur'an is an innovation because it was never used in previous centuries as a source of proof-texts for apocalyptic writings. The earliest commentaries on the Qur'an do not identify Ad with any clarity, although they suggest that the people of Ad were nomads, that they had ambitious building projects, and that God destroyed them for violating the limits he has placed on humankind. There are obvious parallels here to the story of the Tower of Babel in Genesis 11. Bashir Muhammad Abdallah, the writer who first popularized the notion that Ad represents the United States, maintains that God is already judging America for its offenses—its secular humanism; its refusal to convert to Islam; the sexual sins of President Bill Clinton, who was elected in the first place by "the votes of perverts"; American contributions to the supposedly Jewish-controlled International Monetary Fund; and the nation's "unlawful" arrogance, generated by such technological advances as weather forecasting, organized sports, and nuclear weapons.[54]

Muslim speculations about the role of the United States at the end of history take several different forms. One is that the country is ruled by an Antichrist figure called the Dajjal, with the help of the world Zionist conspiracy. It is commonplace for Muslim writers to identify the Dajjal as the current U.S.

president, although some authors name Henry Kissinger, Clint Eastwood, Burt Lancaster, and even the popular magician David Copperfield. At the end of the Dajjal's rule, there will be a great earthquake that will destroy not only the United States but such other enemies of Islam as Hindus, Buddhists, and "sun-and-emperor worshippers in Japan." There will next be two great battles in which the Dajjal's Jewish supporters will be slaughtered in Jerusalem by the victorious Muslims, who will then invade Europe and destroy "the idolatrous church in the Vatican."[55]

A second type of Muslim apocalyptic scenario concerns the Mahdi, a messiah-like figure. In these narratives, the United States is typically punished for resisting the Mahdi's efforts to establish a Muslim empire. An interesting feature of these contemporary Muslim writings is their frequent reference to modern military and transportation technology: The Western powers use flying saucers as well as nuclear missiles in their initial campaigns against the Mahdi, and the Mahdi's victory over the West is accomplished with the use of nuclear weapons. The writers "clearly want to be Westerners, but without the elements of Western civilization which made the technological leap possible in the first place."[56]

Questions to keep in mind:

- What are the literary and cultural sources of the group's view of the end times?
- Who are the writers or compilers of its apocalyptic scenarios?
- What historical or current events appear or are emphasized in its apocalyptic writings?

Belief in Election or Chosenness

Another trait of fundamentalist groups is a belief in their own specialness or election. This conviction is closely related to their dualistic thought patterns, which divide the world's population into the saved and the unsaved, the chosen and the rejected. This pattern has already been noted in the members of the CGP. Fundamentalist or traditionalist groups may refer to themselves by such terms as the "faithful remnant," "the elect," "the righteous few," or similar phrases.

In 1967, some traditionalist Roman Catholic laypeople in Minnesota started a newsletter called *The Remnant,* which takes its name from the reference to "a remnant, chosen by grace" in Romans 11:5. It is considered the oldest traditionalist publication in the United States. *The Remnant* is concerned with fighting what it considers irresponsible innovations in liturgy and doctrine in the Catholic Church, but the editors state that the publication is "not interested in starting its own Church or in crowning its own 'traditional' pope." The editors, however, obviously consider themselves an embattled tiny flock: "The editors of *The Remnant* recognize that it is only a very small and limited instrument against the forces of Modernism which presently have the Bride of Christ by the throat. But it is a small effort that, in its small way, continues to at least try to do something to oppose the prevailing madness within the Church and within the world today."[57]

In some fundamentalist groups, the sense of being special or chosen for divine purposes is reinforced by a division within the group between "ordinary" or less committed members and an inner core of people who are fully committed. The Rashtriya Swayamsevak Sangh (RSS), a Hindu fundamentalist organization for men only, imposes a strict regimen on its members. Training includes education in the ideology of Hindutva, physical exercise, daily worship meetings, and obedience to a hierarchy of leaders. All members wear the same uniform (khaki shorts, white shirts, and a black cap or beret), but only those set aside to recruit new members and start new branches of the RSS are expected to remain celibate. These field workers or organizers are also expected to live on a minimal stipend that pays only their basic living expenses.[58] At the top of the RSS hierarchy is a single leader, the *sarsanghachalak,* who is appointed (for life) by his predecessor.

Questions to keep in mind:

- How does the group define election or chosenness?
- Is the group divided between fully committed and less committed members with less stringent demands made on the latter, or are all members required to observe the same level of discipline?
- Does the group actively recruit new members or does it believe the "chosen ones" will find the group of their own accord?

Separation from the World

Dualistic thinking and a sense of chosenness lead some fundamentalist groups to draw sharp boundaries between themselves and the outside world. These boundaries may be physical, as in the case of the Jewish fundamentalist settlements in Israel, the closing off of urban neighborhoods by the *haredim,* or the building of new communities in rural areas of the West by Mormon fundamentalists. Some of the latter have moved to Mexico or Canada in order to establish settlements beyond the reach of United States law.[59] Other groups may separate themselves from the world by renouncing certain modern inventions and conveniences, as do the Old Order Amish, or by requiring members to live within walking distance of a synagogue, as do the *haredim.* Control over access to television and other communications media is yet another means of enforcing separation. A science teacher who was interviewed by a researcher investigating fundamentalist Mormons called the researcher's attention to a broken television satellite dish lying by the roadside. The teacher explained that members of the group are forbidden to read magazines and newspapers, let alone watch television. But because "forbidden fruit" is always more attractive than what is permitted, people sometimes secretly purchase a dish and watch television as much as they like. "Then one Sunday [the leader of the fundamentalist group] will give one of his sermons about the evils of television. He'll announce that he knows *exactly* who has one, and warn that [they are] putting their eternal souls in serious jeopardy. Every time he does that, a bunch of satellite dishes immediately get dumped in the desert, like this one here."[60]

For fundamentalists who cannot or choose not to separate themselves from the world by geographical or technological restrictions, items of dress may serve as markers instead. In Israel, the knitted skullcap, or *kippah* (yarmulke), was identified with members of GE; some Israeli journalists even spoke of a "knitted skullcap culture" of "self-assured religious youth who are not apologetic about their piety."[61] The young Indian men who belong to the Hindu RSS wear a distinctive uniform that was described in the preceding section. Uniforms are also favored by the members of Christian Identity groups, which are extreme right-wing white-power organizations opposed to the "Zionist occupational government" of the United States. The men of Aryan Nations (AN), a Christian Identity group that built a military-style compound in Hayden Lake, Idaho, in the 1970s, chose uniforms consisting of navy-blue poplin jackets, blue trousers, white shirts, and blue ties, while their wives wore blue or white blouses and skirts.[62]

In Europe and the United States, perhaps the most controversial item of dress as a visual marker of separation is the *hijab,* or head covering, worn by Muslim women. The *hijab* was imposed on the women of Iran after the overthrow of the shah in 1979.[63] Since the events of September 11, 2001, and the July 7, 2005, bombings of the London public transportation system, various institutions and regulatory bodies in the United States and Britain have banned the wearing of *hijabs* on the grounds that they obscure the wearer's face and thus pose problems for security. The best-known instance of this decision in the United States occurred in 2003, when a Florida judge ruled that the head covering must be removed for the photograph on the state driver's license. The judge remarked, "Although the court acknowledges that plaintiff herself most likely poses no threat to national security, there likely are people who would be willing to use a ruling permitting the wearing of full-face cloaks in driver's license photos by pretending to ascribe to religious beliefs in order to carry out activities that would threaten lives."[64] Imperial College London instituted the ban in November 2005,[65] while the European Court of Human Rights upheld Turkey's ban on the *hijab* in universities "to maintain order and avoid giving preference to any religion."[66] The banning of Islamic dress for women in Western countries has provoked controversy because it interferes with the free practice of religion in the eyes of some observers. On the other hand, it appears to contribute to non-Muslims' growing resentment of the Muslim minority in many European countries, particularly after the July 2005 bombings in London. The *Hindu News,* an Indian journal, reported in August 2005 that Muslim women in Britain were being advised to stop wearing head coverings in order to lower the risk of verbal or even physical attacks.[67]

Questions to keep in mind:

- What techniques does the group use to enforce separation from the outside world?
- Does the group seek government recognition of or legal protection for its distinctiveness or separation?
- Are outsiders prohibited from visiting, interviewing, photographing, or communicating with members of the group?

Charismatic Style of Leadership

In general, mainstream religious groups in American Judaism and Christianity are characterized by a high level of specialized training for their clergy. Most bodies require a three- or four-year course of study in a theological school or rabbinical seminary following completion of a bachelor's degree to meet the educational requirements for ordination. In addition to demonstrating intellectual competence, candidates are usually evaluated for psychological stability and spiritual maturity in the course of field placements in local congregations or hospital chaplaincy programs. These evaluations may take the form of meetings with candidacy committees, written reports from the field work supervisor, completing a battery of psychological tests, an interview with a clinical psychologist or psychiatrist, or all four. The length of the candidacy process is partly a reflection of the spread of the therapeutic mindset within the mainstream religious bodies; it is also a response to the sexual misconduct scandals that were widely publicized in the 1980s and 1990s. Numerous books, some of them written by medical rather than religious professionals, poured out of the denominational publishing houses to help bishops and other leaders identify clergy and seminarians at risk of sexual misconduct or a psychiatric disturbance (e.g., depression) that would compromise their ability to minister to parishioners. One author estimated the proportion in the Protestant churches to be as high as 30 percent.[68] What the present academic and psychiatric evaluations demand of ministerial candidates is a high level of self-control and apparent "normality"—students with eccentric or highly emotional personalities, or who claim to speak in tongues or see visions, are likely to be weeded out of most seminary programs long before graduation.

In Christian fundamentalist groups, by contrast, ordination—whether marked by a formal ceremony or simply by acclamation and acceptance by the members of the group—is tied much more closely to demonstrations of spiritual gifts, conversion experiences, and similar phenomena. This model of leadership is called *charismatic,* after the Greek word for "favor" or "grace." It is one reason why women were accepted as ministers in these churches at an earlier point in time than they were in the mainstream bodies.[69] It also helps to explain why fundamentalist churches prefer a congregational polity. It is easier for a pastor with a charismatic personality to establish or increase the membership of a congregation by force of interpersonal charm or compelling sermons when he or she is not constrained by bishops or other denominational higher-ups. In addition, this type of polity simplifies the process of starting a new congregation if one is having difficulty with a senior pastor or the lay leadership in one's present church home.

The drawbacks of a charismatic leadership style, however, are equally obvious. They can lead to a cultlike intensity of relationship between pastor and flock that may end in sexual misconduct or other forms of abuse. One instance from the 1980s that involved "a bright, self-assured, powerful individual whose charisma was instantly infectious" nearly brought about the destruction of an entire congregation.[70] In addition to its potential for interpersonal problems, charismatic leadership encourages and speeds up internal splits within denominations with a congregational polity. When there is no hierarchical church structure to contain the effects of disputes between strong personalities, one or both may simply decide to start a new denomination as well as a congregation. The history of the CGP, for example, contains recurrent episodes of division as a succession of strong-willed leaders broke with the parent body in Tennessee and took their followers with them. The history of splits within the Mormon church after the death of Joseph Smith in 1844 is another example of personality conflicts within the leadership that could not be resolved because the new denomination placed a high value on charisma—particularly the gift of prophecy—as a qualification for succeeding Smith.

Lastly, a charismatic model of leadership presents difficulties for the long-term strength and continuity of a fundamentalist group. Groups drawn together by the force of one individual's personality are likely to be weakened or even dispersed when he or she dies (or is otherwise removed from leadership). For example, Rabbi Moshe Levinger, the acknowledged leader of GE, is widely regarded as having a compelling personality, even by those who regard him as a disturbingly effective troublemaker rather than a servant of God. As "the face of the settlement movement,"[71] Levinger has been chosen as "man of the year" several times by the Israeli press and once as "man of the decade," on a par with Israeli statesman Menachem Begin.[72] The obvious question in the minds of many analysts is what will happen to GE when Levinger is no longer its leader.

At this point, a definition of the terms *church, cult,* and *sect* is in order. Like *fundamentalism* itself, the last two terms have negative overtones. Originally, however, scholars who tried to classify religious groups and movements intended *cult* and *sect* to be neutral descriptions rather than value judgments. Scholars of religion today generally agree on the following definitions[73]:

- *church:* a conventional religious organization
- *sect:* a deviant religious organization with traditional beliefs and practices
- *cult:* a deviant religious organization with novel beliefs and practices

To give some specific examples using fundamentalist groups, the Southern Baptist Convention (SBC) is a church that prefers a charismatic style of leadership but is otherwise conventional in its teaching and forms of worship. Such well-known preachers as Billy Graham and Jerry Falwell were either ordained by or have chosen to affiliate with the SBC. With regard to less conventional fundamentalist groups, those that practice snake-handling (mostly limited to the U.S. South) are considered sects because they share traditional Christian beliefs and such traditional practices as baptism and communion, worship on Sunday, and Bible reading, hymn singing, prayer, and preaching as part of worship. They are deviant insofar as snake-handling is opposed by most Christians and is against the law in almost all the states where it is practiced.

By contrast, Aum Shinrikyō, the Japanese group that released a nerve gas into the Tokyo subway system in 1995, can be fairly described as a cult. Shōkō Asahara, the leader of Aum, had put together an unusual assortment of beliefs taken from Buddhism, New Age thought, Hinduism, and

Christianity. He told his followers that he was the reincarnation of Buddha, Vishnu, and Christ, and that he could control the world by means of his brain waves.[74] In terms of strange practices, Asahara subjected Aum members to violent or punitive treatment as part of their "training" for membership. Some were placed in containers of very hot or cold water, while others were put in solitary confinement for days on end or made to hang by their feet for several hours.[75] The abuse was justified as a way to prepare them for the end of the world. The deviancy of Aum was reflected in the 80 murders it committed from 1988 onward. The individuals marked for death were those who either tried to leave the cult or inform the authorities about previous murders.[76]

Questions to keep in mind when looking at the leadership of a religious group:

- How are the group's leaders identified and trained? Do they undergo any kind of examination process?
- Is anyone in the group a potential leader, or are some persons automatically excluded on the grounds of sex, race, ethnic identity, or other factors?

Strict Behavioral Controls

The last organizational characteristic of fundamentalist groups to consider is behavioral controls. Some forms of control, such as restricting access to secular media or building small communities in remote areas, have already been mentioned. Others include filling the members' time with obligatory meetings or religious rituals, censoring or suppressing the work of educators or other intellectuals, and threatening or carrying out extreme measures—including death—to keep would-be dissidents in line.

With regard to frequent prayer or other meetings, GE is an instance of this method of behavioral control within fundamentalist Judaism. Just as the movement measures a settler's virtue by the number of children in his family and the hardships he endures by choosing to live in a settlement, it evaluates him in regard to the number of hours per day he spends in Torah study or prayer. Members of GE apparently believe that the length of time required to fulfill one of the ceremonial precepts of Judaism is a direct measure of the worshipper's seriousness. The core membership participates in three lengthy daily services as well as more elaborate observances on the Sabbath and holy days, in addition to reciting blessings or prayers over food, when traveling, or when using the bathroom. These pious practices take up far more time than that spent in prayer by most Orthodox Jews.[77]

The RSS offers a Hindu example of this type of behavioral control. Members are expected to attend at least one session of physical exercise (lasting more than an hour) each day as well as participating in a ritual salute to the RSS banner, followed by several hours of instruction and debate. Public marches are another time-consuming activity for RSS members.[78]

A Christian example in the United States is found in the student handbook of Bob Jones University in South Carolina. Students are not only expected to attend all classes and daily chapel but also required to be present for nightly prayer meetings on weekdays, Sunday morning worship and Sunday school on campus, weekly society meetings, and Bible Conference services.[79] They must also take at least one course in Bible every semester to fulfill graduation requirements.[80]

The issue of fundamentalist schools in Western countries leads into a second aspect of behavioral control in fundamentalist groups—limitations on academic freedom, which is considered vital to scholarly research and publication. Curiously, the most restrictive group in the United States with regard to its intellectuals is most likely the mainstream Mormon church rather than the Protestant fundamentalist churches. The LDS as a religious body is admittedly difficult to classify. It can be variously considered "a sect, a mystery cult, a new religion, a church, . . . or an American subculture; indeed, at different times and places it is all of these."[81] Since the 1970s, the LDS has disfellowshipped (a probationary phase prior to excommunication) or excommunicated several history professors or other writers for having published books that bring up unattractive or scandalous aspects of early Mormon history, that take issue with the Mormon church's attitude toward women, or that question certain aspects of Mormon theology.[82] Even though conservative takeovers of such bodies as the Lutheran Church–Missouri Synod (LCMS) in the 1970s and the SBC in the 1980s resulted in the firing or voluntary resignation of some seminary presidents and professors,[83] these churches were more concerned with modern methods of biblical interpretation than with denominational history, and in any event they did not revoke anyone's baptism or excommunicate them.

There are three basic reasons for the LDS church's disciplining of academics and intellectuals, especially historians. One is the relatively short history of Mormonism; of all the major religious groups in the United States, the LDS is the only one younger than the nation itself. This factor means that all the basic documents of Mormonism—its sacred texts as well as early letters, diaries, sermons, court records, and similar written material—are available for examination by modern historical and forensic methods of analysis. The second reason is the Mormon belief in continuing revelation through recent prophets, from Smith to the present "Prophet, Seer, and Revelator" Gordon

B. Hinckley. Because of this doctrine, historical documents that call into question certain aspects of Smith's or Young's character are deeply disturbing to the authorities.

The third reason is the absence of a professionally trained clergy: Mormons do not have theological seminaries or other graduate institutions for the training of ministers. The religious services in an LDS ward (congregation) are conducted by male volunteers who have been admitted to one of the ranks of the Mormon priesthood. Any devout boy over the age of 12 is eligible to become a priest by age 18. If he is then selected to go on a two-year mission to convert others to Mormonism, he receives further instruction and becomes an elder. Elders are expected to support themselves; they are not paid by the church. As a result, Mormons in the upper reaches of the church hierarchy are businessmen, lawyers, accountants, engineers—they are not usually scholarly researchers. And none of them are women.

Problems between the LDS hierarchy and its historians began in 1972, when Leonard Arrington (1917–99) was appointed the denomination's official church historian, the only professional academic to have held that position as of the early 2000s. Arrington had founded the Mormon Historical Association in 1965 and was considered a fine scholar by historians outside the church. As church historian, he opened up the church's archives to younger researchers who began to publish articles on polygamy and other topics not considered "faith-promoting." The authorities responded by cutting funding and eventually transferring Arrington's department to Brigham Young University. Arrington himself was removed from his position in 1982. Clashes between the hierarchy and other scholars and writers continued intermittently in the 1980s and early 1990s, culminating in the expulsion of the so-called September Six in September 1993. Among those disciplined was D. Michael Quinn, widely considered an outstanding historian by his academic peers. According to the *Sunstone Review,* a publication devoted to "open forums of Mormon thought and experience," arguments between the church hierarchy and Mormon intellectuals are an ongoing problem.[84] Others have characterized the Mormon leadership as "obsessed with controlling how the Mormon past is interpreted and presented."[85]

The attitude of the LDS in this regard is quite different from that of other American evangelical and fundamentalist churches, almost all of whose seminaries have moved toward less theological separatism and greater academic respectability.[86] One indication of this change is the number of these institutions that are members of the Association of Theological Schools (ATS), the major accrediting body for graduate programs in religion and theology in Canada as well as in the United States. Of the 251 schools presently accredited by the ATS, somewhere between 30 and 40 of the 193 that are Protestant are either interdenominational evangelical or fundamentalist seminaries, or affiliated with conservative denominations.[87]

The last form of behavior controls to be considered is the use of fear of violence to keep not only dissidents within the group in line but also those outside. This combination is most evident in recent years in regard to Muslim fundamentalism. As was mentioned earlier, there is a tradition within Islam of punishing apostasy with death. One reason commonly given in the Western press for the silence of moderate Muslims following such events as the 1989 fatwa issued in the wake of publication of Salman Rushdie's novel *The Satanic Verses*[88] and the murder of the filmmaker Theo van Gogh in Amsterdam in November 2004 is that the moderates are afraid of being killed also. It was revealed shortly after van Gogh's murder that the Muslim deputy mayor of Amsterdam had been placed on a death list by the same group that had targeted van Gogh.

Questions to keep in mind when looking at the lifestyle of a religious group:

- What types of behavioral controls, if any, are used?
- Are members expected to dress in a distinctive way?
- Is violence used to keep members of the group from leaving?

---

[1] A detailed account and sociological analysis of Operation Rescue may be found in Faye Ginsburg. "Saving America's Souls: Operation Rescue's Crusade against Abortion." In Martin E. Marty and R. Scott Appleby, eds. *Fundamentalisms and the State: Remaking Polities, Economies, and Militance.* Chicago: University of Chicago Press, 1993, pp. 557–580.

[2] James Hitchcock. "Catholic Activist Conservatism in the United States." In Martin E. Marty and R. Scott Appleby, eds. *Fundamentalisms Observed.* Chicago: University of Chicago Press, 1991, p. 101.

[3] Don Lattin. "The End to Innocent Acceptance of Sects." *San Francisco Chronicle,* November 13, 1998, B1.

[4] Karen Armstrong. *Jerusalem: One City, Three Faiths.* New York: Alfred A. Knopf, 1996, pp. 412–413. Rohan had been reared as a Christian but had come under the influence of Herbert Armstrong's Worldwide Church of God in the late 1960s. He claimed that he set fire to the mosque on the basis of instructions in a 1967 editorial by Armstrong.

[5] Alan Feiler. "Catching Up with the Man Who Almost Started World War III." *Baltimore Jewish Times,* March 6, 2003, p. B6. Goodman was arrested and served 15 years in the Israeli prison system. He was released early and returned to the United States in October 1997 after promising not to return to Israel for the next eight years.

[6] The fourth airplane crashed in a field near Shenksville, Pennsylvania. It is thought that the terrorists intended to crash the plane into the White House but were prevented by a group of passengers who rushed the cockpit.

[7] "University Cancels Class on Creationism." *New York Times,* December 1, 2005.

[8] Quoted in Paul Marshall. "Fundamentalists and Other Fun People: To Know Them Is Not to Despise Them." *The Weekly Standard* 10 (November 22, 2004), p. 16.

[9] Ralph W. Hood, Jr., Peter C. Hill, and W. Paul Williamson. *The Psychology of Religious Fundamentalism.* New York: Guilford Press, 2005, pp. 190–204. The explanation and discussion of each point is my own.

[10] "The Fundamentalism Project: A User's Guide." In Marty and Appleby, eds. *Fundamentalisms Observed,* p. ix.

[11] "The Fundamentalism Project: A User's Guide." In Marty and Appleby, eds. *Fundamentalisms Observed,* p. ix. The phrase itself originated with the philosopher Ludwig Wittgenstein, who used it in the *Philosophical Investigations,* written c. 1946 and published in 1953.

[12] Theodor Adorno and Max Horkheimer. *The Authoritarian Personality.* New York: Harper & Row, 1950.

[13] Hood, Hill, and Williamson. *The Psychology of Religious Fundamentalism,* p. 200.

[14] P. J. Watson, Pauline Swayers, Ronald J. Morris, et al. "Reanalysis within a Christian Ideological Surround: Relationships of Intrinsic Religious Orientation with Fundamentalism and Right-Wing Authoritarianism." *Journal of Psychology and Theology* 31 (Winter 2003), p. 315.

[15] Ray F. Paloutzian, J. T. Richardson, and L. R. Rambo. "Religious Conversion and Personality Change." *Journal of Personality* 67 (June 1999), pp. 1,047–1,079.

[16] Quoted in Sydney E. Ahlstrom. *A Religious History of the American People.* New Haven, Conn.: Yale University Press, 1972, pp. 915–916.

[17] "What Does the 'IFCA' in IFCA International Mean?" IFCA International. Available online. URL: http:// www.ifca.org/what_is_ifca_international.htm. Accessed January 5, 2006. The practice of snake-handling, which is derived from Jesus' promise in Mark 16:18 that "tak[ing] up snakes" is one of the "signs" that will accompany true believers, persists in parts of the American South in spite of the fact that six states (Kentucky, Georgia, Tennessee, Virginia, North Carolina, and Alabama) outlawed the practice between 1940 and 1950. The *Kingsport Times-News,* a Virginia newspaper, reported on April 15, 2004, that a local minister had died after being bitten by a rattlesnake during the snake-handling portion of an Easter service.

[18] "Fundamental Intolerance?" *Wilson Quarterly* 23 (Autumn 1999), p. 96.

[19] Gabriel Almond, R. Scott Appleby, and Emmanuel Sivan. *Strong Religion: The Rise of Fundamentalisms around the World.* Chicago: University of Chicago Press, 2003, pp. 93–98.

[20] Almond, Appleby, and Sivan. *Strong Religion,* p. 93.

[21] Samuel C. Heilman. "Jews and Fundamentalism." *Jewish Political Studies Review* 17 (Spring 2005), p. 2.

[22] Samuel C. Heilman and Menachem Friedman. "Religious Fundamentalism and Religious Jews: The Case of the Haredim." In Marty and Appleby, eds., *Fundamentalisms Observed,* p. 239.

[23] Ehud Sprinzak. "Three Models of Religious Violence: Jewish Fundamentalism in Israel." In Marty and Appleby, eds. *Fundamentalisms and the State,* pp. 466–467.

[24] Yehudah Mirsky. "The Inner Life of Religious Zionism." *The New Leader* 78 (December 4, 1995), p. 12.

[25] Angana Chatterji. "Orissa: A Gujarat in the Making." *Dissident Voice* (November 1, 2003). Available online. URL: http://www.dissidentvoice.org/Articles9/Chatterji_Orissa.htm. Accessed December 5, 2005.

[26] Avery Cardinal Dulles. "Religious Freedom: Innovation and Development." *First Things,* no. 118 (December 2001), p. 35.

[27] Patrick Madrid and Pete Vere. *More Catholic Than the Pope: An Inside Look at Extreme Traditionalism.* Huntington, Ind.: Our Sunday Visitor, 2004, p. 10.

[28] "Buddhist Monks." *U.S. Catholic* 69 (April 2004), p. 11.

[29] George M. Marsden. *Fundamentalism—in American Culture: The Shaping of Twentieth-Century Evangelicalism, 1870–1925.* Oxford: Oxford University Press, 1980, pp. 35–36.

[30] Quoted in Paul A. Carter. *The Spiritual Crisis of the Gilded Age.* DeKalb, Ill.: Northern Illinois University Press, 1971, pp. 5–6.

[31] Madrid and Vere. *More Catholic Than the Pope.*

[32] Gideon Aran. "Jewish Zionist Fundamentalism: The Bloc of the Faithful in Israel (Gush Emunim)." In Marty and Appleby, eds. *Fundamentalisms Observed,* pp. 317–318. The heifer must be completely red, including horns and nose; it cannot have so much as a single hair of a different color. In addition, it must never have been used to carry a burden.

[33] Quoted in Ron Dreher. "Red-Heifer Days." *National Review Online* (April 11, 2002). Available online. URL: http://www.nationalreview.com/dreher/dreher041102.asp. Accessed November 22, 2005.

[34] Richard Landes. "The Social Bermuda Triangle: Jews, Modernity, and Apocalypticism." Center for Millennial Studies, Boston University. Available online. URL: http://www.mille.org/people/rlpages/socialtri.html. Accessed November 22, 2005.

[35] H. Richard Niebuhr. *Christ and Culture.* New York: Harper & Row, 1951, p. 45.

[36] Hood, Hill, and Williamson. *The Psychology of Religious Fundamentalism,* p. 100. W. Paul Williamson is a former CGP minister.

[37] Michael J. Ediger. "The Church of God of Prophecy." 1996. Available online. URL: http://www.dtl.org/dtl/article/c-g-p.htm. Accessed November 22, 2005.

[38] Bernard Lewis. "The Enemies of God." *New York Review of Books,* March 25, 1993, p. 31.

[39] Bernard Lewis. "Religion and Murder in the Middle East." In Charles S. Liebman, ed. *Political Assassination: The Murder of Rabin and Political Assassinations in the Middle East.* Tel Aviv, Israel: Yitzhak Rabin Center for Israel Studies, 1998, p. 113.

[40] Karen Armstrong. *The Battle for God.* New York: Ballantine Books, 2000, p. 289.

[41] Armstrong. *The Battle for God,* p. 336.

[42] John O. Voll. "Fundamentalism in the Sunni Arab World: Egypt and the Sudan." In Marty and Appleby, eds. *Fundamentalisms Observed,* p. 345.

[43] Hood, Hill, and Williamson. *The Psychology of Religious Fundamentalism,* p. 193.

[44] Cited in Jerald Tanner and Sandra Tanner. "Mormon Blood Atonement: Fact or Fantasy?" *Salt Lake City Messenger* 92 (April 1997). Available online. URL: http://www.xmission.com/~country/reason/blood.htm. Accessed December 14, 2005.

[45] Cited in Tanner and Tanner. "Mormon Blood Atonement." Sandra Tanner is a great-great-granddaughter of Brigham Young who left the Mormon church partly as a result of reading her ancestor's sermons.

[46] The story is told in detail in Jon Krakauer. *Under the Banner of Heaven.* New York: Anchor Books, 2004.

[47] Robert Lindsey. *A Gathering of Saints.* New York: Bantam Doubleday Dell, 1988, p. 204, pp. 252–253.

[48] Lindsey. *A Gathering of Saints,* pp. 360–361.

[49] Landes. "The Social Bermuda Triangle."

[50] Hisham Kamal Abd al-Hamid. *The Expected Perishing and Ruin of America.* Cited in David Cook. "America, the Second 'Ad: Prophecies about the Downfall of the United States." Available online. URL: http://www.mille.org/scholarship/papers/ADAM.html. Accessed December 8, 2005.

[51] Cook. "America, the Second 'Ad."

[52] Cook. "America, the Second 'Ad."

[53] Quoted in Cook. "America, the Second 'Ad."

[54] Quoted in Cook. "America, the Second 'Ad."

[55] Quoted in Cook. "America, the Second 'Ad."

[56] Cook. "America, the Second 'Ad."

[57] "The Remnant's Statement of Purpose." Available online. URL: http://www.remnantnewspaper.com/about.htm. Accessed November 8, 2005.

[58] Daniel Gold. "Organized Hinduisms: From Vedic Truth to Hindu Nation." In Marty and Appleby, eds. *Fundamentalisms Observed,* pp. 560–561.

[59] Krakauer. *Under the Banner of Heaven,* pp. 22 ff.

[60] Krakauer. *Under the Banner of Heaven,* p. 11.

[61] Federal Research Division, Library of Congress Country Studies. "Israel—Education." Available online. URL: http://countrystudies.us/israel/59.htm. Accessed November 27, 2005.

[62] Stephen Singular. *Talked to Death: The Murder of Alan Berg and the Rise of the Neo-Nazis.* New York: Beech Tree Books, 1987, pp. 44–45.

[63] Majid Tehranian. "Fundamentalist Impact on Education and the Media: An Overview." In Martin E. Marty and R. Scott Appleby, eds. *Fundamentalisms and Society.* Chicago: University of Chicago Press, 1993, p. 337.

[64] CNN. "Judge: Woman Can't Cover Face on Driver's License." June 10, 2003. Available online. URL: http://www.cnn.com/2003/LAW/06/06/florida.license.veil. Accessed December 4, 2005.

[65] "Imperial College London Bans the Hijab, Clothing That Obscures the Wearer's Face." *Guardian,* November 24, 2005. Available online. URL: http://www.guardian.co.uk/uk_news/story/0,3604,1649358,00.html. Accessed December 4, 2005.

[66] "European Court of Human Rights Backs Turkish Headscarf Ban." *BBC News,* November 10, 2005. Available online. URL: http://news.bbc.co.uk/1/hi/world/europe/4424776.stm. Accessed December 4, 2005.

[67] "Muslim Leader in London Urges 'Hijab' Caution for Women." *Hindu News,* August 4, 2005. Available online. URL: http://www.hindu.com/thehindu/holnus/001200508041010.htm. Accessed December 4, 2005.

[68] Conrad W. Weiser. *Healers: Harmed and Harmful.* Minneapolis, Minn.: Augsburg Fortress Press, 1994, pp. 4–5. The title itself reflects the growing tendency to think of clergy as ordained therapists.

[69] Marsden. *Fundamentalism in American Culture,* p. 84.

[70] Marie M. Fortune. *Is Nothing Sacred? The Story of a Pastor, the Women He Sexually Abused, and the Congregation He Nearly Destroyed.* Cleveland, Ohio: United Church Press, 1999, p. 5.

[71] Jeffrey Goldberg. "A Reporter at Large: Among the Settlers." *The New Yorker* (May 31, 2004). Available online. URL: http://www.newyorker.com/fact/content/articles/040531fa_fact2_a. Accessed December 28, 2005.

[72] Aran. "Jewish Zionist Fundamentalism," p. 266.

[73] They were first proposed by Rodney Stark and William S. Bainbridge. "Of Churches, Sects, and Cults: Preliminary Concepts for a Theory of Religious Movements." *Journal for the Scientific Study of Religion* 18, pp. 117–131.

[74] Robert Jay Lifton. *Destroying the World to Save It: Aum Shinrikyō, Apocalyptic Violence, and the New Global Terrorism.* New York: Henry Holt, 2000, p. 27.

[75] Lifton. *Destroying the World,* p. 26.

[76] Lifton. *Destroying the World,* pp. 37–38.

[77] Aran. "Jewish Zionist Fundamentalism," p. 313.

[78] Gold. "Organized Hinduisms," p. 548.

[79] Bob Jones University. "Student Expectations." Available online. URL: http://www.bju.edu/prospective/expect/general.html. Accessed November 15, 2005.

[80] Quentin Schulze. "Two Faces of Fundamentalist Higher Education." In Marty and Appleby, eds. *Fundamentalisms and Society,* p. 498.

[81] Ahlstrom. *A Religious History of the American People,* p. 508.

[82] Peggy Fletcher Stark. "Exiles in Zion." *Salt Lake Tribune,* August 16, 2003.

[83] Nancy T. Ammermann. "North American Protestant Fundamentalism." In Marty and Appleby, eds. *Fundamentalisms Observed,* p. 49.

[84] Elbert Eugene Peck. "The Origin and Evolution of the *Sunstone* Species: Twenty-five Years of Creative Adaptation." Available online. URL: http://www.sunstoneonline.com/sunstone/sun-history.asp. Accessed December 30, 2005.

[85] Krakauer. *Under the Banner of Heaven,* p. 364.

[86] Schulze. "Two Faces of Fundamentalist Higher Education," p. 496.

[87] The list of accredited schools is available on the ATS Web site. URL: http://www.ats.edu/member_schools/denom.asp.

[88] An extended discussion of the Rushdie affair and the reasons underlying Muslim reactions to the novel can be found in Hood, Hill, and Williamson. *Psychology of Religious Fundamentalism,* pp. 155–182.

2

Focus on the United States

INTRODUCTION

The history of fundamentalism in the United States is of special interest because fundamentalism, as a religious reaction to modernity, first developed in North America. For this reason, one question all researchers of other fundamentalist-like movements must ask themselves is whether this term that was first developed to characterize an American Protestant movement can also be used to explain religious movements in other faiths or in other parts of the world. The United States has served for more than two centuries as a unique "laboratory" for the emergence of new religious groups and movements, partly because of its history and partly because of its sheer size.

The large size of the country meant that small religious groups who were in conflict with their neighbors or otherwise unhappy could simply relocate. The early history of New England is filled with accounts of church leaders who disagreed with the Puritanism of the Massachusetts Bay Colony and moved to Rhode Island or Long Island. This pattern was followed by other groups, the last major migration being the westward journey of the Mormons in the 1840s.

One of the reasons for the emergence of fundamentalism in the years following the Civil War, however, was the closing of the American frontier. It was no longer as easy as it had been in the 18th and early 19th centuries for a group of believers to leave their present homes and resettle elsewhere. Nonetheless, the possibility of breaking with an older religious body or tradition remained and with it the potential of adding still another name to the lengthening list of denominations. Add to this spirit of religious independence the various Native American religions and the many different faiths brought to North America by generations of immigrants, and it is not surprising that the United States has a larger number of religious groups than any other country in the world. Even in the 1930s, the German theologian Dietrich Bonhoeffer, who had come to New York for a year of graduate study, remarked, "It has been granted to the Americans less than any other nation on earth to realize the visible unity of the Church of God."[1] The Protestant fundamentalists of the 21st century and their Roman Catholic and Jewish counterparts are part of a vast and ever more complicated American religious mosaic.

HISTORICAL BACKGROUND

Religion in the Colonial Period

ESTABLISHED CHURCHES IN THE COLONIES

The three empires that planted colonies in North America from the end of the 15th through the 18th centuries all had state churches: the Anglican Church in England and the Roman Catholic Church in Spain and France. The Church of England, however, had a different relationship to its monarch than did its Spanish and French counterparts. When King Henry VIII of England broke with the papacy and proclaimed himself "supreme head" of the Anglican Church in 1531, he created something new—an established national church that was no longer Roman Catholic. It was not until the reign of Elizabeth I (1558–1603), however, that the Anglican Church took on a decidedly Protestant character with the Act of Uniformity (1552). The act required all English clergy to use the same form of worship (the Book of Common Prayer) and subscribe to the Thirty-nine Articles (1571), which became the church's doctrinal standard.

THE PURITAN COLONIES

The Elizabethan settlement, as the queen's religious legislation is known, had two important consequences for American religious history. The first is that Elizabeth's restructuring of the Church of England did not go far enough for a group of clergy who had been strongly influenced by Calvinism. This group eventually became known as the Puritans. The queen had retained in the Anglican Church the traditional threefold ministry of bishops, priests, and deacons inherited from the medieval period. Her first Archbishop of Canterbury, Matthew Parker, had been ordained a Catholic priest in 1527, before the break with Rome. The Puritans disapproved of episcopal polity (the church structured as a threefold ministry of bishops, priests, and deacons), however, having accepted John Calvin's teaching that churches should be governed by presbyters, or elders. They also thought that the vestments, musical instruments, and other features of medieval worship that were allowed by the Book of Common Prayer were still too "popish." Eventually some of the Puritans decided to leave England, first for Holland, which had its own version of Calvinism by the early 1600s, and then for England's North American colonies.

The second consequence of the Elizabethan settlement is that Protestant Christianity—specifically, Protestantism of the Reformed (Calvinist) variety—and not Roman Catholicism or Lutheranism, would become the decisive influence on the nation that declared its independence in 1776. One historian has estimated that 75 percent of the American colonists at that time had a Reformed religious background, whether or not they were actual church members.[2]

The Reformed tradition contributed in several ways to the organization as well as the spirituality of the English colonial churches. First, the Puritan desire for religious freedom is better understood as a longing for freedom from religious domination—in this case, domination by the Church of England. It did not mean that the Puritans were radical religious individualists. Although they argued over the proper form of church government, all agreed that a truly godly church must have some kind of lawfully ordered structure and maintain strict discipline over its members. It was also supposed to be a genuine community, "a model of Christian charity," in the words of John Winthrop (1588–1649), the first governor of the Massachusetts Bay Colony.[3] This same communal theme can be found in the Mayflower Compact, the document signed on November 11, 1620, by the members of the Plymouth Colony before disembarking from the ship that had carried them to New England. The compact, which has sometimes been called the first written American constitution, established a civil government as well as a community of the godly.[4]

EARLY STATE CHURCHES

One result of this close association of the Reformed notion of a religious covenant binding humanity to God and faithful believers to one another with the concept of "a civil Body Politick" was the establishment of state churches in the New England colonies. The settlers of Plymouth and the Massachusetts Bay Colony were accustomed to a state religion as part of the general public order in the countries of western Europe. One form or another of Christianity had been the state religion of the West since the Roman emperor Theodosius I outlawed pagan religious practices in 393 C.E. The question in the minds of the New England settlers, and their counterparts in some of the other colonies farther south, was not whether to have an established church, but rather which church to establish. By degrees, Congregationalism became the established church of Massachusetts, Connecticut, and New Hampshire, while the Anglican Church was established in Virginia and received some degree of public support in the Carolinas, New Jersey, Georgia, and New York. Of the original thirteen colonies, only Rhode Island and Maryland were founded without a state church, and in

Maryland the religious freedom originally guaranteed in the 1649 Act of Toleration did not last.

The reader should keep in mind, incidentally, that the Christian notion of a state church implies a distinction between civil and ecclesiastical authority, as well as a relationship between them. This distinction was explained to generations of Christians with reference to Matthew 22, the story of Jesus and the tribute money. When his questioners ask him about the lawfulness of paying taxes to the Roman government, Jesus replies, "Give Caesar what belongs to Caesar, and give God the things that are God's." While the verse does not supply a rule or formula for determining what belongs to Caesar or to God in any specific instance, it nonetheless points to a separation between the two powers. This point will be important in chapter 3 with regard to understanding Islamic fundamentalism.[5]

The Great Awakening

JONATHAN EDWARDS

The Great Awakening was a religious revival that began in Northampton, Massachusetts, in 1734. Inspired by the preaching of its minister, Jonathan Edwards (1703–58), the entire town began to experience "showers of blessings." Edwards's *Faithful Narrative of the Surprising Work of God* stated that "I never saw the Christian spirit in Love to Enemies so exemplified, in all my Life as I have seen it within this half-year."[6]

The author of a sermon preached at Enfield, Connecticut, in 1741 titled "Sinners in the Hands of an Angry God," Edwards is often caricatured as a hellfire-and-damnation preacher. It should be noted, however, that most of Edwards's sermons were not intended to literally scare the hell out of people but rather to urge them to open themselves to God's love. One of his early sermons (1723), in fact, emphasizes the "pleasantness" of religion:

> *Religion does not deny a man the pleasures of sense, only taken moderately and with temperance and in a reasonable manner. God has given us of his redundant bounty many things for the delight of our senses, for our pleasure and gratification. . . . Religion allows us to take the full comfort of our meat and drink, all reasonable pleasures that are to be enjoyed in conversation or recreation; allows of the gratification of all of our natural appetites. . . . The earthly comforts of the Christian are also very much sweetened by the consideration of the love of God, that God is their Father and friend and gives them these blessings from love to them, and because he delights in them. . . . [The godly man] eats and drinks in*

love to God and Jesus Christ, and in peace with his neighbors and charity towards the whole world.[7]

Edwards was concerned with preaching the Gospel to Native Americans in addition to the descendants of English settlers. Between his ministry in Northampton and his acceptance of the presidency of the College of New Jersey (later Princeton University), Edwards lived in Stockbridge, Massachusetts, where he preached to the Mohawk Indians who had settled there. In one sermon from 1751, Edwards told the Mohawk that God had been angered "by the shameful neglect of the white people," who had failed to teach the Indians the Word of God. He added that many of the English and Dutch were opposed to instructing the Indians, "for as long as they keep you in ignorance, 'tis more easy to cheat you in trading with you." He then invited them to "come and enjoy the light of the Word of God, which is ten thousand times better than the light of the sun. There is such a thing as this light's shining into the heart . . . as when you hold a glass out in the light of the sun, the glass will shine . . . like a sweet and beautiful flower in the spring."[8] The Great Awakening was spread as much by people's rediscovery of the positive teachings of Christianity as by fear of personal damnation.

GEORGE WHITEFIELD

The other leader of the Great Awakening was George Whitefield (1714–70), an English minister who had been a member of the Holy Club at Oxford University together with John and Charles Wesley, the founders of the Methodist Church. Ordained in the Church of England in 1736, Whitefield became known as "the apostle of the British Empire" for his frequent travels to North America and other English colonies. His sermons drew crowds as large as 30,000 people—a figure that compares favorably with the size of the modern-day audiences at Billy Graham's crusades, particularly since Whitefield did not have the benefit of microphones or public address systems. In 1740, Whitefield made a six-week tour of New England from Portsmouth, New Hampshire, to Boston (where he preached to a crowd of thousands gathered on the Boston Common) and southward to New Haven, Connecticut, and Staten Island, New York. He took a side trip to Northampton, where he spent several days with Edwards and his family, preaching twice in Edwards's church.

Whitefield's preaching tours introduced two innovations that characterized the later evangelical and fundamentalist movements. The first was the use of a highly emotional style of preaching that appealed to the listener's heart as well as mind. Henry Melchior Muhlenberg (1711–87), the immigrant German pastor who planted Lutheran churches in southeastern Pennsylvania, recorded in his diary that one of his parishioners went to hear

Whitefield preach and said afterward that she had never been so moved by a sermon in her life—and she spoke no English at all![9]

The second innovation was Whitefield's crossing of denominational lines. Although ordained in the Church of England, he was well content to preach in any church that would allow him to do so, as well as preaching in the open air when the size of the crowd made it necessary. In Boston and New Haven, he preached in Congregational meetinghouses; in the South, his sermons were part of Anglican worship services; on Staten Island, he was invited to use the local Presbyterian pulpit. This lack of concern about denominational boundaries would also be a striking feature of 19th-century evangelicalism and fundamentalism.

To some extent, 18th-century interdenominational cooperation was a necessity of frontier life and the slowness of travel on horseback. But more important, this early form of ecumenism (at least among Protestants) issued from the spirit of the evangelical revival itself. John Wesley (1703–91), the English clergyman who is regarded as the founder of the Methodist Church, made his opposition to sectarian rigidity quite plain in his essay on "The Character of a Methodist":

> *If any man say, "Why, these are only the common fundamental principles of Christianity!" thou hast said; so I mean; this is the very truth; I know they are no other. . . . I, and all who follow my judgment, do vehemently refuse to be distinguished from other men by any but the common principles of Christianity,—the plain, old Christianity that I teach, renouncing and detesting all other marks of distinction. . . . From real Christians, of whatsoever denomination they be, we earnestly desire not to be distinguished at all, not from any who sincerely follow after what they know they have not yet attained. . . . Is thy heart right, as my heart is with thine? I ask no farther question. . . . For opinions, or terms, let us not destroy the work of God. Dost thou love and serve God? It is enough. I give thee the right hand of fellowship.*[10]

The Revolutionary Period and the Constitution

The history of the American churches in the period between the end of the Great Awakening in 1745 and the ratification of the constitution of the new nation in 1787 was marked by five characteristics that are important in understanding the development of fundamentalism a century later.[11] They are 1) the growing reality of religious freedom, as distinct from mere toleration; 2) the separation of church and state; 3) the emergence of denominationalism; 4) the acceptance of church membership as voluntary rather than mandated by the state; and 5) the spread of patriotic piety, or what is sometimes called "civil religion."

RELIGIOUS FREEDOM

Only two of the original thirteen colonies—Rhode Island and Maryland—recognized the principle of religious freedom at the time of their original charters in the 1630s. By the end of the 17th century, however, religious freedom was acknowledged in the southern and Middle Atlantic colonies as well. Connecticut, Massachusetts, New Hampshire, Maryland, and Virginia were the only colonies that still had official state churches in 1775, and even they generally practiced an informal toleration of other bodies.

The movement toward complete liberty of belief was accelerated by Virginia's adoption of the Declaration of Rights on June 12, 1776. Many of the articles in the Virginia declaration foreshadow the language of the later Bill of Rights and the Declaration of Independence signed in Philadelphia on July 4, 1776. The 16th and last article in the Virginia document concerns freedom of religion. It reads in its entirety: "That religion, or the duty which we owe to our Creator and the manner of discharging it, can be directed by reason and conviction, not by force or violence; and therefore, all men are equally entitled to the free exercise of religion, according to the dictates of conscience; and that it is the mutual duty of all to practice Christian forbearance, love, and charity towards each other."[12] With the ratification of the United States Constitution in 1787 and the Bill of Rights (the first 10 amendments to the Constitution) in 1791, Protestant Christians of any church tradition had more religious freedom than their counterparts had anywhere else in the world. Roman Catholics still had a few legal disabilities in some states, but they nevertheless enjoyed more freedom to practice their faith than Catholics in any other country with a Protestant state church or majority Protestant population. In addition to the religious freedom granted to members of the various Christian bodies, the Constitution protected the rights of humanists, deists, Unitarians, and persons with no religious convictions to publish their views and to seek public office without restriction. The latter was guaranteed in the third paragraph of Article Six of the Constitution: "The Senators and Representatives before mentioned, and the members of the several state legislatures, and all executive and judicial officers, both of the United States and of the several states, shall be bound by oath or affirmation, to support this Constitution; but no religious test shall ever be required as a qualification to any office or public trust under the United States."[13]

CHURCH AND STATE

The most important article regarding religion in the Bill of Rights, added to the Constitution in 1791, is the First Amendment: "Congress shall make no law respecting an establishment of religion, or prohibiting the free exercise thereof; or abridging the freedom of speech, or of the press; or the right of the people peaceably to assemble, and to petition the Government for a redress of grievances."[14] The first clause is often referred to as the Establishment Clause, and the second, as the Free Exercise Clause.

There is, however, a certain amount of tension between the two parts insofar as the Establishment Clause appears to restrict religion, while the Free Exercise Clause offers it special legal protection. The liberal tradition in American politics has generally resolved this apparent tension by drawing a line between the public and private spheres. It maintains that the Establishment Clause forbids inserting religion into public life, and the Free Exercise Clause protects people against government interference in the practice of their faith—or of no faith at all. One way of understanding fundamentalist political activism in the United States is to see it not as a movement to establish a "theocracy," but rather as a desire to extend the boundaries of the Free Exercise Clause.

The wording of the First Amendment and the principles that underlie it were shaped by several factors at the end of the colonial period. One was the increase in the size of the colonial population as a result of immigration, which in turn brought greater religious diversity with it almost automatically. Historians estimate that there were about 360,000 people of European descent living on the Eastern seaboard in 1713, increasing to 1 million in 1760 and 3 million by 1776. In addition, there were about 500,000 black African slaves living in the thirteen colonies, 89 percent of them south of New Jersey.[15] Second, specialized trades and manufacturing activities were beginning to displace agriculture as the primary means of earning a living. The rise of a merchant class as well as a professional class of lawyers, physicians, clergy, and schoolteachers educated in colonial colleges (there were six that had been founded by 1763 and nine by 1775), rather than in English or Scottish universities, meant that people moved from one colony to another much more often than a hundred years earlier. Increased mobility brought with it the fact that even Christians who favored an established church in theory found themselves religious dissenters if they moved to a colony with a state church different from their own.[16]

Next, there was a small but outspoken group of deists, mostly in the larger cities, who were not atheists but had been influenced by the rationalism of the Enlightenment. Some no longer accepted the authority of biblical revelation, preferring to believe that religion could be grounded in reason alone. Many of them wished to keep religion out of public life altogether on the grounds that it led to fanaticism or persecution. Last, the Anglican Church, which had enjoyed the benefits of official establishment in Maryland and Virginia and a kind of semi-establishment in Georgia and the Carolinas, had been discredited by its ties to the mother country during the American Revolution. This painful history meant that the Anglican Church was the weakest of all possible candidates for establishment in 1787—in spite of the fact that two-thirds of the signers of the Declaration of Independence were at least nominal Anglicans.[17]

Although the Constitution of 1787 refused to establish a state church, it did not thereby require the states that already had established churches to disestablish them. All the established Anglican churches, however, were disestablished by time the Constitution was ratified. The Congregational state churches of New England lingered into the 19th century even though there was increased pressure for disestablishment at the time that these states ratified the Constitution. Connecticut finally drafted and adopted a state constitution in 1818 that disestablished the Congregational Church.[18] Connecticut's example was followed by New Hampshire in 1819 and Massachusetts in 1833.

DENOMINATIONALISM

Denominationalism in the United States means more than simply defining the relationships among the various branches of Christianity (and eventually Judaism) to one another. It also implies an inclusive concept of the church that respects the integrity of each of the distinctive traditions. On the one hand, the acceptance of American Christianity as a community of denominations in which no one member had the right to dominate the others probably hastened the withdrawal of religion from the public sphere. On the other hand, it protected the churches in the United States from the anticlericalism (antagonism toward members of the clergy) and general hostility toward religion that characterized the French Revolution of 1789.

VOLUNTARISM

Voluntarism (or voluntaryism) refers to the notion that churches (and synagogues) should depend on their committed lay members for financial support rather than on subsidies from the state raised by general taxation. Voluntarism tended to increase the independence of local congregations and to weaken the authority of bishops and their counterparts in the hierarchies of other denominations.

Voluntarism also led to an emphasis on efficient church administration as a more desirable quality in a minister than intellectual brilliance. Moreover, voluntary church affiliation meant that the various denominations began to compete with one another for members. This development in turn led to a lowering of the clergy's social status, as the ordained leaders now had to please their congregations rather than receiving automatic respect as authority figures. Nevertheless, in spite of these changes, the churches in the 19th century underwent rapid expansion. Even in the Roman Catholic Church, the general acceptance of the voluntary principle led to such growth in numbers that the 25,000 Catholics who were American citizens in 1790 had more than doubled by 1820.

The second consequence was a new sense of individualism in religion. Voluntarism meant that young adults, whether married or single, had more freedom to join a church of a denomination different from that of their parents, to marry someone from a different faith tradition, and to move from church to church even within the same town if they wished. By the 1830s, when the French visitor Alexis de Tocqueville (1805–59) wrote his well-known *Democracy in America,* he saw the vitality of religious faith in America as primarily an aid in forming the moral character of individual believers, as compared to serving as a "glue" that held entire communities together. He also noted that American individualism in the sphere of religion was a major source of "strange sects": "Here and there in the midst of American society you meet with men full of a fanatical and almost wild spiritualism, which hardly exists in Europe. From time to time strange sects arise which endeavor to strike out extraordinary paths to eternal happiness. Religious insanity is very common in the United States."[19]

CIVIL RELIGION

Civil religion is a term that usually refers to a religious dimension within the common culture of a nation, as in the belief that the United States has a special, even God-given, mission within world history. It can also refer to such patriotic group rituals as the singing of the national anthem at a baseball game, an activity that has no particular religious overtones. The first full-blown example of civil religion was the Roman state religion as restored and promoted by Augustus Caesar (ruled 31 B.C.E.–14 C.E.). What is unique about civil religion in the United States is not that it exists, but that it has had for much of the nation's history a distinctly Judeo-Christian character.

According to sociologist Robert N. Bellah, the biblical strand within American civil religion should not be misunderstood as a contradiction of the Establishment Clause of the First Amendment, but rather as one of the "common elements of religious orientation" held by most citizens: "Although matters of personal religious belief, worship, and association are considered to be strictly private affairs, there are, at the same time, certain common elements of religious orientation that the great majority of Americans share."[20] Some of these common elements can be traced back to the first presidential administrations under the 1787 Constitution. George Washington's first inaugural address (April 30, 1789) reflects the conviction that the newly established nation has been guided by an "Almighty Being" who directs the course of human history:

> *. . . it would be peculiarly improper to omit in this first official act my fervent supplications to that Almighty Being who rules over the universe, who presides in the councils of nations, and whose providential aids can supply every human defect, that His benediction may consecrate to the liberties and happiness of the people of the United States a Government instituted by themselves for these essential purposes. . . . No people can be bound to acknowledge and adore the Invisible Hand which conducts the affairs of men more than those of the United States. Every step by which they have advanced to the character of an independent nation seems to have been distinguished by some token of providential agency.*[21]

Although this address may express certain general religious beliefs derived from Judaism and Christianity, it is not explicitly Christian, let alone specifically Anglican (Washington's nominal religious affiliation). Washington does not mention Jesus Christ, the Trinity, or the Christian church. There is nothing in the inaugural address that could not be accepted by most 18th-century deists. In addition, as Bellah has remarked, the God of American civil religion "is on the austere side, much more related to order, law, and right than to salvation and love."[22] In sum, he is the God of the Enlightenment rather than the Great Awakening, a deity of the rational intellect rather than the religious affections.

The Post–Civil War Era and the Emergence of Fundamentalism

THE TRANSFORMATION OF AMERICAN SOCIETY

The Impact of the Civil War

The Civil War (1861–65) affected the American churches in many ways. One institutional result of the controversy over the abolition of slavery that preceded the war was the division of several of the major Protestant denominations into Northern and Southern branches. The Episcopal Church, for example, separated into the Protestant Episcopal Church in the United States of America and the Episcopal Church in the Confederate States of America in 1861. The Presbyterian, Baptist, and Methodist Churches were also split by the war; some of these divisions were not healed until the 20th century.

The second important aspect of the war as it affected religion in the United States was the intensity of the religious revivals on both sides. It is estimated that there were about 3,000 chaplains on the Union side to meet the religious needs of the soldiers and about 1,100 on the Confederate side. In many places during the war, the chaplains organized preaching services and revival meetings with the help of local clergy. There were somewhere between 100,000 and 200,000 reported religious conversions in the military during the Civil War.[23] The popularity of these army camp revivals was fresh in the minds of many when fundamentalism first began to take shape in the 1870s. In the South in particular, nostalgia for "old-time religion" helped to ease the pain of defeat. Longing for the past helped to make the states of the former Confederacy fertile soil for the eventual spread of fundamentalism in the Methodist and Baptist churches.

The war also affected the American churches by the sheer number of its casualties. It is often forgotten that the Civil War cost more American lives (363,000 Union soldiers and sailors and 200,000 Confederate soldiers and sailors) than any other conflict in the nation's history, including World War II (408,000 U.S. soldiers, sailors and airmen). Moreover, this loss occurred when the total population of the country was only 31.5 million (including slaves).[24] There were many families in both the South and the North that had to cope with grief as well as with the economic dislocations and hardships associated with war. The writers of the period responded in various ways to the human devastation resulting from the war. Some, like Ambrose Bierce, were so traumatized by their combat experiences as to give up belief in any meaning to life at all, let alone a religious significance. John Wesley Powell, the son of a Methodist minister who became a famous explorer and geologist, dismissed the Christianity in which he had been reared as "ghost-lore."[25]

Other writers became interested in the answers offered by the Spiritualist movement to questions raised by the war about life after death. Although American Spiritualism had its beginnings in the 1840s, with the Fox sisters of Hydesville, New York, and their mysterious abilities of "channeling" the spirits of the departed,[26] the movement grew rapidly in the years after 1865, as thousands of bereaved families asked for "messages" from loved ones killed in battle. Mary Todd Lincoln gave the movement additional publicity by consulting Spiritualists after her husband President Abraham Lincoln's assassination in 1865.

Closing of the Frontier

Within four years of the end of the Civil War, the east and west coasts of the United States were joined by the completion of the country's first transcontinental railroad. When the Union Pacific and Central Pacific Railroads were joined by the driving of a golden spike at Promontory Summit, Utah, on May 10, 1869, the nation's western frontier was effectively closed. Another marker of this change was the U.S. Census of 1890: For the first time in American history, the location of the frontier could not be plotted on a demographic map. Before 1890, the statisticians in the Bureau of the Census had been able to identify the slow westward shift of the frontier by drawing a line between the parts of the United States that had more than two inhabitants per square mile and those that had fewer than two. By 1890, there were enough settlers in the western states that a clear line could no longer be drawn.

This demographic transition led to a change in the country's denominational balance. The churches that adapted most rapidly to the challenges of settlement in the far West were the Baptists, Methodists, and Disciples of Christ. These groups tripled their membership between 1860 and 1900.[27] These were also the churches that proved to be most friendly to fundamentalism. The churches that had dominated the eastern seaboard during the colonial period—Congregationalists, Presbyterians, and Episcopalians—grew, too, but much more slowly.[28]

Urbanization and Immigration

The social changes that took place in the United States after 1865 were unsettling to the mainline Protestant churches. One major cause was urbanization, the process that turned a nation of small towns and villages supported by agriculture into large cities based on industry and finance. The churches had thrived in the rural and semirural settings of the early 19th century—even people who were not formal members of any denomination usually had relatives and friends who were. For this reason the beliefs and moral standards of the churches generally had the support of most members of the town. The situation was different in the cities of the late 19th century, which had no tightly knit Protestant community. The members of a city congregation might be drawn from a number of different neighborhoods scattered around the city. In addition, the relative anonymity of city life allowed those who were so inclined to throw off the traditional moral codes of the churches.

Urbanization also brought with it a sharp increase in the numbers of immigrants to the United States. Unlike the majority of immigrants in the colonial period, however, most of these newcomers did not come from English-speaking countries. In addition, a large percentage of the immigrants were Roman Catholics—a fact that was still objectionable to many churchgoing Protestants. The Puritan mindset that persisted among the descendants of the Pilgrims found the drinking, dancing, and easygoing attitude toward Sabbath observance of their Roman Catholic fellow citizens not only personally irritating but a threat to the moral fiber of the country. As the Roman Catholic population of the United States quadrupled from 1860 to 1900, anti-Catholic sentiment grew alongside it.

NEW INTELLECTUAL TRENDS

American Protestantism after the Civil War was disturbed by new intellectual trends, as well as by far-reaching social and economic changes. All three of the major influences in this period were imported from Europe: biblical criticism, Charles Darwin's theory of evolution, and Sigmund Freud's technique of psychoanalysis.

Biblical Criticism

Biblical criticism is an analytical approach to the Hebrew and Christian Scriptures that traditionalists across the Protestant and Roman Catholic spectrum found threatening in the 19th century. The difficulties were posed not so much by so-called lower criticism of the sacred texts as by the development of higher criticism. Lower criticism, which is also sometimes called textual criticism, refers to the process of arriving at the purest or most accurate text of an ancient document. By comparing variant readings of the same passage, dating surviving manuscripts, studying translations of the document into other ancient languages, and checking for errors on the part of the scribes who copied the document by hand, scholars can generally come to a reasonable degree of agreement about the wording of the original text. With a few exceptions, the lower criticism of the Bible did not cause problems for late 19th-century fundamentalists. Some of them, such as conservative Presbyterian minister J. Gresham Machen (1881–1938), were biblical scholars.

It was otherwise with higher criticism, which analyzes the books of the Bible in terms of their date and place of origin, authorship, purpose, possible literary models, and similar concerns. The debates over the methods and purpose of biblical criticism were not limited to the clergy. They also affected educated readers and the next generation of teachers by associating historical criticism with a general belief in the powers of science and an optimistic view of human progress. Acceptance of the findings of biblical criticism led inevitably to the belief that the doctrinal definitions of Christian faith are products of historical development. Historical relativism combined with evolutionary theory was an important source of modernism in theology.

The Challenge of Darwinism

Although *On the Origin of Species* by Charles Darwin was published in 1859, its effects on religion in the United States were not evident at once, partly because of the turmoil of the Civil War. By 1870, however, many American Christians regarded Darwin's book as a blow to human self-esteem and as a direct challenge to a literal reading of the biblical account of creation in the first three chapters of Genesis.

Those who did not reject Darwin's theory of evolution automatically could respond in one of several ways. One option was to abandon religious conviction altogether in favor of a worldview defined entirely by 19th-century scientific knowledge. Thus a person writing under the pen name of "Non-Church-Goer" sent a letter to the editor of the *North American Review* in 1883 claiming that "Science is today doing more for morals than the church."[29] A second approach was to read Genesis as a work of literature rather than history and affirm that the biblical writers were expressing truths of the heart that could not be measured by scientific criteria. A third option involved attempts to reconcile the data of science with the text of Genesis by reinterpreting the Hebrew words for "day" and "night" as eons of time rather than periods of mere hours. These attempts, however, had to be given up when a German scholar named Julius Wellhausen (1844–1918) proposed a theory known as the documentary hypothesis. Wellhausen maintained that the account of creation in Genesis came from at least two different writers and could not have been written by Moses. A fourth response to Darwin was a compromise of sorts, one that accepted evolution as an explanation for the development of animal life but drew the line at applying it to humans. The fifth response avoided direct arguments about evolution in favor of an emphasis on practical morality or social service. It was understandable that many people who were liberal in theology became interested in progressive politics and social reform. The movement that emerged from this combination of interests is known as the Social Gospel.

Freudian Psychoanalysis

Like biblical criticism and evolutionary theory, psychoanalysis was a European import. Sigmund Freud (1856–1939) was a Viennese neurologist who became famous for his theories about the workings of the human mind as they affected human behavior and for his development of a technique—the "talking cure"—for helping emotionally troubled people. Freud's most significant contribution to Western thought is his notion of the unconscious. He showed that human consciousness exists in layers, that people frequently act in ways that have little to do with their conscious awareness at the time, and that they cannot even be fully aware of all their own thoughts. Although many of Freud's theories have since been criticized, his work nonetheless succeeded in shattering the confidence that many Western intellectuals had had in free will, the objectivity of human reason, and the certainty of scientific knowledge.

In addition, Freud's later books explicitly attacked religion as an "illusion," a fantasy from which human beings must be released if they are to grow to full mental maturity. It is not surprising that Freud, like Darwin, came to be regarded by conservative believers as one of the chief enemies of the Christian faith.

CHANGES IN EDUCATIONAL INSTITUTIONS

The emergence of fundamentalism within American Protestantism in the 1870s cannot be fully understood without some understanding of the institutional changes in U.S. higher education. These changes may be briefly summarized: the rapid multiplication of mediocre and poorly funded denominational colleges in the early 19th century; the separation of professional schools of law, medicine, and theology from the undergraduate college; and the emergence of secular universities after 1870 patterned on the German model.

The significance of the spread of denominational colleges after 1790 was twofold. In the first place, there were many more small schools founded than were needed, and most of these were third-rate institutions in terms of quality of instruction. The second consequence was the association of conservative Christianity with academic mediocrity at best and anti-intellectualism at worst.

Graduate schools of law, medicine, and theology did not exist in significant numbers before the 19th century. All students in a college took the same required set of courses—there were no electives—whatever their intended career. Would-be lawyers, physicians, and ministers often learned the specifics of their calling on the job, so to speak, by working with an established practitioner. Edwards, for example, often had young student pastors living in his parsonage. With respect to the ministry, the transition from an apprenticeship system to the option of a professional school degree as preparation for ordination came to play a part in the fundamentalist controversy. First, the new theological education began to separate the denominations that insisted on a learned ministry from those that did not. Second, the seminaries that were affiliated with universities gradually acquired a reputation for theological liberalism, in contrast to the schools that were free-standing and supported by single denominations.

The remaining significant change was the reshaping of the oldest American colleges into universities on the German model. American scholars who had had the opportunity to study in Germany were impressed with the relative freedom of inquiry in the German schools, as well as the opportunities for students and professors to specialize in fields of study that interested them rather than being bound to a set curriculum. As the U.S. colleges expanded into universities, they added science to the undergraduate curriculum, which itself was reorganized to allow for elective as well as required courses. The triumph of Darwin's theory of evolution among the scientists on the university faculties meant that the various Protestant churches no longer determined the content of higher education. In sum, the American university of 1870 was a very different place from the college of 1770. It was larger, better funded, more diversified, and more oriented toward the sciences and "practical" subjects. Furthermore, it focused on academic excellence rather than denominational orthodoxy and posed an even greater threat to fundamentalists because more young adults were going to college than ever before. While the general population of the United States doubled between 1870 and 1910, the number of college students increased fivefold.

FUNDAMENTALISM IN THE UNITED STATES

Defining Fundamentalists and Evangelicals

American fundamentalism first took shape against this background of rapid social, intellectual, demographic, and institutional transformation at the end of the 19th century. The meaning of the term *fundamentalist* shifted over the course of the 20th century, however, particularly in contrast to a larger group of Protestant evangelicals. *Evangelical* originally meant "pertaining to the Gospel" or "Gospel-centered." In 16th-century Germany, it was the term that Luther's followers chose for themselves. In many parts of Germany today, *Evangelisch* often means simply "Lutheran." In Britain and its North American colonies before the Revolution, however, the term *evangelical* came to be associated with the beliefs and missionary activity of the Great Awakening. In the 21st century, American evangelicalism is a much more diverse collection of believers, bound together primarily by a set of traditional beliefs. The church historian George Marsden identifies five core beliefs[30]:

- the Bible as the final doctrinal authority
- God's deeds understood as real historical events
- salvation through Jesus Christ
- the need to carry this message to others
- the importance of spiritual transformation in daily life

It has been estimated that as many as 50 million Americans can be classified as evangelical Christians on the basis of this definition.[31] This large group can be subdivided into those whose religious identity is shaped primarily by their respective denominations (many Southern Baptists, MEMBERS OF THE BLACK CHURCHES, Mennonites, Lutherans, the Dutch Reformed, and Episcopalians) and those who are what Marsden terms *card-carrying evangelicals*—that is, they identify primarily with an interdenominational movement that explicitly calls itself "evangelical."

Fundamentalism is the outgrowth of a split that developed within American evangelical Protestantism after 1870. Some evangelicals began to modify certain traditional teachings (such as the reliability of the Bible) in order to be accepted by people who taught or had been educated in one of the newly expanded and secularized universities, while others remained doctrinally conservative. After World War I ended in 1918, some members of this conservative wing came out fighting, so to speak, and called themselves "fundamentalists." At this time, fundamentalism was almost as varied a group as the evangelicalism from which it had sprung. The fundamentalists of the early 1920s included conservative Episcopalians, Presbyterians, Disciples of Christ, members of Holiness groups, Pentecostals, and others.

However, after the public-relations disaster of the Scopes monkey trial in July 1925, in which biology teacher John T. Scopes was successfully tried for teaching Darwin's theory of evolution in a public school, fundamentalism was identified with willful ignorance and backwoods crudeness. It no longer referred to a coalition of intellectually respectable Protestant traditionalists united in their opposition to modernism. Rather, it was now understood as a rabble of small-town or rural religious extremists. As a result, many moderate or conservative Protestants dropped out of "fundamentalist" organizations after 1925 because they found the label embarrassing.

The next major change in the meaning of *fundamentalist* took place during the 1930s and 1940s, a period when the culture wars in the churches seemed to have quieted down. Fundamentalists began to leave the mainline denominations and set up their own separatist groups. They organized independent missionary organizations and established their own schools. The foundation of Bob Jones University belongs to this period, as does Dallas Theological Seminary and a large group of Bible colleges. By 1960, *fundamentalist* referred primarily to these separatist groups, the largest of which are the General Association of Regular Baptist Churches (GARBC) and IFCA International, formerly known as the Independent Fundamental Churches of America. Their reentry into American politics in response to the social upheavals of the turbulent 1960s led to Jerry Falwell's half-humorous definition of a fundamentalist as "an evangelical who is angry about something."[32] An updated version of the saying defines fundamentalists in the 21st century as "evangelicals with attitude."[33]

World War I and the Postwar Decade

NEW MOVEMENTS AND INSTITUTIONS

Prior to World War I, conservative Protestants who were concerned about modernism and the liberalism of the Social Gospel responded by launching a series of moral crusades that included the temperance movement. Led by such fiery evangelists as Billy Sunday (1862–1935), the temperance movement achieved temporary success with the enactment of Prohibition in 1919. There was also the Sabbatarian movement, which sought to keep businesses and places of amusement from opening on Sunday.

The major evangelical intellectual response to modernism is known as *dispensational premillennialism.* Dispensational premillennialism is a specific way of interpreting the various periods of time mentioned in the Bible. It was first taught by an Englishman named John Nelson Darby (1800–82), who brought his outline of history to the United States in 1862, where it was adopted and elaborated by Cyrus Scofield (1843–1921). Scofield was a Civil War veteran who became a minister and published the first edition of his Reference Bible in 1909. The 1966 revision of this work is still used by American dispensationalists. Scofield's system divided history into seven ages, or dispensations: innocence (before the Fall); conscience (the period between Adam and Noah); human government (the period between the Flood and Abraham); promise (the period of God's covenant with Abraham); law (the covenant with Moses and the giving of the Ten Commandments); grace (the period between the birth of Christ and the Second Coming); and the fullness of time (the millennium, when Christ shall return, restore the kingdom of Israel, and reign for a thousand years).

Dispensationalist premillenialism was important to fundamentalists because it could be used in teaching the thousands of students who enrolled in the new Bible colleges that sprang up during this period. The most outstanding of these was Dwight L. Moody's Bible Institute in Chicago. Dispensationalist leaders also sponsored the publication of *The Fundamentals* (1910–15), a 12-volume series of paperback books that gave the fundamentalist movement its name.

Two other significant developments within American Protestantism during this period are the Holiness and Pentecostal movements. The Holiness movement practically reversed the ethical teachings of modernist clergy.

Instead of maintaining that people are basically good and need only strive to bring their outward behavior into conformity with their inner goodness, the leaders of Holiness groups taught that the supernatural gifts of the Holy Spirit are necessary to overcome humanity's natural inclination to sin. In addition, the Holiness movement believed that a sudden and dramatic conversion experience, followed by a "second blessing," had to take place to fully cleanse the heart.

Pentecostalism originated within American Holiness groups shortly after 1900. Like them, it appealed to the less educated and the socially marginalized. For a brief period after 1905, Pentecostalism was the only American religious group that was fully integrated racially and also accepted women as leaders on an equal basis with men. Where Pentecostalism went beyond the Holiness movement was its insistence that the age of the New Testament miracles is not yet past and that if the Holy Spirit is present, he will manifest himself in such signs as speaking in tongues and miraculous healings. The specific event that touched off the rapid spread of Pentecostalism was the Azusa Street revivals at the Apostolic Faith mission in Los Angeles in 1906. These were led by a black evangelist named William J. Seymour (1870–1922). The largest single denomination that came out of the Pentecostalist movement was the Assemblies of God, established in 1914.

POSTWAR ANXIETY

The armistice that ended World War I in 1918 was followed by what a historian of the postwar decade has called a "revolution in manners and morals."[34] In addition to concerns about the "flaming youth" of the postwar period, Americans were also shaken by industrial unrest, strikes, the spread of communist revolution in Europe, and domestic terrorism. One unnerving episode concerned three dozen package bombs mailed to prominent Americans in April 1919. The worst attack, however, was the explosion that killed 33 people and injured 400 more on September 16, 1920, when a TNT bomb loaded on a horse-drawn cart went off on Wall Street in New York City, 200 feet from the New York Stock Exchange. The bomber escaped and was never found.[35] Many Americans in the postwar years were discouraged or frightened, or both, by the social and political chaos that seemed to be erupting all around them and so were receptive to the pessimistic messages of fundamentalism. Most fundamentalists did not work out a complete political position before World War I, but the Russian Revolution of 1917 and its bloody aftermath led some fundamentalist leaders to associate Bolshevism with the teaching of evolution, the secularism of the universities, and the general "looseness" of contemporary morals as part of a vast cosmic plot against the kingdom of God.[36]

THE BATTLE FOR DENOMINATIONAL CONTROL

The dramatic "made for media" aspect of the Scopes trial has tended to overshadow an equally important struggle between modernists and fundamentalists for institutional control of the mainline Protestant churches. This contest began before the outbreak of World War I but reached its peak in the years between 1922 and 1925. It provides the context for understanding the publication of *The Fundamentals* from 1910 to 1915.

Some churches were relatively unaffected by the struggle. They included the Northern Methodists and the Congregationalists, which were dominated by theological liberals; the Southern Baptists and Southern Methodists, which were dominated by conservatives; the Episcopalians, who were divided by internal quarrels over worship practices; and the Lutheran churches, which were still largely composed of recent German and Scandinavian immigrants and, in any case, had a distinctive approach to theology. The battle between fundamentalism and modernism was most intense within the Disciples of Christ, the Northern Presbyterian, and the Northern Baptist churches.

The Fundamentals, the series of booklets that began to appear in 1910 through the funding of Lyman and Milton Stewart, two wealthy Los Angeles laymen, should not be misunderstood as anti-intellectual tracts. The Stewarts enlisted a distinguished group of conservative Protestants that included the Anglican bishop of Durham, the president of a Baptist seminary, and Benjamin Warfield, a conservative Presbyterian theologian who taught at Princeton Seminary. The articles they produced had "dignity, breadth of subject matter, rhetorical moderation, obvious conviction, and considerable intellectual power. . . . The conservative case was firmly and honorably made."[37] The central issue for *The Fundamentals* was to construct a defense of the authority of the Bible without attacking the legitimate place of science and reason in the life of the mind.

The critical period between 1922 and the Scopes trial in 1925, however, ended with the apparently complete victory of modernism. This phase of the struggle began in May 1922, when Harry Emerson Fosdick (1878–1969), a liberal Baptist minister who was serving as guest preacher at the First Presbyterian Church in New York City, delivered a sermon titled "Shall the Fundamentalists Win?" Fosdick was answered by Clarence Macartney, the senior pastor of the Arch Street Presbyterian Church in Philadelphia, in a sermon called "Shall Unbelief Win?" Macartney then led a successful campaign to have Fosdick expelled from his Presbyterian pulpit. In 1923, J. Gresham Machen, Warfield's successor at Princeton Seminary, published *Christianity and Liberalism.* In it, he argued that liberalism was simply not Christian and that the liberals should be invited to leave the mainline churches. Over the next two years, fundamentalists in both the Northern Baptist and Presbyterian churches came close to winning control of those denominations.

Then came the Scopes trial, which made fundamentalism an object of mockery in many quarters. It was followed in 1927 by Sinclair Lewis's publication of *Elmer Gantry,* a satirical novel that attacked the hypocrisy as well as the pulpit style of fundamentalists. Lewis is thought to have based the character of Gantry on John Roach Straton (1875–1929), the pastor of Calvary Baptist Church in New York City who published a newspaper called the *Fundamentalist.* In 1929, Princeton Seminary reorganized its faculty, causing Machen to withdraw from the school and start a Presbyterian seminary of his own in Philadelphia. By 1936, the division among the Presbyterians led to the formation of a new denomination, the Orthodox Presbyterian Church. On the Baptist side, the modernists were helped by the denomination's loose internal structure. Although the fundamentalists made several attempts between 1923 and 1925 to win majority votes at the annual convention of the Northern Baptists, they did not gain any lasting success on the three issues most important to them—drawing up a formal statement of Baptist doctrine, rooting out modernism among Baptist foreign missionaries, and reversing the liberalism of the seminaries.

FUNDAMENTALISTS AND POLITICS DURING THE DEPRESSION

The Great Depression of the 1930s prompted many anxious citizens to look for extreme political or religious answers to their problems. The new Holiness and Pentecostal denominations grew rapidly in the early 1930s, the Assemblies of God, for example, increasing its membership from 46,000 in 1926 to 148,000 in 1936.[38] The more aggressive fundamentalists within the Baptist, Presbyterian, and Methodist churches began to form interdenominational federations. The American Council of Christian Churches (ACCC) was founded in 1941 by Carl McIntire in direct opposition to the Federal Council of Churches (the forerunner of the present-day National Council of Churches), which had been set up in 1908 by the mainline denominations. The ACCC has remained a militantly separatist group; with a 2006 membership of seven denominations, it continues to refuse membership to any church that belongs to the World Council of Churches, the World Evangelical Fellowship, or any part of the ecumenical movement.

The National Association of Evangelicals (NAE), which was an early sign of the coming split between fundamentalists and evangelicals, was founded in 1942. It could be loosely defined as the continuation of the mainstream fundamentalism represented by Moody. Many of its early leaders had been associated with Moody's Bible Institute, Wheaton College, and Dallas

Theological Seminary. As of 2006, the NAE has 52 member denominations, which are allowed to hold dual membership in the National Council of Churches and other ecumenical organizations.

The second strategy adopted by fundamentalists and evangelicals during the late 1930s and early 1940s was the formation of Bible schools and other forms of ministry that were independent of denominational control. Radio programs were a highly successful innovation. By 1940, Charles E. Fuller, a radio preacher who hosted the "Old-Fashioned Revival Hour," had the largest radio audience in the United States. The Bible Institute set up several local radio stations in the Chicago area. Youth programs were also popular; Youth for Christ International was organized in the early 1940s. The first full-time evangelist for Youth for Christ was a recent graduate of Wheaton College named Billy Graham.

The 1930s were a quiet period for conservative Protestants in terms of political activity. The reason for this relative lack of interest was their attachment to dispensational premillennialism, which implied that political activity on the part of Christians was either doomed to failure or an unnecessary waste of energy in view of the closeness of the Second Coming.

Religious Revival after World War II

Religious faith in the United States underwent a resurgence in the years after 1945. All faith groups benefited, from the large mainline denominations to the smaller sects. Formal membership in a church or synagogue rose from 47 percent of the American population in 1930 to 69 percent in 1960.

The religious revival of the 1950s helped to revitalize American civil religion, in part as a response to the perceived threat of communism during the cold war. Presidential prayer breakfasts first became a part of the Washington landscape under the administration of Dwight D. Eisenhower, and the phrase "under God" was added to the Pledge of Allegiance in 1954. This reawakened civil religion, however, was no more explicitly Christian than its 18th-century version had been. If anything, it was even emptier of biblical content. President Eisenhower made a remark in the course of a speech on Flag Day in 1954 that perfectly reflected the vagueness of 1950s civil religion: "Our government makes no sense unless it is founded on a deeply held religious belief—and I don't care what it is."[39]

FUNDAMENTALISTS AND EVANGELICALS PART WAYS

The relationship between evangelical and fundamentalist Protestants, which had been uneasy since the early 1940s, became an open break in the 1950s. Paradoxically, the separation came about partly because of the very success of the conservative Protestant churches after World War II. Their membership grew by 400 to 700 percent between 1945 and 1965, compared to increases of 75 to 90 percent for the mainline churches.[40] The formation of the NAE in 1942 gave the evangelical bodies an organizational framework that allowed them to speak with one voice on such matters of concern as church-state relationships, the military chaplaincy, and prayer in public schools.

Another factor that increased the visibility of the evangelicals was their concern in overcoming the stereotype of conservative Protestants as poorly educated and anti-intellectual. Fuller Theological Seminary, founded in Pasadena, California, in 1947, was intended to offer a rigorous theological education—including Ph.D. programs—to qualified students.[41] At the level of undergraduate education, evangelicals supported the spread of such interdenominational parachurch organizations as InterVarsity Christian Fellowship and Campus Crusade for Christ. These groups offered opportunities for Bible study, discussion groups, and mission work in inner cities as well as fellowship and worship.

Evangelicals also began to publish interdenominational journals intended for educated laypeople who were not religious professionals. In 1956, Carl F. H. Henry (1913–2003), an evangelical who had entered the Baptist ministry after an early career in journalism, accepted Billy Graham's challenge to start a journal that would be the evangelical counterpart to the liberal *Christian Century.* Henry left his position as the first dean of Fuller Theological Seminary to become the founding editor of *Christianity Today.*

The immediate cause of the split between the evangelicals and the fundamentalists, however, was Graham's decision in 1955 to accept the sponsorship of the New York City Council of Churches for his crusade in the city, scheduled for 1957. The separatist fundamentalists regarded Graham's openness to mainline Protestants as the first step toward modernism, and they withdrew their support of his crusades. Both sides agree that the split has not healed as of the early 2000s.[42]

THE REVIVAL OF FUNDAMENTALISM

The 1960s and 1970s saw a reemergence of fundamentalism in the public sphere and a political realignment of conservative Christians in general. One new area of activity was the establishment of a network of private Christian academies and high schools; it is estimated that the number of such schools reached 10,000 by 1983.[43] These schools were soon followed by a homeschooling movement, which was estimated by a 2000 report of the National Home Education Research Institute of the U.S. Department of Education to include anywhere from 500,000 to 2 million students in 2000.

The next stage in the fundamentalist resurgence was the formation of political action groups and organizations in the Vietnam War era. Fundamentalism benefited from the countercultural protests of the late 1960s because the excesses of the counterculture and its eventual descent into kidnappings, bank robberies, and other forms of urban terrorism after the "Days of Rage" in 1968[44]—as well as the general cultural drift toward greater permissiveness regarding drug use and sexual activity—made conservative forms of Christianity appealing.

Although the Moral Majority, a political action group headed by Falwell that emerged in 1979, is sometimes described as a new type of fundamentalist crusade, it is perhaps better understood as an outgrowth of a political realignment that began to take shape in 1972. The presidential campaign of George McGovern marked a turning point in the religious composition of the Democratic Party. The 1972 convention was the first in which secularists (atheists, agnostics, the unchurched, and others who identified themselves as in some sense irreligious) were the largest "religious" grouping among the delegates; the secularists overwhelmed the ethnic Roman Catholics and Southern Protestant evangelicals who had previously represented important Democratic constituencies.[45] The balance between secularists and religious traditionalists shifted even further in favor of the secularists with each successive election cycle, prompting some religious conservatives to bolt to the Republican Party.

What was even more striking about this political realignment was the formation of a new alliance in the 1980s between Protestant evangelicals and Roman Catholics with regard to family issues and national security. Whereas the Republican Party of the 19th century had been characterized by periodic upsurges of anti-Catholic feeling, anti-Catholicism had all but disappeared by the mid-1970s.[46] In the early 2000s, this faith-based alliance broadened to include a growing number of Jews.[47] Although some American Jews are still uneasy about political cooperation with evangelical Christians, others maintain that Christian support is to be welcomed on the basis of Israel's present-day needs, "so long as evangelicals do not target Jews for proselytization."[48]

CASE STUDY: THE LUTHERAN CHURCH–MISSOURI SYNOD

One aspect of the resurgence of American Protestant fundamentalism that is often overlooked is the fundamentalist takeover of two denominations representing very different ethnic and cultural backgrounds, namely the Lutheran Church–Missouri Synod (LCMS) and the Southern Baptist Convention (SBC).

The case of the LCMS is particularly interesting because Lutheranism as a whole is atypical of American Protestantism. Unlike the churches of the Reformed tradition, Lutherans are not Puritans. Martin Luther had no objection to dancing, drinking, and other human pleasures in moderation; he wished to retain the contributions of the visual arts as well as music to Christian worship; and he kept the basic structure of the Catholic Mass when he translated it into German. In addition, Lutheran theology has been characterized since its beginnings with a high regard for the history of the church and for the authority of a collection of confessional documents (the Book of Concord) as a guide to the proper understanding of the Scriptures. This sense of history and respect for the confessional tradition kept Lutherans apart from the Protestant mainstream during the 19th century, as did their ethnic divisions. The various U.S. Lutheran bodies were founded by settlers speaking five different Scandinavian languages, several different German dialects, Slovak, or Czech. It was not until the 1960s that most of the smaller groups had merged to form three major Lutheran bodies, one of which was the LCMS.

It is possible to regard the schism that took place in 1973 and 1974 within the LCMS as Lutheranism's delayed encounter with the modernist-fundamentalist quarrels that disrupted American evangelicalism in the 1880s and 1920s.[49] The LCMS was German in terms of ethnic origin and reflected the changes within American Lutheranism caused by mass emigration from Europe in the 19th century; the Lutheran population of the United States quintupled in the period between 1870 and 1910, from 500,000 to 2.5 million.[50] The Lutheran immigrants who started the Missouri Synod in 1839 were not motivated by missionary concerns; they had left Prussia to escape the king's forced union of the Lutheran and Reformed Churches in 1817.

As of the early 2000s, the LCMS had 2.7 million members and was the 11th largest Christian denomination in the United States. It has always had a tendency toward separatism in regard to other Lutherans as well as other Christian churches. It still practices closed communion, which means that neither members of other Lutheran bodies nor non-Lutheran Christians can receive Holy Communion in an LCMS congregation. It has never belonged to the National Council of Churches, the World Council of Churches, or even the Lutheran World Federation.

The LCMS differs from other fundamentalist groups, however, in its concern for education. It still maintains the largest non–Roman Catholic parochial school system in the United States, with 62 high schools and 1,786 elementary schools and preschool programs.[51] The LCMS also had, prior to the events of 1973 and 1974, "a system of theological education equal to any in quality and rigor."[52] Far from being a bastion of anti-intellectualism, Concordia Seminary in St. Louis, for example, was one of the most demanding schools of theology in the United States.

The immediate cause of the disruption within the LCMS was a conservative group's insistence on the doctrine of scriptural inerrancy and infallibility, which the Missouri Synod, alone among the American Lutheran churches, had maintained since the 1920s. The conservatives had been organizing since the 1960s and managed to get one of their own, Jacob A. O. Preus, elected as the president of the LCMS in 1969. This politicking was helped by LCMS congregational polity, which gave small rural churches a disproportionate number of delegates at LCMS conventions.[53] John Tietjen (1928–2004), who had become the president of Concordia Seminary in 1969, was the leader of the moderate group. From 1970 to 1974, Preus conducted investigations of the Concordia faculty, accusing various professors of "teaching false doctrine"—behavior that led the Association of Theological Schools (ATS) to put the seminary on academic probation. In February 1974, most of the Concordia students and faculty walked off campus, forming a "seminary in exile," Seminex. The moderates forced out of the LCMS formed the Association of Evangelical Lutheran Churches (AELC) in 1976. That body then merged with the Lutheran Church in America (LCA) and the American Lutheran Church (ALC) in 1988 to form the present Evangelical Lutheran Church in America.

CASE STUDY: THE SOUTHERN BAPTIST CONVENTION

The fundamentalist takeover of the SBC began several years later than its counterpart in the LCMS. Conservatives established a fellowship within the convention and started their own journal in the early 1970s. Like the conservative wing of the LCMS, the SBC conservatives were committed to the doctrine of scriptural inerrancy, but they combined it with acceptance of dispensational premillenialism rather than subscription to a set of confessional documents. Unlike the LCMS, which has its strongest regional concentration in the Midwest, the SBC is particularly strong in the Deep South and Texas, an area of the country deeply affected by the social changes of the 1960s and 1970s—especially the influx of new residents from the North, which meant that fundamentalists now confronted liberals and modernists on their own turf.[54]

The fundamentalists' capture of the denominational administration was made possible in part by the fairly loose structure of the SBC. Paul Pressler, a Texas judge, worked together with Paige Patterson, the president of Southwestern Baptist Theological Seminary, to have a conservative elected president of the SBC. Pressler's study of the denomination's internal structure showed that the president's office was the key to changing the membership of the boards of trustees that run the denomination's seminaries and other agencies, because the president has the authority to nominate new trustees.[55] In 1979, Adrian Rogers (1931–2005) was elected to the presidency of the SBC on a platform of biblical inerrancy. Rogers served as president for three terms, strengthening fundamentalist control over the denomination's publishing house, seminaries, and social welfare agencies. All seminary employees were required to adhere to the Baptist Faith and Message, the SBC's official statement of belief, which Rogers had a hand in revising after he was no longer president. The Baptist Faith and Message was originally composed in 1925 and revised in 1963. The revision of the 1963 text of the statement, which went into effect in October 2000, was sufficiently controversial, particularly with regard to the position of women, to cause former U.S. president Jimmy Carter to leave the SBC.[56] The denomination is still conservative as of the early 2000s in its commitment to temperance (avoiding the use of alcohol and tobacco), biblical inerrancy, evangelism, and the political agenda of the Christian Right.

The New Religious Right

THE MORAL MAJORITY/CHRISTIAN COALITION OF AMERICA

The Moral Majority, organized in 1979 by Falwell, is usually considered the first political manifestation of the Christian Right. The movement was made possible by the growth of mega-churches largely independent of denominational control, combined with fund-raising techniques copied from the televangelists of the 1970s. The Moral Majority was a typical interdenominational venture, its first leaders consisting of a Presbyterian, a Southern Baptist, and two independent Baptists. The movement lobbied politicians and sent direct mailings to voters about such issues as abortion, the Equal Rights Amendment, homosexuality, and media subversion of family values. It has never been clear, however, how much influence the Moral Majority actually had on political developments of the early 1980s.

Falwell dissolved the Moral Majority in 1989. Its successor organization is the Christian Coalition of America (CCA), organized by televangelist Pat Robertson after his failed presidential campaign in 1988. The CCA is somewhat more inclusive than its predecessor organization; its definition of "people of faith" includes Roman Catholics, members of mainline Protestant churches, and Pentecostals, as well as evangelical and fundamentalist Protestants. Its size has been disputed; estimates range between 400,000 and 1.2 million members, while the CCA itself claims a membership of 2 million as of early 2006. Its present efforts emphasize voter education on pro-family issues.

CHRISTIAN RECONSTRUCTIONISM AND DOMINION THEOLOGY

The controversies over abortion following *Roe v. Wade* in 1973 led not only to the formation of such movements as Operation Rescue, a Christian pro-life organization founded in 1986 but also to such extreme actions as the killing of abortion providers. Paul Hill, executed for the shooting of Dr. John Stratton, and several others in the radical anti-abortion movement represent a form of fundamentalist activism called Christian reconstructionism, dominionism, or dominion theology.[57]

Christian reconstructionism is not a denomination but an intellectual trend. Derived from one strand of Calvinist thought, which regarded the moral law of the Old Testament as binding on the state as well as the church, Christian reconstructionism not only mandates biblical law as the basis of civil government but also urges the introduction of Old Testament penalties for such offenses as incest, homosexuality, adultery, and even habitual disobedience on the part of children. In addition, Christian reconstructionism is postmillennial, which means that its adherents believe that the Second Coming will occur after a period of a thousand years of religious utopia. They therefore hold that Christians have a duty to exercise dominion over all areas of political, economic, and intellectual life in order to bring about Christ's return as soon as possible. One reconstructionist, Gary North, has been quoted as saying that Christians have a moral obligation "to recapture every institution for Jesus Christ."[58]

Most of the writers claimed as authorities by Christian reconstructionists are Calvinists. They include Francis Schaeffer (1912–84), a Presbyterian minister and writer whose *Christian Manifesto* (1982) is sometimes regarded as an early form of modern-day reconstructionism. It is plain, however, from a lecture Schaeffer gave in 1982 that he saw Christian political activism more in terms of civil disobedience than revolt. He was also quite definite in his rejection of theocracy:

> *I said it, but let me say it again, we do not want a theocracy! I personally am opposed to a theocracy. On this side of the New Testament I do not believe there is a place for a theocracy 'till Jesus the King comes back. . . . We are only asking for one thing. We are asking for the freedom that the First Amendment guaranteed. That's what we should be standing for. . . . Caesar is not to be put in the place of God and we as Christians, in the name of the Lordship of Christ, and all of life, must so think and act on the appropriate level. It should always be on the appropriate level. We have lots of room to move yet with our court cases, with the people we elect—all the things that we can do in this country. If, unhappily, we come to that place, the appropriate level must also include a disobedience to the state.*[59]

Schaeffer had studied under Cornelius van Til (1895–1987), a conservative Presbyterian theologian claimed as a mentor by Rousas J. Rushdoony

(1916–2001), considered the founder of Christian reconstructionism. Greg Bahnsen (1948–95) was another leader of the movement who borrowed the term *theonomy* (government by God's law) from van Til to describe the movement's approach to political ethics. Van Til himself, however, rejected the type of right-wing political activism that some of his former students advocated.

Rushdoony set up the Chalcedon Foundation, which is basically a Christian reconstructionist think tank, in 1965. Originally interested in homeschooling as a way to turn back the influence of secular humanism, Rushdoony expanded his scope to include research, sponsoring lectureships, and publishing materials on Christian reconstructionism. The foundation's mission statement is forthright: "It is not only our duty as individuals, families and churches to be Christian, but it is also the duty of the state, the school, the arts and sciences, law, economics, and every other sphere to be under Christ the King. Nothing is exempt from His dominion."[60]

As with the CCA, it is not clear how much influence Christian reconstructionists have outside their own circles, although some opponents of the movement claim that they have an influence out of all proportion to their numbers. Most critics concede, however, that the movement is not likely to develop a large following, even among other fundamentalists.[61] In spite of reconstructionism's emphasis on grassroots organizing, much of its literature is written in a dry academic style that has little appeal for most readers. In addition, the movement split internally in 1985 due to disagreements over relatively minor points. The chief significance of Christian reconstructionism for the future seems to be its postmillennial justification of ongoing Christian involvement in the political order.[62]

CHRISTIAN IDENTITY

Christian Identity is not a single organization but a category for identifying various white power groups rejected by mainstream orthodox and evangelical Christians. The various leaders of Christian Identity groups have combined the Genesis story of creation with ideas borrowed from such racist groups as the Ku Klux Klan, political conspiracy theories, millenarian speculation, and even science fiction. Some Christian Identity groups teach that Adam and Eve were white people and that the Jews are the result of Eve's intercourse with Satan (the serpent in the Garden of Eden), while others believe that Jews are aliens from outer space. Another common belief among members of Christian Identity groups is that the commandment forbidding adultery does not refer to sexual intercourse outside marriage but to interracial marriage.

Christian Identity groups are derived from British Israelism (sometimes called Anglo-Israelism), a set of beliefs that holds that the British, or white

Europeans in general, are the direct descendants of the 10 lost tribes of Israel. British Israelism in its origins was not anti-Semitic. Christian Identity in its racist and anti-Semitic form is usually traced to Howard Rand (1889–1991), a second-generation believer in British Israelism who created the Anglo-Saxon Federation of America in 1930, and Wesley Swift (1913–70), who started his own church in California in the 1940s. Some of Rand's early recruits had been members of the Ku Klux Klan, who brought their racist beliefs into the organization.

Swift blended British Israelism with his own racist notions and anti-Semitic conspiracy theories. He taught that the white descendants of the lost tribes are God's chosen people, that present-day Jews are engaged in a conspiracy together with the Freemasons against the true chosen people and have virtually unlimited control over the government and the economy, and that blacks and Asians ("mud people") are inferior to whites because they are descended from animals. In 1957, Swift changed the name of his group to the Church of Jesus Christ Christian, which has been recycled by Aryan Nations (AN) groups.

AN is distinguished by its belief that the catastrophe preceding the end of the world will occur in the United States rather than the Middle East. It is opposed to the federal government, which it routinely refers to as the ZOG, or Zionist occupational government. The original goal of the movement was to take five states in the Pacific Northwest (Oregon, Washington, Idaho, Montana, and Wyoming) by force in order to establish a homeland for whites. This goal is sometimes referred to as the Northwest Territorial Imperative. The headquarters of the AN was located at Hayden Lake, Idaho, until 2001, when it was sold to pay off a lawsuit.

The Hayden Lake compound was started in 1973 by Richard Butler (1918–2004), a former aeronautical engineer who had met Swift in California and decided to join the Christian Identity movement. An annual event at the compound was the World Congress, which attracted a number of extreme right-wing paramilitary and white supremacist groups. The Federal Bureau of Investigation (FBI) estimated that there were at least 75 separate groups of this type in the United States by 1984.[63] In the early 2000s, the larger Christian Identity groups include the Hammerskins, the Kingdom Identity Ministries, the White Separatist Banner, and Jubilee. The AN group reconstituted itself in Alabama prior to Butler's death in 2004.

AN has spawned subgroups within its membership, such as The Order, formed by Robert Jay Mathews (1953–84) in the early 1980s. Mathews had been influenced by an apocalyptic 1978 novel about violent revolution called *The Turner Diaries,* written by physics professor William Pierce (1933–2002).

Although Pierce always denied any connection with Christian Identity, claiming instead to be the founder of the Cosmotheist Community Church (1978), he had been associated with the American Nazi Party and founded a white supremacist group called the National Alliance. Pierce's book proved to be a decisive influence on the Oklahoma City bomber, Timothy McVeigh, as well as Mathews.

The worldview of AN is far more pessimistic and conspiratorial than that of Christian reconstructionism. Members believe that armed revolution is necessary to overthrow the slavery imposed by the ZOG. In this respect AN is unusual among American groups that have been influenced by fundamentalism. Louis Freeh, a former director of the FBI, was sufficiently concerned about the potential for general violence at the end of 1999 that he warned police chiefs across the United States "that in preparation for the new millennium, certain individuals tied to [Christian Identity] groups have been acquiring weapons, storing food and clothing, raising funds, procuring safe houses, preparing compounds, surveying potential targets, and recruiting converts to their cause."[64] Fascination with society-wide revolution helps to explain why the Hayden Lake compound and such other Christian Identity communities as Elohim City in Oklahoma stockpiled weapons and ammunition, conducted survival training courses, and set up paramilitary schools.[65]

Christian Identity and Terrorism

Mathews's The Order was formed with the intention of inciting a race war through targeted assassinations, robberies, and the destruction of such proofs of the worldwide Jewish-Freemason conspiracy as adult movie theaters. After a series of successful holdups of armored cars in early 1984, Mathews and three other members of The Order shot and killed Alan Berg, a controversial radio talk-show host, in Denver on June 18. Mathews eventually died of smoke inhalation in December 1984 when his hideout on an island in Puget Sound was surrounded by the FBI and set on fire.[66]

Not all terrorists influenced by Christian Identity are members of organized groups or cells, however. There are loners on the fringes of the movement, such as Buford Furrow, Jr. (1962–) who lived for a time in the Hayden Lake compound and married Mathews's widow. Furrow attacked a Jewish day-care center in Los Angeles on August 10, 1999, and killed a Filipino-American letter carrier delivering mail in the area an hour later. Furrow was sentenced to life in prison.[67] The absence of a central Christian Identity organization or structure allows mentally unstable individuals to move from one group to another or belong to several at the same time, and allows these groups to relocate quickly in order to continue their activities.

McVeigh (1968–2001) was neither a lone actor nor a member of the inner circle of an established Christian Identity group. Although he met his associates, Terry Nichols and Michael Fortier, during his army training in 1988, his decision to engage in terrorism was apparently triggered by the disastrous end of the siege of the Branch Davidian compound at Waco, Texas, on April 19, 1993. McVeigh had already read Pierce's *Turner Diaries* when he consulted the book as a guide to purchasing and assembling the mixture of fertilizer and fuel oil, described in detail in the novel, to blow up a federal building.[68]

About two weeks before the bombing of the federal building in Oklahoma City, which McVeigh selected as his target because he thought that it contained offices of the Bureau of Alcohol, Tobacco, and Firearms—the agency responsible for the Waco shootout and fire—he contacted the Christian Identity compound at Elohim City. While some observers suggest that McVeigh made the call in order to find out whether he could use the place as a hideout after the bombing, others believe that he was trying to recruit some of the residents as co-conspirators. CBS News reported in February 2004 that a gang of white supremacist bank robbers called the Aryan Republican Army was apparently involved in the Oklahoma City bombing. The gang members lived for a while in the Elohim City camp in 1994 and 1995.[69]

FUTURE

It is difficult to predict the future of fundamentalism in the United States, if only because there are so many different groups with so many different emphases and ways of responding to contemporary cultural and political pressures. With regard to Christian Identity, it is likely that ongoing surveillance by the FBI and the consequent need for secrecy will keep such groups small. On the other hand, another successful terrorist attack on the scale of 9/11 might well make these militant groups attractive to persons—particularly in the rural South and parts of the intermountain West—who do not trust the federal government to protect them.

Such larger fundamentalist churches as the Lutheran Church–Missouri Synod and the Southern Baptist Convention may continue to gain members from mainline Protestant bodies who disapprove of the growing politicization of these denominations. The Protestant fundamentalist bodies are more likely to gain members from the United Church of Christ and the liberal Presbyterian, Baptist, and Methodist Churches, however, as the evidence indicates that disaffected Lutherans and Episcopalians leave their respective churches for Roman Catholicism or Eastern Orthodoxy.[70]

Smaller Protestant fundamentalist groups may well maintain or increase their membership as a result of their interest in the rapidly growing homeschooling movement. As of the early 2000s, the U.S. Census Bureau reported that 33 percent of parents involved in homeschooling mention religion as their primary reason for withdrawing their children from public schools.[71]

Ultratraditionalist Roman Catholicism is not likely to expand its membership in the United States. Pope Benedict XVI's attempts to heal the schism with the Society of St. Pius X and other ultratraditionalist groups have the approval of most American Catholics. In addition, the pope's scholarly defense of Catholic teaching, most evident in his controversial lecture delivered in Regensburg, Germany, on September 12, 2006, has made him an appealing figure to many observers in the United States as well as Europe.[72]

It is possible that political pressure from Muslims in the United States for special treatment in public facilities will lead to new coalitions of conservative Jews and Christians, possibly including some fundamentalist Christian groups. Recent Muslim demands have included the construction of prayer rooms for Muslims in public schools and places of business, the exclusion of men and non-Muslims during special hours for Muslim women in public swimming pools, and the right of Muslim taxi drivers to refuse passengers carrying alcohol or accompanied by seeing-eye dogs.[73]

Unlike other forms of religious separatism, these demands are seen as attempts to impose the beliefs and practices of one faith on others who must share public spaces or transportation. Many nonbelievers, as well as practicing Jews and Christians, are disturbed by what they perceive as Muslim lack of reciprocity and refusal to respect or accept the tradition of religious pluralism in the United States. These perceptions of Muslim intolerance are likely to strengthen existing cooperation between American Jews and Christians in support for the state of Israel as well as other interfaith activities.

---

[1] Dietrich Bonhoeffer. *No Rusty Swords: Letters, Lectures, and Notes, 1928–1936.* Edited by Edwin H. Robinson. New York: Harper & Row, 1965, p. 94.

[2] Sydney E. Ahlstrom. *A Religious History of the American People.* New Haven, Conn.: Yale University Press, 1972, p. 124.

[3] John Winthrop. "A Model of Christian Charity." 1630. Available online. URL: http://religiousfreedom.lib.virginia.edu/sacred/charity.html. Accessed November 5, 2005. Winthrop's scriptural reference is 1 Corinthians 12.

[4] "Mayflower Compact." November 11, 1620. Avalon Project at Yale Law School. Available online. URL: http://www.yale.edu/lawweb/avalon/amerdoc/mayflower.htm. Accessed November 12, 2005. Text is slightly modernized by the host Web site.

[5] Bernard Lewis. *What Went Wrong? The Clash between Islam and Modernity in the Middle East.* New York: HarperCollins, 2002, pp. 100–101.

[6] Quoted in Ahlstrom. *A Religious History of the American People,* p. 282.

[7] Jonathan Edwards. "The Pleasantness of Religion." In Wilson H. Kimnach, Kenneth P. Minkema, and Douglas A. Sweeney. *The Sermons of Jonathan Edwards: A Reader.* New Haven, Conn.: Yale University Press, 1999, pp. 15–18.

[8] Edwards. "Sermon to the Mohawks at the Treaty, August 16, 1751." In Kimnach, Minkema, and Sweeney. *The Sermons of Jonathan Edwards,* pp. 107–109. Edwards corresponded with various officials in England about the exploitation of the Mohawk and other tribes, doing what he could to protect them from unscrupulous traders. One of Edwards's letters was eventually forwarded to the archbishop of Canterbury.

[9] Ahlstrom. *A Religious History of the American People.* p. 283.

[10] John Wesley. "The Character of a Methodist." Available online. URL: http://gbgm-umc.org/umhistory/wesley/charmeth.stm. Accessed November 12, 2005.

[11] Listed in Ahlstrom. *A Religious History of the American People,* p. 379.

[12] "The Virginia Declaration of Rights." Gunston Hall Plantation. Available online. URL: http://www.gunstonhall.org/documents/vdr.html. Accessed October 28, 2005.

[13] "United States Constitution: Article VI." Cornell Law School, Legal Information Institute. Available online. URL: http://www.law.cornell.edu/constitution/constitution.articlevi.html. Accessed October 29, 2005.

[14] "The United States Constitution." USConstitution.net. Available online. URL: http://www.usconstitution.net/const.html. Accessed October 29, 2005.

[15] Figures in Ahlstrom. *A Religious History of the American People,* p. 344.

[16] Robert N. Bellah et al., *Habits of the Heart: Individualism and Commitment in American Life.* New York: Harper & Row, 1985, p. 221.

[17] Ahlstrom. *A Religious History of the American People,* p. 369.

[18] "The Constitution of Connecticut (1818)." State of Connecticut Secretary of the State. Available online. URL: http://www.sots.ct.gov/RegisterManual/SectionI/1818CTCO.HTM. Accessed November 6, 2005.

[19] Alexis de Tocqueville. "Chapter XII: Why Some Americans Manifest a Sort of Fanatical Spiritualism." *Democracy in America.* Vol. II. Available online. URL: http://xroads.virginia.edu/~HYPER/DETOC/ch2_12.htm. Accessed November 12, 2005.

[20] Robert N. Bellah. "Civil Religion in America." *Daedalus* 96 (Winter 1967), p. 3.

[21] George Washington. "First Inaugural Address." Avalon Project at Yale Law School. Available online. URL: http://www.yale.edu/lawweb/avalon/presiden/inaug/wash1.htm. Accessed November 13, 2005.

[22] Bellah. "Civil Religion in America," p. 7.

[23] Ahlstrom. *A Religious History of the American People,* p. 677.

[24] According to the Census of 1860. Available online. URL: http://www.census.gov/prod/www/ab5/decennial/1860.htm. Accessed December 7, 2005.

[25] Quoted in Paul A. Carter. *The Spiritual Crisis of the Gilded Age.* DeKalb, Ill.: Northern Illinois University Press, 1971, p. 5.

[26] The Fox sisters (Kate, Leah, and Margaret) were eventually exposed as frauds, one of them making a dramatic confession onstage at the New York Academy of Music in 1888.

[27] George M. Marsden. *Understanding Fundamentalism and Evangelicalism.* Grand Rapids, Mich.: William B. Eerdmans Publishing, 1991, p. 12.

[28] Ahlstrom. *A Religious History of the American People,* p. 454.

[29] Quoted in Carter. *The Spiritual Crisis of the Gilded Age,* p. 4.

[30] Marsden. *Understanding Fundamentalism and Evangelicalism,* pp. 4–5.

[31] James Davison Hunter. Introduction to *American Evangelicalism: Conservative Religion and the Quandary of Modernity.* New Brunswick, N.J.: Rutgers University Press, 1983.

[32] Quoted in Marsden. *Understanding Fundamentalism and Evangelicalism,* p. 1.

[33] David C. Steinmetz. "Democrats Don't Understand 'Evangelicalism.'" *Pittsburgh Tribune-Review,* November 28, 2004. Available online. URL: http://www.pittsburghlive.com/x/tribune-review/opinion/columnists/guests/print_277011.html. Accessed October 8, 2005.

[34] Frederick Lewis Allen. "The Revolution in Manners and Morals." In *Only Yesterday.* Available online. URL: http://xroads.virginia.edu/~HYPER/ALLEN/ch5.html. Accessed December 12, 2005.

[35] Allen. "The Big Red Scare." In *Only Yesterday.* Available online. URL: http://xroads.virginia.edu/~HYPER/ALLEN/ch3.html. Accessed December 12, 2005. At the time, the Wall Street bombing was the deadliest attack of that type in American history. The Federal Bureau of Investigation finally declared the file on the case inactive in 1940.

[36] George M. Marsden. *Fundamentalism and American Culture: The Shaping of Twentieth-Century Evangelicalism, 1870–1925.* Oxford: Oxford University Press, 1980, p. 211.

[37] Ahlstrom. *A Religious History of the American People,* p. 816.

[38] Figures in Ahlstrom. *A Religious History of the American People,* p. 920.

[39] Quoted in Michael McGough. "Faith and Change—a Paradox for Politics." *Los Angeles Times,* October 17, 2005. Available online. URL: http://www.latimes.com/news/opinion/commentary/la-oe-mcgough17oct17,0,1245506.story?coll=la-news-comment-opinions. Accessed December 7, 2005.

[40] Figures in Ahlstrom. *A Religious History of the American People,* p. 959.

[41] Fuller was accredited by the prestigious Association of Theological Schools in 1957, the first interdenominational evangelical seminary to be accepted.

[42] Ted Olson. "The End of Christian Fundamentalism?" Christianity Today Weblog. Available online. URL: http://www.christianitytoday.com/ct/2002/109/53.0.html. Posted March 15, 2002.

[43] Figures in Nancy T. Ammermann. "North American Protestant Fundamentalism." In Martin E. Marty and R. Scott Appleby, eds. *Fundamentalisms Observed.* Chicago: University of Chicago Press, 1991, p. 42.

[44] John Leonard. "Looking for Mr. Goodbomb." *The Nation* (October 15, 2001). Available online. URL: http://www.thenation.com/docprint.mhtml?i=20011015&s=leonard. Accessed December 20, 2005.

[45] Louis Bolce and Gerald De Maio. "The Politics of Partisan Neutrality." *First Things,* no. 143 (May 2004), p. 10.

[46] Marsden. *Understanding Fundamentalism and Evangelicalism,* p. 96.

[47] Steven Windmueller. "Are American Jews Becoming Republican? Insights into Jewish Political Behavior." *Jerusalem Viewpoints,* no. 509 (December 15, 2003). Available online. URL: http://www.jcpa.org/jl/vp509.htm. Accessed November 3, 2005.

[48] Carl Schrag. "American Jews and Evangelical Christians: Anatomy of a Changing Relationship." *Jewish Political Studies Review* 17 (Spring 2005). Available online. URL: http://www.jcpa.org/cjc/cjc-schrag-s05.htm. Accessed November 3, 2005.

[49] Mark Noll. "The Lutheran Difference." *First Things,* no. 20 (February 1992), pp. 31–40.

[50] Figures in Ahlstrom. *A Religious History of the American People,* p. 756.

[51] Figures in Samuel Nafzger. "An Introduction to the Lutheran Church–Missouri Synod." St. Louis, Mo.: Concordia Publishing, 1994, p. 2.

[52] Richard J. Neuhaus. "Schism and Renewal in American Lutheranism." *Theology Today* 30 (October 1973), p. 292.

[53] Neuhaus. "Schism and Renewal," p. 294.

[54] Ammermann. "North American Protestant Fundamentalism," p. 49.

[55] Ammermann. "North American Protestant Fundamentalism," p. 49.

[56] The texts of all three versions of the Baptist Faith and Message (1925, 1963, and 2000) are available online in parallel-column format. Southern Baptist Convention. URL: http://www.sbc.net/bfm/bfmcomparison.asp. Accessed December 19, 2005.

[57] The relationship of these three names for the movement is fluid; some writers use them virtually interchangeably, while others define Christian reconstructionism as the extreme right wing of dominion theology. *Dominionism* appears to be a term generally used by liberal or left-wing opponents of the movement.

[58] Quoted in Mark Juergensmeyer. *Terror in the Mind of God.* Berkeley: University of California Press, 2003, p. 28.

[59] Francis Schaeffer. "A Christian Manifesto." People for Life. Available online. URL: http://www.peopleforlife.org/francis.html. Accessed December 20, 2005.

[60] Chalcedon Foundation. "The Ministry of Chalcedon." Available online. URL: http://www.chalcedon.edu/ministry.php. Accessed December 19, 2005.

[61] Karen Armstrong. *The Battle for God: A History of Fundamentalism.* New York: Ballantine Books, 2001, p. 362.

[62] Ammermann. "North American Protestant Fundamentalism," p. 55.

[63] Stephen Singular. *Talked to Death: The Murder of Alan Berg and the Rise of the Neo-Nazis.* New York: Beech Tree Books, 1987, p. 87.

[64] David A. Vise and Lorraine Adams. "FBI Warns '2000' May Spark Violence." *Washington Post,* October 31, 1999. Available online. URL: http://www.cesnur.org/testi/FBI_003.htm#Anchor-47857. Accessed November 22, 2005.

[65] Juergensmeyer. *Terror in the Mind of God,* p. 34.

[66] Singular. *Talked to Death,* p. 247.

[67] Heath Foster. "The Hate-Filled Descent of Buford Furrow." *Seattle Post-Intelligencer,* September 17, 1999. Available online. URL: http://seattlepi.nwsource.com/local/furr17.shtml. Accessed December 3, 2005.

[68] Juergensmeyer. *Terror in the Mind of God,* p. 32.

[69] CBS News. "OKC Bombing a Wider Conspiracy?" February 25, 2004. Available online. URL: http://www.cbsnews.com/stories/2004/02/25/national/main602196.shtml. Accessed December 3, 2005.

[70] Jason Byassee, "Going Catholic: Six Journeys to Rome," *Christian Century,* August 22, 2006. Available online. URL: http://www.christiancentury.org/article.lasso?id=2290. Accessed October 10, 2006.

[71] Kurt J. Bauman, U.S. Census Bureau, "Home Schooling in the United States: Trends and Characteristics," Working Paper Series No. 53. Available online. URL: http://www.census.gov/population/www/documentation/twps0053.html. Accessed October 11, 2006.

[72] The official Vatican translation of the lecture, titled "Three Stages in the Program of De-Hellenization" is available on the Web site of the Zenit News Agency at URL: http://www.zenit.org/english/visualizza.phtml?sid=94748. Accessed October 10, 2006.

[73] Lornet Turnbull, "Preserving modesty, in the pool," *Seattle Times,* July 19, 2005. Available online. URL: http://seattletimes.nwsource.com/html/localnews/2002389078_muslimswim.html. Accessed October 10, 2006. John Reinan, "Got wine at the airport? It's harder to grab a cab," *Minneapolis Star Tribune,* September 28, 2006. Available online. URL: http://www.startribune.com/462/story/709262.html. Accessed October 10, 2006. CBC News, "$300 fine for taxi driver who refused guide dog," July 25, 2006. Available online. URL: http://www.cbc.ca/canada/edmonton/story/2006/07/25/fine-taxi.html. Accessed October 10, 2006.

3

Global Perspectives

In this chapter, the reader will be introduced to four fundamentalist or fundamentalist-like movements within four different major religions—Roman Catholic Christianity, Judaism, Islam, and Hinduism—in areas of the world other than the United States.

ULTRATRADITIONALIST ROMAN CATHOLICISM: THE LEFEBVRE SCHISM

Brief Description

Ultratraditionalist (sometimes called extreme traditionalist) Roman Catholicism describes a movement that was formed in response to the changes in that church after the Second Vatican Council (1962–65). These changes included the celebration of Mass in the vernacular rather than in Latin, the opening of leadership roles in worship to the laity, the modernization of the religious orders, and a greater degree of cooperation and fellowship with the Eastern Orthodox Church and the churches of the Reformation. Since then, there have been a number of different extreme traditionalist groups, particularly within American Catholicism, but the largest and most disruptive of these is the Lefebvrist schism, originally headed by Archbishop Marcel-François Lefebvre (1905–91), a Frenchman who had been a missionary bishop in West Africa.

The Lefebvre group wishes to restore the Mass as it was celebrated by the Council of Trent in the 16th century, reverse the Second Vatican Council's openness toward other Christians, and reestablish the clergy's traditional authority over the laity. The size of Lefebvre's following is not precisely known as of the early 2000s. The Vatican estimates that there are 20,000 ultratraditionalist laypeople in the United States and about 1 million worldwide.[1]

Although some observers have compared extreme traditionalism within the Roman Catholic Church to "Protestantism's own fundamentalist reactions to the modern world,"[2] there are some noteworthy differences. To begin with, unlike Protestant fundamentalism, Catholic ultratraditionalism does not have a clearly marked national character. Lefebvre's movement mirrors the internationalism of the Roman Catholic Church. Franz Schmidberger (1946–), Lefebvre's successor as head of the priestly society he founded, is a German. Of the four bishops whose consecration in 1988 led to an open break between Lefebvre and the papacy, one is French, one is Swiss, one is Argentine, and one is a British convert from the Church of England.

Another important difference between American Protestant fundamentalism and extreme Roman Catholic traditionalism is the absence of anything resembling American civil religion in Europe. France in particular—Lefebvre's homeland—underwent much more violent attacks on its state church (which was Roman Catholic) in the course of the French Revolution than any of the American colonies experienced during the peaceful disestablishment of their Protestant state churches. Since the Napoleonic era, the Catholic Church in France has been identified with a monarchical form of government, general political conservatism, and a wish to restore the traditional alliance between church and state.

Still another major difference is the internal structure and legal system of the Roman Catholic Church compared to its American Protestant counterparts. As noted in chapter 2, fundamentalists within the various American Protestant churches either broke away from the parent body to form new denominations or forced out moderates in the few instances in which they succeeded in taking control of the denomination. Lefebvre's followers, however, are defined as a schismatic group rather than a separate "church," according to Roman Catholic canon law. Canon law can be understood as the internal legal system of the Roman Catholic Church. It regulates such matters as the qualifications, duties, and discipline of the clergy; the administration of the sacraments, particularly ordination and marriage; and the care of church buildings and property. Many of the negotiations between the Vatican and Lefebvre or his successors concern points of canon law.

The role of canon law in maintaining the structure of the Roman Catholic hierarchy also helps to explain why the formation and expansion of Lefebvre's movement did not depend on his having a strong or mediagenic personality. Archbishop Lefebvre did not fit the standard model of the charismatic leader. Short in stature and somewhat plump, he has been described as "paternalistic" and a capable administrator[3] rather than a warm or personable father figure.

It would be a mistake, however, to regard extreme Catholic traditionalism as simply a legal struggle over the status of ordained clergy or nostalgia for a certain style of worship. Rather, the movement represents a fundamentalist attitude toward church doctrine itself. The reason why the changes resulting from the Second Vatican Council—particularly a new openness toward other Christians and less emphasis on the authority of the church hierarchy—were disturbing to traditionalists was that they implied changes in the church's teaching. For the ultratraditionalists, the church's teaching is fixed and unchangeable; they therefore tend to interpret developments in its teaching, such as those of the Second Vatican Council, as contradictions rather than expansions of the decrees of earlier councils.[4]

History

LEFEBVRE'S EARLY LIFE AND CAREER

Lefebvre was born into a devout French family in Tourcoing, a city in northern France near the Belgian border. No one was surprised when Marcel-François felt a vocation to the priesthood at an early age. He studied at the French Seminary in Rome in the 1920s, where he came under the influence of a rector who was a strong supporter of Action Française, a right-wing political movement. The rector resigned in 1926.[5] Lefebvre had, however, been marked by the authoritarian and antidemocratic character of Action Française, which was to influence his political opinions for the remainder of his life.

After ordination, Lefebvre served in his home diocese of Lille for a year and then joined the Holy Ghost Fathers (now known as the Spiritans), a missionary order that began in France in 1703. He was sent to West Africa, where he eventually became the rector of a seminary in Gabon. In 1955, Pope Pius XII appointed him the first archbishop of Dakar, Senegal. Lefebvre's organizational skills were evident during this period: He built a number of schools and churches and made an intensive effort to recruit and train native priests. He opposed decolonialization, however, and resigned his archbishopric in 1962 when the Vatican took a different view of the independence of the former French colonies. Back in France, Lefebvre was made archbishop of the small diocese of Tulle, where he became involved with La Cité Catholique, an antimarxist movement started in 1946 by Jean Ousset.

In 1962, Lefebvre was invited to Rome to participate in the Central Preparatory Commission of the Second Vatican Council. He was dismayed when the Council Fathers rejected most of the commission's suggestions. He was even more disturbed by the changes instituted by the council, particularly the redefinition of the bishops' role, the liturgical reforms, and the endorsement of ecumenism. He referred to the new Mass as a "bastard rite" and later spoke of the council itself as "the AIDS of the Church."[6] Father Paul Aulagnier, who first met Lefebvre as a seminarian in 1964, described the archbishop's position in the late 1960s in the following terms:

> *He feared . . . that the spirit of the Reformation was going to corrupt Catholic thinking. In every department—whether liturgical, philosophical, theological, political—he was horrified . . . by a revolutionary world born in 1789. . . . He was horrified by a "free thinking" that was Protestant, Masonic, characteristic of the modern world and which inspires all of modern thinking. He was horrified by philosophical and political liberalism. . . . There was no doubt: the thinking of Archbishop Lefebvre had been formed by the thinking of the Popes of the nineteenth and twentieth centuries—Pius IX, Leo XIII, St. Pius X, Pius XII—these were his masters.*[7]

FOUNDING OF THE SOCIETY OF ST. PIUS X

Lefebvre, who had been the superior general of the Spiritan missionaries as well as archbishop of Tulle, resigned his position in 1968 when the Spiritans began to revise their constitution. Shortly afterward, however, he was approached by Father Aulagnier and others at the French Seminary in Rome who felt that they were being persecuted for their loyalty to traditional doctrines and practices. Asked to recommend a conservative school where the men could complete their studies, Lefebvre suggested the University of Fribourg in Switzerland. In 1970, however, a Dominican theologian named Father Philippe urged Lefebvre to teach the French seminarians himself. Lefebvre then approached François Charrière, the diocesan bishop, for permission to establish a religious institute or society for the young men. This fledgling organization was to become the Society of St. Pius X, or SSPX, named for Lefebvre's papal hero.

The first pope to be declared a saint since the 16th century, Pius X (1835–1914) was also a controversial figure for his opposition to theological modernism. In July 1907, he issued a decree, "Lamentabili sane exitu," which condemned 65 propositions attributed to modernist theology. Proposition 11 expresses a point of view that would have been condemned also by fundamentalist Protestants committed to the doctrine of scriptural inerrancy: "Divine inspiration does not extend to all of Sacred Scriptures so that it renders its parts, each and every one, free from every error."[8] The pope equated modernism with Protestant Christianity in Proposition 65: "Modern Catholicism can be reconciled with true science only if it is transformed into a non-dogmatic Christianity; that is to say, into a broad and liberal Protestantism."[9]

It was this mindset of rejecting modernist changes that Lefebvre hoped to instill in the seminarians committed to his authority as a teacher.

In 1971, the SSPX took direction of an international seminary that Lefebvre had started in Ecône, a small town in the southwest corner of Switzerland near the French and Italian borders. The society was initially quite successful in attracting students to Lefebvre's school.[10] By 1972, the SSPX had a branch in the United States, with the first SSPX priory being established in Michigan in 1973. Others soon followed in Texas, California, and New York.[11] Trouble began, however, in November 1974 when a commission of cardinals appointed by Pope Paul VI (1897–1978) to examine Lefebvre's seminary arrived at Ecône. The reason for the pope's concern was that the SSPX had caused trouble in other parts of Europe by attracting seminarians disappointed with the theological education offered in their own countries. Josef Cardinal Ratzinger (1927–), the future pope Benedict XVI and a member of the commission, acknowledged that the situation in many European seminaries was in fact highly unsatisfactory.[12] The cardinals' visit to Lefebvre's school went as planned—until the archbishop overheard a comment made by one of the visitors and questioned his orthodoxy. Lefebvre then wrote and published a declaration that raised eyebrows in Rome:

> *Because of this adherence to [Eternal Rome], we refuse and have always refused to follow the Rome of neo-Modernist and neo-Protestant tendencies such as were clearly manifested during the Second Vatican Council, and after the Council in all the resulting reforms.*
>
> *All these reforms have indeed contributed and still contribute to the demolition of the Church, to the ruin of the priesthood, to the destruction of the holy Sacrifice of the Mass and the sacraments, to the disappearance of the religious life, and to naturalistic and Teilhardian teaching in universities, seminaries, and catechesis, a teaching born of liberalism and Protestantism many times condemned by the solemn magisterium of the Church.*[13]

The next stage in the widening rift between Lefebvre and Rome came in May 1975, when Pierre Mamie, Charrière's successor as bishop of Fribourg, withdrew the approval of the SSPX that his predecessor had granted. In addition, Lefebvre refused to accept the findings of the commission of cardinals, which urged the closing of the seminary at Ecône as well as suppressing the SSPX itself.

SUPPRESSION OF THE SSPX AND INTERNAL SCHISM

In spite of the recommendations of the commission and the suppression of his society, Lefebvre proceeded with the next academic term at the seminary as if nothing had happened and planned the ordination of the members of its first graduating class in June 1976. Although the archbishop received a very specific warning in early June from the pope's secretary of state, Monsignor Benelli, not to proceed with the ordinations, he disobeyed the letter and went ahead with the ceremony on June 29, 1976. On July 17, Lefebvre sent Paul VI a letter in which he accused the pope of compromising "with the ideas of modern man, an undertaking which originates in a secret understanding between high dignitaries in the Church and those of Masonic lodges since before the Council."[14] Distressed by Lefebvre's attitude, Pope Paul VI suspended Lefebvre from the exercise of his priestly orders. This suspension applied to his administration of any sacrament, not just the ordination of priests.

The pope's action did not stop Lefebvre from his course of action, but it did slow the growth of the extreme traditionalist movement and caused an internal split. The split came about in 1983, when nine American priests in the SSPX rebelled against the archbishop over two questions: whether the Mass authorized by Pope John XXIII (1881–1963) was acceptable, and whether Pope John Paul II (1920–2005) was a "true" pope. Lefebvre insisted that the priests use the 1962 Roman Missal and accept John XXIII, Paul VI, John Paul I, and John Paul II as legitimate popes. The nine priests escalated the conflict by trying to gain legal and financial control of the SSPX in the United States through placing the society's property in their own hands. Lefebvre expelled the nine men from the SSPX in April 1983. Several years of property litigation followed.

The former SSPX priests then formed a society of their own under the leadership of Father Clarence Kelly (1941–), the Society of St. Pius V (SSPV), headquartered at Oyster Bay Cove, New York. Kelly was reportedly consecrated a bishop on October 19, 1993, by Alfredo José Méndez-González, the retired bishop of Arecibo, Puerto Rico. Within a few years after the SSPV was established, however, four of the original nine separated from it and formed a sedevacantist group of their own led by Fathers Daniel Dolan and Donald J. Sanborn. Sedevacantism is the belief that the present pope (or all the popes since Pius XII) is not a true successor of St. Peter and that the See of Rome is empty or vacant.

EXCOMMUNICATION

In 1984, Pope John Paul II attempted a more conciliatory approach to Lefebvre's group by allowing traditionalist Roman Catholics to return to the use of the pre–Vatican II Mass but only under strict control by the local bishop.[15] While the pope's new approach was announced as a pastoral measure, it was also a response to a threat that Lefebvre had made in 1983 to consecrate successor bishops without papal permission. He was 78 that year and wanted to ensure that the SSPX would have a traditionalist bishop to serve as its superior after his death.

In 1987, Lefebvre repeated his threat to consecrate a successor, thus prompting a new set of negotiations with the Vatican, which was represented by Cardinal Ratzinger. In May 1988, Lefebvre signed a protocol with the Vatican that gave him much of what he wanted: regularization of the SSPX as a priestly society, permission to continue the use of the 1962 Latin Mass, and permission to consecrate a priest of Lefebvre's choosing as a bishop to succeed him. The consecration was scheduled for August 1988. Almost immediately, however, Lefebvre began to complain about the document he had just signed, arguing that he needed to consecrate more than one bishop and announced he would do so on June 30. On June 9, the pope sent a personal letter warning Lefebvre not to proceed with the illicit consecrations. Lefebvre went ahead with the June 30 ceremony. He was excommunicated the next day along with the four bishops he had just consecrated. On July 2, the pope sent out an apostolic letter, "Ecclesia Dei afflicta," which confirmed the excommunication of Lefebvre and his followers and urged traditionalists to seek reconciliation with the mainstream church.[16] Lefebvre was never reconciled with the papacy, however, and died of cancer in 1991.

Structure

The SSPX is a priestly society, which means that it does not have lay members. Laypeople may, of course, attend Mass and receive communion from priests belonging to the society. The SSPX and its breakaway group, the SSPV, have borrowed their hierarchical structural pattern from the parent church; neither is democratic in its organization or procedures. Both societies clearly set great store by ecclesiastical titles; the present leaders of the SSPX and SSPV were consecrated as bishops by Lefebvre himself or by a retired bishop, and both men make much of their titles even though they would not be recognized by mainstream Roman Catholics. This emphasis on the unique status of clergy sets extreme Catholic traditionalism apart from Protestant fundamentalism, in that traditionalists are prepared to accept ordained leaders on the juridical basis of their ordination or consecration, whether or not they possess personal charisma.

The SSPX itself is divided into regions or districts, the member clergy in each district being under the oversight of a superior. The society as a whole has a superior general; the current holder of the office is Bishop Bernard Fellay, one of the four bishops consecrated in 1988 by Archbishop Lefebvre. According to the SSPX Web site, as of 2005, it has 336 priests as members in 27 countries, 226 seminarians enrolled in six international seminaries, 130 priories, more than 600 Mass centers where Mass is celebrated regularly, nine retreat houses, 14 major parochial schools, and 50 smaller schools connected to priories or chapels. The main seminary in Ecône reports an enrollment of more than a hundred students as of early 2006. The other five seminaries are located in the United States, France, Germany, Australia, and Argentina.

The reason that extreme traditionalism has not attracted a larger following in recent years is its organizational problems; it consists of a mixture of priestly and lay organizations only loosely related to one another.[17] In addition to Lefebvre's society and its offshoots, there are such other groups as the Catholic Traditionalist Movement, Inc. (CTMI) and the Orthodox Roman Catholic Movement (ORCM), both led by American priests. There are also traditionalist groups led by laypeople, such as Catholics United for the Faith (CUF), founded in 1968, and the Blue Army, which encourages devotion to Our Lady of Fatima and maintains a shrine and retreat center in New Jersey. CUF, for one, has refused to consider aligning itself with the SSPX and has consistently reaffirmed its loyalty to the mainstream Catholic Church.[18]

Goals

Extreme Roman Catholic traditionalists of the Lefebvre type are distinctive among fundamentalist groups in that they do not have secular political objectives of the Christian reconstructionist type. The movement cannot be classified as nationalist, even though the French politician Jean-Marie Le Pen tried to mobilize French Lefebvrists as part of his right-wing political base in the early 2000s. Nor are they motivated to take over the organizational structures of the mainstream church. They seem to ask little more than to be permitted to run their own schools, chapels, and societies as they see fit and to distance themselves from the "errors" of the present hierarchy as much as possible. For this reason Lefebvre's group can be classified as an example of "world-renouncing," as contrasted with "world-conquering," "world-creating," or "world-transforming" fundamentalists.[19] Although some members of the SSPX in the United States or laypersons who worship in SSPX chapels may be active in the pro-life movement, they do so as individuals rather than as representatives of the society.

This attitude of relative passivity toward secular political structures does not mean that extreme Catholic traditionalists do not see "the world" as the enemy. They share a polarized, black-and-white view of the world with fundamentalist Protestants, although they regard Protestants of any type as part of the "world" at enmity with the "true" church. The reader will have noticed references in Lefebvre's writings to a conspiracy between certain members of the Roman hierarchy and such groups as Freemasons, communists, and "free thinkers" as well as Protestants. Extreme Catholic traditionalists are separatists; they will not participate in ecumenical activities with other Christians or interfaith meetings with members of other religions. In 2002, Bernard Fellay, in his capacity as bishop and superior general of the SSPX, condemned Pope John Paul II's invitation to members of other faiths to come to the birthplace of St. Francis and join in praying for peace:

> *Pope John Paul II is inviting all the major religions of the world, the Muslims in particular, to a great prayer meeting in Assisi, in the same spirit of the first meeting for peace that took place there in 1986. We are deeply distressed by this event and condemn it totally.*
>
> *Because it offends God in His first commandment.*
>
> *Because it denies the unity of the Church and Her mission of saving souls.*
>
> *Because it can only lead the faithful into confusion and indifferentism.*
>
> *Because it deceives the unfortunate unfaithful and members of other religions. . . .*
>
> *The only authentic prayer is true prayer addressed to the true God. It is totally wrong to qualify a prayer addressed to the devil as authentic. Can the prayer of a fanatical terrorist, before crashing into the Manhattan tower: "Allah is great" be called authentic? Wasn't he convinced that he was doing the right thing, doesn't that make him sincere?*
>
> *The determination of the Vatican II Council to dispense with the distinction between the order of grace and natural order bears, in this respect, its most poisonous fruits. The result is the worst sort of confusion, that which leads people to think that any religion can finally obtain the greatest favours from God. This is a huge fraud, a ridiculous error.*[20]

Another item of conspiracy thinking among Lefebvre's followers is the repeated suggestion that Pope John Paul I (1912–78), whose pontificate lasted for little more than a month in the summer of 1978, was murdered and the crime covered up by the usual suspects.[21]

Future

The long-term future of Lefebvre's group is dubious. Membership in the SSPX has been dropping since the early 1990s, when the society had about 400 priests.[22] The loss of members can be attributed to four factors: ongoing efforts on the part of the papacy to heal the schism; the tendency of extreme traditionalists to continue to divide among themselves over relatively minor matters; reports of scandals and several bizarre incidents, including a sermon in which American Catholics were told not to vote in elections and that it is wrong for women to drive cars[23]; and the superior general's increasingly high-handed attitude toward other members of the SSPX.

With regard to Vatican policy, the current pope, Benedict XVI, has continued John Paul II's invitations to reconciliation. In August 2005, the pope met for 35 minutes with Bishop Fellay at the bishop's request. There was no breakthrough at the meeting; the bishop was brought into the pope's residence through a side entrance and his name was not listed on the pope's official appointment schedule.[24] In addition, Fellay expressed mistrust of the new pontiff's motives for healing the schism, maintaining that it has more to do with the pope's unenviable position between the extreme traditionalists and the "modernists."[25]

With regard to internal divisions and scandals, several members of the SSPX left to form the Society of St. John in 1997. This society, headquartered in Scranton, Pennsylvania, became in turn the subject of a sex scandal in February 2002 that also involved financial irregularities and alcohol abuse. The society's superior general and its chancellor were reported to have molested a young man who was a minor at the time of the crime. The dormitory manager of a school run by the society also stated that he saw members of the society getting male students drunk.[26]

Still another factor in the decline of the SSPX is Bishop Fellay's increasingly separatist position and his arbitrary expulsion of clergy who disagree with his opinion of the present pope. In fall 2003, Fellay expelled Father Paul Aulagnier, one of Lefebvre's first class of seminary students and the founding superior of the French district of the SSPX. Fellay expelled Aulagnier for airing his disagreement publicly with Fellay's ongoing refusal to be reconciled with the Vatican. A Canadian member of the SSPX, Father Jean Violette, commented on Aulagnier's "weakness" and "lack of spirit."[27] Father Violette's remarks reflect the dualistic, us-against-them mentality characteristic also of Protestant fundamentalist groups.

The Internet is not likely to rescue the SSPX from its present difficulties. Although the Internet has been touted as a medium of communication that allows extreme traditionalists, as well as moderate and liberal believers, to form online discussion groups and recruit new members, the SSPX, SSPV, and similar groups are not likely to increase their numbers through their Web sites. The SSPX's insistence on doctrinally correct liturgy and frequent reception of communion means that virtual communities cannot substitute for a brick-and-mortar congregation.[28]

JEWISH FUNDAMENTALISM: GUSH EMUNIM

Brief Description

JUDAISM IN THE MODERN WORLD

Judaism is the smallest of the world's major religions, with about 12–13 million adherents compared to 2.1 billion Christians, 1.3 billion Muslims, and 900 million Hindus. Jews thus represent less than 0.025 percent of the world's population. Moreover, as of the early 2000s, a majority of the world's Jews live in only two countries, Israel and the United States. This concentration is a relatively recent phenomenon; until 1840, 90 percent of the world's Jews lived in Europe.[29]

Many European Jews did not participate in the complex currents of cultural and religious change in Europe from the 16th through the early 19th centuries. One exception was the Haskalah movement, led by Moses Mendelssohn (1729–86), a Prussian philosopher and man of letters. Mendelssohn urged fellow Jews to learn standard German and reduce their use of Yiddish in order to enter the wider society of educated persons. The Haskalah movement spread beyond Germany into other European countries. Mendelssohn's followers were known as *maskilim*. The movement was controversial because it led to a loss of Jewish communal identity through assimilation and intermarriage. When the Jews were given full civil rights in several western European nations in the 19th century by Napoleon and other rulers, they became involved in political movements as well as intellectual and occupational assimilation. The Zionist movement of the late 19th century, which led eventually to the establishment of the state of Israel in 1948, was one example of Jewish participation in political activity. Other Jews were attracted to the various nationalist and revolutionary uprisings that occurred across Europe in 1848 and 1870.

Anti-Semitism, which had troubled European societies for centuries, persisted after the political emancipation of the Jews, however. It was particularly strong in eastern Europe, which was relatively uninfluenced by Napoleon's political reforms. More than 2 million Jews left Russia and eastern Europe for the United States between 1880 and 1924. Anti-Semitic attitudes, however, were all the more difficult to deal with wherever they were found because they attacked Jews as a people as well as a religion. This dual identity is another aspect of Judaism that differentiates it from other major religions. One effect of anti-Semitic prejudice over the course of the last century has been a decline in religious observance among Jews. A survey conducted in California in 1988 found that only 17 percent of the respondents mentioned "religious observance" as a central aspect of Jewish identity (as opposed to 79 percent for Roman Catholics and 65 percent for Protestants), while 59 percent chose "commitment to social equality."[30] In Israel, fewer than 20 percent of Jews define themselves as religious.[31]

The question of what constitutes Jewish identity is more pressing in Israel than it is in the United States. In 1950, the Knesset (Israeli parliament) passed the Law of Return, which was intended at the time of its passage to provide sanctuary for any Jew elsewhere in the world in danger of persecution. The Nazi Nuremberg laws of 1935 had attempted to define Jewish identity on the basis of a pseudoscientific theory of race. In contrast, the Law of Return does not allow a Jew by birth who has formally converted to another religion to make aliyah (immigrate to Israel), while someone who is not Jewish by birth can claim Israeli citizenship on the basis of a religious conversion to Judaism. An example of this religious distinction took place in May 1991, when Israel admitted about 14,000 Falashas (Ethiopian Jews); those who had converted to Christianity were refused entry.[32] In addition to the issue of whether religious observance or birth should define a person as Jewish, the question of "Who is a Jew?" is complicated by the fact that Reform and Conservative criteria for valid religious conversion to Judaism are not accepted by the Orthodox or Haredi Jews.

THE STATE OF ISRAEL

The nature of the state of Israel is another debated question that has influenced the development of Jewish fundamentalist groups. Israel is technically a secular parliamentary democracy that has guaranteed freedom of religion to its citizens since its establishment on May 14, 1948. The political Zionist movement that was founded in the late 19th century by Theodor Herzl (1860–1904), an Austrian journalist, was essentially secular and was proposed as an answer to the recurrent problem of anti-Semitic persecution, particularly in Russia and eastern Europe. The stirrings of nationalism that had animated so many European ethnic minorities since 1848 suggested a new solution to anti-Semitism. "If the nation—an entity defined by descent, culture, and aspiration—was the only natural and rightful basis of statehood, why then the Jews were also a nation, and must have their own state."[33] For this reason, most Zionists wanted to build a Jewish state in their historic homeland and make Hebrew its official language, although a minority was willing to consider building a nation elsewhere, such as Uganda or Argentina.

In the early years of political Zionism, most Orthodox Jews wanted nothing to do with the movement, believing that the establishment of a Jewish state had to wait for the return of the Messiah. The notion that human beings could bring it about was considered blasphemous. Religious Jews were also generally opposed to political Zionism before the 1930s because they were put off by its secular language and socialist politics. The rise of a religious form of Zionism is usually credited to Rabbi Abraham Isaac Kook (1865–1935), the Chief Rabbi of Palestine after 1921. Kook, who was born in what is now Latvia, immigrated to Israel in 1917. He was able to bridge the gap between the secular Zionists and the religious conservatives by describing the secular pioneers as part of God's divine plan for building up the physical land of Israel and thus preparing the way for the Messiah's spiritual redemption of the Jewish people. Kook was succeeded as leader of the religious Zionists by his son, Zvi (or Tzvi) Yehuda Kook (1891–1982). The younger Kook became the spiritual authority of the fundamentalist settler movement known as Gush Emunim (GE), which can be translated into English as "bloc of the faithful."

TYPES OF JEWISH FUNDAMENTALISM

As of the early 2000s, Jewish fundamentalists can be divided into two large groups, the strictly religious ultra-Orthodox (*haredim*) and the religio-nationalists. The former can be classified as passive fundamentalists, content to barricade themselves behind a wall of strict religious observance, while the religio-nationalists are active fundamentalists who believe in hastening the last day by forming religious settlements throughout the biblically defined area of the land of Israel.[34] Most *haredim* are Ashkenazic Jews; that is, they or their parents came from eastern Europe. They tend to be middle- or lower-middle-class and poorly educated. In the early 1990s, there were about 250,000 *haredim* in Israel.[35] The ultra-Orthodox are opposed to political Zionism and the state of Israel, which they regard as "meaningless at best and terrible sins at worst."[36]

The religio-nationalist fundamentalists can be subdivided into two groups: those associated primarily with the establishment and maintenance of settlements in the land occupied by Israel after 1967 (such as GE) and those belonging to an extreme right-wing movement characterized by ultra-nationalism, strong opposition to Arabs, and a declared intention to pay back Arab terrorism in kind (for example, Kach; others include Zo Artzeinu and Eyal, which influenced Yigal Amir, the assassin of Prime Minister Yitzhak Rabin).

Kach Party

Kach, a political party whose name means "only thus" in Hebrew, was founded by Meir Kahane (1932–90), a rabbi born in Brooklyn who lived in the United States until 1971. Kahane was known primarily as the founder of the Jewish Defense League (JDL), an organization that he started in the late 1960s to protect Jews in New York City from harassment and anti-Semitism by gangs of minority youths. The JDL branched out into domestic terrorism, however, planting pipe bombs, harassing Russian diplomats and businessmen, and targeting Arab-American activists for assassination. Kahane's decision to make aliyah in 1971 was motivated as much by pressure from the FBI, which told the rabbi that it had enough evidence to send him to prison, as by his radical right-wing ideology.[37]

Once settled in Israel, Kahane attracted some favorable attention, succeeding in founding the Kach Party in 1974. Most Israelis, however, regarded him as a racist bigot. What made Kahane unique was not only his commitment to unrestrained violence in pursuit of ultranationalist goals but his openness about seeking revenge. Kahane sought revenge not only against the Arabs but also against Gentiles; in his view of the world, the very establishment of the state of Israel represented God's punishment of the Gentiles.[38] Kahane argued that his glorification of vengefulness was based on Scripture and rabbinic tradition:

> *No trait is more justified than revenge in the right time and place. G-d, Himself, is called NOKEM, Avenger: "The L-rd is a zealous and avenging G-d. The L-rd avenges and is full of wrath. He takes revenge on His adversaries and reserves wrath for His enemies" (Nachum 1:2). Our sages also said (Berachot 33a), "Shall we say that even revenge is great because it appears between two names of G-d? 'A G-d of vengeance is the L-rd' (Psalms 94:1). Rabbi Elazar responded, 'Indeed. Where revenge is necessary, it is a great thing.'"*[39]

Kach was best known for its proposal to forcibly resettle Israel's Arab population beyond its borders. Kahane argued that Arabs should be stripped of any rights as citizens if they choose to continue living within Israel:

> *It is a central tenet of Judaism that G-d wished the Jew to create a unique, total, pure and complete Jewish life, society and state in Eretz Israel. This being so, who can honestly believe that He then sanctioned the democratic right of a non-Jew, who is totally alien and outside the Jewish society and who is free of its religious obligation, to have the slightest say in its workings? . . . Of course, [the Arabs] do not accept the truth of*

Divine ownership of the Land by the G-d of Israel, hence Israel's right to take the Land with sovereignty and ownership. Do we expect them to? Of course the ultimate, only reason that they surrender and live quietly is fear and their understanding that they are too weak AT PRESENT to change the situation. But of course they never accept that situation as permanent and of course they dream of the day when they will return their "stolen land" unto themselves.[40]

Most of those who joined the Kach Party did not, however, read Kahane's writings or study his thought in any systematic way. His followers were generally drawn from the lower economic levels of Israeli society, worried about Arab competition for low-paying jobs and resentful of the educated elites.[41] Many of them were Israeli Jews of Sephardic origin; that is, their ancestors came from Spain or Portugal, in contrast to the eastern European or Rhineland ancestry of the Ashkenazim.[42]

Kach itself split into two groups, Kach and Kahane Chai (Kahane lives), after Kahane was murdered in 1990 in New York City. Both groups disbanded in 1994 after they were banned by antiterrorist laws passed by the Knesset following the massacre of Arab worshippers in Hebron in 1990 by Baruch Goldstein, a Kach activist. Some former members of Kahane Chai maintain an advocacy organization called the Kahane Movement, which has a Web site and distributes the rabbi's writings as well as those of his son Binyamin. The U.S. State Department still lists both Kach and Kahane Chai as "designated foreign terrorist organizations."[43]

History

GE is a religio-nationalist movement that grew out of the religious Zionism taught by Rabbis Abraham Isaac Kook and Zvi Yehuda Kook in the early 1970s. Its membership is small compared to the *haredim,* numbering about 20,000 Israelis. It differs from both Kach and the *haredim* in terms of the socioeconomic status of its adherents. While most members of GE are of Ashkenazic descent, like the *haredim,* they are not marginal to Israeli society, being typically middle or upper-middle class in origin and quite well educated. As a result, they do not have the same fears of contemporary technology that agitate the *haredim.* Members of GE have been described as "positive and optimistic" in their outlook, "rather pleased with the modern world."[44]

RABBI KOOK'S YESHIVA

Because of its roots in religious Zionism, GE has been characterized as a world-transforming, rather than a world-destroying or world-renouncing, fundan st group.[45] GE grew out of a yeshiva (traditional Jewish school) in Jerus Mercaz Harav (or HaRav), founded in 1924 by Abraham Isaac Kook. T inger Kook increased the size of the yeshiva after his father's death in . As has been mentioned earlier, the elder Kook was able to combine ous Zionism with a vision of the secular state as a preparation for the co of the Messiah. The yeshiva that he founded has attempted to blend the tional Haredi respect for Torah study with a civic spirit.[46] The elder Kook fluence may be measured by the fact that Israel's official prayer describes t tate as "the beginning of the flowering of our redemption."[47]

Prior t 967, the future leaders of GE were little more than a close-knit group HaRav alumni committed to religious Zionism. However, the Six-Day W which GE calls the "War of Redemption," transformed the group into ovement that had greater visibility. The war began after Egypt blockaded I li shipping in the Straits of Tiran and deployed a large military force on th raeli border. Israel responded with a preemptive strike on the Egyptian ai rce. By the time the war ended, Israel had gained control of the Gaza St the Golan Heights, the Sinai Peninsula, and the West Bank. Energized b srael's victory in a conflict that could have ended disastrously for the cour , the leaders of GE interpreted the outcome as proof that God not only hac ot deserted the Jewish people but had increased the size of their homeland. I ddition, that the younger Kook had given a prophetic speech at HaRav or three weeks before the outbreak of the 1967 war added to his reputation a livinely inspired. Referring to the date of Israel's founding in 1948, Kook d cried out in yearning for the nation's lost territories:

> *Ninetee ears ago, on the night when news of the United Nations decision in or of the re-establishment of the state of Israel reached us, when th eople streamed into the streets to celebrate and rejoice, I could not go o and join in the jubilation. I sat alone and silent; a burden lay upon me. During those first hours I could not resign myself to what had been done. I could not accept the fact that indeed 'they have . . . divided My land' (Joel 4:2)! Yes [and now after 19 years] where is our Hebron—have we forgotten her?! Where is our Shehem, our Jericho—where?! Have we forgotten them?!*
>
> *And all that lies beyond the Jordan—each and every clod of earth, every region, hill, valley, every plot of land, that is part of Eretz Israel [the Land of Israel]—have we the right to give up even one grain of the Land of God?! On that night, nineteen years ago, during those hours, as I sat trembling in every limb of my body, wounded, cut, torn to pieces—I could not then rejoice.*[48]

Within a matter of weeks, the very places mentioned by Rabbi Kook had been incorporated within Israel's new boundaries. A tape recording of this address is still played at GE celebrations.[49]

THE SETTLEMENT MOVEMENT

The next stage in the development of GE began the following year, when Rabbi Moshe Levinger and some of his followers celebrated Passover in Hebron at an Arab-owned hotel and remained there as squatters. With the help of the Israeli government, Levinger's group built a settlement called Kiryat Arba on the edge of Hebron. By spring 2004, there were about 7,000 settlers living there.[50] Levinger's squat is generally regarded as the beginning of the settlement movement,[51] which distinguished GE from other Jewish fundamentalist groups. While the *haredim* do not think they have the power to shape history, the members of GE regard human beings as able to cooperate with God's plans and thus hasten the coming of the Messiah. The settlement of every part of the land of Israel is one way in which the bloc of the faithful hopes to accomplish this goal. GE's focus on the geographical boundaries of Israel has no real counterpart in any Christian fundamentalist movement.

It was not the Six-Day War of 1967, however, but rather the Yom Kippur War of 1973 that triggered the organizational formation of GE. The Yom Kippur War was a setback for Israel, sometimes referred to as a "semidefeat"[52] or a general crisis of authority.[53] It began when Egypt and Syria mounted a surprise invasion of the Golan Heights and the Sinai Peninsula on October 6, 1967, which was Yom Kippur (Day of Atonement), a major holy day for observant Jews. Although the Israelis had pushed back the invaders by the second week of the war, they felt humiliated by the surprise attack on October 6 and the Egyptian successes of the first two days of combat. After the war ended, a commission was set up to investigate the reasons for Israel's early setbacks. In March 1974, during this period of national introspection, a group of about 200 people met at Kfar Etzion, a religious kibbutz (farming collective) on the West Bank that had been recovered by the Israelis during the Six-Day War. They organized GE as a faction within Israel's National Religious Party (NRP). The slogan of the new bloc of the faithful was "The Land of Israel, for the people of Israel, according to the Torah of Israel."[54] The leaders of the meeting were all former students of Zvi Yehuda Kook. Within a few months, however, GE left the NRP, redefined itself as an independent body, and thus carved out a unique political status within Israeli politics.[55] To protest the government's territorial concessions following the Yom Kippur War, GE members engaged in nonviolent demonstrations, acts of civil disobedience, and the formation of core groups for establishing new settlements in the occupied territories.

Between 1974 and 1977, GE settlers were preoccupied primarily with defending themselves against their Arab neighbors, who obviously could not be counted on to remain passive.[56] After 1977, however, the replacement of the Labor government by Menachem Begin, the leader of the Likud Party, meant that GE now had greater government support. In September 1977, Ariel Sharon, the new agriculture minister, announced a plan to settle more than a million Jews in the West Bank within 20 years.[57] The settlers thus began to move beyond the edge of the occupied territories into the outskirts of Arab towns, setting up industrial parks, yeshivot, and even a college. By 1981, there were about 20 settlements in the territories, occupied by nearly 19,000 settlers.[58] The more isolated settlements were very small, inhabited only by the most committed messianic enthusiasts who were not afraid to settle close to Arab refugee camps.[59]

Begin's approval did not last long, however. In addition to GE's disenchantment with the Likud Party, its members felt betrayed by the Camp David Accords of 1978. The accords provided for a period of transition intended to give the Arabs in the West Bank and Gaza an opportunity for self-government.[60] GE responded with a series of attacks on Palestinian mayors (June 1981), the murder of several students at the Islamic College in Hebron (July 1983), and involvement in a plot to blow up the al-Aqsa Mosque on the Temple Mount in Jerusalem in 1984. Yehuda Etzion, the ringleader of the al-Aqsa plot, was not a typical member of GE; he was preoccupied with messianic rather than vigilante violence. But in addition to hastening the day of the Messiah, Etzion hoped to disrupt the carrying out of the Camp David Accords as well.[61]

AFTER THE INTIFADA

The first Intifada, or Arab uprising in the West Bank in 1987, marked the beginning of a new phase of violence between GE and the Palestinians. Settler vigilantism increased in response to the violent protests, evidenced by Levinger's killing of an Arab shopkeeper in Hebron in 1988. The attitudes of GE members toward the Palestinians began to harden into intense hostility. In addition, the Intifada marked the beginning of recognition among the wider Israeli public that the cost of defending the settlements might be too high to pay.[62] Sharon's plan, as prime minister, to disengage from the settlements in summer 2005 was at least partly motivated by this recognition.

Structure

The origin of GE was within a small and close-knit group of graduates of one specific yeshiva. The men who had attended Mercaz HaRav saw themselves as a trained elite[63]; however, they did not organize GE as a secret or underground society.[64] They formed an inner core of leaders of a group that was never tightly organized and frequently changed its structure. In 1988, GE had a 13-member secretariat elected by a special conference, but the day-to-day affairs of the movement were conducted by Levinger and three other men.[65] This organizational pattern did not last long because the leaders disagreed among themselves about the long-term goals of the movement.

Those outside the GE inner core, moreover, were not a unified group of followers. About 20 percent were not religious at all but were attracted to GE because of its nationalism. As the movement grew in the early 1980s, it drew members from a range of sources—not only from HaRav but also from the population of the West Bank and Gaza settlements, the Bnei Akiva youth movement, the Yeshivot Hesder (schools for religious Israelis that allow them to divide their period of army service between military duty and Torah study), and the secular Labor Zionist movement.[66] The mixed composition of the GE membership and the lack of a long-term internal structure meant that the two organizations that emerged from GE activities in the 1970s became unofficial successor groups.

AMANA

In 1976, the GE settlers in Judea and Samaria (West Bank) formed a legal association called Amana ("covenant," in Hebrew) for joint administration and decision making. Originally intended to be no more than a temporary by-product of GE, it became a self-sufficient organization that gradually replaced the loosely organized leadership of GE. Amana developed an original model—the community settlement—for the GE settlers in the territories. Community settlements are semicooperatives with elected officials, although each family is economically independent.[67] Amana marked the evolution of GE from an ideological fringe group that specialized in civil disobedience to a broader movement with a practical interest in maintaining settled communities.

THE YESHA COUNCIL

The Yesha Council, an organization representing the settlements in both the West Bank and the Gaza Strip, was formed in the 1970s. It has come to be regarded as another successor organization to GE. In 2005, the council had 35 members, 25 mayors, and 10 community leaders. It also had three major tasks: to provide security; oversee the maintenance of roads, electricity, and water supplies; and represent the settlers in the Knesset. The Yesha Council led nonviolent mass protests against Israel's disengagement from Gaza in summer 2005 while carefully distancing itself from violent protestors.

Goals

The members of GE saw themselves as the successors of the pioneers who had come to Israel in the late 1940s. Their central goal was to settle every portion of Israel's God-given land in order to hasten the coming of the Messiah. A position paper written in the mid-1970s defined GE's aims: "To bring about a great awakening of the Jewish People towards full implementation of the Zionist vision . . . realizing that . . . its objective is the full redemption of Israel and of the entire world."[68] In the early years, GE leaders were also concerned with Torah study, the restoration of biblical law, and the rebuilding of the Temple, conspicuous acts of piety, and religious education. The development of Amana and the Yesha Council channeled some of the movement's energy into practical political concerns as well.

Future

It is difficult to picture a long-term future for GE as a formal organization. Its original leaders are now elderly. Furthermore, the growth of Amana and the Yesha Council overshadowed GE itself in the 1980s and 1990s. More important, the long-term problems created by 20 years of fundamentalist protests and violence have damaged the fabric of Israeli society.[69] Israel's withdrawal from the settlements in summer 2005 may bring about the complete dissolution of GE and its successor organizations. Gideon Aran, an expert who has studied GE since the 1970s remarked in a 2005 interview that its messianic enthusiasm is not what it was several decades ago: "Obviously the messianic impulse of Jewish religiosity has been knocked down."[70] In light of Prime Minister Sharon's sudden stroke in January 2006, however, it is too early to tell whether a religious form of Israeli nationalism may yet reemerge from the present crisis. The Israeli media generally refer to religious Zionists in 2006 as Ne'emanei Eretz Yisrael, "those who are faithful to the land of Israel," rather than as members of GE.

ISLAMIC FUNDAMENTALISM: HAMAS

Brief Description

Islamic fundamentalism differs from its Christian and Jewish counterparts because of Islam's very different history as a religion. Whereas both Judaism and Christianity were marked by centuries of powerlessness and persecution before returning to the homeland (Judaism) or converting the secular ruler (Christianity), Muhammad, the founder of Islam, succeeded in winning political and military victories in his own lifetime: "He conquered his promised land, and created his own state, of which he himself was supreme sovereign."[71] This unification of prophetic revelation, religious authority, and political rule in the person of one leader had important consequences.

The first is the absence of the distinction between church and state, which occasioned so many power struggles between popes and monarchs in the history of Europe and which is summarized in the First Amendment of the U.S. Constitution. In Islam, rather, "the state was the church, and the church was the state, and God was head of both, with the Prophet as his representative on earth."[72] This lack of separation between church and state, and the corresponding lack of a distinction between civil and canon law, meant that one code of law—the sharia—governed all areas of life. The religious professionals of Islam, the ulema (or ulama), are not clergy in the sense of having priestly or sacramental functions. They are jurists, experts in the holy law of their religion. These teachers may be expected to be more learned than most Muslims, but they are not regarded as having a higher spiritual status.[73]

Second, the close relationship between religious and political authority in Islam meant that defeat on the battlefield or the loss of cultural superiority would be experienced as a profound religious humiliation. For a long period after Muhammad's death in 632 C.E., Muslim armies advanced across North Africa and even into Europe. Turned back by Charles Martel at Tours (France) in 732, Muslim rulers were not driven out of Spain until 1492, the year that Christopher Columbus arrived in the New World. Even then, the Ottoman Turks were able to control much of southeastern Europe. Having captured Constantinople (present-day Istanbul, in Turkey) in 1453, they besieged the city of Vienna (Austria) twice, in 1529 and 1683. The Treaty of Carlowitz in 1699 marked a decisive shift in the balance of military power between Islam and the West: After 1700, the Muslim rulers of the Middle East were on the defensive.[74] In addition to Western successes on the battlefield, the West overtook and surpassed Muslim cultural achievements. During the Middle Ages, the West had to import medical and mathematical information and skills from the Arab world, but after the Renaissance and the technological revolution of the 17th century, the European countries (and their American colonies) forged far ahead of their Muslim counterparts. Moreover, the acquisition of colonies in Asia and Africa, as well as North and South America, gave the European powers a decisive economic advantage over the Ottoman Empire.

Muslims remained largely unaware of the magnitude of this transition until the late 18th century, but when they finally recognized that "everything had changed," in the words of Bernard Lewis, the feelings of shame and anger cut deep: "Muslims, instead of invading and dominating Christendom, were invaded and dominated by Christian powers. The resulting frustration and anger at what seemed to them *a reversal of both natural and divine law* have been growing for centuries, and have reached a climax in our own time."[75] Since the 18th century, Muslims also had to confront the ongoing colonial ambitions of Great Britain and France; the expansionist ambitions of czarist Russia; the decline and corruption of the Ottoman Empire in the 19th century; the establishment of autocratic governments in the Middle East in the 20th century, particularly in Egypt and Iran; and the humiliating outcome of the Six-Day War in 1967. One result was the emergence of fundamentalist groups in Muslim countries.

These groups varied widely in their goals and approaches; only a few can be briefly summarized here. Some fundamentalist groups, such as the Egyptian Muslim Brotherhood, began as charitable and educational social service organizations in the 1920s and focused on religious and moral reform as the key to remaking Egypt as an Islamic nation. Only in the late 1930s did the Brotherhood begin to discuss the use of violence as a way to extend its teachings and influence. Sayyid Qutb, a member of the Brotherhood who was executed by the government of Egyptian president Gamal Abdel Nasser in 1966, taught a radical doctrine of violent revolution and total rejection of the West. Qutb's teachings were controversial, however, and were not accepted by all members of the Muslim Brotherhood.

In Saudi Arabia, those who followed the Wahhabi version of Islamic fundamentalism—named for Muhammad Ibn Abd-al-Wahhab (1703–92), a scholar from central Arabia—practiced an austere form of worship that forbade honoring local saints, visiting the tombs of holy men, practicing magic, and a number of other popular religious practices. Wahhabism also urged the Islamization of society as a whole and the formation of a state based on formal recognition of Islam. Saudi Arabia, however, is unique insofar as it is an Islamic state that was not created as a result of conflict with Western powers.

Pakistan is an example of an Islamic state that came into being during the period of decolonialization. As early as 1906, Muslims in what was then British India were concerned that their interests would never be addressed by the Hindu majority. As plans were made in the 1940s for Indian independence, Muslim leaders as well as Hindu nationalists pressed for the creation of two separate states. In 1947, the British Parliament finally passed an act legitimizing the partition arrangement. The central figure in the Islamization of Pakistan was Abul Ala Mawdudi (1903–79), the founder of the Jamaat-e-Islami, a political movement that was originally opposed to the creation of Pakistan in 1947. After the partition, however, the Jamaat redefined its goal as the establishment of an Islamic constitution in Pakistan.

In Iran, the Westernizing and repressive monarchy of the shah Mohammad Reza Pahlavi was overthrown in 1979 by revolutionaries who invited the ayatollah (Shiite Muslim religious leader) Ruhollah Khomeini (1900–89) to return from exile and become the supreme leader of the nation. The monarchy was replaced with an Islamic republic, sharia law was introduced, and dress codes were enforced on both men and women. Khomeini came under criticism for his 1989 fatwa (decree) calling for the assassination of the writer Salman Rushdie following the publication of *The Satanic Verses,* a novel that Khomeini considered blasphemous.

The size of Islamic fundamentalist groups is difficult to estimate because many do not keep membership lists or statistics. In addition, the number of people who sympathize with the goals of these groups is often many times larger than the core membership. For example, the military wing of Hamas, the Palestinian branch of the Muslim Brotherhood, is estimated to number about a thousand men.[76] Yet, more than 200,000 people crowded the streets for the funeral procession of Hamas's leader, Sheikh Ahmed Ismail Yassin, in 2004.

FUNDAMENTALIST LEADERSHIP

The question of a political leader's religious role in Islam is related to the history of the caliphate. *Caliph* comes from an Arabic word that means "successor" or "deputy." After Muhammad's death, his successors were chosen by tribal agreement. The caliph had both political and spiritual power as the head of a community that was a church and state combined, but he did not have the prophetic powers attributed to Muhammad. There were several dynasties of caliphs, the last being the Abbasid dynasty, which fled to Egypt when the Mongols captured Baghdad in 1258. When the Ottoman Turks invaded Egypt in 1517, the Ottoman sultan took the title of caliph. His successors kept the title until the last sultan, Mehmet VI, was deposed by the Turkish National Assembly in 1922. Mehmet's cousin became the caliph until 1924, when Turkey abolished the caliphate.

Since 1924, Muslims have made periodic proposals to reestablish the institution. Al-Qaeda leader Osama bin Laden's remark about "tasting humiliation and contempt for more than 80 years" in the video he released after 9/11, is a reference to the abolition of the caliphate.[77] Some Muslim fundamentalists long for the restoration of the caliphate on the grounds that it would unite Muslims presently divided by their respective nation-states and bring back the golden age of Islam by overcoming "the empire of the United States and the world's Jewish government."[78] In November 1998, a group of Muslim extremists in Turkey planned to hijack a plane and fly it into a Turkish national monument as a first step toward restoring the caliphate.[79]

In addition to the caliphate, Muslim fundamentalists typically want to introduce sharia, the traditional religious law of Islam, not only in countries with majority-Muslim populations but also in the West. Pressure to introduce sharia for the governance of Muslim communities within Western countries has predictably aroused fears on the part of other groups that the ultimate goal is the imposition of sharia on the entire society. For example, there have been disputes in several Canadian provinces in the early 2000s regarding the use of sharia in the Canadian family court system. Opponents of sharia law maintain that its rules regarding inheritance, divorce, child custody, and remarriage are inherently unfair to women. In 2005, the Quebec National Assembly voted unanimously to block the introduction of sharia law in Quebec courts.[80] Such other practices as honor killings (the murder of female members of a family who resist forced marriages or date or marry non-Muslim men), which are carried out by some Muslims living in western European countries, have also created tensions between non-Muslim Europeans and Muslim minorities. In June 2006, a Danish court made headlines by sentencing all nine members of a Muslim family to prison for the premeditated murder of Ghazala Khan in September 2005, even though only one brother fired the shot that ended her life. The trial was also unusual because the judge had to warn Muslims in the courtroom audience several times that he would not tolerate intimidation of witnesses or jurors.[81]

The leaders of Islamic fundamentalist groups also differ from their American fundamentalist counterparts in another critical respect: They are usually not religious leaders who have decided to enter politics (such as Pat Robertson or Jerry Falwell) but political strategists and secular intellectuals who have entered the sphere of religion. Neither bin Laden nor the early leaders of political Islam in the 1940s were clerics.[82] The writer regarded as the founder of political Islam, Mawdudi, was a journalist, politician, and scholar who wrote on fundamentalist Islam as an alternative to both Western political systems and Soviet Marxism. Mawdudi was influenced by the Deobandi movement, a response to British colonialism that emphasized the importance of sharia. The movement took its name from Darul Uloom Deoband, an Islamic madrassa, or seminary, founded in Uttar Pradesh, India, in 1866.

In August 1941, Mawdudi founded the Jamaat-e-Islami, an organization in what is now Pakistan dedicated to "the establishment of the Islamic way so as to achieve God's pleasure and seek salvation in the hereafter."[83] Mawdudi was opposed to nationalism, which he saw as a threat to the unity of Islam. He was particularly opposed to feminism and religious pluralism; among his many writings is a 1963 treatise on the fitness of the death penalty as the traditional Islamic penalty for apostasy from Islam.[84] Mawdudi maintained that the Muslim world should cleanse itself of all foreign elements and wage jihad (holy war) until all of humanity is united under Islamic rule. He was willing to endorse violence to achieve this goal.[85]

Mawdudi's work had a profound influence on Qutb, an Egyptian intellectual who turned from being a secular social reformer in the 1930s to joining the Muslim Brotherhood and becoming a radical fundamentalist in the 1950s. He studied in the United States for a master's degree from 1948 to 1950. The visit left him disgusted with the open mingling of the sexes permitted in American society. Back in Egypt, Qutb published several radical books urging the duty of jihad and arguing that killing in the name of religion is morally correct. He denounced Nasser's government as satanic and was executed as a danger to the Egyptian state in 1966.

History

HAMAS AND THE MUSLIM BROTHERHOOD

The history of Hamas reflects a pattern of political leaders appealing to preexisting religious ideals rather than of teachers from the ulema entering politics. Sheikh Yassin (1937?–2004), one of the two founders of Hamas, had been educated at an Islamic university in Egypt, while Abdel Aziz Rantisi (1947–2004), the other cofounder, was a pediatrician. The organization was originally called the Palestinian wing of the Muslim Brotherhood. The Muslim Brotherhood, which Sheikh Yassin had joined during his student years in Cairo, was founded in 1928 by Hassan al-Banna (1906–49), a schoolteacher who wanted to reform Egyptian society by recalling it to pure Islamic faith and practice. In addition to offering educational and spiritual programs, the Brotherhood spread rapidly in the 1930s because it also set up social services. The movement, which never became a formal political party, was composed mostly of devout men who were not members of the ulema[86]; it eventually became anti-intellectual as a result.[87] The Brotherhood was opposed to the secular nationalism represented by such leaders as Nasser and Anwar Sadat. In 1954, one of the Brothers attempted to assassinate Nasser, who then suppressed the Brotherhood.[88]

The Muslim Brotherhood established branches in Palestine, Syria, and Sudan. Yassin was a member of the Palestinian branch, as was Rantisi, who had joined the Brotherhood during his years in medical school in Alexandria, Egypt. Rantisi read Mawdudi during those years, later acknowledging him as the most important influence on his own thinking.[89] The name of the Palestinian branch of the Brotherhood was changed to Hamas in 1987, when the movement backed the Intifada, or uprising against Israeli occupation. The word *hamas* in Arabic means "zeal" or "fervor," but it is also an acronym for the Arabic name of the movement—Harakat al-Muqawama as-Islamiya, or "Islamic resistance movement." According to Rantisi, the Intifada began in 1987 as a protest against the accidental killing of four children who were throwing stones at an Israeli tank.[90]

By February 1988, the Muslim Brotherhood had accepted Hamas as its military arm.[91] In August, Hamas issued its charter (or covenant), a document in which it declared its intention to destroy Israel. It summarized its position as follows: "Allah is its target, the Prophet is its model, the Koran its constitution: Jihad is its path and death for the sake of Allah is the loftiest of its wishes."[92] The intense anti-Semitism of Hamas is reflected in a conversation that Rantisi had with an American reporter in March 2004. Rantisi said, "The Jews are worse than Hitler. . . . I believe that more than fifty percent of the world doesn't believe in the Holocaust, and I am one of them. . . . The Germans were the victims of the Jews. . . . The Jews are the enemy of God, and God is the enemy of the Jews."[93]

Like its Egyptian model, Hamas extended its influence by offering social services to the Palestinians but found itself in the late 1980s in a power struggle with the Palestine Liberation Organization (PLO), a nationalist group. After the Israeli government succeeded in suppressing a rival group called Islamic Jihad, Hamas emerged as the religious alternative to the PLO.[94]

USE OF SUICIDE BOMBERS

Hamas became infamous in the 1990s for its strategic use of suicide bombing, a tactic which it borrowed from a guerrilla organization in Sri Lanka called the Tamil Tigers. The first Hamas suicide bombing took place in April 1994, when a member of the group drove a car loaded with explosives into a bus in Afula, Israel. The number of suicide bombings increased dramatically after the beginning of the so-called Second Intifada in September 2000. Other attacks involving Hamas operatives included a bus in Haifa and a restaurant in Jerusalem, both in 2001. In response to the bombings, the Israeli government approved a plan to construct a security fence along the West Bank in July 2001 to prevent illegal entry into Israel. The first stage of the fence was completed in summer 2003.

Most observers agree that the persons recruited as suicide bombers are neither poor nor mentally ill.[95] With regard to religious motives, the lack of a central religious authority in Islam means that members of the ulema disagree among themselves as well as with the political leaders of Hamas. Many clerics maintain that the Qur'an forbids suicide under any circumstance, while others argue that it is justified when it targets "oppressors." One imam in London said after the bombings of the London public transportation system in July

2005 that "there should be a clear distinction between the suicide bombing of those who are trying to defend themselves from occupiers, which is something different from those who kill civilians, which is a big crime."[96]

Rantisi and Yassin appealed to the concepts of jihad and martyrdom to justify Hamas's use of suicide bombers. Yassin told an American interviewer that "The jihad against Israel is the duty of every individual Muslim."[97] He stated in 2001 that "The Israelis will fall to their knees. You can sense the fear in Israel already; they are worried about where and when the next attacks will come. Ultimately, Hamas will win."[98] The concept of martyrdom, however, appears to be more significant to the bombers themselves than the notion of a holy war. Their families and friends typically maintain that they are proud of their dead kin.[99] Rantisi himself told an American scholar that the phrase *suicide bombings* is incorrect. People should refer to them as *istishadi,* or "self-chosen martyrs." He added that "all Muslims seek to be martyrs."[100]

Structure

Hamas is a controversial organization because of its combination of social service activities with terrorist acts. Most analysts, however, maintain that the division of the organization into military and social wings is more apparent than real. Yassin himself was reported as saying repeatedly that "Hamas is one body."[101] Both the military operatives and the social organizations answer to the political leadership. The major sources of Hamas's funding are Iran and Saudi Arabia; its total annual budget is about $70 million, 85 percent of which comes from outside Palestine.[102] The organization distributes $2 to $3 million in monthly handouts to the families of suicide bombers.[103]

The military operatives themselves are divided into three groups: one that gathers intelligence about Palestinians suspected of collaborating with Israel, a second that pursues violators of Islamic law, and a third known as the Izz al-Din al-Qassam brigades. These brigades were first set up in 1991 by Zaccaria Walid Akel, a Hamas member living in Gaza. The Izz al-Din members at first carried out kidnappings and executions of suspected collaborators. In December 1991, they escalated their activities by killing Israelis; their first known victim was Doron Shorshan, a resident of Kfar Darom. The brigades then began to kidnap and murder Israeli soldiers until 1994, when they turned to suicide bombings.[104] In 2005, the brigades started to carry out joint operations with such other groups as Islamic Jihad and the al-Aqsa Martyr Brigades. This switch in tactics has been attributed to the effectiveness of Israel's security fence in stopping suicide bombers.

As of early 2007, the command structure of Hamas appears to be coming apart, largely as a result of Israel's targeted assassination of Salah Shehada, the head of Izz al-Din al-Qassam, in July 2002, and the 2004 killings of Yassin and Rantisi.[105] It is difficult to predict, however, what may happen following Israel's arrest of Hamas leaders at the end of June 2006. As of mid-2006 most Hamas leaders who have not been arrested by the Israeli Defense Force (IDF) are reported to be in hiding.

Goals

The central goal of Hamas is the establishment of an Islamic state in Palestine. It disagreed with its parent organization, the Muslim Brotherhood, about the priority of war with Israel. The Muslim Brotherhood maintained that the establishment of an Islamic state (the caliphate) throughout the Muslim world would be followed by jihad against Israel, whereas Hamas emphasizes jihad as the only way to solve the Palestinian problem. Article 13 of the Hamas covenant states: "There is no solution for the Palestinian question except through Jihad. Initiatives, proposals and international conferences are all a waste of time and vain endeavors."[106] In addition, the organization rejects any notion of a divided state: "The Islamic Resistance Movement believes that the land of Palestine is an Islamic Waqf consecrated for future Moslem generations until Judgment Day. It, or any part of it, should not be squandered: it, or any part of it, should not be given up."[107]

Since the early 2000s, Hamas has moved its goals beyond the borders of Palestine to call for a "great Islamic state," with Palestine being a part of it. It has become much more open about identifying with the project of a global jihad.[108] Although Hamas candidates toned down calls for the destruction of Israel during the December 2005 election campaign, several spokesmen for the group threatened a new intifada in May 2006.

Future

The future of Hamas has been openly discussed since the deaths of Yassin and Rantisi in 2004. One possibility is that Hamas will take over the entire Gaza Strip after Israel's withdrawal and join forces with al-Qaeda.[109] Others have remarked that Hamas's political gains in the 2006 election place it in a dilemma: It must decide whether to participate in the Palestinian Legislative Council. If it does so, it will have to give up some of its religious objectives in order to function within a parliamentary system.[110] The present disagreements among Hamas leaders may be related to this dilemma. Hassan Yusif, a sheikh living on the West Bank, is reported to favor the possibility of coexistence with Israel, while Khaled Mashal, a senior Hamas member based in Damascus, Syria, refuses to abandon the hard line of the 1988 covenant. In early 2006, Hamas's official election campaign omitted calls for the destruction of

Israel and focused instead on such internal issues as financial corruption and lawlessness.[111]

An additional possibility is that Hamas may continue to lose popular support among the Palestinians. Its inability to avenge the deaths of Yassin and Rantisi in 2004 is said to have damaged its prestige in the eyes of the local population.[112] Moreover, its use of suicide bombers has cost it goodwill, even among some Muslims. Ongoing struggles between Hamas and Fatah members (known as Fauda, or "anarchy" in Arabic, Fatah is the secular political party of the PLO) since the recent elections have led to a number of deaths. In addition, Israel's withholding of tax receipts from the Palestinian Authority and the West's temporary cutoff of financial aid in spring 2006 have increased economic instability.

A third possibility is open warfare between Israel and the Palestinian Authority. The kidnapping of Gilad Shalit, an Israeli soldier, on June 25, 2006, has led to an increasingly tense series of confrontations between Hamas and the government of Israel. On June 28, the IDF began Operation Summer Rains, a ground entrance into the Gaza Strip to secure Shalit's release. This move was followed by the arrest of 28 members of the Hamas government on June 29. The ongoing bombardment of Israeli towns by Izz al-Din al-Qassam rockets fired from the settlements that the Israelis evacuated in 2005 led the Israeli cabinet to approve a deeper military incursion into the Gaza Strip on July 5.

HINDU FUNDAMENTALISM: HINDUTVA

Brief Description

HINDUISM AS A RELIGION

Fundamentalism within Hinduism is difficult to isolate because of the nature of the religion itself. Movements resembling fundamentalism have emerged over the past century, however, in connection with India's political aspirations—first for independence from Britain and later for national unity. Some scholars prefer the phrase *Hindu revivalism* or *organized Hinduisms* to describe contemporary right-wing nationalist movements among Indian Hindus. In early 2006, it was estimated that there are between 900 million and 1 billion Hindus in the world, 98 percent of them living in India (which is 79 percent Hindu). This concentration of population is one reason for the current close alliance between Hindu revivalism and Indian nationalism.

Unlike Christianity, Judaism, and Islam, Hinduism does not have a normative collection of holy writings or a systematic outline of religious teachings accepted by all adherents. In fact, the attempts made by various

20th-century Hindus to assemble a definitive collection of texts or beliefs reflect the influence of Islam and Christianity.[113] The basic sacred texts of Hinduism are the Vedas, a body of religious texts written in Sanskrit between 1500 and 500 B.C.E., although the oral tradition behind them goes back at least as far as 2500 B.C.E. The word *veda* means "knowledge." The Vedas, which are considered shruti, or "divinely revealed," include hymns, prayers, ritual chants, charms, and philosophical writings (the Aranyakas and Upanishads) composed by various sages and holy people. There is no single author regarded as the founder of Hinduism. The various sects that did accept the Vedas as sacred writings came to be grouped together as followers of the Sanatana Dharma, which can be translated as "eternal way" or "eternal values." The Sanatana Dharma is now known as Hinduism. Some beliefs held by most Hindus include dharma (a set of duties and obligations); samsara (reincarnation or rebirth); karma (cause and effect in life related to one's actions); and moksha (salvation). The soul attains moksha after a number of reincarnations determined by the laws of karma. Virtuous actions in life bring one closer to release from the cycle of birth and death, while vicious actions guarantee rebirth into a form of life with a lower level of consciousness.

There is no normative or established school of thought for interpreting the Vedas, which are written in an allegorical or mystical style. Only one major strand of Hinduism, Vaishnavism, favors the literal sense of the text over mystical or poetic interpretations, while other groups within Hinduism maintain that the Vedas should be read creatively. In addition, Hinduism lacks a central doctrinal authority and a body of trained scriptural interpreters corresponding to the Christian clergy, Jewish rabbinate, or Muslim ulema. Unfortunately, this lack makes it easier for demagogues or opportunistic politicians to stir up mob violence related to religious beliefs for their own purposes.[114]

Hinduism has also been associated with a system of classes, or castes (*varnas*), based on callings or professions and known as the Varna Vyasvatha. There are four major castes: Brahmans (teachers and priests), Kshatriyas (kings, warriors, and administrators), Vaishyas (farmers, traders, and merchants), and Shudras (servants and laborers). One group of people—the Dalits (also known as the untouchables)—were defined as being completely outside the caste system. Scholars do not agree as to whether the caste system is a necessary part of Hinduism or whether it can be justified on the basis of a few texts in the Vedas. The caste system has not been completely eliminated in contemporary India even though the country's constitution strictly prohibits caste-based discrimination. Caste still influences political decisions in many parts of India.

INDIA'S COLONIAL HISTORY: THE BRITISH RAJ

The history of India—particularly the Raj, or period of British colonial rule—is another factor that influenced the development of Hindu revivalism. Britain first acquired a foothold in India in 1757, when Colonel Robert Clive defeated the nawab (provincial governor) of Bengal at the Battle of Plassey in 1757. Clive's troops were funded by the British East India Company, which took advantage of his victory to monopolize trade. Bengal then became a protectorate under direct British rule. The Raj itself began in 1858, when territories under the control of the British East India Company were transferred to the British Crown. The Raj lasted until 1947, when India became an independent republic and adopted a secular constitution.

The Raj changed India in a number of ways. First, it broke down the older notion of Hinduism as a collection of different religious communities living together in varying degrees of harmony. By recruiting educated Indians to serve as administrators and clerks, the British created a new type of hierarchy in the cities that began to replace the older land-based aristocracy. A Western education soon became essential for social and professional advancement. Second, the British administrators reserved a certain number of government positions for Dalits and low-caste Indians. This practice of job reservations made genuine social mobility possible for numbers of lower-class Indians, but it also separated caste from economic class. Many high-caste Indians resent what they consider unfair privileges given to the Dalits by the reservation system.[115]

Third, the political unity imposed on India by the Raj was more apparent than real. The complex network of competing communal, religious, and social obligations and loyalties that had existed for thousands of years before the Raj did not disappear; in fact, it persists in contemporary India. Loyalty is generally given to local customs and institutions rather than to such abstractions as a "universal state."[116] This situation made it easier for Hindu nationalists to preach the notion of a "Hindu community" as defining the nation's identity. Because of its connection with Hindu nationalism, the word *communalism* has become a synonym in Indian usage for fundamentalist movements.[117] According to writer Krishna Kumar, "What we are witnessing today is less the resurgence of religion than of communalism, where a community of believers has not only a religious affiliation but also social, economic, and political interests in common."[118]

The Raj also made Indians more aware of the religious differences among themselves because the British defined the largest groups according to the British definition of "a religion," a definition that was inevitably shaped by Christianity. The British administrators then used a threefold division of

Indian religions into Hindu, Muslim, and Sikh, combined with stereotypes of each of the three groups, as a guide to filling official positions. In 1909, the British carried this classification even further by assigning separate electoral constituencies to the different religions based on census data. This arrangement made it quite clear that political power was associated with religious identity. Consequently, the more educated members in each religious group began organizing themselves along broader religious lines.[119] Christian missionary activity and the formation of the Muslim League in 1906 provided additional reasons for Hindus to organize themselves politically.[120]

History

ARYA SAMAJ

The first reform movement within Hinduism, the Arya Samaj, or Arya Society, began in the late 19th century. It was started in 1875 by Swami Dayananda Sarasvati (1824–83) in Bombay (Mumbai), on the western coast of India. Dayananda wanted to purify Hinduism of what he regarded as later additions by returning to the Vedas as the basic source of religious authority. His was essentially a world-renouncing form of fundamentalism, emphasizing the virtue of chastity (*brahmacharya*) and detachment from the material world (*sannyasa*) in order to escape the cycle of death and rebirth. The Arya Samaj was opposed to such practices as child marriage, the caste system, temple offerings, and animal sacrifices. It became a form of missionary Hinduism under the slogan "Make this world noble."

In 1909, some members of Arya Samaj formed the first political Hindu group, the Punjab Provincial Hindu Sabha, or council. The group's formation was triggered by the results of several successive censuses that showed the Hindu population of the area dropping in comparison to a rise in the Muslim population.[121] This provincial council was renamed the All-India Hindu Mahasabha, or great council, in 1915. The Mahasabha was intended to counter the growing power of the Muslim League as well as the secular Indian National Congress. Outbreaks of violence between Hindus and Muslims became more frequent in the 1920s.

SAVARKAR AND HEDGEWAR

Hindutva, a right-wing Hindu nationalist ideology, emerged from the Mahasabha through the work of Vinayak Damodar Savarkar (1883–1966), who became a hero to many Indians struggling for independence from British rule. Savarkar had been imprisoned in 1911 for the murder of a British customs official and transferred to a jail in Ratnagiri, Maharashtra, in 1921. There he wrote *Hindutva* (Hinduness), the book that became the foundational text of right-wing Hindu nationalism. Savarkar defined Hinduness as a basic communal identity based on "earth" and "birth" that submerged all differences of caste, language, and regional custom. Savarkar wrote in *Hindutva,* "A Hindu means a person who regards this land of Bharatavarsha, from the Indus [River] to the seas, as his Fatherland as well as his Holy Land, that is the cradle-land of his religion."[122]

Savarkar's ideas were taken up by Keshav Baliram Hedgewar (1889–1940), a politician who was distressed by the lack of any sense of national solidarity in India and disillusioned with Mohandas K. Gandhi's policy of nonviolence. Hedgewar had joined the Hindu Mahasabha in 1923 and remained a member until 1929. He decided, after reading *Hindutva,* that turning the Mahasabha into a political party was counterproductive. To him, the best way to restore communal unity based on "Hinduness" was to transform individuals by physical discipline and spiritual revitalization, which he proposed to do by forming a brotherhood of such committed persons.

In contrast to Dayananda's regard for the Vedas as the core of Hindu teaching, Hedgewar made the warrior (Kshatriya) ideal contained in such epics as the *Ramayana* central to his program. He founded the Rashtriya Swayamsevak Sangh (RSS) in September 1925 for "propagating Hindu culture." Hedgewar recruited idealistic preadolescent males, called *swayamsevaks* (self-servants), who were trained to serve the goals of Hindutva through rigorous physical, mental, and spiritual exercises, including paramilitary training. The youths were expected to swear oaths of loyalty to the organization's banner, its supreme director, and various Hindu saints. The first RSS recruits were drawn from Brahman families in Nagpur. By 1939, the RSS had 60,000 active members organized into 500 *shakhas,* or branches[123]; as of 2004, the number of *shakhas* had grown to 48,000.[124] It is thought that there are about 50,000 *shakhas* as of 2006.

Hedgewar was succeeded as supreme head of the RSS in 1940 by Madhav Sadashiv Golwarkar (1906–73), who is significant for publishing a book, *We, or Our Nationhood Defined.* This 1939 publication showed that Hindutva was intolerant toward other faith traditions:

> *The non-Hindu peoples in Hindustan must adopt the Hindu culture and language, must learn to respect and hold in reverence the Hindu religion, must entertain no idea but glorification of the Hindu race and culture; i. e., they must not only give up their attitude of intolerance and ungratefulness towards this land and its age-old traditions, but must also cultivate a positive attitude of love and devotion instead. . . . they must cease to be foreigners, or must stay in this country wholly subordinated to the Hindu nation.*[125]

HINDUTVA AND THE MUSLIMS

The cause of Hindu nationalism was certainly strengthened by India's move toward independence in 1947. The Muslim League's involvement since 1907 in the drive to divide the territory of British India into two states, one for Muslims and the other for Hindus, was reinforced by the activism of Hindu nationalists, who also regarded partition as an answer to the political struggles between the two religious groups. The nationalist cause, however, was set back by the involvement of Hindutva extremists in the assassination of Gandhi in 1948. Gandhi was targeted because he wanted to protect the rights of the Muslim minority in India.[126] Savarkar was arrested as a coconspirator in the assassination but was released for lack of evidence. It was not until the 1970s and 1980s that members of Hindu nationalist organizations became more militant. There were several events and developments during those years that reawakened Hindu opposition to Muslims in particular[127]:

- A large influx of Muslim refugees from Bangladesh in 1971 that made Hindus a minority in some of India's eastern states
- The impact of the Sikh militant movement in 1980–84 on Hindus, which culminated in the assassination of Prime Minister Indira Gandhi
- Ethnic cleansing in the disputed region of Kashmir and a rise in the number of Islamic schools in northern India
- An increase in the Muslim population of northern India and group conversions of Dalits to Islam
- Advances in mass communications, which disrupt old ways of life and increase people's awareness of economic and social inequalities

The result of growing hostility toward Muslims was the destruction of a 16th-century Muslim mosque, the Babri Masjid, in Ayodhya by a mob of Hindutva activists in December 1992. The mosque had been constructed on the site of an ancient temple that Hindus believed had marked the birthplace of Rama, an incarnation of the god Vishnu. The demolition of the temple, which was the culmination of a 10-year campaign by the Bajrang Dal, a paramilitary group founded in 1984 specifically for that purpose, sparked riots throughout India in which at least 2,000 people were killed. The anti-Muslim riots in Gujarat in February 2002, which followed a Muslim attack on a train carrying Hindu pilgrims from Ayodhya, are widely regarded as a sequel to the destruction of the mosque in 1992.[128]

The other religion that Hindutva activists consider a threat is Christianity. Hindu attacks on Christians have increased significantly since the late 1990s.

In 1999, an Australian missionary who had worked among the leper community in Orissa for nearly 30 years was burned alive in his station wagon, along with his two young sons. In the years since 1999, there have been cases of sexual assaults on Roman Catholic nuns, the killing of priests and missionaries, the burning of churches, and desecrations of Christian cemeteries.[129] The Bharatiya Janata Party (BJP), the political party most closely associated with Hindutva, has tried to impose a government ban on conversions to Christianity. The BJP appoints school officials in the states it controls to alter textbooks and course outlines to emphasize the role of Hinduism in India's history.[130] This tactic is known as "saffronization," the name being derived from the golden yellow color that has symbolized Hinduism for centuries.

Structure

The ideology of Hindutva, spread by the RSS, gave rise to a group of organizations ranging from political parties to trade unions and militias. This collection of groups is called the Sangh Parivar, or the Sangh family of organizations. In the early 21st century, the Sangh has attempted to recruit Hindus living abroad, particularly in the United States and the United Kingdom. The major entities in the Sangh Parivar, in addition to the RSS itself, are the BJP, the Sangh's political wing; the Vishwa Hindu Parishad (VHP), a cultural-religious organization; the paramilitary Bajrang Dal; and the Seva Vibhag, a service organization. The BJP, founded on April 5, 1980, grew out of a predecessor political organization known as the Jana Sangh, formed by members of the Hindu Mahasabha, the Arya Samaj, and the RSS in 1951. The VHP was founded by Golwarkar in 1964 as a missionary society to draw Dalits and members of "backward" tribes into Hinduism and intimidate converts to Christianity, Buddhism, or Islam. It was involved in the agitation leading to the destruction of the Babri Masjid in Ayodhya in 1992.[131] As a result of the VHP's involvement in stirring up mob violence, it was banned for two years under India's Unlawful Activities Act. The organization continued to increase its strength after the ban expired, however, and claims to have branches in 25 countries outside India as of the early 2000s.[132]

The RSS is the only organization within the Sangh Parivar whose members are distinguished by wearing uniforms (white shirts, khaki shorts, and black berets) and maintaining a regimented lifestyle. They are expected to participate in daily physical drills, to participate in a short religious ceremony honoring the saffron-colored banner of the RSS, and to attend periodic ideological lectures. The *pracharaks,* or upper-level organizers, are expected to remain celibate and receive only basic living expenses as compensation for their work.[133]

Goals

The goals of Hindutva activists in the early 2000s included a proposal to change the constitution of India in order to "Hinduize" the country. The proposed changes would have outlawed conversions to Christianity among the Dalits, struck down the permission granted to Muslims since 1950 to use sharia rather than Indian civil law to regulate such matters as marriage and inheritance, and allowed Hindus to purchase land or start businesses in Kashmir, which is heavily Muslim. If the BJP had won several major electoral victories after 2002 and had been able to amend the constitution as it desired, India might have been subjected to a massive wave of violence.[134] Instead, the secular Congress Party gained control of the central government.

Other goals of the BJP include "purifying" India of Christians, deporting Muslims to Bangladesh, and building a Hindu temple to Rama on the site of the Babri mosque in Ayodhya. Only a makeshift temple has been built as of early 2006. It was heavily damaged in July 2005 when six Muslim terrorists disguised as Hindu worshippers rammed a jeep loaded with explosives into the security wall surrounding the temple.[135]

Future

Hindutva may have a more limited future than seemed to be the case as recently as 2002. In the aftermath of the Gujarat riots, some observers seemed to think that Hindutva-sponsored violence would succeed in reducing India to anarchy.[136] Others thought that Hindutva would continue to appeal to Indians as a ready-made "identity kit" in a country whose economic transition means that caste is no longer a reliable marker of one's position in society.[137] In 2003, the U.S. Commission on International Religious Freedom recommended adding India to the list of the worst religious persecutors under the International Religious Freedom Act for its "egregious, systematic and ongoing" violations of religious freedom.[138]

The BJP suffered a major electoral setback in 2004, however. It lost control not only of the central government but also of the ministry of education, which had been its chief ally in rewriting school textbooks to conform to Hindutva ideology. The BJP's loss of power to the Congress Party is said to be a reaction against Hindu nationalism because of the high death toll in the Gujarat riots.[139] The U.S. State Department's 2005 report on religious freedom in India noted that the new central government is taking steps to "desaffronize" educational materials but that the VHP continues its policy of trying to force all Christians in states ruled by the BJP to convert to Hinduism.[140] A spokesman for the VHP told a reporter that the aim of the organization is to establish "a Hindu state and Hindu glory."[141] One result of this and other hard-line pronouncements has been an open quarrel between the BJP, which wants to take a more moderate line on religious issues in order to broaden its appeal to voters, and the VHP, which refuses to soften its demands. As of early 2006, the BJP appeared to have lost its direction as well as its morale; its new leaders are uncertain about their ongoing loyalty to the ideology of Hindutva.[142]

---

[1] Figures in William D. Dinges. "'We Are What You Were': Roman Catholic Traditionalism in America." In Mary Jo Weaver and R. Scott Appleby, eds. *Being Right: Conservative Catholics in America.* Bloomington: Indiana University Press, 1995, p. 242.

[2] William D. Dinges. "Roman Catholic Traditionalism." In Martin E. Marty and R. Scott Appleby, eds. *Fundamentalisms Observed.* Chicago: University of Chicago Press, 1991, p. 67.

[3] Desmond O'Grady. "A Tale of Two Prelates: An Ecumenist and a Schismatic." *Commonweal* 124 (January 31, 1997), p. 22.

[4] Dinges. "Roman Catholic Traditionalism," p. 83.

[5] Quoted in O'Grady. "A Tale of Two Prelates," p. 21.

[6] Quoted in O'Grady. "A Tale of Two Prelates," p. 23.

[7] Quoted in Patrick Madrid and Pete Vere. *More Catholic than the Pope: An Inside Look at Extreme Traditionalism.* Huntington, Ind.: Our Sunday Visitor, 2004, pp. 26–27. Vere, a canon lawyer, was associated with Lefebvre's movement for eight years until he returned to the mainstream Catholic Church in the early 2000s.

[8] Pius X. "Syllabus Condemning the Errors of the Modernists: Lamentabili sane." Papal Encyclicals Online. Available online. URL: http://www.papalencyclicals.net/Pius10/p10lamen.htm. Accessed October 3, 2005.

[9] Pius X. "Syllabus Condemning the Errors of the Modernists."

[10] Marcel Lefebvre. "An Open Letter to Confused Catholics." Quoted in Madrid and Vere. *More Catholic than the Pope,* p. 21.

[11] Dinges. "'We Are What You Were,'" p. 249.

[12] Vere. "Canonical History of the Lefebvrite Schism," p. 6.

[13] Marcel Lefebvre. "La Déclaration du 21 novembre 1974, Itinéraires, no. 195." Translated in *The Collected Works of His Excellency Archbishop Marcel Lefebvre.* Vol. 1. Dickinson, Tex.: Angelus Press, 1985, p. 34.

[14] Quoted in Madrid and Vere. *More Catholic than the Pope,* p. 54.

[15] Dinges. "'We Are What You Were,'" p. 245.

[16] Pope John Paul II. "Ecclesia Dei adflicta." Adoremus. Available online. URL: http://www.adoremus.org/EcclesiaDei.html. Accessed December 2, 2005.

[17] Gabriel Almond, R. Scott Appleby, and Emmanuel Sivan. *Strong Religion: The Rise of Fundamentalisms around the World.* Chicago: University of Chicago Press, 2003, p. 186.

[18] James A. Sullivan. "Catholics United for the Faith: Dissent and the Laity." In Mary Jo Weaver and R. Scott Appleby, eds. *Being Right: Conservative Catholics in America.* Bloomington: Indiana University Press, 1995, p. 119.

[19] Almond, Appleby, and Sivan. *Strong Religion,* p. 185.

[20] Bishop Bernard Fellay. "Statement from Bishop Bernard Fellay Concerning the Interdenominational Day of Prayer in Assisi on 24th January 2002." Society of St. Pius X Canada. Available online. URL: http://www.sspx.ca/Documents/Bishop-Fellay/Bishop_Fellay_on_Assisi.htm. Accessed December 1, 2005.

[21] "Tower of Trent Hall of Honor, Bishop Bernard Fellay, Superior General of the Society of St. Pius X." *Daily Catholic* 15, no. 144 (May 25, 2004). Available online. URL: http://www.dailycatholic.org/issue/04May/may25ttt.htm. Accessed December 1, 2005. The medical evidence indicates that John Paul I died of a pulmonary embolism. Conspiracy theories that he was given poisoned coffee or an intentional overdose of digitalis (a heart medication) have been generally rejected.

[22] Dinges. "'We Are What You Were,'" p. 249.

[23] Matt C. Abbott. "Schismatic Traditionalists." *Homiletic and Pastoral Review* (March 1999), p. 57.

[24] John L. Allen. "Pope Meets with Schismatic Leader." *National Catholic Reporter* 41 (September 9, 2005), p. 13.

[25] Bishop Bernard Fellay. "Interview Concerning His Meeting with Pope Benedict XVI." Society of St. Pius X Canada. Available online. URL: http://www.sspx.ca/Documents/Bishop-Fellay/DICI_Interview_Sept_2005.htm. Accessed November 30, 2005.

[26] Rod Dreher. "Scranton Scandal: Traditionalist Catholics Are Not Immune to Sex Scandals." *National Review Online,* February 7, 2002. Available online. URL: http://www.nationalreview.com/dreher/dreher020702.shtml. Accessed December 6, 2005.

[27] Jean Violette. "Fr. Violette's Letter to the Faithful." Society of St. Pius X Canada. December 2003. Available online. URL: http://www.sspx.ca/Documents/Fr-Violettes-Letters/2003_December.htm. Accessed November 30, 2005.

[28] Jonathan V. Last. "God on the Internet." *First Things,* no. 158 (December 2005), p. 40. Available online. URL: http://www.firstthings.com/ftissues/ft0512/articles/last.html. Accessed November 30, 2005.

[29] Jonathan Sacks. "Judaism and Politics in the Modern World." In Peter L. Berger, ed. *The Desecularization of the World: Resurgent Religion and World Politics.* Washington, D.C.: Ethics and Public Policy Center, 1999, p. 52.

[30] Seymour M. Lipset and Earl Raab. *Judaism and the New American Scene.* Cambridge, Mass.: Harvard University Press, 1995, p. 40.

[31] Charles S. Liebman. "Jewish Fundamentalism and the Israeli Polity." In Martin E. Marty and R. Scott Appleby, eds. *Fundamentalisms and the State.* Chicago: University of Chicago Press, 1993, p. 68.

[32] David C. Rapoport. "Comparing Militant Fundamentalist Movements and Groups." In Marty and Appleby, eds. *Fundamentalisms and the State,* p. 437.

[33] Bernard Lewis. "The Emergence of Modern Israel." *Middle Eastern Studies* 8 (October 1972), p. 423.

[34] Samuel C. Heilman. "Jews and Fundamentalism." *Jewish Political Studies Review* 17 (Spring 2005). Available online. URL: http://www.jcpa.org/cjc/cjc-heilman-s05.htm. Accessed December 31, 2005.

[35] Ehud Sprinzak. "Three Models of Religious Violence: The Case of Jewish Fundamentalism in Israel." In Marty and Appleby, eds. ***Fundamentalisms and the State,*** p. 469.

[36] Sprinzak. "Three Models of Religious Violence," p. 464.

[37] Sprinzak. "Three Models of Religious Violence," pp. 477–478.

[38] Sprinzak. "Three Models of Religious Violence," p. 479.

[39] Meir Kahane. "Revenge—the Jewish Approach." Kahane.org. Available online. URL: http://www.kahane.org/meir/revenge.html. Accessed December 15, 2005.

[40] Kahane. "The Arabs in Eretz Israel." Kahane.org. Available online. URL: http://www.kahane.org/meir/arabs.html. Accessed December 5, 2005.

[41] Sprinzak. "Three Models of Religious Violence," p. 484.

[42] Almond, Appleby, and Sivan. ***Strong Religion,*** p. 162.

[43] United States Department of State. "Appendix B: Background Information on Terrorist Groups." Available online. URL: http://www.state.gov/s/ct/rls/pgtrpt/2000/2450.htm. Accessed November 30, 2005.

[44] Sprinzak. "Three Models of Religious Violence," p. 469.

[45] Almond, Appleby, and Sivan. ***Strong Religion,*** p. 160.

[46] Michael Rosenak. "Jewish Fundamentalism in Israeli Education." In Martin E. Marty and R. Scott Appleby, eds. ***Fundamentalisms and Society.*** Chicago: University of Chicago Press, 1993, p. 396.

[47] Quoted in Harvey Sicherman. "The Sacred and the Profane: Judaism and International Relations." 2001 Templeton Lecture on Religion and World Affairs, Foreign Policy Research Institute, February 21, 2001. Available online. URL: http://www.fpri.org/fpriwire/1001.200291.sicherman.judaismintlrelations.html. Accessed October 29, 2005.

[48] Quoted in Rabbi Ed Snitkoff. "Settling All the Land: The Birth and Growth of Gush Emunim." MyJewishLearning.com. Available online. URL: http://www.myjewishlearning.com/ideas_belief/LandIsrael/modern_landisrael/ReligiousZionism /GushEmunim.htm. Accessed November 3, 2005.

[49] Gideon Aran. "Jewish Zionist Fundamentalism: The Bloc of the Faithful in Israel (Gush Emunim)." In Marty and Appleby, eds. ***Fundamentalisms Observed,*** p. 268.

[50] Jeffrey Goldberg. "A Reporter at Large: Among the Settlers." Part 1. *The New Yorker* (May 31, 2004) Available online. URL: http://www.newyorker.com/fact/content/articles/040531fa_fact2_a. Accessed December 2, 2005.

[51] Aran. "Jewish Zionist Fundamentalism," p. 269.

[52] Almond, Appleby, and Sivan. ***Strong Religion,*** p. 161.

[53] Aran. "Jewish Zionist Fundamentalism," p. 278.

[54] Snitkoff. "Settling All the Land."

[55] Ehud Sprinzak. "Gush Emunim: The Tip of the Iceberg." *Jerusalem Quarterly* 21 (Fall 1981). Available online. URL: http://www.geocities.com/alabasters_archive/gush_iceberg.html#author. Accessed December 12, 2005.

[56] Sprinzak. "Three Models of Religious Violence," p. 473.

[57] Ian S. Lustick. "The Evolution of Gush Emunim and Related Groups." In *For the Land and the Lord: Jewish Fundamentalism in Israel.* New York: Council on Foreign Relations, 1988.

[58] Karen Armstrong. *The Battle for God: A History of Fundamentalism.* New York: Ballantine Books, 2000, p. 285.

[59] Israel Shahak and Norton Mesvinsky. "The Nature of Gush Emunim Settlements." In *Jewish Fundamentalism in Israel.* London: Pluto Press, 1999.

[60] "Camp David Accords; September 17, 1978." Avalon Project of the Yale Law School. Available online. URL: http://www.yale.edu/lawweb/avalon/mideast/campdav.htm. Accessed December 3, 2005.

[61] Sprinzak. "Three Models of Religious Violence," p. 476.

[62] Sprinzak. "Three Models of Religious Violence," p. 486.

[63] Rosenak. "Jewish Fundamentalism in Israeli Education," p. 396.

[64] Aran. "Jewish Zionist Fundamentalism," p. 303.

[65] United States Library of Congress Country Studies. "Gush Emunim." *Israel.* Washington, D.C.: Department of the Army, 1988. Available online. URL: http://countrystudies.us/israel/102.htm. Accessed November 24, 2005.

[66] Lustick. "The Evolution of Gush Emunim and Related Groups."

[67] Aran. "Jewish Zionist Fundamentalism," pp. 282–283.

[68] Quoted in Aran. "Jewish Zionist Fundamentalism," p. 290.

[69] Sprinzak. "Three Models of Religious Violence," pp. 486–487.

[70] Interview by Jean-Marc Flükiger. "Jewish Messianism and the Settler Movement after Gaza Withdrawal: Interview with Gideon Aran." *Religioscope* (November 29, 2005). Available online. URL: http://religion.info/english/interviews/article_212.shtml. Accessed January 3, 2006.

[71] Bernard Lewis. *What Went Wrong? The Clash between Islam and Modernity in the Middle East.* New York: HarperCollins, 2002, p. 101.

[72] Lewis. *What Went Wrong?,* p. 101.

[73] Steve Bruce. *Fundamentalism.* Malden, Mass.: Polity Press, 2000, pp. 42–43.

[74] Bernard Lewis. "The Roots of Muslim Rage." *Atlantic Monthly* (September 1990), p. 48.

[75] Bernard Lewis. "Targeted by a History of Hatred." *Washington Post,* September 10, 2002, p. A15. Emphasis mine.

[76] Council on Foreign Relations. "Backgrounder: Hamas." Available online. URL: http://www.cfr.org/publication/8968/. Updated June 14, 2006.

[77] Anton LaGuardia. "Fanatics around the World Dream of the Caliph's Return." *The Telegraph,* January 8, 2005. Available online. URL: http://www.telegraph.co.uk/news/main.jhtml?xml=/news/2005/08/01/wislam101.xml. Accessed October 22, 2005.

[78] Quoted in Daniel Pipes. "What Do the Terrorists Want? [A Caliphate]." *New York Sun,* July 26, 2005. Available online. URL: http://www.danielpipes.org/article/2798. Accessed January 3, 2006.

[79] Karl Vick. "Reunified Islam: Unlikely but Not Entirely Radical." *Washington Post,* January 14, 2006, p. A1. Available online. URL: http://www.washingtonpost.com/wp-dyn/content/article/2006/01/13/AR2006011301816_pf.html. Accessed January 14, 2006.

[80] CBC News Online. "In Depth: Islam." May 26, 2005. Available online. URL: http://www.cbc.ca/news/background/islam/shariah-law.html. Accessed January 12, 2006.

[81] "Alle ni kendt skyldige i 'aeresdrab.'" *Jyllands-Posten,* June 27, 2006. Available online. URL: http://www.jp.dk/indland/artikel:aid=3812570/. Accessed June 28, 2006.

[82] *AsiaSource. "Good Muslim, Bad Muslim: AsiaSource* Interview with Mahmood Mamdani." May 5, 2004. Available online. URL: http://www.asiasource.org/news/special_reports/mamdani.cfm. Accessed January 2, 2006.

[83] Quoted in Mumtaz Ahmad. "Islamic Fundamentalism in South Asia: The Jamaat-i-Islami and the Tablighi Jamaat of South Asia." In Marty and Appleby, eds. *Fundamentalisms Observed,* p. 467.

[84] Abul Ala Mawdudi. *The Punishment of the Apostate According to Islamic Law.* Translated by Syed Silas Husain and Ernest Hahn. Mississauga, Canada: 1994. Available online. URL: http://www.answering-islam.org/Hahn/Mawdudi/. Accessed November 22, 2005.

[85] *AsiaSource. "Good Muslim, Bad Muslim."*

[86] John O. Voll. "Fundamentalism in the Sunni Arab World: Egypt and the Sudan." In Marty and Appleby, eds. *Fundamentalisms Observed,* p. 362.

[87] Karen Armstrong. *The Battle for God,* p. 223.

[88] Voll. "Fundamentalism in the Sunni Arab World," p. 370.

[89] Mark Juergensmeyer. *Terror in the Mind of God: The Global Rise of Religious Violence.* Berkeley: University of California Press, 2003, p. 84.

[90] Juergensmeyer. *Terror in the Mind of God,* p. 75.

[91] Jean-François Legrain. "A Defining Moment: Palestinian Islamic Fundamentalism." In James Piscatori, ed. *Islamic Fundamentalisms and the Gulf Crisis.* Chicago: American Academy of Arts and Sciences, the Fundamentalism Project, 1991, p. 74.

[92] "Hamas Covenant, 1988: The Covenant of the Islamic Resistance Movement." Avalon Project at Yale Law School. Available online. URL: http://www.yale.edu/lawweb/avalon/mideast/hamas.htm. Accessed November 6, 2005.

[93] Jeffrey Goldberg. "A Reporter at Large: The Sheikh." *The New Yorker* (May 31, 2004). Available online. URL: http://www.newyorker.com/fact/content/articles/040531fa_fact2_d. Accessed December 2, 2005.

[94] Almond, Appleby, and Sivan. *Strong Religion,* p. 179.

[95] Yoram Schweitzer. "Suicide Bombings: The Ultimate Weapon?" August 7, 2001. Institute for Counter-Terrorism. Available online. URL: http://www.ict.org.il/articles/articledet.cfm?articleid=373. Accessed January 2, 2006.

[96] Sayed Mohammed Musawi, quoted in Mona Eltahawy. "After London, Tough Questions for Muslims." *Washington Post,* July 24, 2005, p. B7. Available online. URL: http://www.washingtonpost.com/wp-dyn/content/article/2005/07/22/AR2005072201629.html. Accessed January 3, 2006.

[97] Quoted in Goldberg. "A Reporter at Large: The Sheikh."

[98] Bruce Hoffman. "The Logic of Suicide Terrorism." *Atlantic Monthly* (June 2003). Available online. URL: http://www.theatlantic.com/doc/200306/hoffman. Accessed January 3, 2006.

[99] Avishai Margalit. "The Suicide Bombers." *New York Review of Books* 50 (January 16, 2003). Available online. URL: http://www.nybooks.com/articles/15979. Accessed January 3, 2006.

[100] Juergensmeyer. *Terror in the Mind of God,* pp. 73–74.

[101] Quoted in Matthew A. Levitt. "Hamas from Cradle to Grave." *Middle East Quarterly* 10 (Winter 2004). Available online. URL: http://www.meforum.org/article/582. Accessed January 4, 2006.

[102] Anti-Defamation League. *Hamas Fact Sheet.* March 22, 2004. Available online. URL: http://www.adl.org/Israel/hamas_facts.asp. Accessed January 4, 2006.

[103] Levitt. "Hamas from Cradle to Grave."

[104] Bradley Burston. "Background/Hamas vs. Abbas: The Lethal Wild Card, a Profile." *Haaretz,* January 19, 2006. Available online. URL: http://www.haaretz.com/hasen/pages/ShArt.jhtml?itemNo=529909&displayTypeCd=1 &sideCd=1&contrassID=2. Accessed January 20, 2006.

[105] Burston. "Background/Hamas vs. Abbas."

[106] "Hamas Covenant, 1988."

[107] "Hamas Covenant, 1988."

[108] Dore Gold. "America's Hamas Dilemma: Spreading Democracy or Combating Terrorism?" *Jerusalem Issue Brief* 5 (November 1, 2005). Available online. URL: http://www.jcpa.org/brief/brief005-8.htm. Accessed January 6, 2006.

[109] Major General Yaakov Amidror and David Keyes. "Will a Gaza 'Hamas-stan' Become a Future al-Qaeda Sanctuary?" *Jerusalem Issue Brief* 4, no. 7 (November 8, 2004). Available online. URL: http://www.jcpa.org/brief/brief004-7.htm. Accessed January 6, 2006.

[110] Asaf Maliach. "Hamas and the 'Two-Level' Strategy." January 7, 2006. Institute for Counter-Terrorism. Available online. URL: http://www.ict.org.il/. Accessed January 7, 2006.

[111] Khaled abu Toameh and staff members. "US to Cut Funding If Hamas Elected." *Jerusalem Post,* January 14, 2006. Available online. URL: http://www.jpost.com/servlet/Satellite?cid=1136361077792&pagename=JPost%2FJP Article%2FShowFull. Accessed January 15, 2006.

[112] Burston. "Background/Hamas vs. Abbas."

[113] Krishna Kumar. "Hindu Revivalism and Education in North-Central India." In Marty and Appleby, eds. *Fundamentalisms and Society,* p. 537.

[114] N. J. Demerath. "The Pitfalls of Pluralism: Talibanization and Saffronization in India." *Harvard International Review* 25 (Winter 2004), p. 18.

[115] Demerath. "The Pitfalls of Pluralism," p. 20.

[116] Robert Erik Frykenberg. "Hindu Fundamentalism and the Structural Stability of India." In Marty and Appleby, eds. *Fundamentalisms and the State,* p. 234.

[117] Special correspondent. "NDA Fostered Communalism, Says Sonia Gandhi." *The Hindu,* November 12, 2005. Available online. URL: http://www.hindu.com/2005/11/12/stories/2005111206661200.htm. Accessed January 18, 2006. Interestingly, the *Hindu*'s masthead describes it as "India's National Newspaper."

[118] Krishna Kumar. "Religious Fundamentalism in India and Beyond." *Parameters* 32 (Autumn 2002), p. 30.

[119] Daniel Gold. "Organized Hinduisms: From Vedic Truth to Hindu Nation." In Marty and Appleby, eds. *Fundamentalisms Observed,* p. 537.

[120] Frykenberg. "Hindu Fundamentalism and the Structural Stability of India," pp. 238–239.

[121] Gold. "Organized Hinduisms," p. 539.

[122] Quoted in Koenraad Elst. "Hindutva." In *Who Is a Hindu? Hindu Revivalist Views of Animism, Buddhism, Sikhism and Other Offshoots of Hinduism.* New Delhi: Voice of India, 2001. Available online. URL: http://koenraadelst.voiceofdharma.com/books/wiah/ch4.htm. Accessed January 18, 2006.

[123] Frykenberg. "Hindu Fundamentalism and the Structural Stability of India," p. 241.

[124] John Lancaster. "Hindu Nationalists Regroup after Loss." *Washington Post,* June 6, 2004. p. A22. Available online. URL: http://www.washingtonpost.com/wp-dyn/articles/A18954-2004Jun5.html. Accessed January 18, 2006.

[125] Quoted in Frykenberg. "Hindu Fundamentalism and the Structural Stability of India," p. 242.

[126] Kumar. "Religious Fundamentalism in India," p. 28.

[127] Kumar. "Religious Fundamentalism in India," pp. 29–30.

[128] Richard Bonney. "Introduction." In Richard Bonney, ed. *Ayodhya 1992: The Assertion of Cultural and Religious Hegemony.* Leicester, England: University of Leicester, 2003, p. 8.

[129] Manpreet Singh. "Hindu Radical Redux: Church Leaders Report More Than 200 New Incidents of Persecution." *Christianity Today* 49 (May 2005), p. 19.

[130] Paul Marshall. "Hinduism and Terror." *First Things,* no. 144 (June–July 2004), pp. 10–13.

[131] United States Library of Congress Country Studies. "Modern Transformations." *India.* Washington, D.C.: Department of the Army, 1996. Also available online.

[132] Almond, Appleby, and Sivan. *Strong Religion,* p. 137.

[133] Lancaster. "Hindu Nationalists Regroup."

[134] Demerath. "The Pitfalls of Pluralism," p. 19.

[135] Onkar Singh. "6 Militants Storm Ayodhya, Killed." Rediff.com. July 5, 2005. Available online. URL: http://in.rediff.com/news/2005/jul/05ayo.htm. Accessed January 6, 2006.

[136] Swami Agnivesh and the Reverend Valson Thampu. "Are We Creating an Anarchic Society?" *The Hindu Magazine* (March 31, 2002). Available online. URL: http://www.hinduonnet.com/thehindu/mag/2002/03/31/stories/2002033100010100.htm. Accessed January 6, 2006.

[137] Demerath. "The Pitfalls of Pluralism," p. 18.

[138] Freedom House, Center for Religious Freedom. *The Rise of Hindu Extremism and the Repression of Christian and Muslim Minorities in India.* Washington, D.C.: Freedom House, 2003, p. 22.

[139] Lancaster. "Hindu Nationalists Regroup," p. A22.

[140] United States Department of State. "India: International Religious Freedom Report 2005." Available online. URL: http://www.state.gov/g/drl/rls/irf/2005/51618.htm. Accessed January 6, 2006.

[141] Quoted in "The Struggle for the Hindu Soul: A Family Squabble, or the Beginning of the End for Hindu Nationalism?" *The Economist* (August 4, 2005). Available online. URL: http://www.economist.com/printedition/displayStory.cfm?story_id=4254416. Accessed January 2, 2006.

[142] Anjana Pasricha. "A New President Takes Over India's Main Opposition Party." *Voice of America News,* January 2, 2006. Available online. URL: http://www.voanews.com/english/2006-01-02-voa15.cfm. Accessed January 3, 2006.

PART II

Primary Sources

4

United States Documents

The primary sources in this chapter are divided into three sections: constitutional documents, including colonial charters that are related to the separation of church and state; presidential speeches and addresses that illustrate some of the features of American civil religion during different periods of U.S. history; and sermons from different periods that exemplify evangelical and fundamentalist preaching. The documents are arranged in chronological order within each section. Documents that have been excerpted are identified as such; all others are reproduced in full.

I. CHARTERS AND CONSTITUTIONAL DOCUMENTS

The Mayflower Compact (1620)

The Mayflower Compact was the first governing document of the Plymouth Colony. It was signed aboard the Mayflower *on November 11, 1620, as the ship lay at anchor in what is now Provincetown Harbor near Cape Cod, Massachusetts. John Adams, second president of the United States, occasionally spoke of the Mayflower Compact as the foundation of the Constitution of the United States. The Pilgrims aboard the* Mayflower *knew that earlier settlements in North America had come to grief because of a lack of central leadership, and the compact represented an agreement to abide by the rules of government for the sake of the colony's survival.*

> IN THE NAME OF GOD, AMEN. We, whose names are underwritten, the Loyal Subjects of our dread Sovereign Lord King *James,* by the Grace of God, of *Great Britain, France,* and *Ireland,* King, *Defender of the Faith,* &c. Having undertaken for the Glory of God, and Advancement of the Christian Faith, and the Honour of our King and Country, a Voyage to plant

the first Colony in the northern Parts of *Virginia;* Do by these Presents, solemnly and mutually, in the Presence of God and one another, covenant and combine ourselves together into a civil Body Politick, for our better Ordering and Preservation, and Furtherance of the Ends aforesaid: And by Virtue hereof do enact, constitute, and frame, such just and equal Laws, Ordinances, Acts, Constitutions, and Officers, from time to time, as shall be thought most meet and convenient for the general Good of the Colony; unto which we promise all due Submission and Obedience. IN WITNESS whereof we have hereunto subscribed our names at *Cape-Cod* the eleventh of November, in the Reign of our Sovereign Lord King *James,* of *England, France,* and *Ireland,* the eighteenth, and of *Scotland* the fifty-fourth, *Anno Domini;* 1620.

Source: "Mayflower Compact, 1620." Avalon Project of Yale Law School. Available online. URL: http://www.yale.edu/lawweb/avalon/amerdoc/mayflower.htm. Accessed July 3, 2006.

Maryland Toleration Act (September 21, 1649) (excerpts)

The Maryland Toleration Act, which is sometimes regarded as a precursor of the First Amendment to the United States Constitution, was passed by the colonial assembly of the Province of Maryland in September 1649. Mandating tolerance for all Christian denominations, the act was passed in part to protect the rights of Roman Catholics. Maryland had been founded as a refuge for English Catholics, but the need to attract more settlers made it evident that Protestants would soon form a majority of the population. Although the act prevented outright persecution of any group, it did not succeed in preventing political struggles for control of the assembly.

An Act Concerning Religion.

Forasmuch as in a well governed and Christian Common Weath [sic] matters concerning Religion and the honor of God ought in the first place to bee taken, into serious consideracion and endeavoured to bee settled, Be it therefore ordered and enacted by the Right Honourable Cecilius Lord Baron of Baltemore absolute Lord and Proprietary of this Province with the advise and consent of this Generall Assembly:

That whatsoever person or persons within this Province and the Islands thereunto helonging shall from henceforth blaspheme God, that is Curse him, or deny our Saviour Jesus Christ to bee the sonne of God, or shall deny the holy Trinity the father sonne and holy Ghost, or the Godhead of any of the said Three persons of the Trinity or the Unity of the Godhead, or shall use or utter any reproachfull Speeches, words or language concerning the said Holy Trinity, or any of the said three persons thereof, shalbe punished with death and confiscation or forfeiture of all his or her lands and goods to the Lord Proprietary and his heires.

And bee it also Enacted by the Authority and with the advise and assent aforesaid, That whatsoever person or persons shall from henceforth use or utter any reproachfull words or Speeches concerning the blessed Virgin Mary the Mother of our Saviour or the holy Apostles or Evangelists or any of them shall in such case for the first offence forfeit to the said Lord Proprietary and his heirs Lords and Proprietaries of this Province the summe of five pound Sterling or the value thereof to be Levyed on the goods and chattells of every such person soe offending, but in case such Offender or Offenders, shall not then have goods and chattells sufficient for the satisfyeing of such forfeiture, or that the same bee not otherwise speedily satisfyed that then such Offender or Offenders shalbe publiquely whipt and bee imprisoned during the pleasure of the Lord Proprietary or the Lieutenant or cheife Governor of this Province for the time being. And that every such Offender or Offenders for every second offence shall forfeit tenne pound sterling or the value thereof to bee levyed as aforesaid, or in case such offender or Offenders shall not then have goods and chattells within this Province sufficient for that purpose then to bee publiquely and severely whipt and imprisoned as before is expressed. And that every person or persons before mentioned offending herein the third time, shall for such third Offence forfeit all his lands and Goods and bee for ever banished and expelled out of this Province.

And be it also further Enacted by the same authority advise and assent that whatsoever person or persons shall from henceforth uppon any occasion of Offence or otherwise in a reproachful manner or Way declare call or denominate any person or persons whatsoever inhabiting, residing, traffiqueing, trading or comerceing within this Province or within any the Ports, Harbors, Creeks or Havens to the same belonging an heritick, Scismatick, Idolator, puritan, Independant, Prespiterian popish prest, Jesuite, Jesuited papist, Lutheran, Calvenist, Anabaptist, Brownist, Antinomian, Barrowist, Roundhead, Separatist, or any other name or terme in a reproachfull manner relating to matter of Religion shall for every such Offence forfeit and loose the somme of tenne shillings sterling or the value thereof to bee levyed on the goods and chattells of every such Offender and Offenders, the one half thereof to be forfeited and paid unto the person and persons of whom such reproachfull words are or shalbe spoken or uttered, and the other half thereof to the Lord Proprietary and his heires Lords and Proprietaries of this Province. But if such person or persons who shall at any time utter or speake any such reproachfull words or Language shall not have Goods or Chattells sufficient and overt within this Province to bee taken to satisfie the penalty aforesaid or that the same bee not otherwise speedily satisfyed, that then the person or persons soe offending shalbe publickly whipt, and shall suffer imprisonment without baile or maineprise [bail] untill hee, shee or they respectively shall satisfy the party soe offended or greived by such reproachfull Language by asking him or her respectively forgivenes publiquely for such his Offence before the Magistrate of cheife Officer or Officers of the Towne or place where such Offence shalbe given.

And be it further likewise Enacted by the Authority and consent aforesaid That every person and persons within this Province that shall at any time hereafter prophane the Sabbath or Lords day called Sunday by frequent swearing, drunkennes or by any uncivill or disorderly recreacion, or by working on that day when absolute necessity doth not require it shall for every such first offence forfeit 2s 6d sterling or the value thereof, and for the second offence 5s sterling or the value thereof, and for the third offence and soe for every time he shall offend in like manner afterwards 10s sterling or the value thereof. And in case such offender and offenders shall not have sufficient goods or chattells within this Province to satisfy any of the said Penalties respectively hereby imposed for prophaning the Sabbath or Lords day called Sunday as aforesaid, That in Every such case the partie soe offending shall for the first and second offence in that kinde be imprisoned till hee or shee shall publickly in open Court before the cheife Commander Judge or Magistrate, of that County Towne or precinct where such offence shalbe committed acknowledg the Scandall and offence he hath in that respect given against God and the good and civill Governement of this Province, And for the third offence and for every time after shall also bee publickly whipt.

And whereas the inforceing of the conscience in matters of Religion hath frequently fallen out to be of dangerous Consequence in those commonwealthes where it hath been practised, And for the more quiett and peaceable governement of this Province, and the better to preserve mutuall Love and amity amongst the Inhabitants thereof, Be it Therefore also by the Lord Proprietary with the advise and consent of this Assembly Ordeyned and enacted (except as in this present Act is before Declared and sett forth) that noe person or persons whatsoever within this Province, or the Islands, Ports, Harbors, Creekes, or havens thereunto belonging professing to beleive in Jesus Christ, shall from henceforth bee any waies troubled, Molested or discountenanced for or in respect of his or her religion nor in the free exercise thereof within this Province or the Islands thereunto belonging nor any way compelled to the beleife or exercise of any other Religion against his or her consent, soe as they be not unfaithfull to the Lord Proprietary, or molest or conspire against the civill Governement established or to bee established in this Province under him or his heires. And that all and every person and persons that shall presume Contrary to this Act and the true intent and meaning thereof directly or indirectly either in person or estate willfully to wrong disturbe trouble or molest any person whatsoever within this Province professing to beleive in Jesus Christ for or in respect of his or her religion or the free exercise thereof within this Province other than is provided for in this Act that such person or persons soe offending, shalbe compelled to pay trebble damages to the party soe wronged or molested, and for every such offence shall also forfeit 20s sterling in money or the value thereof, half thereof for the use of the Lord Proprietary, and his heires Lords and Proprietaries of this Province, and the other half for the use of the party soe wronged or molested as aforesaid, Or if the partie soe offending as aforesaid shall refuse or bee unable to recompense the party soe wronged, or to satisfy such fyne or forfeiture, then such Offender shalbe severely punished by publick whipping and imprisonment during the pleasure of the Lord Proprietary, or his Lieutenant or cheife Governor of this Province for the tyme being without baile or maineprise. . . .

The freemen have assented.

Source: "Maryland Toleration Act of 1649; September 21, 1649." Avalon Project of Yale Law School. Available online. URL: http://www.yale.edu/lawweb/avalon/amerdoc/maryland_toleration.htm. Accessed July 3, 2006.

Constitution of the United States (1787): Article VI

With the ratification of the U.S. Constitution in 1787 and the Bill of Rights (the first 10 amendments to the Constitution) in 1791, Protestant Christians of any church tradition had more religious freedom than their counterparts anywhere else in the world. Roman Catholics still had a few legal disabilities in some states, but they nevertheless enjoyed more freedom to practice their faith than Catholics in any other country with a Protestant state church or majority Protestant population. In addition to the religious freedom granted to members of the various Christian bodies, the Constitution protected the rights of humanists, deists, Unitarians, and persons with no religious convictions to publish their views and to seek public office without restriction. The latter was guaranteed in Article VI, which is reprinted here.

All debts contracted and engagements entered into, before the adoption of this Constitution, shall be as valid against the United States under this Constitution, as under the Confederation.

This Constitution, and the laws of the United States which shall be made in pursuance thereof; and all treaties made, or which shall be made, under the authority of the United States, shall be the supreme law of the land; and the judges in every state shall be bound thereby, anything in the Constitution or laws of any State to the contrary notwithstanding.

The Senators and Representatives before mentioned, and the members of the several state legislatures, and all executive and judicial officers, both of the United States and of the several states, shall be bound by oath or affirmation, to support this Constitution; but no religious test shall ever be required as a qualification to any office or public trust under the United States.

Source: McMillan Law Library Electronic Reference Desk. "Constitution of the United States." School of Law, Emory. Available online. URL: http://www.law.emory.edu/FEDERAL/usconst.html. Accessed June 27, 2006. The full text of the Constitution of 1787, as well as the Bill of Rights and later amendments, is available online through a number of Web sites. The most useful online versions are those at the Law School of Emory University (http://www.law.emory.edu/FEDERAL/usconst.html), which includes the text of amendments that were never ratified; FindLaw (http://www.findlaw.com/casecode/constitution/), which contains analysis and interpretation of the various articles as well as links to relevant Supreme Court cases; and the Avalon Project of Yale Law School (http://www.yale.edu/lawweb/avalon/usconst.htm).

Constitution of the United States: The Bill of Rights (1791)

The Bill of Rights was first proposed as an addition to the newly ratified Constitution of the United States in 1788. It was a controversial proposal, opposed by such leaders as Alexander Hamilton, who favored a strong federal government and did not think that certain specific rights, including freedom of religion, needed explicit protection in the Constitution. The anti-Federalist party, led by Patrick Henry and Thomas Jefferson, was concerned about the lack of such explicit protection. They were influenced by the English philosopher John Locke (1632–1704), who had argued in his Two Treatises of Government *(1689) that all people have certain natural rights by virtue of being human, including life, liberty, the pursuit of safety and happiness, and ownership of private property. James Madison submitted to Congress on June 8, 1789, a proposal for 12 constitutional amendments securing these natural rights. New Jersey became the first state to ratify 11 of the 12 amendments on November 20, 1791, rejecting the second of Madison's 12 articles. Other states rejected the proposed first amendment. The Bill of Rights became law on December 15, 1791, when Virginia became the last state to ratify the 10 amendments that were approved by all the states, articles III through XII of Madison's draft.*

Amendment I

Congress shall make no law respecting an establishment of religion, or prohibiting the free exercise thereof; or abridging the freedom of speech, or of the press; or the right of the people peaceably to assemble, and to petition the government for a redress of grievances.

Amendment II

A well regulated militia, being necessary to the security of a free state, the right of the people to keep and bear arms, shall not be infringed.

Amendment III

No soldier shall, in time of peace be quartered in any house, without the consent of the owner, nor in time of war, but in a manner to be prescribed by law.

Amendment IV

The right of the people to be secure in their persons, houses, papers, and effects, against unreasonable searches and seizures, shall not be violated, and no warrants shall issue, but upon probable cause, supported by oath or affirmation, and particularly describing the place to be searched, and the persons or things to be seized.

Amendment V

No person shall be held to answer for a capital, or otherwise infamous crime, unless on a presentment or indictment of a grand jury, except in cases arising in the land or naval forces, or in the militia, when in actual service in time of war or public danger; nor shall any person be subject for the same offense to be twice put in jeopardy of life or limb; nor shall be compelled in any criminal case to be a witness against himself, nor be deprived of life, liberty, or property, without due process of law; nor shall private property be taken for public use, without just compensation.

Amendment VI

In all criminal prosecutions, the accused shall enjoy the right to a speedy and public trial, by an impartial jury of the state and district wherein the crime shall have been committed, which district shall have been previously ascertained by law, and to be informed of the nature and cause of the accusation; to be confronted with the witnesses against him; to have compulsory process for obtaining witnesses in his favor, and to have the assistance of counsel for his defense.

Amendment VII

In suits at common law, where the value in controversy shall exceed twenty dollars, the right of trial by jury shall be preserved, and no fact tried by a jury, shall be otherwise reexamined in any court of the United States, than according to the rules of the common law.

Amendment VIII

Excessive bail shall not be required, nor excessive fines imposed, nor cruel and unusual punishments inflicted.

Amendment IX

The enumeration in the Constitution, of certain rights, shall not be construed to deny or disparage others retained by the people.

Amendment X

The powers not delegated to the United States by the Constitution, nor prohibited by it to the states, are reserved to the states respectively, or to the people.

Source: "Constitution of the United States: Bill of Rights." Avalon Project of Yale Law School. Available online. URL: http://www.yale.edu/lawweb/avalon/rights1.htm. Accessed July 3, 2006.

Constitution of the State of Connecticut (1818) (excerpts)

Connecticut did not have a formal state constitution until 1818, having been governed during the colonial period by a charter that continued to serve as the framework of the state's government after 1776. Since the charter had never been approved by popular vote, however, as well as having been granted originally by a king, Connecticut held a constitutional convention in the summer of 1818. The draft constitution was duly approved by the voters and signed into law by Governor Oliver Wolcott, Jr., in October 1818. It formally disestablished the Congregational Church as the state church of Connecticut.

ARTICLE SEVENTH

Of Religion.

Sec. 1. It being the duty of all men to worship the Supreme Being, the great Creator and Preserver of the Universe, and their right to render that worship in the mode most consistent with the dictates of their consciences: no person shall, by law, be compelled to join or support, nor be classed with, or associated to, any congregation, church, or religious association. But every person now belonging to such congregation, church, or religious association, shall remain a member thereof, until he shall have separated himself therefrom, in the manner hereinafter provided. And each and every society or denomination of Christians in this state, shall have and enjoy the same and equal powers, rights, and privileges; and shall have power and authority to support and maintain the ministers or teachers of their respective denominations, and to build and repair houses for public worship, by a tax on the members of any such society only, to be laid by a major vote of the legal voters assembled at any society meeting, warned and held according to law, or in any other manner.

Sec. 2. If any Person shall choose to separate himself from the society or denomination of Christians to which he may belong, and shall leave a written notice thereof with the clerk of such society, he shall there upon be no longer liable for any future expenses which may be incurred by said society. . . .

Done in convention, on the fifteenth day of September, in the year of our Lord one thousand eight hundred and eighteen, and of the Independence of the United States the forty-third.

By order of the convention.

Oliver Wollcott, President.
James Lanman, Robert Fairchild, Clerks.

Source: "The Constitution of Connecticut (1818)." State of Connecticut, Office of the Secretary of the State. Available online. URL: http://www.sots.ct.gov/RegisterManual/SectionI/1818CTCO.HTM. Accessed July 3, 2006.

II. PRESIDENTIAL SPEECHES AND ADDRESSES

George Washington: First Inaugural Address (April 30, 1789)

George Washington delivered his first inaugural address in New York City, the new nation's temporary seat of government, on April 30, 1789. After the oath of office had been administered by the chancellor of New York on the balcony of Federal Hall in the presence of a large crowd assembled to witness the occasion, Washington gave his address to a joint session of the first United States Congress. One of the senators from Pennsylvania noted that Washington, so calm and resolute on the battlefield, was nervous to the point of trembling as he spoke to the legislators. Following the address, the new president and Congress proceeded up Broadway for a worship service in St. Paul's Church. The speech reflects the deistic Christianity of the Enlightenment rather than any specific denominational character; at the same time, it set a precedent for the inclusion of civil religion in the public political rituals of the United States.

Fellow-Citizens of the Senate and of the House of Representatives:

Among the vicissitudes incident to life no event could have filled me with greater anxieties than that of which the notification was transmitted by your order, and received on the 14th day of the present month. On the one hand, I was summoned by my Country, whose voice I can never hear but with veneration and love, from a retreat which I had chosen with the fondest predilection, and, in my flattering hopes, with an immutable decision, as the asylum of my declining years—a retreat which was rendered every day more necessary as well as more dear to me by the addition of habit to inclination, and of frequent interruptions in my health to the gradual waste committed on it by time. On the other hand, the magnitude and difficulty of the trust to which the voice of my country called me, being sufficient to awaken in the wisest and most experienced of her citizens a distrustful scrutiny into his qualifications, could not but overwhelm with despondence one who (inheriting inferior endowments from nature and unpracticed in the duties of civil administration) ought to be peculiarly conscious of his own deficiencies. In this conflict of emotions all I dare aver is that it has been my faithful study to collect my duty from a just appreciation of every circumstance by which it might be affected. All I dare hope is that if, in executing this task, I have been too much swayed by a grateful remembrance of former instances, or by an affectionate sensibility to this transcendent proof of the confidence of my fellow-citizens, and have thence too little consulted my incapacity as well as disinclination for the weighty and untried cares before me, my error will be palliated by the motives which mislead me, and its consequences be judged by my country with some share of the partiality in which they originated.

Such being the impressions under which I have, in obedience to the public summons, repaired to the present station, it would be peculiarly improper to omit in this first official act my fervent supplications to that Almighty Being who rules over the universe, who presides in the councils of nations, and whose providential aids can supply every human defect, that His benediction may consecrate to the liberties and happiness of the people of the United States a Government instituted by themselves for these essential purposes, and may enable every instrument employed in its administration to execute with success the functions allotted to his charge. In tendering this homage to the Great Author of every public and private good,

I assure myself that it expresses your sentiments not less than my own, nor those of my fellow-citizens at large less than either. No people can be bound to acknowledge and adore the Invisible Hand which conducts the affairs of men more than those of the United States. Every step by which they have advanced to the character of an independent nation seems to have been distinguished by some token of providential agency; and in the important revolution just accomplished in the system of their united government the tranquil deliberations and voluntary consent of so many distinct communities from which the event has resulted can not be compared with the means by which most governments have been established without some return of pious gratitude, along with an humble anticipation of the future blessings which the past seem to presage. These reflections, arising out of the present crisis, have forced themselves too strongly on my mind to be suppressed. You will join with me, I trust, in thinking that there are none under the influence of which the proceedings of a new and free government can more auspiciously commence.

By the article establishing the executive department it is made the duty of the President "to recommend to your consideration such measures as he shall judge necessary and expedient." The circumstances under which I now meet you will acquit me from entering into that subject further than to refer to the great constitutional charter under which you are assembled, and which, in defining your powers, designates the objects to which your attention is to be given. It will be more consistent with those circumstances, and far more congenial with the feelings which actuate me, to substitute, in place of a recommendation of particular measures, the tribute that is due to the talents, the rectitude, and the patriotism which adorn the characters selected to devise and adopt them. In these honorable qualifications I behold the surest pledges that as on one side no local prejudices or attachments, no separate views nor party animosities, will misdirect the comprehensive and equal eye which ought to watch over this great assemblage of communities and interests, so, on another, that the foundation of our national policy will be laid in the pure and immutable principles of private morality, and the preeminence of free government be exemplified by all the attributes which can win the affections of its citizens and command the respect of the world. I dwell on this prospect with every satisfaction which an ardent love for my country can inspire, since there is no truth more thoroughly established than that there exists in the economy and course of nature an indissoluble union between virtue and happiness; between duty and advantage; between the genuine maxims of an honest and magnanimous policy and the solid rewards of public prosperity and felicity; since we ought to be no less persuaded that the propitious smiles of Heaven can never be expected on a nation that disregards the eternal rules of order and right which Heaven itself has ordained; and since the preservation of the sacred fire of liberty and the destiny of the republican model of government are justly considered, perhaps, as deeply, as finally, staked on the experiment entrusted to the hands of the American people.

Besides the ordinary objects submitted to your care, it will remain with your judgment to decide how far an exercise of the occasional power delegated by the fifth article of the Constitution is rendered expedient at the present juncture by the nature of objections which have been urged against the system, or by the degree of inquietude which has given birth to them. Instead of undertaking particular recommendations on this subject, in which I could be guided by no lights derived from official opportunities, I shall again give way to my entire confidence in your discernment and pursuit of the public good; for I assure myself that whilst you carefully avoid every alteration which might endanger the benefits of an united and effective government, or which ought to await the future lessons of experience, a reverence for the characteristic rights of freemen and a regard for the public harmony will sufficiently influence your deliberations on the question how far the former can be impregnably fortified or the latter be safely and advantageously promoted.

To the foregoing observations I have one to add, which will be most properly addressed to the House of Representatives. It concerns myself, and will therefore be as brief as possible. When I was first honored with a call into the service of my country, then on the eve of an arduous struggle for its liberties, the light in which I contemplated my duty required that I should renounce every pecuniary compensation. From this resolution I have in no instance departed; and being still under the impressions which produced it, I must decline as inapplicable to myself any share in the personal emoluments which may be indispensably included in a permanent provision for the executive department, and must accordingly pray that the pecuniary estimates for the station in which I am placed may during my continuance in it be limited to such actual expenditures as the public good may be thought to require.

Having thus imparted to you my sentiments as they have been awakened by the occasion which brings us together, I shall take my present leave; but not without resorting once more to the benign Parent of the Human Race in humble supplication that, since He has been pleased to favor the American people with opportunities for deliberating in perfect tranquillity, and dispositions for deciding with unparalleled unanimity on a form of government for the security of their union and the advancement of their happiness, so His divine blessing may be equally conspicuous in the enlarged views, the temperate consultations, and the wise measures on which the success of this Government must depend.

Source: "First Inaugural Address of George Washington." Avalon Project of Yale Law School. Available online. URL: http://www.yale.edu/lawweb/avalon/presiden/inaug/wash1.htm. Accessed July 4, 2006.

Abraham Lincoln: Second Inaugural Address (March 4, 1865)

One of the shortest inaugural addresses in the history of the presidency, Abraham Lincoln's second inaugural address is also one of the most religiously intense documents in U.S. political history. Delivered from the east portico of the Capitol, it was received by the spectators in almost complete silence. A journalist who was present on the occasion was struck by the fact that the sky, which had been overcast all morning, brightened, and the sun came out just as Lincoln left his seat, providing a sudden burst of light as he began to speak.

Fellow-Countrymen:

At this second appearing to take the oath of the Presidential office there is less occasion for an extended address than there was at the first. Then a statement somewhat in detail of a course to be pursued seemed fitting and proper. Now, at the expiration of four years, during which public declarations have been constantly called forth on every point and phase of the great contest which still absorbs the attention and engrosses the energies of the nation, little that is new could be presented. The progress of our arms, upon which all else chiefly depends, is as well known to the public as to myself, and it is, I trust, reasonably satisfactory and encouraging to all. With high hope for the future, no prediction in regard to it is ventured.

On the occasion corresponding to this four years ago all thoughts were anxiously directed to an impending civil war. All dreaded it, all sought to avert it. While the inaugural address was being delivered from this place, devoted altogether to saving the Union without war, insurgent agents were in the city seeking to destroy it without war—seeking to dissolve the Union and divide effects by negotiation. Both parties deprecated war, but one of them would make war rather than let the nation survive, and the other would accept war rather than let it perish, and the war came.

One-eighth of the whole population were colored slaves, not distributed generally over the Union, but localized in the southern part of it. These slaves constituted a peculiar and powerful interest. All knew that this interest was somehow the cause of the war. To strengthen, perpetuate, and extend this interest was the object for which the insurgents would rend the Union even by war, while the Government claimed no right to do more than to restrict the territorial enlargement of it. Neither party expected for the war the magnitude or the duration which it has already attained. Neither anticipated that the cause of the conflict might cease with or even before the conflict itself should cease. Each looked for an easier triumph, and a result less fundamental and astounding. Both read the same Bible and pray to the same God, and each invokes His aid against the other. It may seem strange that any men should dare to ask a just God's assistance in wringing their bread from the sweat of other men's faces, but let us judge not, that we be not judged. The prayers of both could not be answered. That of neither has been answered fully. The Almighty has His own purposes. "Woe unto the world because of offenses; for it must needs be that offenses come, but woe to that man by whom the offense cometh." If we shall suppose that American slavery is one of those offenses which, in the providence of God, must needs come, but which, having continued through His appointed time, He now wills to remove, and that He gives to both North and South this terrible war as the woe due to those by whom the offense came, shall we discern therein any departure from those divine attributes which the believers in a living God always ascribe to Him? Fondly do we hope, fervently do we pray, that this mighty scourge of war may speedily pass away. Yet, if God wills that it continue until all the wealth piled by the bondsman's two hundred and fifty years of unrequited toil shall be sunk, and until every drop of blood drawn with the lash shall be paid by another drawn with the sword, as was said three thousand years ago, so still it must be said "the judgments of the Lord are true and righteous altogether."

With malice toward none, with charity for all, with firmness in the right as God gives us to see the right, let us strive on to finish the work we are in, to bind up the nation's wounds, to care for him who shall have borne the battle and for his widow and his orphan, to do all which may achieve and cherish a just and lasting peace among ourselves and with all nations.

Source: "Second Inaugural Address of Abraham Lincoln." Avalon Project of Yale Law School. Available online. URL: http://www.yale.edu/lawweb/avalon/presiden/inaug/lincoln2.htm. Accessed July 4, 2006.

Franklin D. Roosevelt: State of the Union Address (January 6, 1941) (excerpts)

President Franklin D. Roosevelt delivered the "Four Freedoms" speech as the annual State of the Union address to Congress on January 6, 1941. The United

States had not entered World War II at that point, as the Japanese attack on Pearl Harbor did not occur until December 7, 1941. Most of the speech deals with the necessity of putting a nation still nominally at peace on a wartime footing. Roosevelt warns, "I have recently pointed out how quickly the tempo of modern warfare could bring into our very midst the physical attack which we must eventually expect if the dictator nations win this war." The four freedoms are not enunciated until the closing section of the speech.

Mr. President, Mr. Speaker, members of the 77th Congress:

I address you, the members of this new Congress, at a moment unprecedented in the history of the union. I use the word "unprecedented" because at no previous time has American security been as seriously threatened from without as it is today.

Since the permanent formation of our government under the Constitution in 1789, most of the periods of crisis in our history have related to our domestic affairs. And, fortunately, only one of these—the four-year war between the States—ever threatened our national unity. Today, thank God, 130,000,000 Americans in 48 States have forgotten points of the compass in our national unity.

It is true that prior to 1914 the United States often has been disturbed by events in other continents. We have even engaged in two wars with European nations and in a number of undeclared wars in the West Indies, in the Mediterranean and in the Pacific, for the maintenance of American rights and for the principles of peaceful commerce. But in no case had a serious threat been raised against our national safety or our continued independence.

What I seek to convey is the historic truth that the United States as a nation has at all times maintained opposition—clear, definite opposition—to any attempt to lock us in behind an ancient Chinese wall while the procession of civilization went past. Today, thinking of our children and of their children, we oppose enforced isolation for ourselves or for any other part of the Americas.

That determination of ours, extending over all these years, was proved, for example, in the early days during the quarter century of wars following the French Revolution. While the Napoleonic struggles did threaten interests of the United States because of the French foothold in the West Indies and in Louisiana, and while we engaged in the War of 1812 to vindicate our right to peaceful trade, it is nevertheless clear that neither France nor Great Britain nor any other nation was aiming at domination of the whole world.

And in like fashion, from 1815 to 1914—ninety-nine years—no single war in Europe or in Asia constituted a real threat against our future or against the future of any other American nation. . . .

I suppose that every realist knows that the democratic way of life is at this moment being directly assailed in every part of the world—assailed either by arms or by secret spreading of poisonous propaganda by those who seek to destroy unity and promote discord in nations that are still at peace. During 16 long months this assault has blotted out the whole pattern of democratic life in an appalling number of independent nations, great and small. And the assailants are still on the march, threatening other nations, great and small.

Therefore, as your President, performing my constitutional duty to "give to the Congress information of the state of the union," I find it unhappily necessary to report that the future and the safety of our country and of our democracy are overwhelmingly involved in events far beyond our borders.

Armed defense of democratic existence is now being gallantly waged in four continents. If that defense fails, all the population and all the resources of Europe and Asia, and Africa and Austral-Asia will be dominated by conquerors. And let us remember that the total of those populations in those four continents, the total of those populations and their resources greatly exceed the sum total of the population and the resources of the whole of the Western Hemisphere—yes, many times over.

In times like these it is immature—and, incidentally, untrue—for anybody to brag that an unprepared America, single-handed and with one hand tied behind its back, can hold off the whole world.

No realistic American can expect from a dictator's peace international generosity, or return of true independence, or world disarmament, or freedom of expression, or freedom of religion—or even good business. Such a peace would bring no security for us or for our neighbors. Those who would give up essential liberty to purchase a little temporary safety deserve neither liberty nor safety.

As a nation we may take pride in the fact that we are soft-hearted; but we cannot afford to be soft-headed. We must always be wary of those who with sounding brass and a tinkling cymbal preach the "ism" of appeasement. We must especially beware of that small group of selfish men who would clip the wings of the American eagle in order to feather their own nests. . . .

In the future days, which we seek to make secure, we look forward to a world founded upon four essential human freedoms.

The first is freedom of speech and expression—everywhere in the world.

The second is freedom of every person to worship God in his own way everywhere in the world.

The third is freedom from want, which, translated into world terms, means economic understandings which will secure to every nation a healthy peacetime life for its inhabitants—everywhere in the world.

The fourth is freedom from fear, which, translated into world terms, means a world-wide reduction of armaments to such a point and in such a thorough fashion that no nation will be in a position to commit an act of physical aggression against any neighbor—anywhere in the world.

That is no vision of a distant millennium. It is a definite basis for a kind of world attainable in our own time and generation. That kind of world is the very antithesis of the so-called "new order" of tyranny which the dictators seek to create with the crash of a bomb.

To that new order we oppose the greater conception—the moral order. A good society is able to face schemes of world domination and foreign revolutions alike without fear.

Since the beginning of our American history we have been engaged in change, in a perpetual, peaceful revolution, a revolution which goes on steadily, quietly, adjusting itself to changing conditions without the concentration camp or the quicklime in the ditch. The world order which we seek is the cooperation of free countries, working together in a friendly, civilized society.

This nation has placed its destiny in the hands and heads and hearts of its millions of free men and women, and its faith in freedom under the guidance of God. Freedom means the supremacy of human rights everywhere. Our support goes to those who struggle to gain those rights and keep them. Our strength is our unity of purpose. To that high concept there can be no end save victory.

Source: Top 100 American Speeches Online Speech Bank. "Franklin Delano Roosevelt: The Four Freedoms." American Rhetoric. Available online. URL: http://www.americanrhetoric.com/speeches/fdrthefourfreedoms.htm. Accessed June 27, 2006.

John F. Kennedy: Inaugural Address (January 20, 1961)

It is almost forgotten in the early 21st century that John F. Kennedy's 1960 presidential candidacy aroused fears in a significant minority of the population that his Roman Catholicism posed a danger to the First Amendment. His inaugural address, however, continued the tradition begun by George Washington of invoking a nonsectarian form of civil religion.

Vice President Johnson, Mr. Speaker, Mr. Chief Justice, President Eisenhower, Vice President Nixon, President Truman, reverend clergy, fellow citizens, we observe today not a victory of party, but a celebration of freedom—symbolizing an end, as well as a beginning—signifying renewal, as well as change. For I have sworn before you and Almighty God the same solemn oath our forebears prescribed nearly a century and three quarters ago.

The world is very different now. For man holds in his mortal hands the power to abolish all forms of human poverty and all forms of human life. And yet the same revolutionary beliefs for which our forebears fought are still at issue around the globe—the belief that the rights of man come not from the generosity of the state, but from the hand of God.

We dare not forget today that we are the heirs of that first revolution. Let the word go forth from this time and place, to friend and foe alike, that the torch has been passed to a new generation of Americans—born in this century, tempered by war, disciplined by a hard and bitter peace, proud of our ancient heritage—and unwilling to witness or permit the slow undoing of those human rights to which this Nation has always been committed, and to which we are committed today at home and around the world.

Let every nation know, whether it wishes us well or ill, that we shall pay any price, bear any burden, meet any hardship, support any friend, oppose any foe, in order to assure the survival and the success of liberty.

This much we pledge—and more.

To those old allies whose cultural and spiritual origins we share, we pledge the loyalty of faithful friends. United, there is little we cannot do in a host of cooperative ventures. Divided, there is little we can do—for we dare not meet a powerful challenge at odds and split asunder.

To those new States whom we welcome to the ranks of the free, we pledge our word that one form of colonial control shall not have passed away merely to be replaced by a far more iron tyranny. We shall not always expect to find them supporting our view. But we shall always hope to find them strongly supporting their own freedom—and to remember that, in the past, those who foolishly sought power by riding the back of the tiger ended up inside.

To those peoples in the huts and villages across the globe struggling to break the bonds of mass misery, we pledge our best efforts to help them help themselves, for whatever period is required—not because the Communists may be doing it, not because we seek their votes, but because it is right. If a free society cannot help the many who are poor, it cannot save the few who are rich.

To our sister republics south of our border, we offer a special pledge—to convert our good words into good deeds—in a new alliance for progress—to assist free men and free governments in casting off the chains of poverty. But this peaceful revolution of hope cannot become the prey of hostile powers. Let all our neighbors know that we shall join with them to oppose aggression or subversion anywhere in the Americas. And let every other power know that this Hemisphere intends to remain the master of its own house.

To that world assembly of sovereign states, the United Nations, our last best hope in an age where the instruments of war have far outpaced the instruments of peace, we renew our pledge of support—to prevent it from becoming merely a forum for invective—to strengthen its shield of the new and the weak—and to enlarge the area in which its writ may run.

Finally, to those nations who would make themselves our adversary, we offer not a pledge but a request: that both sides begin anew the quest for peace, before the dark powers of destruction unleashed by science engulf all humanity in planned or accidental self-destruction.

We dare not tempt them with weakness. For only when our arms are sufficient beyond doubt can we be certain beyond doubt that they will never be employed.

But neither can two great and powerful groups of nations take comfort from our present course—both sides overburdened by the cost of modern weapons, both rightly alarmed by the steady spread of the deadly atom, yet both racing to alter that uncertain balance of terror that stays the hand of mankind's final war.

So let us begin anew—remembering on both sides that civility is not a sign of weakness, and sincerity is always subject to proof. Let us never negotiate out of fear. But let us never fear to negotiate.

Let both sides explore what problems unite us instead of belaboring those problems which divide us.

Let both sides, for the first time, formulate serious and precise proposals for the inspection and control of arms—and bring the absolute power to destroy other nations under the absolute control of all nations.

Let both sides seek to invoke the wonders of science instead of its terrors. Together let us explore the stars, conquer the deserts, eradicate disease, tap the ocean depths, and encourage the arts and commerce.

Let both sides unite to heed in all corners of the earth the command of Isaiah—to "undo the heavy burdens. . . and to let the oppressed go free."

And if a beachhead of cooperation may push back the jungle of suspicion, let both sides join in creating a new endeavor, not a new balance of power, but a new world of law, where the strong are just and the weak secure and the peace preserved.

All this will not be finished in the first 100 days. Nor will it be finished in the first 1,000 days, nor in the life of this Administration, nor even perhaps in our lifetime on this planet. But let us begin.

In your hands, my fellow citizens, more than in mine, will rest the final success or failure of our course. Since this country was founded, each generation of Americans has been summoned to give testimony to its national loyalty. The graves of young Americans who answered the call to service surround the globe.

Now the trumpet summons us again—not as a call to bear arms, though arms we need; not as a call to battle, though embattled we are—but a call to bear the burden of a long twilight struggle, year in and year out, "rejoicing in hope, patient in tribulation"—a struggle against the common enemies of man: tyranny, poverty, disease, and war itself.

Can we forge against these enemies a grand and global alliance, North and South, East and West, that can assure a more fruitful life for all mankind? Will you join in that historic effort?

In the long history of the world, only a few generations have been granted the role of defending freedom in its hour of maximum danger. I do not shrink from this responsibility—I welcome it. I do not believe that any of us would exchange places with any other people or any other generation. The energy, the faith, the devotion which we bring to this endeavor will light our country and all who serve it—and the glow from that fire can truly light the world.

And so, my fellow Americans: ask not what your country can do for you—ask what you can do for your country.

My fellow citizens of the world: ask not what America will do for you, but what together we can do for the freedom of man.

Finally, whether you are citizens of America or citizens of the world, ask of us the same high standards of strength and sacrifice which we ask of you. With a good conscience our only sure reward, with history the final judge of our deeds, let us go forth to lead the land we love, asking His blessing and His help, but knowing that here on earth God's work must truly be our own.

Source: "Inaugural Address of John F. Kennedy." Avalon Project of Yale Law School. Available online. URL: http://www.yale.edu/lawweb/avalon/presiden/inaug/kennedy.htm. Accessed July 4, 2006.

Ronald W. Reagan: Farewell Address (January 11, 1989) (excerpts)

President Ronald Reagan's farewell to the nation at the end of his second term of office in 1989 is one of two major speeches in which he referred directly to

John Winthrop's sermon of 1630, excerpted below. Reagan reintroduced the image of the United States as a "shining city on a hill" to the traditions of American civil religion.

My fellow Americans:

This is the 34th time I'll speak to you from the Oval Office and the last. We've been together eight years now, and soon it'll be time for me to go. But before I do, I wanted to share some thoughts, some of which I've been saving for a long time.

It's been the honor of my life to be your president. So many of you have written the past few weeks to say thanks, but I could say as much to you. Nancy and I are grateful for the opportunity you gave us to serve.

One of the things about the presidency is that you're always somewhat apart. You spend a lot of time going by too fast in a car someone else is driving, and seeing the people through tinted glass—the parents holding up a child, and the wave you saw too late and couldn't return. And so many times I wanted to stop and reach out from behind the glass, and connect. Well, maybe I can do a little of that tonight. . . .

An informed patriotism is what we want. And are we doing a good enough job teaching our children what America is and what she represents in the long history of the world? Those of us who are over 35 or so years of age grew up in a different America. We were taught, very directly, what it means to be an American. And we absorbed, almost in the air, a love of country and an appreciation of its institutions. If you didn't get these things from your family, you got them from the neighborhood, from the father down the street who fought in Korea or the family who lost someone at Anzio. Or you could get a sense of patriotism from school. And if all else failed, you could get a sense of patriotism from popular culture. The movies celebrated democratic values and implicitly reinforced the idea that America was special. TV was like that, too, through the mid-'60s.

But now, we're about to enter the '90s, and some things have changed. Younger parents aren't sure that an unambivalent appreciation of America is the right thing to teach modern children. And as for those who create the popular culture, well-grounded patriotism is no longer the style. Our spirit is back, but we haven't reinstitutionalized it. We've got to do a better job of getting across that America is freedom—freedom of speech, freedom of religion, freedom of enterprise. And freedom is special and rare. It's fragile; it needs protection.

So, we've got to teach history based not on what's in fashion but what's important: Why the Pilgrims came here, who Jimmy Doolittle was, and what those 30 seconds over Tokyo meant. You know, four years ago on the 40th anniversary of D-Day, I read a letter from a young woman writing of her late father, who'd fought on Omaha Beach. Her name was Lisa Zanatta Henn, and she said, "We will always remember, we will never forget what the boys of Normandy did." Well, let's help her keep her word. If we forget what we did, we won't know who we are. I'm warning of an eradication of the American memory that could result, ultimately, in an erosion of the American spirit. Let's start with some basics: more attention to American history and a greater emphasis on civic ritual. And let me offer lesson No. 1 about America: All great change in America begins at the dinner table. So, tomorrow night in the kitchen I hope the talking begins. And children, if your parents haven't been teaching you what it means to be an American, let 'em know and nail 'em on it. That would be a very American thing to do.

And that's about all I have to say tonight. Except for one thing. The past few days when I've been at that window upstairs, I've thought a bit of the "shining city upon a hill." The phrase comes from John Winthrop, who wrote it to describe the America he imagined. What he imagined was important because he was an early Pilgrim, an early freedom man. He journeyed here on what today we'd call a little wooden boat; and like the other Pilgrims, he was looking for a home that would be free.

I've spoken of the shining city all my political life, but I don't know if I ever quite communicated what I saw when I said it. But in my mind it was a tall proud city built on rocks stronger than oceans, wind-swept, God-blessed, and teeming with people of all kinds living in harmony and peace, a city with free ports that hummed with commerce and creativity, and if there had to be city walls, the walls had doors and the doors were open to anyone with the will and the heart to get here. That's how I saw it and see it still.

And how stands the city on this winter night? More prosperous, more secure, and happier than it was eight years ago. But more than that; after 200 years, two centuries, she still stands strong and true on the granite ridge, and her glow has held steady no matter what storm. And she's still a beacon, still a magnet for all who must have freedom, for all the pilgrims from all the lost places who are hurtling through the darkness, toward home.

We've done our part. And as I walk off into the city streets, a final word to the men and women of the Reagan revolution, the men and women across America who for eight years did the work that brought America back. My friends: We did it. We weren't just marking time. We made a difference. We made the city stronger. We made the city freer, and we left her in good hands. All in all, not bad, not bad at all.

And so, good-bye, God bless you, and God bless the United States of America.

Source: "Farewell Address to the Nation." Ronald Reagan Presidential Library. Available online. URL: http://www.reagan.utexas.edu/archives/speeches/1989/011189i.htm. Accessed July 4, 2006.

George W. Bush: Remarks at National Day of Prayer and Remembrance (September 14, 2001)

Delivered from the pulpit of the National Cathedral in Washington, D.C., only three days after the terrorist attacks of September 11, 2001, this address resembles Abraham Lincoln's second inaugural speech in its use of biblical themes to express resolve as well as the need for consolation at a time of national tragedy.

We are here in the middle hour of our grief. So many have suffered so great a loss, and today we express our nation's sorrow. We come before God to pray for the missing and the dead, and for those who love them.

On Tuesday, our country was attacked with deliberate and massive cruelty. We have seen the images of fire and ashes, and bent steel.

Now come the names, the list of casualties we are only beginning to read. They are the names of men and women who began their day at a desk or in an airport, busy with life. They are the names of people who faced death, and in their last moments called home to say, be brave, and I love you.

They are the names of passengers who defied their murderers, and prevented the murder of others on the ground. They are the names of men and women who wore the uniform of the United States, and died at their posts.

They are the names of rescuers, the ones whom death found running up the stairs and into the fires to help others. We will read all these names. We will linger over them, and learn their stories, and many Americans will weep.

To the children and parents and spouses and families and friends of the lost, we offer the deepest sympathy of the nation. And I assure you, you are not alone.

Just three days removed from these events, Americans do not yet have the distance of history. But our responsibility to history is already clear: to answer these attacks and rid the world of evil.

War has been waged against us by stealth and deceit and murder. This nation is peaceful, but fierce when stirred to anger. This conflict was begun on the timing and terms of others. It will end in a way, and at an hour, of our choosing.

Our purpose as a nation is firm. Yet our wounds as a people are recent and unhealed, and lead us to pray. In many of our prayers this week, there is a searching, and an honesty. At St. Patrick's Cathedral in New York on Tuesday, a woman said, "I prayed to God to give us a sign that He is still here." Others have prayed for the same, searching hospital to hospital, carrying pictures of those still missing.

God's signs are not always the ones we look for. We learn in tragedy that his purposes are not always our own. Yet the prayers of private suffering, whether in our homes or in this great cathedral, are known and heard, and understood.

There are prayers that help us last through the day, or endure the night. There are prayers of friends and strangers, that give us strength for the journey. And there are prayers that yield our will to a will greater than our own.

This world He created is of moral design. Grief and tragedy and hatred are only for a time. Goodness, remembrance, and love have no end. And the Lord of life holds all who die, and all who mourn.

It is said that adversity introduces us to ourselves. This is true of a nation as well. In this trial, we have been reminded, and the world has seen, that our fellow Americans are generous and kind, resourceful and brave. We see our national character in rescuers working past exhaustion; in long lines of blood donors; in thousands of citizens who have asked to work and serve in any way possible.

And we have seen our national character in eloquent acts of sacrifice. Inside the World Trade Center, one man who could have saved himself stayed until the end at the side of his quadriplegic friend. A beloved priest died giving the last rites to a firefighter. Two office workers, finding a disabled stranger, carried her down sixty-eight floors to safety. A group of men drove through the night from Dallas to Washington to bring skin grafts for burn victims.

In these acts, and in many others, Americans showed a deep commitment to one another, and an abiding love for our country. Today, we feel what Franklin Roosevelt called the warm courage of national unity. This is a unity of every faith, and every background.

It has joined together political parties in both houses of Congress. It is evident in services of prayer and candlelight vigils, and American flags, which are displayed in pride, and wave in defiance.

Our unity is a kinship of grief, and a steadfast resolve to prevail against our enemies. And this unity against terror is now extending across the world.

America is a nation full of good fortune, with so much to be grateful for. But we are not spared from suffering. In every generation, the world has produced enemies of human freedom. They have attacked America, because we are freedom's home and defender. And the commitment of our fathers is now the calling of our time.

On this national day of prayer and remembrance, we ask almighty God to watch over our nation, and grant us patience and resolve in all that is to come. We pray that He will comfort and console those who now walk in sorrow. We thank Him for each life we now must mourn, and the promise of a life to come.

As we have been assured, neither death nor life, nor angels nor principalities nor powers, nor things present nor things to come, nor height nor depth, can separate us from God's love. May He bless the souls of the departed. May He comfort our own. And may He always guide our country.

God bless America.

Source: "September 11, 2001: Attack on America. President's Remarks at National Day of Prayer and Remembrance 1:00 P.M. EDT; September 14, 2001." Avalon Project of Yale Law School. Available online. URL: http://www.yale.edu/lawweb/avalon/sept_11/president_001.htm. Accessed July 4, 2006.

III. SERMONS

John Winthrop: "A Modell of Christian Charity" (1630) (excerpts)

"A Modell of Christian Charity" was preached by John Winthrop, the governor of the Massachusetts Bay Colony, in 1630 on board the ship Arabella. *It is sometimes called the "City on a Hill" sermon because of its application of the words of Matthew 5:14: "For we must consider that we shall be as a city upon a hill. The eyes of all people are upon us. So that if we shall deal falsely with our God in this work we have undertaken, and so cause Him to withdraw His present help from us, we shall be made a story and a by-word through the world." Excerpts from the sermon are often reproduced in anthologies of American literature, but the reader should read the sermon in its entirety—even though it is long by contemporary standards—in order to understand the logical structure and careful exposition of Scripture that characterized Puritan preaching. Winthrop emphasizes the importance of mutual affection within the Puritan community: "We must delight in each other; make others' conditions our own; rejoice together, mourn together, labor and suffer together, always having before our eyes our commission and community in the work,*

as members of the same body." Winthrop's sermon was often cited by President Ronald Reagan; his references to it in a 1974 speech to the Conservative Political Action Conference and in his 1989 farewell address to the nation are available online (http://reagan2020.us/speeches/City_Upon_A_Hill.asp and http://www.reagan.utexas.edu/archives/speeches/1989/011189i.htm, respectively).

GOD ALMIGHTY in His most holy and wise providence, hath so disposed of the condition of mankind, as in all times some must be rich, some poor, some high and eminent in power and dignity; others mean and in submission.

The Reason hereof:

1st Reason. First to hold conformity with the rest of His world, being delighted to show forth the glory of his wisdom in the variety and difference of the creatures, and the glory of His power in ordering all these differences for the preservation and good of the whole, and the glory of His greatness, that as it is the glory of princes to have many officers, so this great king will have many stewards, counting himself more honored in dispensing his gifts to man by man, than if he did it by his own immediate hands.

2nd Reason. Secondly, that He might have the more occasion to manifest the work of his Spirit: first upon the wicked in moderating and restraining them, so that the rich and mighty should not eat up the poor, nor the poor and despised rise up against and shake off their yoke. Secondly, in the regenerate, in exercising His graces in them, as in the great ones, their love, mercy, gentleness, temperance etc., and in the poor and inferior sort, their faith, patience, obedience etc.

3rd Reason. Thirdly, that every man might have need of others, and from hence they might be all knit more nearly together in the bonds of brotherly affection. From hence it appears plainly that no man is made more honorable than another or more wealthy etc., out of any particular and singular respect to himself, but for the glory of his Creator and the common good of the creature, man. Therefore God still reserves the property of these gifts to Himself as Ezek. 16:17, He there calls wealth, His gold and His silver, and Prov. 3:9, He claims their service as His due, "Honor the Lord with thy riches," etc.—All men being thus (by divine providence) ranked into two sorts, rich and poor; under the first are comprehended all such as are able to live comfortably by their own means duly improved; and all others are poor according to the former distribution.

There are two rules whereby we are to walk one towards another: Justice and Mercy. These are always distinguished in their act and in their object, yet may they both concur in the same subject in each respect; as sometimes there may be an occasion of showing mercy to a rich man in some sudden danger or distress, and also doing of mere justice to a poor man in regard of some particular contract, etc. . . .

Thus stands the cause between God and us. We are entered into covenant with Him for this work. We have taken out a commission. The Lord hath given us leave to draw our own articles. We have professed to enterprise these and those accounts, upon these and those ends. We have hereupon besought Him of favor and blessing. Now if the Lord shall please to hear us, and bring us in peace to the place we desire, then hath He ratified this covenant and sealed our commission, and will expect a strict performance of the articles contained in it; but if we shall neglect the observation of these articles which are the ends we have propounded, and, dissembling with our God, shall fall to embrace this present world and prosecute our carnal intentions, seeking great things for ourselves and our posterity, the Lord will surely break out in wrath against us, and be revenged of such a people, and make us know the price of the breach of such a covenant.

Now the only way to avoid this shipwreck, and to provide for our posterity, is to follow the counsel of Micah, to do justly, to love mercy, to walk humbly with our God. For this end, we must be knit together, in this work, as one man. We must entertain each other in brotherly affection. We must be willing to abridge ourselves of our superfluities, for the supply of others' necessities. We must uphold a familiar commerce together in all meekness, gentleness, patience and liberality. We must delight in each other; make others' conditions our own; rejoice together, mourn together, labor and suffer together, always having before our eyes our commission and community in the work, as members of the same body. So shall we keep the unity of the spirit in the bond of peace. The Lord will be our God, and delight to dwell among us, as His own people, and will command a blessing upon us in all our ways, so that we shall see much more of His wisdom, power, goodness and truth, than formerly we have been acquainted with. We shall find that the God of Israel is among us, when ten of us shall be able to resist a thousand of our enemies; when He shall make us a praise and glory that men shall say of succeeding plantations, "may the Lord make it like that of New England." For we must consider that we shall be as a city upon a hill. The eyes of all people are upon us. So that if we shall deal falsely with our God in this work we have undertaken, and so cause Him to withdraw His present help from us, we shall be made a story and a by-word through the world. We shall open the mouths of enemies to speak evil of the ways of God, and all professors for God's sake. We shall shame the faces of many of God's worthy servants, and cause their prayers to be turned into curses upon us till we be consumed out of the good land whither we are going.

And to shut this discourse with that exhortation of Moses, that faithful servant of the Lord, in his last farewell to Israel, Deut. 30. "Beloved, there is now set before us life and death, good and evil," in that we are commanded this day to love the Lord our God, and to love one another, to walk in his ways and to keep his Commandments and his ordinance and his laws, and the articles of our Covenant with Him, that we may live and be multiplied, and that the Lord our God may bless us in the land whither we go to possess it. But if our hearts shall turn away, so that we will not obey, but shall be seduced, and worship other Gods, our pleasure and profits, and serve them; it is propounded unto us this day, we shall surely perish out of the good land whither we pass over this vast sea to possess it.

Therefore let us choose life, that we and our seed may live, by obeying His voice and cleaving to Him, for He is our life and our prosperity.

Source: "A Model of Christian Charity." Religious Freedom Page. Available online. URL: http://religiousfreedom.lib.virginia.edu/sacred/charity.html. Accessed June 27, 2006.

George Whitefield: "The Heinous Sin of Drunkenness" (1740s) (excerpts)

"The Heinous Sin of Drunkenness" is one of George Whitefield's sermons, with Ephesians 5:18 as its text. The reader may find it interesting to compare Whitefield's treatment with Billy Sunday's sermon on the same subject. Like Jonathan Edwards's sermons, Whitefield's are organized rather than free flowing; he lists six reasons why drunkenness is a sin and three means for avoiding it. Another characteristic of Whitefield's style is his frequent use of expressions or phrases derived from the Bible without direct citation, such as "this kind of sin goeth not forth but by prayer and fasting" and "partakers of this inheritance with the saints in light." Whitefield is preaching in a period of history when he can expect his listeners to know that the first phrase is an echo of Matthew 17:21 and the second, of Colossians 1:12. Billy Sunday, by contrast, cannot assume that his listeners know the Bible as well as Whitefield's did.

Ephesians 5:18—"Be not drunk with Wine, wherein is Excess; but be filled with the Spirit."

The persons to whom these words were written, were the inhabitants of Ephesus, as we are told in the Acts, had been worshippers of the great goddess Diana, and, in all probability, worshipped the God Baccbus also; at the celebration of whose festivals, it was always customary, nay, part of their religion, to get drunk; as though there was no other way to please their God, but by turning themselves into brutes.

The apostle therefore in this chapter, amongst many other precepts more especially applicable to them, lays down this in the text; and exhorts them, as they had now, by the free grace of God, been turned from heathenish darkness to the light of the gospel, to walk as children of light, and no longer make it part of their religion or practice to be "drunk with wine, wherein is excess;" but, on the contrary, strive to "be filled with the Spirit" of that Savior, after whose name they were called, and whose religion taught them to abstain from a filthy sin, and to live soberly as they ought to live.

The world being now Christian, and the doctrines of the gospel every where received, one would imagine, there should be no reason for repeating the precept now before us. But alas, Christians! I mean Christians falsely so called, are led captive by all sin in general, and by this or drunkenness in particular; that was St. Paul to rise again from the dead, he might be tempted to think most of us were turned back to the worship of dumb idols; had set up temples in honor of Bacchus; and made it part of our religion, as the Ephesians did of theirs, "to be drunk with wine, wherein is excess."

Some of our civil magistrates have not been wanting to use the power given them from above, for the punishment and restraint of such evil doings; and I wish it could be said this plague of drinking, by what they have done, had been stayed amongst us. But alas! though their labor, we trust, has not been altogether in vain in the Lord, yet thousands, and I could almost say ten thousands, fall daily at our right-hand, by this sin of drunkenness, in our streets; nay, men seem to have made a covenant with hell, and though the power of the civil magistrate is exerted against them, nay, though they cannot but daily see the companions of their riot hourly, by this sin, brought to the grave, yet "they will rise up early to follow strong drink, and cry, To-morrow shall be as today, and so much the more abundantly; when we awake, we will seek it yet again."

It is high time therefore, for thy ministers, O God, to lift up their voices like a trumpet; and since human threats cannot prevail, to set before them the terrors of the Lord, and try if these will not persuade them to cease from the evil of their doings.

But alas! how shall I address myself to them? I fear excess of drinking has made them such mere Nabals, that there is no speaking to them. And many of God's servants have toiled all their life-time in dissuading them from this sin of drunkenness, yet they will not forbear. However, at thy command, I will speak also, though they be a rebellious house. Magnify thy strength, O Lord, in my weakness, and grant that I may speak with such demonstration of the Spirit, and power, that from henceforward they may cease to act so unwisely, and this sin of drunkenness may not be their ruin. . . .

First, Drunkenness is a sin which must be highly displeasing to God; because it is an abuse of his good creatures. . . . Of every beast of the field, every fish of the sea, and whatsoever flieth in the air, or moveth on the face of the earth, that is fit for food, "we may freely eat," without scruple take and eat; but then, with this limitation, that we use them moderately. For God, by the death of Jesus, has given no man license to be intemperate; but, on the contrary, has laid us under the strongest obligations to live soberly, as well as godly, in this present world.

But the drunkard, despising the goodness and bounty of God, in restoring to us what we had so justly forfeited, turns his grace into wantonness; and as though the creature was not of itself enough subject to vanity, by being cursed for our sake, he abuses it still more, by making it administer to his lusts; and turns that wine which was intended to make glad his heart, into a deadly poison. . . .

Secondly, What makes drunkenness more exceedingly sinful, is, that a man, by falling into it, sinneth against his own body. When the apostle would dissuade the Corinthians from fornication, he urges this as an argument, "Flee fornication, brethren; for he that committeth fornication, sinneth against his own body." And may not I as justly cry out, Flee drunkenness, my brethren, since he that committeth that crime, sinneth against his own body? For, from whence come so many diseases and distempers in your bodies? Come they not from hence, even from your intemperance in drinking? Who hath pains in the head? Who hath rottenness in the bones? Who hath redness of eyes? He that tarries long at the wine, he that rises early to seek new wine. How many walking skeletons have you seen, whose bodies were once exceeding fair to look upon, fat and well-favored; but, by this sin of drinking, how has their beauty departed from them, and how have they been permitted to walk to and fro upon the earth, as though God intended to set them up, as he did Lot's wife, for monuments of his justice, that others might learn not to get drunk? . . .

Thirdly, What renders drunkenness more inexcusable, is, that it robs a man of his reason. Reason is the glory of a man; the chief thing whereby God has made us to differ from the brute creation. And our modern unbelievers have exalted it to such a high degree, as even to set it in opposition to revelation, and so deny the Lord that bought them. But though, in doing this, they greatly err, and whilst they profess themselves wise, become real fools; yet we must acknowledge, that reason is the candle of the Lord, and whosoever puts it out, shall bear his punishment, whosoever he be. But yet, this the drunkard does. Nebuchadnezzar's curse he makes his choice, his reason departeth from him; and then what is he better than a brute? . . .

Fourthly, There is a farther aggravation of this crime, that it is an inlet to, and forerunner of many other sins; for it seldom comes alone. We may say of drunkenness, as Solomon does in strife, that it is like the letting out of water; for we know not what will be the end thereof. Its name is Legion; behold a troop of sins cometh after it. And, for my own part, when I see a drunkard, with the holy Prophet, when he looked in Hazael's face, I can hardly forbear weeping, to consider how many vices he may fall into, ere he comes to himself again. . . .

Fifth consideration, which highly aggravates the sin of drunkenness, it separates the Holy Spirit from us. It is to be hoped, that no one here present need be informed, that before we can be assured we are Christians indeed, we must receive the Holy Ghost, must be born again from above, and have the Spirit of God witnessing with our spirits, that we are the sons of God. This, this alone is true Christianity; and without the cohabitation of this blessed Spirit in our hearts, our righteousness does not exceed the righteousness of the Scribes and Pharisees, and we shall in no wise enter into the kingdom of God.

But now, drunkards do in effect bid this blessed Spirit to depart from them: for what has he to do with such filthy swine? They have no log of share in the Spirit of the Son of David. They have chased him out of their hearts, by defiling his temple; I mean their bodies. . . .

Sixth reason against the sin of drunkenness; it absolutely unfits a man for the enjoyment of God in heaven, and exposes him to his eternal wrath. . . . But think you, O ye drunkards, that you shall ever be partakers of this inheritance with the saints in light? Do you flatter yourselves, that you, who have made them often the subject of your drunken songs, shall now be exalted to sing with them the heavenly songs of Zion? No, as by drunkenness you have made your hearts cages of unclean birds, with impure and unclean spirits must you dwell. . . .

And now, by way of conclusion, I cannot but exhort all persons, high and low, rich and poor, to practice a strict self-denial in eating and drinking. For though "the kingdom of God consists not in meats and drinks," yet an abstemious [moderate, sober, temperate] use of God's good creatures, greatly promotes the spiritual life.

Source: "Sermon 52: The Heinous Sin of Drunkenness." The Whitefield Sermon Archive. Available online. URL: http://www.pioneernet.net/rbrannan/whitefield/sermons/WITF_052.HTM. Accessed June 27, 2006.

Jonathan Edwards: "Sinners in the Hands of an Angry God" (1741) (excerpts)

"Sinners in the Hands of an Angry God," the best known of all of Jonathan Edwards's sermons, was preached to the members of the Congregational church at Enfield, Connecticut, in July 1741—for which reason it is sometimes referred to in biographies of Edwards as the "Enfield sermon." It has given him an undeserved reputation as an 18th-century version of a hate-filled fundamentalist. In the context of the Great Awakening, this type of sermon was called an "awakening" sermon, meant to convince listeners of the vital importance of the Christian message so that they would then be prepared for "converting" or "edifying" sermons. Using Deuteronomy 32:35 ("Their foot shall slide in due time, for the day of their calamity is at hand") as his text, Edwards organized the sermon into two parts, the doctrine (teaching) and the application. "Sinners" is thus a good example of the structure of colonial sermons as well as content. It should, however, be read together with one or more of Edwards's other sermons in order to have a clearer and more balanced picture of Edwards as a pastor.

Their foot shall slide in due time. —DEUT. 32:35.

. . . The observation from the words that I would now insist upon is this.

There is nothing that keeps wicked men at any one moment out of hell, but the mere pleasure of God.

By the mere pleasure of God, I mean his sovereign pleasure, his arbitrary will, restrained by no obligation, hindered by no manner of difficulty, any more than if nothing else but God's mere will had in the least degree, or in any respect whatsoever, any hand in the preservation of wicked men one moment. . . .

There is no want of *power* in God to cast wicked men into hell at any moment. Men's hands cannot be strong when God rises up. The strongest have no power to resist him, nor can any deliver out of his hands.

He is not only able to cast wicked men into hell, but he can most easily do it. Sometimes an earthly prince meets with a great deal of difficulty to subdue a rebel, who has found means to fortify himself, and has made himself strong by the numbers of his followers. But it is not so with God. There is no fortress that is any defense from the power of God. Though hand join in hand, and vast multitudes of God's enemies combine and associate themselves, they are easily broken in pieces. They are as great heaps of light chaff before the whirlwind; or large quantities of dry stubble before devouring flames. We find it easy to tread on and crush a worm that we see crawling on the earth; so it is easy for us to cut or singe a slender thread that any thing hangs by: thus easy is it for God, when he pleases, to cast his enemies down to hell. What are we, that we should think to stand before him, at whose rebuke the earth trembles, and before whom the rocks are thrown down?. . .

God has laid himself under *no obligation,* by any promise to keep any natural man out of hell one moment. God certainly has made no promises either of eternal life, or of any deliverance or preservation from eternal death, but what are contained in the covenant of grace, the promises that are given in Christ, in whom all the promises are yea and amen. But surely they have no interest in the promises of the covenant of grace who are not the children of the covenant, who do not believe in any of the promises, and have no interest in the *mediator* of the covenant.

So that whatever some have imagined and pretended about promises made to natural men's earnest seeking and knocking, it is plain and manifest, that whatever pains a natural man takes in religion, whatever prayers he makes, till he believes in Christ, God is under no manner of obligation to keep him a moment from eternal destruction.

So that thus it is, that natural men are held in the hand of God over the pit of hell; they have deserved the fiery pit, and are already sentenced to it; and God is dreadfully provoked, his anger is as great towards them as to those that are actually suffering the executions of the fierceness of his wrath in hell, and they have done nothing in the least to appease or abate that anger, neither is God in the least bound by any promise to hold them up one moment; the devil is waiting for them, hell is gaping for them, the flames gather and flash about them, and would fain lay hold on them, and swallow them up; the fire pent up in their own hearts is struggling to break out: and they have no interest in any mediator, there are no means within reach that can be any security to them. In short, they have no refuge, nothing to take hold of, all that preserves them every moment is the mere arbitrary will, and uncovenanted, unobliged forbearance of an incensed God.

APPLICATION.

The use may be of *awakening* to unconverted persons in this congregation. This that you have heard is the case of every one of you that are out of Christ. That world of misery, that lake of burning brimstone, is extended abroad under you. There is the dreadful pit of the glowing flames of the wrath of God; there is hell's wide gaping mouth open; and you have nothing to stand upon, nor any thing to take hold of, there is nothing between you and hell but the air; it is only the power and mere pleasure of God that holds you up. . . .

The God that holds you over the pit of hell, much as one holds a spider, or some loathsome insect over the fire, abhors you, and is dreadfully provoked: his wrath towards you burns like fire; he looks upon you as worthy of nothing else, but to be cast into the fire; he is of purer eyes than to bear to have you in his sight; you are ten thousand times more abominable in his eyes, than the most hateful venomous serpent is in ours. You have offended him infinitely more than ever a stubborn rebel did his prince; and yet it is nothing but his hand that holds you from falling into the fire every moment. It is to be ascribed to nothing else, that you did not go to hell the last night; that you was suffered to awake again in this world, after you closed your eyes to sleep. And there is no other reason to be given, why you have not dropped into hell since you arose in the morning, but that God's hand has held you up. There is no other reason to be given why you have not gone to hell, since you have sat here in the house of God, provoking his pure eyes by your sinful wicked manner of attending his solemn worship. Yea, there is nothing else that is to be given as a reason why you do not this very moment drop down into hell.

O sinner! Consider the fearful danger you are in: it is a great furnace of wrath, a wide and bottomless pit, full of the fire of wrath, that you are held over in the hand of that God, whose wrath is provoked and incensed as much against you, as against many of the damned in hell. You hang by a slender thread, with the flames of divine wrath flashing about it, and ready every moment to singe it, and burn it asunder; and you have no interest in any mediator, and nothing to lay hold of to save yourself, nothing to keep off the flames of wrath, nothing of your own, nothing that you ever have done, nothing that you can do, to induce God to spare you one moment. . . .

And now you have an extraordinary opportunity, a day wherein Christ has thrown the door of mercy wide open, and stands in calling and crying with a loud voice to poor sinners; a day wherein many are flocking to him, and pressing into the kingdom of God. Many are daily coming from the east, west, north and south; many that were very lately in the same miserable condition that you are in, are now in a happy state, with their hearts filled with love to him who has loved them, and washed them from their sins in his own blood, and rejoicing in hope of the glory of God. How awful is it to be left behind at such a day! To see so many others feasting, while you are pining and perishing! To see so many rejoicing and singing for joy of heart, while you have cause to mourn for sorrow of heart, and howl for vexation of spirit! How can you rest one moment in such a condition? Are not your souls as precious as the souls of the people at Suffield, where they are flocking from day to day to Christ? . . .

Therefore, let every one that is out of Christ, now awake and fly from the wrath to come. The wrath of Almighty God is now undoubtedly hanging over a great part of this congregation: let every one fly out of Sodom: "Haste and escape for your lives, look not behind you, escape to the mountain, lest you be consumed" [Gen. 19:17].

Source: "Sinners in the Hands of an Angry God (1741)." The Jonathan Edwards Center at Yale University. Available online. URL: http://edwards.yale.edu/images/pdf/sinners.pdf. Accessed June 27, 2006. (A good paperback edition of selected sermons is Wilson H. Kimnach, Kenneth P. Minkema, and Douglas A. Sweeney, eds., *The Sermons of Jonathan Edwards: A Reader.* New Haven, Conn.: Yale University Press, 1999.)

Dwight L. Moody: "The Qualifications for Soul Winning" (1873) (excerpts)

"The Qualifications for Soul Winning" is a sermon preached by Dwight L. Moody in Edinburgh, Scotland, on December 7, 1873, during an evangelistic tour of Great Britain. The sermon does not have a base scriptural text but is rather organized around a central theme. Moody has several basic points that he enumerates, illustrating each with some simple anecdotes and illustrations. The sermon is a good example of Moody's fairly low-key preaching style; he communicates his message through sincerity and personal warmth rather than by theatrical gestures or highly emotional appeals. It also illustrates his emphasis on the positive aspects of Christian faith: "Let us not go about, hanging our heads like a bulrush; if Christ gives joy, let us live it! The whole world is in all matters for the very best thing—you always want to get the best possible thing for your money; let us show, then, that our religion is the very best thing: men with long, gloomy faces are never wise in the winning of souls."

1. Shake off the vipers that are in the Church, formalism, pride, and self-importance, etc.
2. It is the only happy life to live for the salvation of souls.
3. We must be willing to do little things for Christ.
4. Must be of good courage.
5. Must be cheerful.

God had no children too weak, but a great many too strong to make use of. God stands in no need of our strength or wisdom, but of our ignorance, of our weakness; let us but give these to Him, and He can make use of us in winning souls. "And they that be wise shall shine as the brightness of the firmament; and they that turn many to righteousness as the stars for ever and ever." Daniel 12:3.

Now we all want to shine; the mother wishes it for her boy, when she sends him to school, the father for his lad, when he goes off to college; and here God tells us who are to shine—not statesmen, or warriors, or such like, that shine but for a season—but such as will shine for ever and ever; those, namely, who win souls to Christ; the little boy even who persuades one to come to Christ.

Speaking of this, Paul counts up five things (1 Cor. 1:27–9) that God makes use of—the weak things, the foolish things, the base things, the despised things, and the things which are not, and for this purpose, that no flesh might glory in his sight—all five being just such as we should despise. He can and will use us, just when we are willing to be humble for Christ's sake, and so for six thousand years God has been teaching men; so with an ass's jawbone Samson slew his thousands (Judges 15:15), so at the blowing of rams' horns the walls of Jericho fell (Joshua 6:20). Let God work in His own way, and with His own instruments; let us all rejoice that He should, and let us too get into the position in which God can use us.

There is much mourning to-day over false "isms," infidelity, and the like, but sum them all up, and I do not fear them one half so much as that dead and cold formalism that has crept into the Church of God. The unbelieving world, and these skeptics holding out their false lights, are watching you and me: when Jacob put away his idols, he could go up to Bethel and get strength and the blessing—so will it be with the Church of God. A viper fixes upon the hand of the shipwrecked Paul; immediately he is judged by the barbarians some criminal unfit to live; but he shakes it off into the fire, and suffers no harm, and now they are ready to worship him, and ready too to hear and receive his message: the Church of God must shake off the vipers that have fastened on hand and heart too, ere men will hear. Where one ungodly man reads this Bible, a hundred read you and me: and if they find nothing in us, they set the whole thing aside as a myth. . . .

And further, we must be ready to *do little things* for God; many are willing to do the great things. I dare say hundreds would have been ready to occupy this pulpit to-day. How many of them would be as willing to teach a dirty class in the ragged school?

I remember, one afternoon I was preaching, observing a young lady from the house I was staying at, in the audience. I had heard she taught in the Sabbath-school, which I knew was at the same hour; and so I asked her, after service, how she came to be there? "Oh," said she, "my class is but five little boys, and I thought it did not matter for them." And yet among these there might have been, who knows, a Luther or a Knox, the beginning of a stream of blessing, that would have gone on widening and ever widening; and besides, one soul is worth all the kingdoms of the earth. . . .

Another thing we want is, to be *of good courage.* Three or four times this comes out in the first chapter of Joshua; and I have observed that God never uses a man that is always looking on the dark side of things: what we do for Him let us do cheerfully, not because it is our duty—not that we should sweep away the word but because it is our privilege. What would my wife or children say if I spoke of loving them because it was my *duty* to do so? And my mother—if I go to see her once a year, and were to say—"Mother, I am come all this way to discharge what I feel to be my duty in visiting you;" might she not rightly reply—"My son, if this is all that has brought you, you might have spared coming at all!" and go own in broken-hearted sorrow to the grave?

A London minister, a friend of mine, lately pointed out a family of seven, all of whom he was just receiving into the Church. Their story was this: going to church, he had to pass by a window, looking up at which one day, he saw a baby looking out; he smiled—the baby smiled again. Next time he passes he looks up again, smiles, and the baby smiles back. A third time going by, he looks up, and seeing the baby, throws it a kiss—which the baby returns to him. Time after time he has to pass the window, and now cannot refrain from looking up each time: and each time there are more faces to receive his smiling greeting; till by-and-by he sees the whole family grouped at the window—father, mother, and all. The father conjectures the happy, smiling stranger must be a minister, and so, next Sunday morning, after they have received at the window the usual greeting, two of the children, ready dressed, are sent out to follow him: they enter his church, hear him preach, and carry back to their parents the report that they never heard such preaching; and what preaching could equal that of one who had so smiled on them? Soon the rest come to the church too, and are brought in—all by a smile. Let us not go about, hanging our heads like a bulrush; if Christ gives joy, let us live it! The whole world is in all matters for the very best thing—you always want to get the best possible thing for your money; let us show, then, that our religion is the very best thing: men with long, gloomy faces are never wise in the winning of souls. . . .

"They that be wise shall shine, as the brightness of the firmament; and they that turn many to righteousness as the stars for ever and ever." (Daniel 12:3). The Lord help us as humbly, devoutly, and cheerfully to abound in His work!

Source: "D. L. Moody: The Qualifications for Soul Winning." Biblebelievers.com. Available online. URL: http://www.biblebelievers.com/moody_sermons/m1.html. Accessed June 27, 2006.

Billy Sunday: The "Booze Sermon" (c. 1907) (excerpts)

From the 1890s through the end of World War I, Billy Sunday was one of the foremost opponents of the liquor trade as well as a well-known Protestant fundamentalist preacher. It is said that no other single individual did as much to convince Americans to vote for Prohibition as he did. A one-time professional baseball player, Sunday did not preach while standing sedately in a pulpit but stripped off his suit jacket (a shocking informality for a preacher in the early 1900s) and acted more like an athlete on the stage than a minister. He delivered the "Booze Sermon" hundreds of times in the course of three decades of preaching.

Here [Matthew 8:28–34] we have one of the strangest scenes in all the Gospels. Two men, possessed of devils, confront Jesus, and while the devils are crying out for Jesus to leave them, he commands the devils to come out, and the devils obey the command of Jesus. The devils ask permission to enter into a herd of swine feeding on the hillside. This is the only record we have of Jesus ever granting the petition of devils, and he did it for the salvation of men.

Then the fellows that kept the hogs went back to town and told the peanut-brained, weasel-eyed, hog-jowled, beetle-browed, bull-necked lobsters that owned the hogs, that "a long-haired fanatic from Nazareth, named Jesus, has driven the devils out of some men and the devils have gone into the hogs, and the hogs into the sea, and the sea into the hogs, and the whole bunch is dead."

And then the fat, fussy old fellows came out to see Jesus and said that he was hurting their business. A fellow says to me, "I don't think Jesus Christ did a nice thing."

You don't know what you are talking about.

Down in Nashville, Tennessee, I saw four wagons going down the street, and they were loaded with stills, and kettles, and pipes.

"What's this?" I said.

"United States revenue officers, and they have been in the moonshine district and confiscated the illicit stills, and they are taking them down to the government scrap heap."

Jesus Christ was God's revenue officer. Now the Jews were forbidden to eat pork, but Jesus Christ came and found that crowd buying and selling and dealing in pork, and confiscated the whole business, and he kept within the limits of the law when he did it. Then the fellows ran back to those who owned the hogs to tell what had befallen them and those hog-owners said to Jesus: "Take your helpers and hike. You are hurting our business." And they looked into the sea and the hogs were bottom side up, but Jesus said, "What is the matter?" And they answered, "Leave our hogs and go." A fellow says it is rather a strange request for the devils to make, to ask permission to enter into hogs. I don't know, if I was a devil I would rather live in a good, decent hog than in lots of men. If you will drive the hog out you won't have to carry slop to him, so I will try to help you get rid of the hog.

And they told Jesus to leave the country. They said: "You are hurting our business." . . .

That is the attitude of the liquor traffic toward the Church, and State, and Government, and the preacher that has the backbone to fight the most damnable, corrupt institution that ever wriggled out of hell and fastened itself on the public.

I am a temperance Republican down to my toes. Who is the man that fights the whisky business in the South? It is the Democrats! They have driven the business from Kansas, they have driven it from Georgia, and Maine and Mississippi and North Carolina and North Dakota and Oklahoma and Tennessee and West Virginia. And they have driven it out of 1,756 counties. And it is the rock-ribbed Democratic South that is fighting the saloon. They started this fight that is sweeping like fire over the United States. You might as well try and dam Niagara Falls with toothpicks as to stop the reform wave sweeping our land. The Democratic party of Florida has put a temperance plank in its platform and the Republican party of every state would nail that plank in their platform if they thought it would carry the election. It is simply a matter of decency against poverty, sobriety against drunkenness, honesty against thieving, heaven, against hell. Don't you want to see men sober? Brutal, staggering men transformed into respectable citizens? . . .

I challenge you to show me where the saloon has ever helped business, education, church, morals or anything we hold dear. . . .

Listen! Seventy-five per cent of our idiots come from intemperate parents; eighty per cent of the paupers, eighty-two per cent of the crime is committed by men under the influence of liquor; ninety per cent of the adult criminals are whisky-made. The *Chicago Tribune* kept track for ten years and found that 53,556 murders were committed by men under the influence of liquor.

Archbishop Ireland, the famous Roman Catholic, of St. Paul, said of social crime today, that "75 per cent is caused by drink, and 80 per cent of the poverty."

I go to a family and it is broken up, and I say, "What caused this?" Drink! I step up to a young man on the scaffold and say, "What brought you here?" Drink! Whence all the misery and sorrow and corruption? Invariably it is drink. . . .

The saloon is the sum of all villanies [sic]. It is worse than war or pestilence. It is the crime of crimes. It is the parent of crimes and the mother of sins. It is the appalling source of misery and crime in the land. And to license such an incarnate fiend of hell is the dirtiest, low-down, damnable business on top of this old earth. There is nothing to be compared to it.

The legislature of Illinois appropriated $6,000,000 in 1908 to take care of the insane people in the state, and the whisky business produces seventy-five per cent of the insane. That is what you go down in your pockets for to help support. Do away with the saloons and you will close these institutions. The saloons make them necessary, and they make the poverty and fill the jails and the penitentiaries. Who has to pay the bills? The landlord who doesn't get the rent because the money goes for whisky; the butcher and the grocer and the charitable person who takes pity on the children of drunkards, and the taxpayer who supports the insane asylums and other institutions, that the whisky business keeps full of human wrecks. . . .

Several years ago in the city of Chicago a young man of good parents, good character, one Sunday crossed the street and entered a saloon, open against the law. He found there boon companions. There were laughter, song and jest and much drinking. After awhile, drunk, insanely drunk, his money gone, he was kicked into the street. He found his way across to his mother's home. He importuned her for money to buy more drink. She refused him. He seized from the sideboard a revolver and ran out into the street and with the expressed determination of entering the saloon and getting more drink, money or no money. His fond mother followed him into the street. She put her hand upon him in a loving restraint. He struck it from him in anger, and then his sister came and added her entreaty in vain. And then a neighbor, whom he knew, trusted and respected, came and put his hand on him in gentleness and friendly kindness, but in an insanity of drunken rage he raised the revolver and shot his friend dead in his blood upon the street. There was a trial; he was found guilty of murder. He was sentenced to life imprisonment, and when the little mother heard the verdict—a frail little bit of a woman—she threw up her hands and fell in a swoon. In three hours she was dead.

In the streets of Freeport, Illinois, a young man of good family became involved in a controversy with a lewd woman of the town. He went in a drunken frenzy to his father's home, armed himself with a deadly weapon and set out for the city in search of the woman with whom he had quarreled. The first person he met upon the public square in the city, in the daylight, in a place where she had a right to be, was one of the most refined and cultured women of Freeport. She carried in her arms her babe—motherhood and babyhood, upon the streets of Freeport in the day time, where they had a right to be—but this young man in his drunken insanity mistook her for the woman he sought and shot her dead upon the streets with her babe in her arms. He was tried and Judge Ferand, in sentencing him to life imprisonment said: "You are the seventh man in two years to be sentenced for murder while intoxicated." . . .

I tell you, gentlemen, the American home is the dearest heritage of the people, for the people, and by the people, and when a man can go from home in the morning with the kisses of wife and children on his lips, and come back at night with an empty dinner bucket to a happy home, that man is a better man, whether white or black. Whatever takes away the comforts of home—whatever degrades that man or woman—whatever invades the sanctity of the home, is the deadliest foe to the home, to church, to state and school, and the saloon is the deadliest foe to the home, the church and the state, on top of God Almighty's dirt. And if all the combined forces of hell should assemble in conclave, and with them all the men on earth that hate and despise God, and purity, and virtue—if all the scum of the earth could mingle with the denizens of hell to try to think of the deadliest institution to home, to church and state, I tell you, sir, the combined hellish intelligence could not conceive of or bring an institution that could touch the hem of the garment of the open licensed saloon to damn the home and manhood, and womanhood, and business and every other good thing on God's earth. . . .

The saloon is a liar. It promises good cheer and sends sorrow. It promises health and causes disease. It promises prosperity and sends adversity. It promises happiness and sends misery. Yes, it sends the husband home with a lie on his lips to his wife; and the boy home with a lie on his lips to his mother; and it causes the employee to lie to his employer. It degrades. It is God's worst enemy and the devil's best friend. It spares neither youth nor old age. It is waiting with a dirty blanket for the baby to crawl into the world. It lies in wait for the unborn.

It cocks the highwayman's pistol. It puts the rope in the hands of the mob. It is the anarchist of the world and its dirty red flag is dyed with the blood of women and children. It sent the bullet through the body of Lincoln; it nerved the arm that sent the bullets through Garfield and William McKinley. Yes, it is a murderer. Every plot that was ever hatched against the government and law, was born and bred, and crawled out of the grog-shop to damn this country. . . .

I want every man to say, "God, you can count on me to protect my wife, my home, my mother and my children and the manhood of America."

By the mercy of God, which has given to you the unshaken and unshakable confidence of her you love, I beseech you, make a fight for the women who wait until the saloons spew out their husbands and their sons, and send them home maudlin, brutish, devilish, stinking, blear-eyed, bloated-faced drunkards.

You say you can't prohibit men from drinking. Why, if Jesus Christ were here today some of you would keep on in sin just the same. But the law can be enforced against whisky just the same as it can be enforced against anything else, if you have honest officials to enforce it. Of course it doesn't prohibit. There isn't a law on the books of the state that prohibits. We have laws against murder. Do they prohibit? We have laws against burglary. Do they prohibit? We have laws against arson, rape, but they do not prohibit. Would you introduce a bill to repeal all the laws that do not prohibit? Any law will prohibit to a certain extent if honest officials enforce it. But no law will absolutely prohibit. We can make a law against liquor prohibit as much as any law prohibits. . . .

By the grace of God I have strength enough to pass the open saloon, but some of you can't, so I owe it to you to help you.

I've stood for more sneers and scoffs and insults and had my life threatened from one end of the land to the other by this God-forsaken gang of thugs and cutthroats because I have come out uncompromisingly against them. I've taken more dirty, vile insults from this low-down bunch than from any one on earth, but there is no one that will reach down lower, or reach higher up or wider, to help you out of the pits of drunkenness than I.

Source: "Booze." Christians Unite Articles. Available online. URL: http://articles.christiansunite.com/article415.shtml. Accessed September 8, 2006. (An audio file of about two minutes of the sermon in WAV format is available online at http://billysunday.org/audio.php3. As the Web site notes, the sound quality is not the best, but the clip does give the listener a sense of Sunday's preaching style.)

Billy Graham: "America's Greatest Sin" (1958) (excerpts)

The following sermon was preached by Billy Graham on September 24, 1958, at an evangelistic meeting in Charlotte, North Carolina. It is one of a relatively small number of Graham's sermons that have been transcribed for print reproduction, whereas there are literally thousands available in audio or video format. Graham's preaching style is simple and straightforward in comparison to the formality of Jonathan Edwards or the dramatic flourishes of Billy Sunday. It is interesting that Graham pointed to covetousness (greed or excessive craving for something) as the central spiritual disorder of the United States as early as the 1950s: "Americans are considered all over the world as materialistic, worldly, secular, greedy, and covetous. We are guilty of that sin as a nation, as a people, and as individuals." Another significant feature of this sermon is the absence of theological separatism; Graham's words are accessible to Christians from mainline denominations (including Roman Catholics) as well as members of evangelical churches: "God doesn't want you to go around with a long face. God is not interested in any legalism. God is not interested in any rules. God wants you to just love Him. And when you love Him supremely, the rest will take care of itself."

Now, tonight I want you to turn with me to the 12th chapter of the gospel according to Luke. How many of you have your Bibles? Lift them up, way up. Wonderful. We want you to bring your Bible every night. The 12th chapter of the gospel according to Luke, beginning at verse 15. Now, let's begin at the 1st verse. I will read the first three verses, then skip over to verse 15.

This is Christ talking. Now Christ has been going up and down the country making the blind to see, and the deaf to hear, and the dumb to speak, and the lame to walk, and the dead to rise. He has been feeding the hungry. And as He is going around, of course, Christ is also teaching the people. And so on this occasion, He is teaching a great group of people. . . .

Jesus said, "Beware of covetousness." And the tenth commandment says, "Thou shalt not covet" [Exodus 20:17]. And I believe tonight that the greatest sin in America is the sin of covetousness.

Americans are considered all over the world as materialistic, worldly, secular, greedy, and covetous. We are guilty of that sin as a nation, as a people, and as individuals. Americans have the highest standard of living the world has ever known. Never in history—in Rome, in Babylon, in the great nations of the past—has there ever been a standard of living like we enjoy in America.

You say, "But, Billy, I'm not a rich person." You have shoes, don't you? You have a suit of clothes; you have a dress. Then you are rich by the world's standards. You had something to eat, didn't you? In India tonight, over a hundred million people will go to bed hungry tonight—if they have a bed to go to. And when they drive the trucks down the streets of Calcutta tomorrow morning, they will pick up people that died of starvation, as I have seen them in India. The poorest person in this audience tonight is rich by the world's standards.

And in spite of our riches, in spite of our high standard of living, our whole economy is geared to getting *more*. The capitalist wants more profit. The laboring man wants more wages for less hours. And all of us are engaged in a mad race—trampling over each other, cheating each other, lying, stealing, any way we can get it—to get another dollar. The Bible says it's the sin of covetousness. "Thou shall not covet."

The word "covetousness" means to delight in something. It's the object of your attention—to wish for, to desire it, to love, to set your heart on. Something that fascinates, something that you long for, something that you are looking for; to get more of this world's goods, even if it means the starvation of your own soul.

You are a rich man, and you are a rich person now. I'm not talking about the millionaire now. I'm talking about the man that makes twenty-five dollars a week. I am talking about a rich American. . . .

God says that covetousness is actually idolatry, and He says a covetous person has no place in the kingdom of God. No place in the kingdom of God—the Bible says that in Ephesians 5:3 and 5. I just read it to you. If words mean anything, it means that a covetous person shall not go to heaven, shall not be saved. You say, "Well, Billy, isn't a man supposed to take care of his family?" Yes. The Bible says, "Give me not poverty lest I steal" [Proverbs 30:8–9].

We are to have enough, but we're not to give our full attention to the things of the world. Our first attention is to be on Christ. We are to seek first the kingdom of God and his righteousness, then all of these things shall be added unto us [Matthew 6:33].

Is that what you're doing? Are you seeking God's kingdom first? Are you seeking the things of Christ first? Or is your business, your pleasure, your amusement—the things of this world—first in your life? . . .

We used to think that worldliness was summed up in not doing certain things. But I tell you worldliness is deeper than that. Worldliness is a spirit. It's the spirit of iniquity; it's the mystery of lawlessness; it is the world system round about us. I know a man that doesn't drink, he doesn't even smoke, he doesn't even go to the theater. And he thinks he's separated. He is one of the most worldly men I know today, because he is taken up continually with the things of this world. He thinks about making money; he thinks about his new car. He is given entirely to the things of this world. Oh, he goes religiously to church every Sunday morning, carries the Bible with him. But I tell you he is a worldly man; he is a covetous man. And the Bible says a covetous man is an idolater, and an idolater is hated by God, and no idolater shall inherit the kingdom of God.

You may be able to pronounce all the shibboleths. You may be able to pronounce all the cliches. You may be an orthodox of the orthodox. You may be able to split all the theological hairs. You may be a theological bloodhound. But I tell you tonight, unless we are separated from the temper, and the lusts, and the evils of this world, we cannot call ourselves God's children. We must be separated.

I don't mean that pious, false separation that is a stumbling block to the world's finding the Savior. I mean a separation of hearts, a sanctification of heart, separated not so much from, but to God. God is first in our lives. "Seek ye first the kingdom of God"—and if you put God first, then all of these other things will be added [see Matthew 6:33]. And the enjoyment of these things will be far deeper and greater if God is first.

God doesn't want you to go around with a long face. God is not interested in any legalism. God is not interested in any rules. God wants you to just love Him. And when you love Him supremely, the rest will take care of itself. . . .

And today in America the world is on fire. Mr. Nehru has said the world may blow up. Mr. Truman says we hang on the brink of hell. Our leaders are warning us every day that we could blow up any moment. And what are we doing? Spending our time at ease, spending our time before our television sets, spending our time filling the night clubs and the theaters, spending our time getting a better automobile, a better job, more money, all the things of the world. We are like a man on a sinking ship that is trying to make his cabin more comfortable. We are covetous, and that is our greatest sin tonight. And it may be your sin.

The Scripture tells us that our Lord Jesus Christ had no covetousness in Him. He "thought it not robbery to be equal with God . . . He humbled himself . . . even to the death of the cross" [Philippians 2:5, 8]. I see Jesus Christ emptying Himself at the cross, giving Himself for you and for me in dying on that cross. And I must confess tonight that I have been guilty of breaking God's law, of falling short. And I want to tell you that if I was going to be saved by the way I have lived, I would be lost. I am saved simply and wholly by the blood that was shed at the cross, because the blood symbolized the life that was given. And Jesus Christ died on that cross. . . .

You may be the richest man in town. You may be a political leader. You may be a bank president. You may be a union leader. You may be a baseball player. You may be a football hero at the high school. Whoever you are, you've got to humble yourself and come to Christ. And I'm going to ask you in a moment, all of you that will come and say, "I have sinned against God. I want to receive Christ as my Lord and Savior. I want to be forgiven. I want to seek the kingdom of God."

And the reason that I ask you to come is because Jesus said if we are not willing to confess Him before men, He'll not confess us before the Father which is in heaven [see Matthew 10:32, 33]. And when Jesus healed the man with the withered arm, He could have healed him by saying, "Be healed." But He didn't do it. He said, "Stretch it forth." Now that man had tried to stretch it forth, and he had tried to be brave. He had tried to strengthen his arm many times, but he had failed. But by faith in the Word of Christ, he stretched it forth and he was healed. [Matthew 12:10–13.]

I am asking you to stretch your life forth to Christ. God wants you to do something as evidence that you are giving your life to Him. I am asking you to do something tonight to make it clear and definite by coming and giving your life to Christ.

Source: "America's Greatest Sins." Billy Graham Center Archives. Available online. URL: http://www.wheaton.edu/bgc/archives/docs/bg-charlotte/0924.html. Accessed June 27, 2006.

Jerry Falwell: "A Good Christian Should Be a Good Citizen" (2005)

*This sermon was preached at Thomas Road Baptist Church, Falwell's home congregation in Lynchburg, Virginia, on November 6, 2005. The reader should note that Falwell's second text is the passage from Matthew that contains the reference to the "city on a hill." In spite of Falwell's reference to the United States as a "Christian nation," he is careful to cite the passage in Matthew 22, in which Jesus speaks of the distinction between "Caesar's things" and God's. It is not always easy to analyze the theological content of Falwell's sermons because of their loose organizational structure, but it seems clear that his call to his listeners to be informed voters and potential candidates for office should not be identified as Christian reconstructionism. Falwell's specific immediate concerns (*Roe v. Wade*, local controversies over Christmas displays, etc.) reflect the increasing tension between secularists and religious believers* *(including non-fundamentalists) since 1972. There is one interesting respect in which Falwell's sermon reflects a major social change since 1972—the role of women in politics. He specifically mentions "the God-given right of each man and woman to the pursuit of happiness," and he seems to assume the legitimacy of women serving in public office.*

Following my conversion to faith in Christ as an 18-year-old college student, I was taught that religion and politics don't mix. Later, as a young pastor, I was discouraged from speaking out on the moral issues facing the culture. There was a deafening silence in my pulpit.

As election days came and went, I was careful never to even make mention to my congregation that they had a duty to be informed voters.

TEXT- I Samuel 17:29, "And David said, What have I now done? Is there not a cause?"

TEXT- Matthew 5:13–16, "Ye are the salt of the earth: but if the salt have lost his savour, wherewith shall it be salted? it is thenceforth good for nothing, but to be cast out, and to be trodden under foot of men. 14 Ye are the light of the world. A city that is set on an hill cannot be hid. 15 Neither do men light a candle, and put it under a bushel, but on a candlestick; and it giveth light unto all that are in the house. 16 Let your light so shine before men, that they may see your good works, and glorify your Father which is in heaven."

What is an American? Anonymous.

"An American is English, or French, or Italian, Irish, German, Spanish, Polish, Russian, or Greek. An American may also be Canadian, Mexican, African, Indian, Chinese, Japanese, Australian, Iranian, Asian, or Arab, or Pakistani, or Afghan.

["]An American may also be a Cherokee, Blackfoot, Navajo, Apache or one of the many other tribes known as native Americans. An American is Christian, or he could be Jewish, or Buddhist, or Muslim. In fact, there are more Muslims in America than in Afghanistan. The only difference is that in America, they are free to worship as each of them chooses. An American is also free to believe in no religion. For that, he will answer only to God, not to the government, or to armed thugs claiming to speak for the government and for God. An American is from the most prosperous land in the history of the world. The root of that prosperity can be found in the Declaration of Independence, which recognizes the God-given right of each man and woman to the pursuit of happiness. An American is generous. Americans have helped out just about every other nation in the world in their time of need. When Afghanistan was overrun by the Soviet army 24 years ago, Americans came with arms and supplies to enable the people to win back their country. As of the morning of September 11, 2001, Americans had given more than any other nation to the poor in Afghanistan. Americans welcome the best—the best products, the best books, the best music, the best food, the best athletes.

["]But they also welcome the least. The national symbol of America, the Statue of Liberty, welcomes your tired and your poor, the wretched refuse of your teeming shores, the homeless, tempest-tossed. These, in fact, are the people who built America. Some of them were working in the Twin Towers the morning of September 11, earning a better life for their families. I've been told that the World Trade Center victims were from at least thirty other countries, cultures, and first languages—including those that aided and abetted the terrorists. So, you can try to kill an American if you must. Hitler did. So did General Tojo, and Stalin, and Mao, and every blood thirsty tyrant in the history of the world. But, in doing so, you would just be killing yourself, because Americans are not a particular people from a particular place. They are the embodiment of the human spirit and freedom. Everyone who holds to that spirit, everywhere, is an American."

A GOOD LETTER TO AN EDITOR

I am going to read you a letter which was written to the editor of an American newspaper which then appeared on the op-ed page.

"AMERICA IS A CHRISTIAN NATION."

"As you walk up the steps to the building which houses the U.S. Supreme Court, you can see near the top of the building a row of the world's law givers and each one is facing one in the middle who is facing forward with a full frontal view . . . it is Moses and he is holding the Ten Commandments!

["]As you enter the Supreme Court courtroom, the two huge oak doors have the Ten Commandments engraved on each lower portion of each door.

["]As you sit inside the courtroom, you can see the wall, right above where the Supreme Court judges sit, a display of the Ten Commandments!

["]There are Bible verses etched in stone all over the Federal Buildings and Monuments in Washington, D.C.

["]James Madison, the fourth president, known as the father of our constitution made the following statement:

"We have staked the whole of all our political institutions upon the capacity of mankind for self-government, upon the capacity of each and all of us to govern ourselves, to control ourselves, to sustain ourselves according to the Ten Commandments of God." James Madison.

["]Patrick Henry, that patriot and founding father of our country said:

"It cannot be emphasized too strongly or too often that this great nation was founded not by religionists but by Christians, not on religions but on the Gospel of Jesus Christ". Patrick Henry.

["]Every session of Congress begins with a prayer led by a paid preacher, whose salary has been paid by the taxpayer since 1777.

["]Fifty-two of the 55 framers of the Constitution were members of the established orthodox churches in the colonies. Thomas Jefferson worried that the Courts would overstep their authority and instead of interpreting the law would begin making law . . . an oligarchy . . . the rule of few over many.

["]The very first Supreme Court Justice, John Jay, said:

"Americans should select and prefer Christians as their rulers." John Jay.

["]Jay was also the first President of the American Bible Society.

["]THE BIG QUESTION?

["]How, then, have we gotten to the point that everything we have done for our first 200 years to recognize and emphasize our religious heritage in this country has now, in one generation, become suddenly wrong and unconstitutional?"

A great and thought-provoking letter.

WHAT CAN I AS ONE PERSON DO TO HELP MY NATION?

We must pray for America's leaders.

I Timothy 2:1–2, "I exhort therefore, that, first of all, supplications, prayers, intercessions, and giving of thanks, be made for all men; 2 For kings, and for all that are in authority; that we may lead a quiet and peaceable life in all godliness and honesty."

We must participate in the political process. As we approach election day each cycle, we must be informed and registered voters.

Matthew 22:17–21, "Tell us therefore, What thinkest thou? Is it lawful to give tribute unto Caesar, or not? 18 But Jesus perceived their wickedness, and said, Why tempt ye me, ye hypocrites? 19 Shew me the tribute money.

And they brought unto him a penny. 20 And he saith unto them, Whose is this image and superscription? 21 They say unto him, Caesar's. Then saith he unto them, Render therefore unto Caesar the things which are Caesar's; and unto God the things that are God's."

USE EVERY PLATFORM TO SPEAK UP FOR AMERICA!!

We can write letters to op-ed pages. We can use every platform God provides us. This past week, I decided to stop the grinches who, every year, attempt to steal Christmas.

This week, I decided to purchase two full-page ads in our local newspaper, the *Lynchburg News & Advance,* with a SPECIAL CHALLENGE.

The ad can be seen at this link: http://www.falwell.com/christmas.pdf

I am calling on pastors, churches and individuals to join Liberty Counsel's "Friend or Foe Christmas Campaign" by purchasing ads in newspapers across the country.

We need to draw a line in the sand and resist bullying tactics by the American Civil Liberties Union, Americans United for the Separation of Church and State, the American Atheists and other leftist organizations that intimidate school and government officials by spreading misinformation about Christmas.

Celebrating Christmas is constitutional!

SOME MUST ANSWER THE CALL TO PUBLIC SERVICE.

I Corinthians 1:26–29, "For ye see your calling, brethren, how that not many wise men after the flesh, not many mighty, not many noble, are called: 27 But God hath chosen the foolish things of the world to confound the wise; and God hath chosen the weak things of the world to confound the things which are mighty; 28 And base things of the world, and things which are despised, hath God chosen, yea, and things which are not, to bring to nought things that are: 29 That no flesh should glory in his presence."

MORAL MAJORITY BORN 26 YEARS AGO.

Francis Schaeffer-LaHaye, Stanley, Kennedy. Reagan- 12 Senators- Religious Right was born.

November 8 crucial. 2–4 Supreme Court justices. FMA is a must. *Roe vs Wade* must be overturned.

IS THERE NOT A CAUSE? IS AMERICA WORTH SAVING?
I Samuel 17:29, "And David said, What have I now done? Is there not a cause?"

Source: "A Good Christian Should Be a Good Citizen." Thomas Road Baptist Church. Available online. URL: http://sermons.trbc.org/20051106.html Accessed July 3, 2006.

5

International Documents

The primary sources in this chapter are divided into three sections: international documents and covenants regarding religious freedom; excerpts from the constitutions or basic laws of specific countries related to religious freedom and the country's state religion, if any; and documents of religious groups. The documents are arranged in chronological order within the first section. In the second section, they are arranged alphabetically by country. In the third section, the religious groups follow the order established in chapter 3. Documents that have been excerpted are identified as such; all others are reproduced in full.

I. INTERNATIONAL DOCUMENTS AND COVENANTS

United Nations Universal Declaration of Human Rights (1948)

The declaration was adopted by the General Assembly of the United Nations on December 10, 1948, at the Palais de Chaillot in Paris. Following its adoption, the General Assembly called upon all member countries to publicize the text of the declaration and "to cause it to be disseminated, displayed, read and expounded principally in schools and other educational institutions, without distinction based on the political status of countries or territories." Eleanor Roosevelt, who was one of the drafters of the document, referred to the declaration as "a Magna Carta for all mankind."

Preamble

Whereas recognition of the inherent dignity and of the equal and inalienable rights of all members of the human family is the foundation of freedom, justice and peace in the world,

Whereas disregard and contempt for human rights have resulted in barbarous acts which have outraged the conscience of mankind, and the advent of a world in which human beings shall enjoy freedom of speech and belief and freedom from fear and want has been proclaimed as the highest aspiration of the common people,

Whereas it is essential, if man is not to be compelled to have recourse, as a last resort, to rebellion against tyranny and oppression, that human rights should be protected by the rule of law,

Whereas it is essential to promote the development of friendly relations between nations,

Whereas the peoples of the United Nations have in the Charter reaffirmed their faith in fundamental human rights, in the dignity and worth of the human person and in the equal rights of men and women and have determined to promote social progress and better standards of life in larger freedom,

Whereas Member States have pledged themselves to achieve, in cooperation with the United Nations, the promotion of universal respect for and observance of human rights and fundamental freedoms,

Whereas a common understanding of these rights and freedoms is of the greatest importance for the full realization of this pledge,

Now, therefore,

The General Assembly,

Proclaims this Universal Declaration of Human Rights as a common standard of achievement for all peoples and all nations, to the end that every individual and every organ of society, keeping this Declaration constantly in mind, shall strive by teaching and education to promote respect for these rights and freedoms and by progressive measures, national and international, to secure their universal and effective recognition and observance, both among the peoples of Member States themselves and among the peoples of territories under their jurisdiction.

Article 1

All human beings are born free and equal in dignity and rights. They are endowed with reason and conscience and should act towards one another in a spirit of brotherhood.

Article 2

Everyone is entitled to all the rights and freedoms set forth in this Declaration, without distinction of any kind, such as race, colour, sex, language, religion, political or other opinion, national or social origin, property, birth or other status. Furthermore, no distinction shall be made on the basis of the political, jurisdictional or international status of the country or territory to which a person belongs, whether it be independent, trust, non-self-governing or under any other limitation of sovereignty.

Article 3

Everyone has the right to life, liberty and security of person.

Article 4

No one shall be held in slavery or servitude; slavery and the slave trade shall be prohibited in all their forms.

Article 5

No one shall be subjected to torture or to cruel, inhuman or degrading treatment or punishment.

Article 6

Everyone has the right to recognition everywhere as a person before the law.

Article 7

All are equal before the law and are entitled without any discrimination to equal protection of the law. All are entitled to equal protection against any discrimination in violation of this Declaration and against any incitement to such discrimination.

Article 8

Everyone has the right to an effective remedy by the competent national tribunals for acts violating the fundamental rights granted him by the constitution or by law.

Article 9

No one shall be subjected to arbitrary arrest, detention or exile.

Article 10

Everyone is entitled in full equality to a fair and public hearing by an independent and impartial tribunal, in the determination of his rights and obligations and of any criminal charge against him.

Article 11

1. Everyone charged with a penal offence has the right to be presumed innocent until proved guilty according to law in a public trial at which he has had all the guarantees necessary for his defence.

2. No one shall be held guilty of any penal offence on account of any act or omission which did not constitute a penal offence, under national or international law, at the time when it was committed. Nor shall a heavier penalty be imposed than the one that was applicable at the time the penal offence was committed.

Article 12

No one shall be subjected to arbitrary interference with his privacy, family, home or correspondence, nor to attacks upon his honour and reputation. Everyone has the right to the protection of the law against such interference or attacks.

Article 13

1. Everyone has the right to freedom of movement and residence within the borders of each state.

2. Everyone has the right to leave any country, including his own, and to return to his country.

Article 14

1. Everyone has the right to seek and to enjoy in other countries asylum from persecution.

2. This right may not be invoked in the case of prosecutions genuinely arising from non-political crimes or from acts contrary to the purposes and principles of the United Nations.

Article 15

1. Everyone has the right to a nationality.

2. No one shall be arbitrarily deprived of his nationality nor denied the right to change his nationality.

Article 16

1. Men and women of full age, without any limitation due to race, nationality or religion, have the right to marry and to found a family. They are entitled to equal rights as to marriage, during marriage and at its dissolution.

2. Marriage shall be entered into only with the free and full consent of the intending spouses.

3. The family is the natural and fundamental group unit of society and is entitled to protection by society and the State.

Article 17

1. Everyone has the right to own property alone as well as in association with others.

2. No one shall be arbitrarily deprived of his property.

Article 18

Everyone has the right to freedom of thought, conscience and religion; this right includes freedom to change his religion or belief, and freedom, either alone or in community with others and in public or private, to manifest his religion or belief in teaching, practice, worship and observance.

Article 19

Everyone has the right to freedom of opinion and expression; this right includes freedom to hold opinions without interference and to seek, receive and impart information and ideas through any media and regardless of frontiers.

Article 20

1. Everyone has the right to freedom of peaceful assembly and association.

2. No one may be compelled to belong to an association.

Article 21

1. Everyone has the right to take part in the government of his country, directly or through freely chosen representatives.

2. Everyone has the right of equal access to public service in his country.

3. The will of the people shall be the basis of the authority of government; this will shall be expressed in periodic and genuine elections which shall be

by universal and equal suffrage and shall be held by secret vote or by equivalent free voting procedures.

Article 22

Everyone, as a member of society, has the right to social security and is entitled to realization, through national effort and international cooperation and in accordance with the organization and resources of each State, of the economic, social and cultural rights indispensable for his dignity and the free development of his personality.

Article 23

1. Everyone has the right to work, to free choice of employment, to just and favourable conditions of work and to protection against unemployment.

2. Everyone, without any discrimination, has the right to equal pay for equal work.

3. Everyone who works has the right to just and favourable remuneration ensuring for himself and his family an existence worthy of human dignity, and supplemented, if necessary, by other means of social protection.

4. Everyone has the right to form and to join trade unions for the protection of his interests.

Article 24

Everyone has the right to rest and leisure, including reasonable limitation of working hours and periodic holidays with pay.

Article 25

1. Everyone has the right to a standard of living adequate for the health and well-being of himself and of his family, including food, clothing, housing and medical care and necessary social services, and the right to security in the event of unemployment, sickness, disability, widowhood, old age or other lack of livelihood in circumstances beyond his control.

2. Motherhood and childhood are entitled to special care and assistance. All children, whether born in or out of wedlock, shall enjoy the same social protection.

Article 26

1. Everyone has the right to education. Education shall be free, at least in the elementary and fundamental stages. Elementary education shall be compulsory. Technical and professional education shall be made generally available and higher education shall be equally accessible to all on the basis of merit.

2. Education shall be directed to the full development of the human personality and to the strengthening of respect for human rights and fundamental freedoms. It shall promote understanding, tolerance and friendship among all nations, racial or religious groups, and shall further the activities of the United Nations for the maintenance of peace.

3. Parents have a prior right to choose the kind of education that shall be given to their children.

Article 27

1. Everyone has the right freely to participate in the cultural life of the community, to enjoy the arts and to share in scientific advancement and its benefits.

2. Everyone has the right to the protection of the moral and material interests resulting from any scientific, literary or artistic production of which he is the author.

Article 28

Everyone is entitled to a social and international order in which the rights and freedoms set forth in this Declaration can be fully realized.

Article 29

1. Everyone has duties to the community in which alone the free and full development of his personality is possible.

2. In the exercise of his rights and freedoms, everyone shall be subject only to such limitations as are determined by law solely for the purpose of securing due recognition and respect for the rights and freedoms of others and of meeting the just requirements of morality, public order and the general welfare in a democratic society.

3. These rights and freedoms may in no case be exercised contrary to the purposes and principles of the United Nations.

Article 30

Nothing in this Declaration may be interpreted as implying for any State, group or person any right to engage in any activity or to perform any act aimed at the destruction of any of the rights and freedoms set forth herein.

Source: "Universal Declaration of Human Rights." Office of the High Commissioner for Human Rights. Available online. URL: http://www.unhchr.ch/udhr/lang/eng.htm. Accessed July 4, 2006.

United Nations International Covenant on Civil and Political Rights (opened for signature 1966; entered into force 1976) (excerpts)

The International Covenant on Civil and Political Rights (ICCPR) is a United Nations treaty based on the Universal Declaration of Human Rights of 1948. The ICCPR is monitored by the Human Rights Committee, composed of 18 experts who meet three times per year to consider periodic reports submitted by member states regarding compliance with the treaty. The 18 members of the Human Rights Committee are elected by member states but do not represent any states. The United States ratified the ICCPR in 1992 with a number of reservations. While the treaty is binding on the United States as a matter of international law, it does not affect domestic law.

Preamble

The States Parties to the present Covenant,

Considering that, in accordance with the principles proclaimed in the Charter of the United Nations, recognition of the inherent dignity and of the equal and inalienable rights of all members of the human family is the foundation of freedom, justice and peace in the world,

Recognizing that these rights derive from the inherent dignity of the human person,

Recognizing that, in accordance with the Universal Declaration of Human Rights, the ideal of free human beings enjoying civil and political freedom and freedom from fear and want can only be achieved if conditions are created whereby everyone may enjoy his civil and political rights, as well as his economic, social and cultural rights,

Considering the obligation of States under the Charter of the United Nations to promote universal respect for, and observance of, human rights and freedoms,

Realizing that the individual, having duties to other individuals and to the community to which he belongs, is under a responsibility to strive for the promotion and observance of the rights recognized in the present Covenant,

Agree upon the following articles:

Article 1

1. All peoples have the right of self-determination. By virtue of that right they freely determine their political status and freely pursue their economic, social and cultural development. . . .

Article 2

1. Each State Party to the present Covenant undertakes to respect and to ensure to all individuals within its territory and subject to its jurisdiction the rights recognized in the present Covenant, without distinction of any kind, such as race, colour, sex, language, religion, political or other opinion, national or social origin, property, birth or other status. . . .

3. Each State Party to the present Covenant undertakes:

(a) To ensure that any person whose rights or freedoms as herein recognized are violated shall have an effective remedy, notwithstanding that the violation has been committed by persons acting in an official capacity;

(b) To ensure that any person claiming such a remedy shall have his right thereto determined by competent judicial, administrative or legislative authorities, or by any other competent authority provided for by the legal system of the State, and to develop the possibilities of judicial remedy;

(c) To ensure that the competent authorities shall enforce such remedies when granted.

Article 3

The States Parties to the present Covenant undertake to ensure the equal right of men and women to the enjoyment of all civil and political rights set forth in the present Covenant. . . .

Article 18

1. Everyone shall have the right to freedom of thought, conscience and religion. This right shall include freedom to have or to adopt a religion or belief of his choice, and freedom, either individually or in community with others and in public or private, to manifest his religion or belief in worship, observance, practice and teaching.

2. No one shall be subject to coercion which would impair his freedom to have or to adopt a religion or belief of his choice.

3. Freedom to manifest one's religion or beliefs may be subject only to such limitations as are prescribed by law and are necessary to protect public safety, order, health, or morals or the fundamental rights and freedoms of others.

4. The States Parties to the present Covenant undertake to have respect for the liberty of parents and, when applicable, legal guardians to ensure the religious and moral education of their children in conformity with their own convictions.

Article 19

1. Everyone shall have the right to hold opinions without interference.

2. Everyone shall have the right to freedom of expression; this right shall include freedom to seek, receive and impart information and ideas of all kinds, regardless of frontiers, either orally, in writing or in print, in the form of art, or through any other media of his choice.

3. The exercise of the rights provided for in paragraph 2 of this article carries with it special duties and responsibilities. It may therefore be subject to certain restrictions, but these shall only be such as are provided by law and are necessary:

(a) For respect of the rights or reputations of others;

(b) For the protection of national security or of public order, or of public health or morals.

Article 20

1. Any propaganda for war shall be prohibited by law.

2. Any advocacy of national, racial or religious hatred that constitutes incitement to discrimination, hostility or violence shall be prohibited by law.

Article 21

The right of peaceful assembly shall be recognized. No restrictions may be placed on the exercise of this right other than those imposed in conformity with the law and which are necessary in a democratic society in the interests of national security or public safety, public order, the protection of public health or morals or the protection of the rights and freedoms of others. . . .

Article 26

All persons are equal before the law and are entitled without any discrimination to the equal protection of the law. In this respect, the law shall prohibit any discrimination and guarantee to all persons equal and effective protection against discrimination on any ground such as race, colour, sex, language, religion, political or other opinion, national or social origin, property, birth or other status.

Article 27

In those States in which ethnic, religious or linguistic minorities exist, persons belonging to such minorities shall not be denied the right, in community with the other members of their group, to enjoy their own culture, to profess and practise their own religion, or to use their own language. . . .

Source: "International Covenant on Civil and Political Rights." Office of the United Nations High Commissioner for Human Rights. Available online. URL: http://www.ohchr.org/english/law/ccpr.htm. Accessed July 4, 2006.

United Nations Declaration on the Elimination of All Forms of Intolerance and of Discrimination Based on Religion or Belief (1981)

The eight articles of the 1981 declaration are intended to protect the rights of children and of groups of persons (that is, religious communities) as well as the human rights of individuals guaranteed by the 1948 declaration. Article 3 links this declaration to the ICCPR of 1976. Some observers have noted that this 1981 document does not address several sensitive issues, including freedom of missionary activity, the right of conscientious objection to military service, the status of women, and the right to change one's religious affiliation.

The General Assembly,

Considering that one of the basic principles of the Charter of the United Nations is that of the dignity and equality inherent in all human beings, and that all Member States have pledged themselves to take joint and separate action in co-operation with the Organization to promote and encourage universal respect for and observance of human rights and fundamental freedoms for all, without distinction as to race, sex, language or religion,

Considering that the Universal Declaration of Human Rights and the International Covenants on Human Rights proclaim the principles of nondiscrimination and equality before the law and the right to freedom of thought, conscience, religion and belief,

Considering that the disregard and infringement of human rights and fundamental freedoms, in particular of the right to freedom of thought, conscience, religion or whatever belief, have brought, directly or indirectly, wars and great suffering to mankind, especially where they serve as a means of foreign interference in the internal affairs of other States and amount to kindling hatred between peoples and nations,

Considering that religion or belief, for anyone who professes either, is one of the fundamental elements in his conception of life and that freedom of religion or belief should be fully respected and guaranteed,

Considering that it is essential to promote understanding, tolerance and respect in matters relating to freedom of religion and belief and to ensure that the use of religion or belief for ends inconsistent with the Charter of the United Nations, other relevant instruments of the United Nations and the purposes and principles of the present Declaration is inadmissible,

Convinced that freedom of religion and belief should also contribute to the attainment of the goals of world peace, social justice and friendship among peoples and to the elimination of ideologies or practices of colonialism and racial discrimination,

Noting with satisfaction the adoption of several, and the coming into force of some, conventions, under the aegis of the United Nations and of the specialized agencies, for the elimination of various forms of discrimination,

Concerned by manifestations of intolerance and by the existence of discrimination in matters of religion or belief still in evidence in some areas of the world,

Resolved to adopt all necessary measures for the speedy elimination of such intolerance in all its forms and manifestations and to prevent and combat discrimination on the ground of religion or belief,

Proclaims this Declaration on the Elimination of All Forms of Intolerance and of Discrimination Based on Religion or Belief:

Article 1

1. Everyone shall have the right to freedom of thought, conscience and religion. This right shall include freedom to have a religion or whatever belief of his choice, and freedom, either individually or in community with others and in public or private, to manifest his religion or belief in worship, observance, practice and teaching.

2. No one shall be subject to coercion which would impair his freedom to have a religion or belief of his choice.

3. Freedom to manifest one's religion or belief may be subject only to such limitations as are prescribed by law and are necessary to protect public safety, order, health or morals or the fundamental rights and freedoms of others.

Article 2

1. No one shall be subject to discrimination by any State, institution, group of persons, or person on the grounds of religion or other belief.

2. For the purposes of the present Declaration, the expression "intolerance and discrimination based on religion or belief" means any distinction, exclusion, restriction or preference based on religion or belief and having as its purpose or as its effect nullification or impairment of the recognition, enjoyment or exercise of human rights and fundamental freedoms on an equal basis.

Article 3

Discrimination between human being on the grounds of religion or belief constitutes an affront to human dignity and a disavowal of the principles of the Charter of the United Nations, and shall be condemned as a violation of the human rights and fundamental freedoms proclaimed in the Universal Declaration of Human Rights and enunciated in detail in the International Covenants on Human Rights, and as an obstacle to friendly and peaceful relations between nations.

Article 4

1. All States shall take effective measures to prevent and eliminate discrimination on the grounds of religion or belief in the recognition, exercise and enjoyment of human rights and fundamental freedoms in all fields of civil, economic, political, social and cultural life.

2. All States shall make all efforts to enact or rescind legislation where necessary to prohibit any such discrimination, and to take all appropriate measures to combat intolerance on the grounds of religion or other beliefs in this matter.

Article 5

1. The parents or, as the case may be, the legal guardians of the child have the right to organize the life within the family in accordance with their religion or belief and bearing in mind the moral education in which they believe the child should be brought up.

2. Every child shall enjoy the right to have access to education in the matter of religion or belief in accordance with the wishes of his parents or, as the case may be, legal guardians, and shall not be compelled to receive teaching on religion or belief against the wishes of his parents or legal guardians, the best interests of the child being the guiding principle.

3. The child shall be protected from any form of discrimination on the ground of religion or belief. He shall be brought up in a spirit of understanding, tolerance, friendship among peoples, peace and universal brotherhood,

respect for freedom of religion or belief of others, and in full consciousness that his energy and talents should be devoted to the service of his fellow men.

4. In the case of a child who is not under the care either of his parents or of legal guardians, due account shall be taken of their expressed wishes or of any other proof of their wishes in the matter of religion or belief, the best interests of the child being the guiding principle.

5. Practices of a religion or belief in which a child is brought up must not be injurious to his physical or mental health or to his full development, taking into account article 1, paragraph 3, of the present Declaration.

Article 6

In accordance with article 1 of the present Declaration, and subject to the provisions of article 1, paragraph 3, the right to freedom of thought, conscience, religion or belief shall include, *inter alia,* the following freedoms:

(a) To worship or assemble in connection with a religion or belief, and to establish and maintain places for these purposes;

(b) To establish and maintain appropriate charitable or humanitarian institutions;

(c) To make, acquire and use to an adequate extent the necessary articles and materials related to the rites or customs of a religion or belief;

(d) To write, issue and disseminate relevant publications in these areas;

(e) To teach a religion or belief in places suitable for these purposes;

(f) To solicit and receive voluntary financial and other contributions from individuals and institutions;

(g) To train, appoint, elect or designate by succession appropriate leaders called for by the requirements and standards of any religion or belief;

(h) To observe days of rest and to celebrate holidays and ceremonies in accordance with the precepts of one's religion or belief;

(i) To establish and maintain communications with individuals and communities in matters of religion and belief at the national and international levels.

Article 7

The rights and freedoms set forth in the present Declaration shall be accorded in national legislation in such a manner that everyone shall be able to avail himself of such rights and freedoms in practice.

Article 8

Nothing in the present Declaration shall be construed as restricting or derogating from any right defined in the Universal Declaration of Human Rights and the International Covenants on Human Rights.

Source: "Declaration on the Elimination of All Forms of Intolerance and Discrimination Based on Religion and Belief." Office of the United Nations High Commissioner for Human Rights. Available online. URL: http://www.ohchr.org/english/law/religion.htm. Accessed July 4, 2006.

II. CONSTITUTIONAL DOCUMENTS AND BASIC LAWS OF SPECIFIC COUNTRIES

Egypt

Constitution (following 1980 and 2005 amendments) (excerpts)

Egypt has had six different constitutions or provisional constitutions in the period from 1923 to the early 2000s. The present constitution was first adopted in 1971 under President Anwar Sadat and amended in 1980 and 2005. The amendments largely concerned the independence of the Egyptian judiciary and the manner of electing the president.

Constitutional Proclamation

We, the people of Egypt, who have been toiling on this great land since the dawn of history and the beginning of civilization, we, the people working in Egypt's villages, cities, plants, centres of education, industry and in any field of work which contributes to create life on its soil or which plays a part in the honour of defending this land,

We, the people who believe in our immortal and spiritual heritage, and who are confident in our profound faith, and cherish the honour of man and of humanity at large,

We, the people, who in addition to preserving the legacy of history, bear the responsibility of great present and future objectives whose seeds are embedded in the long and arduous struggle, with which the banners of liberty, socialism and unity along the path of the great march of the Arab Nation,

We, the Egyptian people, in the name of God and with His assistance, pledge indefinitely and unconditionally to exert every effort to realise:

Peace to our world

Being determined that peace can only be based on justice and that political and social progress of all peoples can only be realized through the freedom and independent will of these peoples, and that any civilization is not worthy of its name unless it is free from exploitation whatever its form.

Union

The hope of our Arab Nation, being convinced that Arab Unity is a call of history and future, and an inevitable destiny which can only materialize through an Arab Nation capable of warding off any threat whatever may be the source or the pretexts justifying it.

The constant development of life in our nation. . . .

Freedom for the humanity of the Egyptian man. . . .

We the working masses of the people of Egypt—out of determination, confidence and faith in all our national and international responsibilities, and in acknowledgment of God's right and His messages, and in recognition of the right of our nation, as well as of the principle and responsibility of mankind, and in the name of God and with His assistance, declare on the Eleventh of September 1971 that we accept and grant ourselves this Constitution, asserting our firm determination to defend and protect it, assuring our respect for it.

Chapter one: The State

Art. 1: The Arab Republic of Egypt is a Socialist Democratic State based on the alliance of the working forces of the people. The Egyptian people are part of the Arab Nation and work for the realization of its comprehensive unity.

Art. 2: Islam is the Religion of the State. Arabic is its official language, and the principal source of legislation is Islamic jurisprudence. . . .

Chapter two: Basic Constituents of the Society

. . . **Art. 12:** Society shall be committed to safeguarding and protecting morals, promoting the genuine Egyptian traditions and abiding by the high standards of religious education, moral and national values, historical heritage of the people, scientific facts, socialist conduct and public manners within the limits of the law. The State is committed to abiding by these principles and promoting them. . . .

Art. 18: Education is a right guaranteed by the State. It is obligatory in the primary stage. The State shall work to extend obligation to other stages. The State shall supervise all branches of education and guarantee the independence of universities and scientific research centers, with a view to linking all this with the requirements of society and production.

Art. 19: Religious education shall be a principal subject in the courses of general education. . . .

Chapter three: Public Freedoms, Rights and Duties

Art. 40: All citizens are equal before the law. They have equal public rights and duties without discrimination due to race, ethnic origin, language, religion or creed. . . .

Art. 46: The State shall guarantee the freedom of belief and the freedom of practising religious rights.

Art. 47: Freedom of opinion shall be guaranteed. Every individual shall have the right to express his opinion and to publicise it verbally, in writing, by photography or by other means of expression within the limits of the law. Self criticism and constructive criticism shall guarantee the safety of the national structure. . . .

Source: "Egypt Constitution: Index." Government of Egypt. Available online. URL: http://www.egypt.gov.eg/english/laws/constitution/index.asp. Accessed July 4, 2006.

India

Constitution (1949) (excerpt)

The constitution of India, which was adopted on November 26, 1949, and amended most recently on June 6, 2004, defines the country as "a sovereign socialist secular democratic republic." Article 25 establishes the right to religious freedom for all citizens, while Article 26 guarantees the freedom of "every religious denomination or section thereof" to manage its own affairs and property in matters of religion.

PREAMBLE

WE, THE PEOPLE OF INDIA, having solemnly resolved to constitute India into a SOVEREIGN SOCIALIST SECULAR DEMOCRATIC REPUBLIC and to secure to all its citizens:

JUSTICE, social, economic and political;

LIBERTY of thought, expression, belief, faith and worship;

EQUALITY of status and of opportunity;

and to promote among them all

FRATERNITY assuring the dignity of the individual and the unity and integrity of the Nation;

IN OUR CONSTITUENT ASSEMBLY this twenty-sixth day of November, 1949, do HEREBY ADOPT, ENACT AND GIVE TO OURSELVES THIS CONSTITUTION. . . .

PART III: FUNDAMENTAL RIGHTS

. . . Right to Equality. . .

15. Prohibition of discrimination on grounds of religion, race, caste, sex or place of birth.—(1) The State shall not discriminate against any citizen on grounds only of religion, race, caste, sex, place of birth or any of them.

(2) No citizen shall, on grounds only of religion, race, caste, sex, place of birth or any of them, be subject to any disability, liability, restriction or condition with regard to

(a) access to shops, public restaurants, hotels and places of public entertainment; or

(b) the use of wells, tanks, bathing ghats, roads and places of public resort maintained wholly or partly out of State funds or dedicated to the use of the general public.

(3) Nothing in this article shall prevent the State from making any special provision for women and children.

(4) Nothing in this article or in clause (2) of article 29 shall prevent the State from making any special provision for the advancement of any socially and educationally backward classes of citizens or for the Scheduled Castes and the Scheduled Tribes. . . .

Right to Freedom of Religion

25. Freedom of conscience and free profession, practice and propagation of religion.—(1) Subject to public order, morality and health and to the other provisions of this Part, all persons are equally entitled to freedom of conscience and the right freely to profess, practise and propagate religion.

(2) Nothing in this article shall affect the operation of any existing law or prevent the State from making any law—

(a) regulating or restricting any economic, financial, political or other secular activity which may be associated with religious practice;

(b) providing for social welfare and reform or the throwing open of Hindu religious institutions of a public character to all classes and sections of Hindus.

Explanation I. The wearing and carrying of kirpans shall be deemed to be included in the profession of the Sikh religion.

Explanation II. In sub-clause (b) of clause (2), the reference to Hindus shall be construed as including a reference to persons professing the Sikh, Jaina or Buddhist religion, and the reference to Hindu religious institutions shall be construed accordingly.

26. Freedom to manage religious affairs—Subject to public order, morality and health, every religious denomination or any section thereof shall have the right—

(a) to establish and maintain institutions for religious and charitable purposes;

(b) to manage its own affairs in matters of religion;

(c) to own and acquire movable and immovable property; and

(d) to administer such property in accordance with law.

27. Freedom as to payment of taxes for promotion of any particular religion—No person shall be compelled to pay any taxes, the proceeds of which are specifically appropriated in payment of expenses for the promotion or maintenance of any particular religion or religious denomination.

28. Freedom as to attendance at religious instruction or religious worship in certain educational institutions—(1) No religious instruction shall be provided in any educational institution wholly maintained out of State funds.

(2) Nothing in clause (1) shall apply to an educational institution which is administered by the State but has been established under any endowment or trust which requires that religious instruction shall be imparted in such institution.

(3) No person attending any educational institution recognised by the State or receiving aid out of State funds shall be required to take part in any religious instruction that may be imparted in such institution or to attend any religious worship that may be conducted in such institution or in any premises attached thereto unless such person or, if such person is a minor, his guardian has given his consent thereto. . . .

Source: "Constitution of India." Government of India. Available online. URL: http://india.gov.in/govt/constitutions_india_bak.php#eng. Accessed June 27, 2006.

Israel

Declaration of Independence (1948)

Israel is unusual in not having (as of the early 2000s) a complete written constitution but rather a set of constitutional documents that are a "work in progress." The Declaration of the Establishment of the State of Israel (May

14, 1948) mentions a draft constitution to be prepared by a committee and adopted in October 1948. By early 1949, however, the constitutional assembly was unable to agree on a written constitution, largely as a result of the division between secular and religious Israelis. It was feared that a complete written constitution would make the split worse because any such document would have to define the relationship between religion and the state in very specific terms. Some observers think that the lack of a full constitution made it easier for such fundamentalist groups as Gush Emunim to gain the power that they did in the 1970s and 1980s. Israel does, however, have a set of so-called Basic Laws that are considered the "building blocks" of a constitution, adopted and modified between 1958 and 2001. These Basic Laws deal with such matters as the Knesset, the army, the judiciary, and elections. (They are available online in English at http://www.oefre.unibe.ch/law/icl/is__indx.html.) In addition to the Basic Laws, the Knesset has also passed ordinary laws. The laws related most closely to religion are the Law of Return (1950) and the Protection of Holy Places Law (1967), which follow this declaration.

ERETZ-ISRAEL (the Land of Israel) was the birthplace of the Jewish people. Here their spiritual, religious and political identity was shaped. Here they first attained to statehood, created cultural values of national and universal significance and gave to the world the eternal Book of Books.

After being forcibly exiled from their land, the people remained faithful to it throughout their Dispersion and never ceased to pray and hope for their return to it and for the restoration in it of their political freedom.

Impelled by this historic and traditional attachment, Jews strove in every successive generation to re-establish themselves in their ancient homeland. In recent decades they returned in their masses. Pioneers, ma'pilim (immigrants coming to Eretz-Israel in defiance of restrictive legislation) and defenders, they made deserts bloom, revived the Hebrew language, built villages and towns, and created a thriving community controlling its own economy and culture, loving peace but knowing how to defend itself, bringing the blessings of progress to all the country's inhabitants, and aspiring towards independent nationhood.

In the year 5657 (1897), at the summons of the spiritual father of the Jewish State, Theodore Herzl, the First Zionist Congress convened and proclaimed the right of the Jewish people to national rebirth in its own country. This right was recognized in the Balfour Declaration of the 2nd November, 1917, and reaffirmed in the Mandate of the League of Nations which, in particular, gave international sanction to the historic connection between the Jewish people and Eretz-Israel and to the right of the Jewish people to rebuild its National Home.

The catastrophe which recently befell the Jewish people—the massacre of millions of Jews in Europe—was another clear demonstration of the urgency of solving the problem of its homelessness by re-establishing in Eretz-Israel the Jewish State, which would open the gates of the homeland wide to every Jew and confer upon the Jewish people the status of a fully privileged member of the comity of nations.

Survivors of the Nazi holocaust in Europe, as well as Jews from other parts of the world, continued to migrate to Eretz-Israel, undaunted by difficulties, restrictions and dangers, and never ceased to assert their right to a life of dignity, freedom and honest toil in their national homeland. In the Second World War, the Jewish community of this country contributed its full share to the struggle of the freedom- and peace-loving nations against the forces of Nazi wickedness and, by the blood of its soldiers and its war effort, gained the right to be reckoned among the peoples who founded the United Nations.

On the 29th November, 1947, the United Nations General Assembly passed a resolution calling for the establishment of a Jewish State in Eretz-Israel; the General Assembly required the inhabitants of Eretz-Israel to take such steps as were necessary on their part for the implementation of that resolution. This recognition by the United Nations of the right of the Jewish people to establish their State is irrevocable. This right is the natural right of the Jewish people to be masters of their own fate, like all other nations, in their own sovereign State.

ACCORDINGLY WE, MEMBERS OF THE PEOPLE'S COUNCIL, REPRESENTATIVES OF THE JEWISH COMMUNITY OF ERETZ-ISRAEL AND OF THE ZIONIST MOVEMENT, ARE HERE ASSEMBLED ON THE DAY OF THE TERMINATION OF THE BRITISH MANDATE OVER ERETZ-ISRAEL AND, BY VIRTUE OF OUR NATURAL AND HISTORIC RIGHT AND ON THE STRENGTH OF THE RESOLUTION OF THE UNITED NATIONS GENERAL ASSEMBLY, HEREBY DECLARE THE ESTABLISHMENT OF A JEWISH STATE IN ERETZ-ISRAEL, TO BE KNOWN AS THE STATE OF ISRAEL.

WE DECLARE that, with effect from the moment of the termination of the Mandate being tonight, the eve of Sabbath, the 6th Iyar, 5708 (15th May, 1948), until the establishment of the elected, regular authorities of the State in accordance with the Constitution which shall be adopted by the Elected Constituent Assembly not later than the 1st October 1948, the People's Council shall act as a Provisional Council of State, and its executive organ, the People's Administration, shall be the Provisional Government of the Jewish State, to be called "Israel."

THE STATE OF ISRAEL will be open for Jewish immigration and for the Ingathering of the Exiles; it will foster the development of the country for the benefit of all its inhabitants; it will be based on freedom, justice and peace as envisaged by the prophets of Israel; it will ensure complete equality of social and political rights to all its inhabitants irrespective of religion, race or sex; it will guarantee freedom of religion, conscience, language, education and culture; it will safeguard the Holy Places of all religions; and it will be faithful to the principles of the Charter of the United Nations.

THE STATE OF ISRAEL is prepared to cooperate with the agencies and representatives of the United Nations in implementing the resolution of the General Assembly of the 29th November, 1947, and will take steps to bring about the economic union of the whole of Eretz-Israel.

WE APPEAL to the United Nations to assist the Jewish people in the building-up of its State and to receive the State of Israel into the comity of nations.

WE APPEAL—in the very midst of the onslaught launched against us now for months—to the Arab inhabitants of the State of Israel to preserve peace and participate in the upbuilding of the State on the basis of full and equal citizenship and due representation in all its provisional and permanent institutions.

WE EXTEND our hand to all neighboring states and their peoples in an offer of peace and good neighborliness, and appeal to them to establish bonds of cooperation and mutual help with the sovereign Jewish people settled in its own land. The State of Israel is prepared to do its share in a common effort for the advancement of the entire Middle East.

WE APPEAL to the Jewish people throughout the Diaspora to rally round the Jews of Eretz-Israel in the tasks of immigration and upbuilding and to stand by them in the great struggle for the realization of the age-old dream—the redemption of Israel.

PLACING OUR TRUST IN THE ALMIGHTY, WE AFFIX OUR SIGNATURES TO THIS PROCLAMATION AT THIS SESSION OF THE PROVISIONAL COUNCIL OF STATE, ON THE SOIL OF THE HOMELAND, IN THE CITY OF TEL-AVIV, ON THIS SABBATH EVE, THE 5TH DAY OF IYAR, 5708 (14TH MAY, 1948).

Source: "The Declaration of the Establishment of the State of Israel." Jewish Virtual Library. Available online. URL: http://www.jewishvirtuallibrary.org/jsource/History/Dec_of_Indep.html. Accessed June 27, 2006.

Law of Return (1950)

The Law of Return was passed by the Knesset in 1950, which was only five years after the end of the Holocaust, in order to provide a refuge for Jews seeking protection from anti-Semitic persecution anywhere in the world. The law was amended in 1970 by the addition of the following statement: "The rights of a Jew under this Law and the rights of an oleh under the Nationality Law . . . are also vested in a child and a grandchild of a Jew, the spouse of a Jew, the spouse of a child of a Jew and the spouse of a grandchild of a Jew." In other words, persons within those degrees of relationship to a Jew, and who would have been considered Jews under the Nuremberg Laws, may emigrate to Israel even if they do not regard themselves as Jews. Some observers regard the 1970 amendment as Israel's attempt to offset the rapid demographic growth of the Palestinian population.

1. Every Jew has the right to come to this country as an oleh [a Jew immigrating to Israel].

2. (a) Aliyah shall be by oleh's visa.

(b) An oleh's visa shall be granted to every Jew who has expressed his desire to settle in Israel, unless the Minister of Immigration is satisfied that the applicant:

(1) is engaged in an activity directed against the Jewish people; or

(2) is likely to endanger public health or the security of the State.

3. (a) A Jew who has come to Israel and subsequent to his arrival has expressed his desire to settle in Israel may, while still in Israel, receive an oleh's certificate.

(b) The restrictions specified in section 2(b) shall apply also to the grant of an oleh's certificate, but a person shall not be regarded as endangering public health on account of an illness contracted after his arrival in Israel.

4. Every Jew who has immigrated into this country before the coming into force of this Law, and every Jew who was born in this country, whether before or after the coming into force of this Law, shall be deemed to be a person who has come to this country as an oleh under this Law.

5. The Minister of Immigration is charged with the implementation of this Law and may make regulations as to any matter relating to such implementation and also as to the grant of oleh's visas and oleh's certificates to minors up to the age of 18 years.

Source: "The Law of Return 5710 (1950)." The Knesset English. Available online. URL: http://www.knesset.gov.il/laws/special/eng/return.htm. Accessed July 4, 2006.

Protection of Holy Places Law (1967)

The Law of Protection of the Holy Places was passed by the Knesset in 1967 to guarantee equal freedom of access to places considered holy by Jews,

Christians, and Muslims and to safeguard such places from desecration or other harm. Fundamentalist Jews regard the limitations placed on their visits to the Temple Mount by the Muslim Waqf as a violation of this law and have repeatedly petitioned Israel's High Court of Justice for permission to pray openly and wear their traditional prayer shawls on the Temple Mount.

1. The Holy Places shall be protected from desecration and any other violation and from anything likely to violate the freedom of access of the members of the different religions to the places sacred to them or their feelings with regard to those places.

2.

a. Whosoever desecrates or otherwise violates a Holy Place shall be liable to imprisonment for a term of seven years.

b. Whosoever does anything likely to violate the freedom of access of the members of the different religions to the places sacred to them or their feelings with regard to those places shall be liable to imprisonment for a term of five years.

3. This Law shall add to, and not derogate from, any other law.

4. The Minister of Religious Affairs is charged with the implementation of this Law, and he may, after consultation with, or upon the proposal of, representatives of the religions concerned and with the consent of the Minister of Justice make regulations as to any matter relating to such implementation.

5. This Law shall come into force on the date of its adoption by the Knesset.

Source: "Protection of Holy Places 5727 (1967)." The Knesset English. Available online. URL: http://www.knesset.gov.il/laws/special/eng/HolyPlaces.htm. Accessed July 4, 2006.

Pakistan

Constitution (1973, amended 2004) (excerpts)

Pakistan has had two constitutions since it became independent; the documents were drafted and adopted in 1956 and 1973, respectively. The 1956 constitution declared Pakistan to be an Islamic republic. The 1973 constitution, was promulgated on August 14, 1973, the 26th anniversary of the country's independence. It has been modified by a set of 17 amendments.

Preamble

Whereas sovereignty over the entire Universe belongs to Almighty Allah alone, and the authority to be exercised by the people of Pakistan within the limits prescribed by Him is a sacred trust;

And whereas it is the will of the people of Pakistan to establish an order:

Wherein the State shall exercise its powers and authority through the chosen representatives of the people;

Wherein the principles of democracy, freedom, equality, tolerance and social justice, as enunciated by Islam, shall be fully observed;

Wherein the Muslims shall be enabled to order their lives in the individual and collective spheres in accordance with the teachings and requirements of Islam as set out in the Holy Quran and Sunnah;

Wherein adequate provision shall be made for the minorities freely to profess and practise their religions and develop their cultures;

Wherein the territories now included in or in accession with Pakistan and such other territories as may hereafter be included in or accede to Pakistan shall form a Federation wherein the units will be autonomous with such boundaries and limitations on their powers and authority as may be prescribed;

Therein shall be guaranteed fundamental rights, including equality of status, of opportunity and before law, social, economic and political justice, and freedom of thought, expression, belief, faith, worship and association, subject to law and public morality;

Wherein adequate provision shall be made to safeguard the legitimate interests of minorities and backward and depressed classes;

Wherein the independence of the judiciary shall be fully secured;

Wherein the integrity of the territories of the Federation, its independence and all its rights, including its sovereign rights on land, sea and air, shall be safeguarded;

So that the people of Pakistan may prosper and attain their rightful and honoured place amongst the nations of the World and make their full contribution towards international peace and progress and happiness of humanity:

Now, therefore, we, the people of Pakistan, cognisant of our responsibility before Almighty Allah and men;

Congnisant of the sacrifices made by the people in the cause of Pakistan; faithful to the declaration made by the Founder of Pakistan, Quaid-i-Azam Mohammad Ali Jinnah, that Pakistan would be a democratic State based on Islamic principles of social justice;

Dedicated to the preservation of democracy achieved by the unremitting struggle of the people against oppression and tyranny; inspired by the resolve to protect our national and political unity and solidarity by creating an egalitarian society through a new order;

Do hereby, through our representatives in the National Assembly, adopt, enact and give to ourselves, this Constitution.

PART I: Introductory

1. (1) Pakistan shall be a Federal Republic to be known as the Islamic Republic of Pakistan, hereinafter referred to as Pakistan. . . .

2. Islam shall be the State religion of Pakistan. . . .

PART II: Fundamental Rights and Principles of Policy

. . . 19. Every citizen shall have the right to freedom of speech and expression, and there shall be freedom of the press, subject to any reasonable restrictions imposed by law in the interest of the glory of Islam or the integrity, security or defence of Pakistan or any part thereof, friendly relations with foreign States, public order, decency or morality, or in relation to contempt of court, commission of or incitement to an offence.

20. Subject to law, public order and morality:-

(a) every citizen shall have the right to profess, practise and propagate his religion; and

(b) every religious denomination and every sect thereof shall have the right to establish, maintain and manage its religious institutions.

21. No person shall be compelled to pay any special tax the proceeds of which are to be spent on the propagation or maintenance of any religion other than his own.

22. (1) No person attending any educational institution shall be required to receive religious instruction, or take part in any religious ceremony, or attend religious worship, if such instruction, ceremony or worship relates to a religion other than his own.

(2) In respect of any religious institution, there shall be no discrimination against any community in the granting of exemption or concession in relation to taxation.

(3) Subject to law:

(a) no religious community or denomination shall be prevented from providing religious instruction for pupils of that community or denomination in any educational institution maintained wholly by that community or denomination; and

(b) no citizen shall be denied admission to any educational institution receiving aid from public revenues on the ground only of race, religion, caste or place of birth. . . .

PART IX: Islamic Provisions

227. (1) All existing laws shall be brought in conformity with the Injunctions of Islam as laid down in the Holy Quran and Sunnah, in this Part referred to as the Injunctions of Islam, and no law shall be enacted which is repugnant to such Injunctions.

(2) Effect shall be given to the provisions of clause (1) only in the manner provided in this Part.

(3) Nothing in this Part shall affect the personal laws of non-Muslim citizens or their status as citizens.

228. (1) There shall be constituted within a period of ninety days from the commencing day a Council of Islamic Ideology, in this part referred to as the Islamic Council.

(2) The Islamic Council shall consist of such members, being not less than eight and not more than twenty, as the President may appoint from amongst persons having knowledge of the principles and philosophy of Islam as enunciated in the Holy Quran and Sunnah, or understanding of the economic, political, legal or administrative problems of Pakistan. . . .

229. The President or the Governor of a Province may, or if two-fifths of its total membership so requires, a House or a Provincial Assembly shall, refer to the Islamic Council for advice any question as to whether a proposed law is or is not repugnant to the Injunctions of Islam. . . .

Source: "The Constitution of the Islamic Republic of Pakistan." Pakistani.org. Available online. URL: http://www.pakistani.org/pakistan/constitution/. Accessed July 4, 2006.

III. DOCUMENTS OF RELIGIOUS GROUPS

Roman Catholicism

"Lamentabili sane exitu" (1907) (excerpts)

"Lamentabili sane exitu" was a decree issued by Pope Pius X in July 1907, condemning the errors of the so-called modernist theologians, most of whom were European Roman Catholics rather than American Roman Catholics. Archbishop Marcel Lefebvre regarded "Lamentabili" as a guide to orthodox Catholic teaching and as a standard for evaluating the decrees of the Second Vatican Council in 1964.

With truly lamentable results, our age, casting aside all restraint in its search for the ultimate causes of things, frequently pursues novelties so ardently that it rejects the legacy of the human race. Thus it falls into very serious errors, which are even more serious when they concern sacred authority, the interpretation of Sacred Scripture, and the principal mysteries of Faith. The fact that many Catholic writers also go beyond the limits determined by the Fathers and the Church herself is extremely regrettable. In the name of higher knowledge and historical research (they say), they are looking for that progress of dogmas which is, in reality, nothing but the corruption of dogmas.

These errors are being daily spread among the faithful. Lest they captivate the faithful's minds and corrupt the purity of their faith, His Holiness, Pius X, by Divine Providence, Pope, has decided that the chief errors should be noted and condemned by the Office of this Holy Roman and Universal Inquisition.

Therefore, after a very diligent investigation and consultation with the Reverend Consultors, the Most Eminent and Reverend Lord Cardinals, the General Inquisitors in matters of faith and morals have judged the following propositions to be condemned and proscribed. In fact, by this general decree, they are condemned and proscribed.

1. The ecclesiastical law which prescribes that books concerning the Divine Scriptures are subject to previous examination does not apply to critical scholars and students of scientific exegesis of the Old and New Testament.

2. The Church's interpretation of the Sacred Books is by no means to be rejected; nevertheless, it is subject to the more accurate judgment and correction of the exegetes.

3. From the ecclesiastical judgments and censures passed against free and more scientific exegesis, one can conclude that the Faith the Church proposes contradicts history and that Catholic teaching cannot really be reconciled with the true origins of the Christian religion.

4. Even by dogmatic definitions the Church's magisterium cannot determine the genuine sense of the Sacred Scriptures.

5. Since the deposit of Faith contains only revealed truths, the Church has no right to pass judgment on the assertions of the human sciences. . . .

9. They display excessive simplicity or ignorance who believe that God is really the author of the Sacred Scriptures. . . .

11. Divine inspiration does not extend to all of Sacred Scriptures so that it renders its parts, each and every one, free from every error.

12. If he wishes to apply himself usefully to Biblical studies, the exegete must first put aside all preconceived opinions about the supernatural origin of Sacred Scripture and interpret it the same as any other merely human document. . . .

15. Until the time the canon was defined and constituted, the Gospels were increased by additions and corrections. Therefore there remained in them only a faint and uncertain trace of the doctrine of Christ. . . .

19. Heterodox exegetes have expressed the true sense of the Scriptures more faithfully than Catholic exegetes. . . .

22. The dogmas the Church holds out as revealed are not truths which have fallen from heaven. They are an interpretation of religious facts which the human mind has acquired by laborious effort.

23. Opposition may, and actually does, exist between the facts narrated in Sacred Scripture and the Church's dogmas which rest on them. Thus the critic may reject as false facts the Church holds as most certain. . . .

27. The divinity of Jesus Christ is not proved from the Gospels. It is a dogma which the Christian conscience has derived from the notion of the Messias. . . .

31. The doctrine concerning Christ taught by Paul, John, and the Councils of Nicea, Ephesus and Chalcedon is not that which Jesus taught but that which the Christian conscience conceived concerning Jesus. . . .

35. Christ did not always possess the consciousness of His Messianic dignity.

36. The Resurrection of the Savior is not properly a fact of the historical order. It is a fact of merely the supernatural order (neither demonstrated nor demonstrable) which the Christian conscience gradually derived from other facts.

37. In the beginning, faith in the Resurrection of Christ was not so much in the fact itself of the Resurrection as in the immortal life of Christ with God. . . .

40. The Sacraments have their origin in the fact that the Apostles and their successors, swayed and moved by circumstances and events, interpreted some idea and intention of Christ.

41. The Sacraments are intended merely to recall to man's mind the ever-beneficent presence of the Creator. . . .

45. Not everything which Paul narrates concerning the institution of the Eucharist (I Cor. 11:23–25) is to be taken historically. . . .

49. When the Christian supper gradually assumed the nature of a liturgical action those who customarily presided over the supper acquired the sacerdotal character. . . .

52. It was far from the mind of Christ to found a Church as a society which would continue on earth for a long course of centuries. On the contrary, in the mind of Christ the kingdom of heaven together with the end of the world was about to come immediately.

53. The organic constitution of the Church is not immutable. Like human society, Christian society is subject to a perpetual evolution.

54. Dogmas, Sacraments and hierarchy, both their notion and reality, are only interpretations and evolutions of the Christian intelligence which have increased and perfected by an external series of additions the little germ latent in the Gospel.

55. Simon Peter never even suspected that Christ entrusted the primacy in the Church to him.

56. The Roman Church became the head of all the churches, not through the ordinance of Divine Providence, but merely through political conditions.

57. The Church has shown that she is hostile to the progress of the natural and theological sciences.

58. Truth is no more immutable than man himself, since it evolved with him, in him, and through him.

59. Christ did not teach a determined body of doctrine applicable to all times and all men, but rather inaugurated a religious movement adapted or to be adapted to different times and places. . . .

62. The chief articles of the Apostles' Creed did not have the same sense for the Christians of the first ages as they have for the Christians of our time. . . .

64. Scientific progress demands that the concepts of Christian doctrine concerning God, creation, revelation, the Person of the Incarnate Word, and Redemption be re-adjusted.

65. Modern Catholicism can be reconciled with true science only if it is transformed into a non-dogmatic Christianity; that is to say, into a broad and liberal Protestantism.

The following Thursday, the fourth day of the same month and year, all these matters were accurately reported to our Most Holy Lord, Pope Pius X. His Holiness approved and confirmed the decree of the Most Eminent Fathers and ordered that each and every one of the above-listed propositions be held by all as condemned and proscribed.

Source: "Syllabus Condemning the Errors of the Modernists." Papal Encyclicals Online. Available online. URL: http://www.papalencyclicals.net/Pius10/p10lamen.htm. Accessed July 5, 2006.

Decree on Ecumenism (1964) (excerpts)

"Unitatis Redintegratio" is the Latin title of the Second Vatican Council's Decree on Ecumenism. It was promulgated on November 21, 1964, by Pope Paul VI, although an early draft of the decree had been read by Pope John

XXIII before his death in June 1963. The original version of the document contained five sections, the first three dealing with Rome's relationships with Eastern Orthodoxy and the churches of the Reformation, the fourth with Judaism, and the fifth with religious freedom. After some discussion, the Council Fathers decided to treat the fourth and fifth sections as separate documents, which eventually became the Decree on the Relationship of the Church to Non-Christian Religions (October 1965) and the Declaration on Religious Freedom (December 1965). The final version of the Decree on Ecumenism is remarkable for its positive appreciation of other Christian bodies and for its description of the Roman Catholic Church as a "pilgrim" rather than a perfect church to which all others must eventually return. It was precisely this modesty that offended Archbishop Marcel Lefebvre and other ultratraditionalists and led them to accuse the council of "Protestantizing."

INTRODUCTION

1. The restoration of unity among all Christians is one of the principal concerns of the Second Vatican Council. Christ the Lord founded one Church and one Church only. However, many Christian communions present themselves to men as the true inheritors of Jesus Christ; all indeed profess to be followers of the Lord but differ in mind and go their different ways, as if Christ Himself were divided. Such division openly contradicts the will of Christ, scandalizes the world, and damages the holy cause of preaching the Gospel to every creature.

But the Lord of Ages wisely and patiently follows out the plan of grace on our behalf, sinners that we are. In recent times more than ever before, He has been rousing divided Christians to remorse over their divisions and to a longing for unity. Everywhere large numbers have felt the impulse of this grace, and among our separated brethren also there increases from day to day the movement, fostered by the grace of the Holy Spirit, for the restoration of unity among all Christians. This movement toward unity is called "ecumenical." Those belong to it who invoke the Triune God and confess Jesus as Lord and Savior, doing this not merely as individuals but also as corporate bodies. For almost everyone regards the body in which he has heard the Gospel as his Church and indeed, God's Church. All however, though in different ways, long for the one visible Church of God, a Church truly universal and set forth into the world that the world may be converted to the Gospel and so be saved, to the glory of God.

The Sacred Council gladly notes all this. It has already declared its teaching on the Church, and now, moved by a desire for the restoration of unity among all the followers of Christ, it wishes to set before all Catholics the ways and means by which they too can respond to this grace and to this divine call.

CHAPTER I: CATHOLIC PRINCIPLES ON ECUMENISM

2. What has revealed the love of God among us is that the Father has sent into the world His only-begotten Son, so that, being made man, He might by His redemption give new life to the entire human race and unify it. Before offering Himself up as a spotless victim upon the altar, Christ prayed to His Father for all who believe in Him: "that they all may be one; even as thou, Father, art in me, and I in thee, that they also may be one in us, so that the world may believe that thou has sent me." In His Church He instituted the wonderful sacrament of the Eucharist by which the unity of His Church is both signified and made a reality. He gave His followers a new commandment to love one another, and promised the Spirit, their Advocate, who, as Lord and life-giver, should remain with them forever.

After being lifted up on the cross and glorified, the Lord Jesus poured forth His Spirit as He had promised, and through the Spirit He has called and gathered together the people of the New Covenant, who are the Church, into a unity of faith, hope and charity, as the Apostle teaches us: "There is one body and one Spirit, just as you were called to the one hope of your calling; one Lord, one faith, one Baptism." For "all you who have been baptized into Christ have put on Christ . . . for you are all one in Christ Jesus." It is the Holy Spirit, dwelling in those who believe and pervading and ruling over the Church as a whole, who brings about that wonderful communion of the faithful. He brings them into intimate union with Christ, so that He is the principle of the Church's unity. The distribution of graces and offices is His work too, enriching the Church of Jesus Christ with different functions "in order to equip the saints for the work of service, so as to build up the body of Christ.". . .

3. Even in the beginnings of this one and only Church of God there arose certain rifts, which the Apostle strongly condemned. But in subsequent centuries much more serious dissensions made their appearance and quite large communities came to be separated from full communion with the Catholic Church—for which, often enough, men of both sides were to blame. The children who are born into these Communities and who grow up believing in Christ cannot be accused of the sin involved in the separation, and the Catholic Church embraces upon them as brothers, with respect and affection. For men who believe in Christ and have been truly baptized are in communion with the Catholic Church even though this communion is imperfect. The differences that exist in varying degrees between them and

the Catholic Church—whether in doctrine and sometimes in discipline, or concerning the structure of the Church—do indeed create many obstacles, sometimes serious ones, to full ecclesiastical communion. The ecumenical movement is striving to overcome these obstacles. But even in spite of them it remains true that all who have been justified by faith in Baptism are members of Christ's body, and have a right to be called Christian, and so are correctly accepted as brothers by the children of the Catholic Church.

Moreover, some and even very many of the significant elements and endowments which together go to build up and give life to the Church itself, can exist outside the visible boundaries of the Catholic Church: the written word of God; the life of grace; faith, hope and charity, with the other interior gifts of the Holy Spirit, and visible elements too. All of these, which come from Christ and lead back to Christ, belong by right to the one Church of Christ.

The brethren divided from us also use many liturgical actions of the Christian religion. These most certainly can truly engender a life of grace in ways that vary according to the condition of each Church or Community. These liturgical actions must be regarded as capable of giving access to the community of salvation.

It follows that the separated Churches and Communities as such, though we believe them to be deficient in some respects, have been by no means deprived of significance and importance in the mystery of salvation. For the Spirit of Christ has not refrained from using them as means of salvation which derive their efficacy from the very fullness of grace and truth entrusted to the Church.

Nevertheless, our separated brethren, whether considered as individuals or as Communities and Churches, are not blessed with that unity which Jesus Christ wished to bestow on all those who through Him were born again into one body, and with Him quickened to newness of life—that unity which the Holy Scriptures and the ancient Tradition of the Church proclaim. For it is only through Christ's Catholic Church, which is "the all-embracing means of salvation," that they can benefit fully from the means of salvation. We believe that Our Lord entrusted all the blessings of the New Covenant to the apostolic college alone, of which Peter is the head, in order to establish the one Body of Christ on earth to which all should be fully incorporated who belong in any way to the people of God. This people of God, though still in its members liable to sin, is ever growing in Christ during its pilgrimage on earth, and is guided by God's gentle wisdom, according to His hidden designs, until it shall happily arrive at the fullness of eternal glory in the heavenly Jerusalem.

4. Today, in many parts of the world, under the inspiring grace of the Holy Spirit, many efforts are being made in prayer, word and action to attain that fullness of unity which Jesus Christ desires. The Sacred Council exhorts all the Catholic faithful to recognize the signs of the times and to take an active and intelligent part in the work of ecumenism.

The term "ecumenical movement" indicates the initiatives and activities planned and undertaken, according to the various needs of the Church and as opportunities offer, to promote Christian unity. These are: first, every effort to avoid expressions, judgments and actions which do not represent the condition of our separated brethren with truth and fairness and so make mutual relations with them more difficult; then, "dialogue" between competent experts from different Churches and Communities. At these meetings, which are organized in a religious spirit, each explains the teaching of his Communion in greater depth and brings out clearly its distinctive features. In such dialogue, everyone gains a truer knowledge and more just appreciation of the teaching and religious life of both Communions. In addition, the way is prepared for cooperation between them in the duties for the common good of humanity which are demanded by every Christian conscience; and, wherever this is allowed, there is prayer in common. Finally, all are led to examine their own faithfulness to Christ's will for the Church and accordingly to undertake with vigor the task of renewal and reform. . . .

Catholics, in their ecumenical work, must assuredly be concerned for their separated brethren, praying for them, keeping them informed about the Church, making the first approaches toward them. But their primary duty is to make a careful and honest appraisal of whatever needs to be done or renewed in the Catholic household itself, in order that its life may bear witness more clearly and faithfully to the teachings and institutions which have come to it from Christ through the Apostles.

For although the Catholic Church has been endowed with all divinely revealed truth and with all means of grace, yet its members fail to live by them with all the fervor that they should, so that the radiance of the Church's image is less clear in the eyes of our separated brethren and of the world at large, and the growth of God's kingdom is delayed. All Catholics must therefore aim at Christian perfection and, each according to his station, play his part that the Church may daily be more purified and renewed. For the Church must bear in her own body the humility and dying of Jesus, against the day when Christ will present her to Himself in all her glory without spot or wrinkle.

All in the Church must preserve unity in essentials. But let all, according to the gifts they have received enjoy a proper freedom, in their various forms of spiritual life and discipline, in their different liturgical rites, and even in their theological elaborations of revealed truth. In all things let charity prevail. If they are true to this course of action, they will be giving ever better expression to the authentic catholicity and apostolicity of the Church.

On the other hand, Catholics must gladly acknowledge and esteem the truly Christian endowments from our common heritage which are to be found among our separated brethren. It is right and salutary to recognize the riches of Christ and virtuous works in the lives of others who are bearing witness to Christ, sometimes even to the shedding of their blood. For God is always wonderful in His works and worthy of all praise.

Nor should we forget that anything wrought by the grace of the Holy Spirit in the hearts of our separated brethren can be a help to our own edification. Whatever is truly Christian is never contrary to what genuinely belongs to the faith; indeed, it can always bring a deeper realization of the mystery of Christ and the Church. . . .

This Sacred Council is gratified to note that the participation by the Catholic faithful in ecumenical work is growing daily. It commends this work to the bishops everywhere in the world to be vigorously stimulated by them and guided with prudence.

CHAPTER II: THE PRACTICE OF ECUMENISM

5. The attainment of union is the concern of the whole Church, faithful and shepherds alike. This concern extends to everyone, according to his talent, whether it be exercised in his daily Christian life or in his theological and historical research. This concern itself reveals already to some extent the bond of brotherhood between all Christians and it helps toward that full and perfect unity which God in His kindness wills.

6. Every renewal of the Church is essentially grounded in an increase of fidelity to her own calling. Undoubtedly this is the basis of the movement toward unity. . . .

Church renewal has therefore notable ecumenical importance. Already in various spheres of the Church's life, this renewal is taking place. The Biblical and liturgical movements, the preaching of the word of God and catechetics, the apostolate of the laity, new forms of religious life and the spirituality of married life, and the Church's social teaching and activity—all these should be considered as pledges and signs of the future progress of ecumenism.

7. There can be no ecumenism worthy of the name without a change of heart. For it is from renewal of the inner life of our minds, from self-

denial and an unstinted love that desires of unity take their rise and develop in a mature way. We should therefore pray to the Holy Spirit for the grace to be genuinely self-denying, humble, gentle in the service of others, and to have an attitude of brotherly generosity towards them. St. Paul says: "I, therefore, a prisoner for the Lord, beg you to lead a life worthy of the calling to which you have been called, with all humility and meekness, with patience, forbearing one another in love, eager to maintain the unity of the spirit in the bond of peace". (29) This exhortation is directed especially to those raised to sacred Orders precisely that the work of Christ may be continued. He came among us "not to be served but to serve.". . .

9. We must get to know the outlook of our separated brethren. To achieve this purpose, study is of necessity required, and this must be pursued with a sense of realism and good will. Catholics, who already have a proper grounding, need to acquire a more adequate understanding of the respective doctrines of our separated brethren, their history, their spiritual and liturgical life, their religious psychology and general background. Most valuable for this purpose are meetings of the two sides—especially for discussion of theological problems—where each can treat with the other on an equal footing—provided that those who take part in them are truly competent and have the approval of the bishops. From such dialogue will emerge still more clearly what the situation of the Catholic Church really is. In this way too the outlook of our separated brethren will be better understood, and our own belief more aptly explained.

10. Sacred theology and other branches of knowledge, especially of an historical nature, must be taught with due regard for the ecumenical point of view, so that they may correspond more exactly with the facts.

It is most important that future shepherds and priests should have mastered a theology that has been carefully worked out in this way and not polemically, especially with regard to those aspects which concern the relations of separated brethren with the Catholic Church. This importance is the greater because the instruction and spiritual formation of the faithful and of religious depends so largely on the formation which their priests have received.

Moreover, Catholics engaged in missionary work in the same territories as other Christians ought to know, particularly in these times, the problems and the benefits in their apostolate which derive from the ecumenical movement. . . .

CHAPTER III: CHURCHES AND ECCLESIAL COMMUNITIES SEPARATED FROM THE ROMAN APOSTOLIC SEE

13. We now turn our attention to the two chief types of division as they affect the seamless robe of Christ.

The first divisions occurred in the East, when the dogmatic formulae of the Councils of Ephesus and Chalcedon were challenged, and later when ecclesiastical communion between the Eastern Patriarchates and the Roman See was dissolved.

Other divisions arose more than four centuries later in the West, stemming from the events which are usually referred to as "The Reformation." As a result, many Communions, national or confessional, were separated from the Roman See. Among those in which Catholic traditions and institutions in part continue to exist, the Anglican Communion occupies a special place.

These various divisions differ greatly from one another not only by reason of their origin, place and time, but especially in the nature and seriousness of questions bearing on faith and the structure of the Church. Therefore, without minimizing the differences between the various Christian bodies, and without overlooking the bonds between them which exist in spite of divisions, this holy Council decides to propose the following considerations for prudent ecumenical action.

I. The Special Consideration of the Eastern Churches

14. For many centuries the Church of the East and that of the West each followed their separate ways though linked in a brotherly union of faith and sacramental life; the Roman See by common consent acted as guide when disagreements arose between them over matters of faith or discipline. Among other matters of great importance, it is a pleasure for this Council to remind everyone that there flourish in the East many particular or local Churches, among which the Patriarchal Churches hold first place, and of these not a few pride themselves in tracing their origins back to the apostles themselves. Hence a matter of primary concern and care among the Easterns, in their local churches, has been, and still is, to preserve the family ties of common faith and charity which ought to exist between sister Churches. . . .

II. Separated Churches and Ecclesial Communities in the West

19. In the great upheaval which began in the West toward the end of the Middle Ages, and in later times too, Churches and ecclesial Communities came to be separated from the Apostolic See of Rome. Yet they have retained a particularly close affinity with the Catholic Church as a result of the long centuries in which all Christendom lived together in ecclesiastical communion. However, since these Churches and ecclesial Communities,

on account of their different origins, and different teachings in matters of doctrine on the spiritual life, vary considerably not only with us, but also among themselves, the task of describing them at all adequately is extremely difficult; and we have no intention of making such an attempt here.

Although the ecumenical movement and the desire for peace with the Catholic Church have not yet taken hold everywhere, it is our hope that ecumenical feeling and mutual esteem may gradually increase among all men. It must however be admitted that in these Churches and ecclesial Communities there exist important differences from the Catholic Church, not only of an historical, sociological, psychological and cultural character, but especially in the interpretation of revealed truth. To make easier the ecumenical dialogue in spite of these differences, we wish to set down some considerations which can, and indeed should, serve as a basis and encouragement for such dialogue.

20. Our thoughts turn first to those Christians who make open confession of Jesus Christ as God and Lord and as the sole Mediator between God and men, to the glory of the one God, Father, Son and Holy Spirit. We are aware indeed that there exist considerable divergences from the doctrine of the Catholic Church concerning Christ Himself, the Word of God made flesh, the work of redemption, and consequently, concerning the mystery and ministry of the Church, and the role of Mary in the plan of salvation. But we rejoice to see that our separated brethren look to Christ as the source and center of Church unity. Their longing for union with Christ inspires them to seek an ever closer unity, and also to bear witness to their faith among the peoples of the earth.

21. A love and reverence of Sacred Scripture which might be described as devotion, leads our brethren to a constant meditative study of the sacred text. For the Gospel "is the power of God for salvation to every one who has faith, to the Jew first and then to the Greek." While invoking the Holy Spirit, they seek in these very Scriptures God as it were speaking to them in Christ, Whom the prophets foretold, Who is the Word of God made flesh for us. They contemplate in the Scriptures the life of Christ and what the Divine Master taught and did for our salvation, especially the mysteries of His death and resurrection. . . .

22. Whenever the Sacrament of Baptism is duly administered as Our Lord instituted it, and is received with the right dispositions, a person is truly incorporated into the crucified and glorified Christ, and reborn to a sharing of the divine life, as the Apostle says: "You were buried together with Him in Baptism, and in Him also rose again—through faith in the working of God, who raised Him from the dead."

Baptism therefore establishes a sacramental bond of unity which links all who have been reborn by it. But of itself Baptism is only a beginning, an inauguration wholly directed toward the fullness of life in Christ. Baptism, therefore, envisages a complete profession of faith, complete incorporation in the system of salvation such as Christ willed it to be, and finally complete ingrafting in eucharistic communion.

Though the ecclesial Communities which are separated from us lack the fullness of unity with us flowing from Baptism, and though we believe they have not retained the proper reality of the eucharistic mystery in its fullness, especially because of the absence of the sacrament of Orders, nevertheless when they commemorate His death and resurrection in the Lord's Supper, they profess that it signifies life in communion with Christ and look forward to His coming in glory. Therefore the teaching concerning the Lord's Supper, the other sacraments, worship, the ministry of the Church, must be the subject of the dialogue. . . .

24. Now that we have briefly set out the conditions for ecumenical action and the principles by which it is to be directed, we look with confidence to the future. This Sacred Council exhorts the faithful to refrain from superficiality and imprudent zeal, which can hinder real progress toward unity. Their ecumenical action must be fully and sincerely Catholic, that is to say, faithful to the truth which we have received from the apostles and Fathers of the Church, in harmony with the faith which the Catholic Church has always professed, and at the same time directed toward that fullness to which Our Lord wills His Body to grow in the course of time. . . .

Each and all these matters which are set forth in this Decree have been favorably voted on by the Fathers of the Council. And We, by the apostolic authority given Us by Christ and in union with the Fathers, approve, decree and establish them in the Holy Spirit and command that they be promulgated for the glory of God.

Given in Rome at St. Peter's, November 21, 1964

Source: "Decree on Ecumenism: *Unitatis Redintegratio.*" Vatican Web site. Available online. URL: http://www.vatican.va/archive/hist_councils/ii_vatican_council/documents/vat-ii_decree_19641121_unitatis-redintegratio_en.html. Accessed December 5, 2005. It is also available in print, with a brief introduction by Walter M. Abbott, S. J., in Walter M. Abbott, S.J., ed., *The Documents of Vatican II.* New York: Guild Press, America Press, and Association Press, 1966.

Declaration on Religious Freedom (1965) (excerpts)

"Dignitatis humanae," or the Declaration on Religious Freedom, was promulgated by Pope Paul VI on December 7, 1965. Its full title is "On the Right of the

Person and of Communities to Social and Civil Freedom in Matters Religious." Although the document's affirmations about "immunity from [religious] coercion in civil society" do not sound remarkable to most Americans, they nonetheless made "Dignitatis humanae" the single most controversial document of the Second Vatican Council. The reason for the controversy is that the document openly acknowledged that Christian doctrine undergoes development: "To this end, [the Vatican Council] searches into the sacred tradition and doctrine of the Church—the treasury out of which the Church continually brings forth new things that are in harmony with the things that are old." What was scandalous to such ultraconservatives as Marcel Lefebvre was not the concept of religious freedom itself but the notion of the development of church teaching. To Lefebvre, "Dignitatis humanae" could not be seen as anything other than a flat contradiction of Pope Pius X's writings and the earlier Syllabus of Errors, promulgated by Pope Pius IX in 1864.

1. A sense of the dignity of the human person has been impressing itself more and more deeply on the consciousness of contemporary man, and the demand is increasingly made that men should act on their own judgment, enjoying and making use of a responsible freedom, not driven by coercion but motivated by a sense of duty. The demand is likewise made that constitutional limits should be set to the powers of government, in order that there may be no encroachment on the rightful freedom of the person and of associations. This demand for freedom in human society chiefly regards the quest for the values proper to the human spirit. It regards, in the first place, the free exercise of religion in society. This Vatican Council takes careful note of these desires in the minds of men. It proposes to declare them to be greatly in accord with truth and justice. To this end, it searches into the sacred tradition and doctrine of the Church—the treasury out of which the Church continually brings forth new things that are in harmony with the things that are old.

First, the council professes its belief that God Himself has made known to mankind the way in which men are to serve Him, and thus be saved in Christ and come to blessedness. We believe that this one true religion subsists in the Catholic and Apostolic Church, to which the Lord Jesus committed the duty of spreading it abroad among all men. Thus He spoke to the Apostles: "Go, therefore, and make disciples of all nations, baptizing them in the name of the Father and of the Son and of the Holy Spirit, teaching them to observe all things whatsoever I have enjoined upon you" (Matt. 28: 19–20). On their part, all men are bound to seek the truth, especially in what concerns God and His Church, and to embrace the truth they come to know, and to hold fast to it.

This Vatican Council likewise professes its belief that it is upon the human conscience that these obligations fall and exert their binding force. The truth cannot impose itself except by virtue of its own truth, as it makes its entrance into the mind at once quietly and with power.

Religious freedom, in turn, which men demand as necessary to fulfill their duty to worship God, has to do with immunity from coercion in civil society. Therefore it leaves untouched traditional Catholic doctrine on the moral duty of men and societies toward the true religion and toward the one Church of Christ. . . .

2. This Vatican Council declares that the human person has a right to religious freedom. This freedom means that all men are to be immune from coercion on the part of individuals or of social groups and of any human power, in such wise that no one is to be forced to act in a manner contrary to his own beliefs, whether privately or publicly, whether alone or in association with others within due limits.

The council further declares that the right to religious freedom has its foundation in the very dignity of the human person as this dignity is known through the revealed word of God and by reason itself. This right of the human person to religious freedom is to be recognized in the constitutional law whereby society is governed and thus it is to become a civil right. . . .

3. Further light is shed on the subject if one considers that the highest norm of human life is the divine law—eternal, objective and universal—whereby God orders, directs and governs the entire universe and all the ways of the human community by a plan conceived in wisdom and love. Man has been made by God to participate in this law, with the result that, under the gentle disposition of divine Providence, he can come to perceive ever more fully the truth that is unchanging. Wherefore every man has the duty, and therefore the right, to seek the truth in matters religious in order that he may with prudence form for himself right and true judgments of conscience, under use of all suitable means. . . .

4. The freedom or immunity from coercion in matters religious which is the endowment of persons as individuals is also to be recognized as their right when they act in community. Religious communities are a requirement of the social nature both of man and of religion itself.

Provided the just demands of public order are observed, religious communities rightfully claim freedom in order that they may govern themselves according to their own norms, honor the Supreme Being in public worship, assist their members in the practice of the religious life, strengthen them by instruction, and promote institutions in which they may join together for the purpose of ordering their own lives in accordance with their religious principles.

Religious communities also have the right not to be hindered, either by legal measures or by administrative action on the part of government, in the selection, training, appointment, and transferal of their own ministers, in communicating with religious authorities and communities abroad, in erecting buildings for religious purposes, and in the acquisition and use of suitable funds or properties. . . .

5. The family, since it is a society in its own original right, has the right freely to live its own domestic religious life under the guidance of parents. Parents, moreover, have the right to determine, in accordance with their own religious beliefs, the kind of religious education that their children are to receive. Government, in consequence, must acknowledge the right of parents to make a genuinely free choice of schools and of other means of education, and the use of this freedom of choice is not to be made a reason for imposing unjust burdens on parents, whether directly or indirectly. Besides, the rights of parents are violated, if their children are forced to attend lessons or instructions which are not in agreement with their religious beliefs, or if a single system of education, from which all religious formation is excluded, is imposed upon all. . . .

The protection and promotion of the inviolable rights of man ranks among the essential duties of government. Therefore government is to assume the safeguard of the religious freedom of all its citizens, in an effective manner, by just laws and by other appropriate means. Government is also to help create conditions favorable to the fostering of religious life, in order that the people may be truly enabled to exercise their religious rights and to fulfill their religious duties, and also in order that society itself may profit by the moral qualities of justice and peace which have their origin in men's faithfulness to God and to His holy will.

If, in view of peculiar circumstances obtaining among peoples, special civil recognition is given to one religious community in the constitutional order of society, it is at the same time imperative that the right of all citizens and religious communities to religious freedom should be recognized and made effective in practice.

Finally, government is to see to it that equality of citizens before the law, which is itself an element of the common good, is never violated, whether openly or covertly, for religious reasons. Nor is there to be discrimination among citizens.

It follows that a wrong is done when government imposes upon its people, by force or fear or other means, the profession or repudiation of any religion, or when it hinders men from joining or leaving a religious community. All the more is it a violation of the will of God and of the sacred rights of the person and the family of nations when force is brought to bear in any way in order to destroy or repress religion, either in the whole of mankind or in a particular country or in a definite community. . . .

May the God and Father of all grant that the human family, through careful observance of the principle of religious freedom in society, may be brought by the grace of Christ and the power of the Holy Spirit to the sublime and unending and "glorious freedom of the sons of God" (Rom. 8:21).

Source: "Declaration on Religious Freedom: *Dignitatis Humanae.*" Vatican Website. Available online. URL: http://www.vatican.va/archive/hist_councils/ii_vatican_council/documents/vat-ii_decl_19651207_dignitatis-humanae_en.html. Accessed December 6, 2005. It is available in print, with a brief introduction by John Courtney Murray. Walter M. Abbott, ed. *The Documents of Vatican II.* New York: Guild Press, America Press, and Association Press, 1966.

"Ecclesia Dei afflicta" (Excommunication of Archbishop Marcel Lefebvre, 1988)

"Ecclesia Dei afflicta" is an apostolic letter, also called a motu proprio *because the pope issued it of his own accord rather than as a response to a request from others. Pope John Paul II issued this document in July 1988 following Archbishop Marcel Lefebvre's consecration of four members of the Society of St. Pius X as bishops.*

1. With great affliction the Church has learned of the unlawful episcopal ordination conferred on 30 June last by Archbishop Marcel Lefebvre, which has frustrated all the efforts made during the previous years to ensure the full communion with the Church of the Priestly Fraternity of St. Pius X founded by the same Mons. Lefebvre. These efforts, especially intense during recent months, in which the Apostolic See has shown comprehension to the limits of the possible, were all to no avail.

2. This affliction was particularly felt by the Successor of Peter, to whom in the first place pertains the guardianship of the unity of the Church, even though the number of persons directly involved in these events might be few. For every person is loved by God on his own account and has been redeemed by the blood of Christ shed on the Cross for the salvation of all. The particular circumstances, both objective and subjective in which Archbishop Lefebvre acted, provide everyone with an occasion for profound reflection and for a renewed pledge of fidelity to Christ and to his Church.

3. In itself, this act was one of *disobedience* to the Roman Pontiff in a very grave matter and of supreme importance for the unity of the church, such as is the ordination of bishops whereby the apostolic succession is

sacramentally perpetuated. Hence such disobedience—which implies in practice the rejection of the Roman primacy—constitutes a *schismatic* act. In performing such an act, notwithstanding the formal *canonical warning* sent to them by the Cardinal Prefect of the Congregation for Bishops on 17 June last, Mons. Lefebvre and the priests Bernard Fellay, Bernard Tissier de Mallerais, Richard Williamson, and Alfonso de Galarreta, have incurred the grave penalty of excommunication envisaged by ecclesiastical law.

4. The *root* of this schismatic act can be discerned in an incomplete and contradictory notion of Tradition. Incomplete, because it does not take sufficiently into account the *living* character of Tradition, which, as the Second Vatican Council clearly taught, "comes from the apostles and progresses in the Church with the help of the Holy Spirit. There is a growth in insight into the realities and words that are being passed on. This comes about in various ways. It comes through the contemplation and study of believers who ponder these things in their hearts. It comes from the intimate sense of spiritual realities which they experience. And it comes from the preaching of those who have received, along with their right of succession in the episcopate, the sure charism of truth."

But especially contradictory is a notion of Tradition which opposes the universal Magisterium of the Church possessed by the Bishop of Rome and the Body of Bishops. It is impossible to remain faithful to the Tradition while breaking the ecclesial bond with him to whom, in the person of the Apostle Peter, Christ himself entrusted the ministry of unity in his Church.

5. Faced with the situation that has arisen I deem it my duty to inform all the Catholic faithful of some aspects which this sad event has highlighted.

a) The outcome of the movement promoted by Mons. Lefebvre can and must be, for all the Catholic faithful, a motive for sincere reflection concerning their own fidelity to the Church's Tradition, authentically interpreted by the ecclesiastical Magisterium, ordinary and extraordinary, especially in the Ecumenical Councils from Nicaea to Vatican II. From this reflection all should draw a renewed and efficacious conviction of the necessity of strengthening still more their fidelity by rejecting erroneous interpretations and arbitrary and unauthorized applications in matters of doctrine, liturgy and discipline.

To the bishops especially it pertains, by reason of their pastoral mission, to exercise the important duty of a clear-sighted vigilance full of charity and firmness, so that this fidelity may be everywhere safeguarded. However, it is necessary that all the Pastors and the other faithful have a new awareness, not only of the lawfulness but also of the richness for the

Church of a diversity of charisms, traditions of spirituality and apostolate, which also constitutes the beauty of unity in variety: of that blended "harmony" which the earthly Church raises up to Heaven under the impulse of the Holy Spirit.

b) Moreover, I should like to remind theologians and other experts in the ecclesiastical sciences that they should feel themselves called upon to answer in the present circumstances. Indeed, the extent and depth of the teaching of the Second Vatican Council call for a renewed commitment to deeper study in order to reveal clearly the Council's continuity with Tradition, especially in points of doctrine which, perhaps because they are new, have not yet been well understood by some sections of the Church.

c) In the present circumstances I wish especially to make an appeal both solemn and heartfelt, paternal and fraternal, to all those who until now have been linked in various ways to the movement of Archbishop Lefebvre, that they may fulfil the grave duty of remaining united to the Vicar of Christ in the unity of the Catholic Church, and of ceasing their support in any way for that movement. Everyone should be aware that formal adherence to the schism is a grave offence against God and carries the penalty of excommunication decreed by the Church's law.

To all those Catholic faithful who feel attached to some previous liturgical and disciplinary forms of the Latin tradition I wish to manifest my will to facilitate their ecclesial communion by means of the necessary measures to guarantee respect for their rightful aspirations. In this matter I ask for the support of the bishops and of all those engaged in the pastoral ministry in the Church.

6. Taking account of the importance and complexity of the problems referred to in this document, by virtue of my Apostolic Authority I decree the following:

a) a *Commission* is instituted whose task it will be to collaborate with the bishops, with the Departments of the Roman Curia and with the circles concerned, for the purpose of facilitating full ecclesial communion of priests, seminarians, religious communities or individuals until now linked in various ways to the Fraternity founded by Mons. Lefebvre, who may wish to remain united to the Successor Peter in the Catholic Church, while preserving their spiritual and liturgical traditions, in the light of the Protocol signed on 5 May last by Cardinal Ratzinger and Mons. Lefebvre;

b) this Commission is composed of a Cardinal President and other members of the Roman Curia, in a number that will be deemed opportune according to circumstances;

c) moreover, respect must everywhere be shown for the feelings of all those who are attached to the Latin liturgical tradition, by a wide and generous application of the directives already issued some time ago by the Apostolic See for the use of the Roman Missal according to the typical edition of 1962.

7. As this year specially dedicated to the Blessed Virgin is now drawing to a close, I wish to exhort all to join in unceasing prayer that the Vicar of Christ, through the intercession of the Mother of the church, addresses to the Father in the very words of the Son: "That they all may be one!"

Given at Rome, at St. Peter's. 2 July 1988, the tenth year of the pontificate.

Source: "Apostolic Letter: *'Ecclesia Dei.'*" Vatican Web site. Available online. URL: http://www.vatican.va/holy_father/john_paul_ii/motu_proprio/documents/hf_jp-ii_motu-propri o_02071988_ecclesia-dei_en.html. Accessed July 4, 2006.

Judaism

Gush Emunim Statement of Principles (1970s)

Fundamentalist groups within Judaism do not usually draw up statements of belief or organizational principles, in part because many of their goals are related to the geographical boundaries of the state of Israel as described in the Old Testament and so do not need additional definition or justification. In the case of Gush Emunim (GE), many of its leaders were intellectuals who were not particularly concerned with organizational structure. In the 1970s, however, some of the leaders of GE drafted a statement of principles that is reproduced here. It has no formal title.

Aims: To bring about a great awakening of the Jewish People towards full implementation of the Zionist vision, realizing that this vision originates in Israel's Jewish heritage, and that its objective is the full redemption of Israel and of the entire world.

Background: The Jewish People is now engaged in a fierce struggle for survival in its land and for its right to full sovereignty therein. Yet we are witnessing a process of decline and retreat from realization of the Zionist ideal, in word and deed. Four related factors are responsible for this crisis: mental weariness and frustration induced by the extended conflict; the lack of challenge; preference for selfish goals over national objectives; the attenuation of Jewish faith. The latter is the key to understanding the uniqueness and destiny of the people and its land.

Principles of Action:
(a) Education and publicity (a link with Torah and Jewish ethics; love of the Jewish People and the Land of Israel; Zionist consciousness and the vision of redemption; national missions and Fulfillment).
(b) Love of Israel.
(c) *Aliyah* [Jewish immigration to Israel].
(d) Settlement throughout the Land of Israel.
(e) An assertive foreign and security policy.
"Let us be strong on behalf of our people and the cities of our God, and the good Lord will do what is best." [2 Samuel 10:12]

Source: Gideon Aran. "Jewish Zionist Fundamentalism: The Bloc of the Faithful in Israel (Gush Emunim)." In Martin E. Marty and R. Scott Appleby, eds. *Fundamentalisms Observed.* Chicago: University of Chicago Press, 1991, p. 290.

Islam

Abul Ala Mawdudi: *The Punishment of the Apostate According to Islamic Law* (1963) (excerpts)

First published in the Urdu language in India in 1963, The Punishment of the Apostate *was written by Abul Ala Mawdudi, widely regarded as one of the most influential theorists of fundamentalist Islam. The document was translated into English by Ernest Hahn, a Canadian, and Syed Silas Husain, an Indian convert from Islam to Christianity, in 1994. Hahn and Husain justify the translation on the grounds that Westerners need to familiarize themselves with the traditional Islamic penalty for apostasy (execution) as well as Mawdudi's arguments justifying its continuation. The translators' introduction is worth reading in its own right as an example of responsible discussion of a sensitive issue. They point out that their purpose is "not to malign Islam" but to invite Western Christians to understand the difficulty that converts from Islam face in some parts of the world, and also to introduce Mawdudi's work to readers who may be unfamiliar with him.*

To everyone acquainted with Islamic law it is no secret that according to Islam the punishment for a Muslim who turns to *kufr* (infidelity, blasphemy) is execution. Doubt about this matter first arose among Muslims during the final portion of the nineteenth century as a result of speculation. Otherwise, for the full twelve centuries prior to that time the total Muslim community remained unanimous about it. The whole of our religious literature clearly testifies that ambiguity about the matter of the apostate's execution never existed among Muslims. The expositions of the Prophet, the Rightly-Guided Caliphs (*Khulafa'-i Rashidun*), the great Companions (*Sahaba*) of the Prophet, their Followers (*Tabi'un*), the leaders among the *mujtahids* and, following them, the doctors of the *shari'ah* of every century are available on record. All these collectively will assure you that from the time of the Prophet to the present day one injunction only has been continuously and uninterruptedly operative and that no room whatever remains to suggest that perhaps the punishment of the apostate is not execution.

Some people have been influenced by the so-called enlightenment of the present age to the point that they have opened the door to contrary thoughts on such proven issues. Their daring is truly very astonishing. They have not considered that if doubts arise even about such matters which are supported by such a continuous and unbroken series of witnesses, this state of affairs will not be confined to one or two problems. Hereafter anything whatever of a past age which has come down to us through verbal tradition will not be protected from doubt, be it the Qur'an or ritual prayer (*namaz*) or fasting (*roza*). It will come to the point that even Muhammad's mission to this world will be questioned. In fact a more reasonable way for these people, rather than creating doubt of this kind, would have been to accept as fact what is fact and is proven through certified witnesses, and then to consider whether or not to follow the religion which punishes the apostate by death. The person who discovers any established or wholesome element of his religion to conflict with his intellectual standards and then tries to prove that this element is not really a part of the religion, already proves that his affliction is such that, "You cannot become a *kafir* (infidel); since there is no other choice, become a Muslim" (*kafer natavani shod nachar Musalman sho*). In other words, though his manner of thought and outlook has deviated from the true path of his religion, he insists on remaining in it only because he has inherited it from his forefathers.

A. The Proof from the Qur'an for the Commandment to Execute the Apostate

Here I wish briefly to offer proof that will quiet the doubt in the hearts of those who, for lack of sources of information, may think that perhaps the punishment of death did not exist in Islam but was added at a later time by the *"mawlawis"* (religious leaders) on their own.

God Most High declares in the Qur'an:

But if they repent and establish worship and pay the poor-due, then are they your brethren in religion. We detail our revelations for a people who have knowledge. And if they break their pledges after their treaty (hath been made with you) and assail your religion, then fight the heads of disbelief—Lo! they have no binding oaths in order that they may desist. (9:11,12)[1]

The following is the occasion for the revelation of this verse: During the pilgrimage (*hajj*) in A.H. 9 God Most High ordered a proclamation of an immunity. By virtue of this proclamation all those who, up to that time, were fighting against God and His Apostle and were attempting to obstruct the way of God's religion through all kinds of excesses and false covenants, were granted from that time a maximum respite of four months. During this period they were to ponder their own situation. If they wanted to accept Islam, they could accept it and they would be forgiven. If they wanted to leave the country, they could leave. Within this fixed period nothing would hinder them from leaving. Thereafter those remaining, who would neither accept Islam nor leave the country, would be dealt with by the sword. In this connection it was said: "If they repent and uphold the practice of prayer and almsgiving, then they are your brothers in religion. If after this, however, they break their covenant, then war should be waged against the leaders of *kufr* (infidelity). Here "covenant breaking" in no way can be construed to mean "breaking of political covenants." Rather, the context clearly determines its meaning to be "confessing Islam and then renouncing it." Thereafter the meaning of "fight the heads of disbelief" (9:11,12) can only mean that war should be waged against the leaders instigating apostasy.[2]

B. Proof from the Hadith (Canonical Tradition) for the Commandment to Execute the Apostate

After the Qur'an we turn to the Hadith. This is the command of the Prophet:

1. Any person (i.e., Muslim) who has changed his religion, kill him.[3]

This tradition has been narrated by Abu Bakr, Uthman, Ali, Muadh ibn Jabal, Abu Musa Ashari, Abdullah ibn Abbas, Khalid ibn Walid and a number of other Companions, and is found in all the authentic Hadith collections.

2. Abdullah ibn Masud reports:

The Messenger of God stated: In no way is it permitted to shed the blood of a Muslim who testifies that "there is no god except God" and "I am the Apostle of God" except for three crimes: a. he has killed someone and his act merits retaliation; b. he is married and commits adultery; c. he abandons his religion and is separated from the community.[4]

3. Aisha reports:

The Messenger of God stated that it is unlawful to shed the blood of a Muslim other than for the following reasons: a. although married, he commits adultery or b. after being a Muslim he chooses *kufr,* or c. he takes someone's life.[5]

4. Uthman reports:

I heard the Messenger of God saying that it is unlawful to shed the blood of a Muslim except in three situations: a. a person who, being a Muslim, becomes a *kafir;* b. one who after marriage commits adultery; c. one who commits murder apart from having an authorization to take life in exchange for another life.[6]

Uthman further reports:

I heard the Messenger of God saying that it is unlawful to shed the blood of a Muslim with the exception of three crimes: a. the punishment of someone who after marriage commits adultery is stoning; b. retaliation is required against someone who intentionally commits murder; c. anyone who becomes an apostate after being a Muslim should be punished by death.[7]

All the reliable texts of history clearly prove that Uthman, while standing on the roof of his home, recited this tradition before thousands of people at a time when rebels had surrounded his house and were ready to kill him. His argument against the rebels was based on the point of this tradition that apart from these three crimes it was unlawful to put a Muslim to death for a fourth crime, "and I have committed none of these three. Hence after killing me, you yourself will be found guilty." It is evident that in this way this tradition became a clear argument in favour of Uthman against the rebels. Had there been the slightest doubt about the genuineness of this tradition, hundreds of voices would have cried out: "Your statement is false or doubtful!" But not even one person among the whole gathering of the rebels could raise an objection against the authenticity of this tradition.

5. Abu Musa Ashari reports:

The Prophet appointed and sent him (Abu Musa) as governor of Yemen. Then later he sent Muadh ibn Jabal as his assistant. When Muadh arrived there, he announced: People, I am sent by the Messenger of God for you. Abu Musa placed a cushion for him to be comfortably seated.

Meanwhile a person was presented who previously had been a Jew, then was a Muslim and then became a Jew. Muadh said: I will not sit unless this person is executed. This is the judgement of God and His Messenger.

Muadh repeated the statement three times. Finally, when he was killed, Muadh sat.[8]

It should be noted that this incident took place during the blessed life of the Prophet. At that time Abu Musa represented the Prophet as governor and Muadh as vice-governor. If their action had not been based on the decision of God and His Messenger, surely the Prophet would have objected.

6. Abdullah ibn Abbas reports:

Abdullah ibn Abi Sarh was at one time secretary to the Messenger of God. Then Satan seized him and he joined the *kuffar.* When Mecca was conquered the Messenger of God ordered that he be killed. Later, however, Uthman sought refuge for him and the Messenger of Allah gave him refuge.[9]

We find the commentary on this last incident in the narration of Sad ibn Abi Waqqas:

When Mecca was conquered, Abdullah ibn Sad ibn Abi Sarh took refuge with Uthman ibn Affan. Uthman took him and they presented themselves to the Prophet, requesting: O Messenger of God, accept the allegiance of Abdullah. The Prophet lifted his head, looked in his direction and remained silent. This happened three times and he (the Prophet) only looked in his direction. Finally after three times he accepted his allegiance. Then he turned towards his Companions and said: Was there no worthy man among you who, when he saw me withholding my hand from accepting his allegiance, would step forward and kill this person? The people replied: O Messenger of God, we did not know your wish. Why did you not signal with your eyes? To this the Prophet replied: It is unbecoming of a Prophet to glance in a stealthy manner.[10]

7. Aisha narrates:

On the occasion of the battle of Uhud (when the Muslims suffered defeat), a woman apostatized. To this the Prophet responded: Let her repent. If she does not repent, she should be executed.[11]

8. Jabir ibn Abdullah narrates:

A woman Umm Ruman (or Umm Marwan) apostatized. Then the prophet ordered that it would be better that she be offered Islam again and then repent. Otherwise she should be executed.[12]

A second report of Bayhaqi with reference to this reads:

She refused to accept Islam. Therefore she was executed. . . .

The Fundamental Objective of Islamic Rule

Islam establishes its rule not only with the purpose of organizing a nation but with a clear and fixed objective which it explains in these words:

He it is who hath sent His messenger with the guidance and the Religion of Truth, that He may cause it to prevail over all religion, however much the idolaters may be averse. (9:33)

And fight them until persecution is no more, and religion is all for Allah. . . . (8:39)

Thus We have appointed you a middle nation, that ye may be witnesses against mankind, and that the messenger may be a witness against you. . . . (2:143)

According to these verses the true purpose of the Messenger's mission is to ensure the victory of the guidance and Religion of Truth, which he has brought from God over every other competing order of life of a religious nature. From this it necessarily follows that where the Messenger achieves success in his mission, there he cannot let any movement arise which competes with God's guidance and His religion and strives for the ascendancy of another religion or order of life.

As the successors of the Messenger after the Messenger's departure are heirs of the religion which he had brought from God, in the same way they are heirs of the mission for which God had ordained him. The very purpose of all their struggles, it is agreed, is to make all religion the sole preserve of God.

Hence, wherever they control the affairs of this life and must be fully answerable to God for the administration of a particular country or territory, in no way during their tenure of supervision can they there legally provide an opportunity to any other religion to spread its message as competition to the religion of God, because the provision of such an opportunity will certainly mean that all religion will not be for God and whatever evil of any false order of life remains will further grow. In the end, to what will they testify before God? Will they testify: Where You have granted us the power to rule, there we have provided evil an opportunity to raise its head against Your religion? . . .

Source: "The Punishment of the Apostate According to Islamic Law." Answering Islam. Available online. URL: http://www.answering-islam.org/Hahn/Mawdudi/. Accessed July 4, 2006.

Hamas Charter (1988) (excerpts)

The Hamas Charter (also called the Hamas Covenant) was adopted on August 18, 1988. The covenant begins by invoking Allah and then proceeds to outline the movement's structure and goals in 36 articles. Its unrelenting opposition to "the Zionist entity" runs throughout the document, although readers may be interested to learn in Article 22 that Israel is responsible for creating "secret societies, such as Freemasons, Rotary Clubs, the Lions and others . . . for the purpose of sabotaging societies and achieving Zionist interests." Hamas's attitude toward the Palestine Liberation Organization is spelled out in Article 27: "We are unable to exchange the present or future Islamic Palestine with the secular idea. The Islamic nature of Palestine is part of our religion and whoever takes his religion lightly is a loser."

In The Name Of The Most Merciful Allah

"Ye are the best nation that hath been raised up unto mankind: ye command that which is just, and ye forbid that which is unjust, and ye believe in Allah. And if they who have received the scriptures had believed, it had surely been the better for them: there are believers among them, but the greater part of them are transgressors. They shall not hurt you, unless with a slight hurt; and if they fight against you, they shall turn their backs to you, and they shall not be helped. They are smitten with vileness wheresoever they are found; unless they obtain security by entering into a treaty with Allah, and a treaty with men; and they draw on themselves indignation from Allah, and they are afflicted with poverty. This they suffer, because they disbelieved the signs of Allah, and slew the prophets unjustly; this, because they were rebellious, and transgressed." (Al-Imran—verses 109–111).

"Israel will exist and will continue to exist until Islam will obliterate it, just as it obliterated others before it" (The Martyr, Imam Hassan al-Banna, of blessed memory).

"The Islamic world is on fire. Each of us should pour some water, no matter how little, to extinguish whatever one can without waiting for the others." (Sheikh Amjad al-Zahawi, of blessed memory). . . .

Introduction

Praise be unto Allah, to whom we resort for help, and whose forgiveness, guidance and support we seek; Allah bless the Prophet and grant him salvation, his companions and supporters, and to those who carried out his message and adopted his laws—everlasting prayers and salvation as long as the earth and heaven will last. Hereafter:

O People:

Out of the midst of troubles and the sea of suffering, out of the palpitations of faithful hearts and cleansed arms; out of the sense of duty, and in response to Allah's command, the call has gone out rallying people together and making them follow the ways of Allah, leading them to have determined will in order to fulfill their role in life, to overcome all obstacles, and surmount the difficulties on the way. Constant preparation has continued and so has the readiness to sacrifice life and all that is precious for the sake of Allah.

Thus it was that the nucleus (of the movement) was formed and started to pave its way through the tempestuous sea of hopes and expectations, of wishes and yearnings, of troubles and obstacles, of pain and challenges, both inside and outside.

When the idea was ripe, the seed grew and the plant struck root in the soil of reality, away from passing emotions, and hateful haste. The Islamic Resistance Movement emerged to carry out its role through striving for the sake of its Creator, its arms intertwined with those of all the fighters for the liberation of Palestine. The spirits of its fighters meet with the spirits of all the fighters who have sacrificed their lives on the soil of Palestine, ever since it was conquered by the companions of the Prophet, Allah bless him and grant him salvation, and until this day.

This Covenant of the Islamic Resistance Movement (HAMAS), clarifies its picture, reveals its identity, outlines its stand, explains its aims, speaks about its hopes, and calls for its support, adoption and joining its ranks. Our struggle against the Jews is very great and very serious. It needs all sincere efforts. It is a step that inevitably should be followed by other steps. The Movement is but one squadron that should be supported by more and more squadrons from this vast Arab and Islamic world, until the enemy is vanquished and Allah's victory is realised.

Thus we see them coming on the horizon "and you shall learn about it hereafter" "Allah hath written, Verily I will prevail, and my apostles: for Allah is strong and mighty." (The Dispute—verse 21).

"Say to them, This is my way: I invite you to Allah, by an evident demonstration; both I and he who followeth me; and, praise be unto Allah! I am not an idolator." (Joseph—verse 107).

Definition of the Movement. . .

Article One:

The Islamic Resistance Movement: The Movement's programme is Islam. From it, it draws its ideas, ways of thinking and understanding of the universe, life and man. It resorts to it for judgement in all its conduct, and it is inspired by it for guidance of its steps. . . .

Article Two:

The Islamic Resistance Movement is one of the wings of Moslem Brotherhood in Palestine. Moslem Brotherhood Movement is a universal organization which constitutes the largest Islamic movement in modern times. It is characterised by its deep understanding, accurate comprehension and its complete embrace of all Islamic concepts of all aspects of life, culture, creed, politics, economics, education, society, justice and judgment, the spreading of Islam, education, art, information, science of the occult and conversion to Islam. . . .

Article Three:

The basic structure of the Islamic Resistance Movement consists of Moslems who have given their allegiance to Allah whom they truly worship,—"I have created the jinn and humans only for the purpose of worshipping"—who know their duty towards themselves, their families and country. In all that, they fear Allah and raise the banner of Jihad in the face of the oppressors, so that they would rid the land and the people of their uncleanliness, vileness and evils.

"But we will oppose truth to vanity, and it shall confound the same; and behold, it shall vanish away." (Prophets—verse 18).

Article Four:

The Islamic Resistance Movement welcomes every Moslem who embraces its faith, ideology, follows its programme, keeps its secrets, and wants to belong to its ranks and carry out the duty. Allah will certainly reward such one. . . .

Article Five:

Time extent of the Islamic Resistance Movement: By adopting Islam as its way of life, the Movement goes back to the time of the birth of the Islamic message, of the righteous ancestor, for Allah is its target, the Prophet is its example and the Koran is its constitution. Its extent in place is anywhere that there are Moslems who embrace Islam as their way of life everywhere in the globe. This being so, it extends to the depth of the earth and reaches out to the heaven.

"Dost thou not see how Allah putteth forth a parable; representing a good word, as a good tree, whose root is firmly fixed in the earth, and whose branches reach unto heaven; which bringeth forth its fruit in all seasons, by the will of its Lord? Allah propoundeth parables unto men, that they may be instructed." (Abraham—verses 24–25). . . .

Article Six:

The Islamic Resistance Movement is a distinguished Palestinian movement, whose allegiance is to Allah, and whose way of life is Islam. It strives to raise the banner of Allah over every inch of Palestine, for under the wing of Islam followers of all religions can coexist in security and safety where their lives, possessions and rights are concerned. In the absence of Islam, strife will be rife, oppression spreads, evil prevails and schisms and wars will break out.

How excellent was the Moslem poet, Mohamed Ikbal, when he wrote:

"If faith is lost, there is no security and there is no life for him who does not adhere to religion. He who accepts life without religion, has taken annihilation as his companion for life." . . .

Article Seven:

As a result of the fact that those Moslems who adhere to the ways of the Islamic Resistance Movement spread all over the world, rally support for it and its stands, strive towards enhancing its struggle, the Movement is a universal one. It is well-equipped for that because of the clarity of its ideology, the nobility of its aim and the loftiness of its objectives.

On this basis, the Movement should be viewed and evaluated, and its role be recognised. He who denies its right, evades supporting it and turns a blind eye to facts, whether intentionally or unintentionally, would awaken to see that events have overtaken him and with no logic to justify his attitude. One should certainly learn from past examples. . . .

The Islamic Resistance Movement is one of the links in the chain of the struggle against the Zionist invaders. It goes back to 1939, to the emergence of the martyr Izz al-Din al Kissam and his brethren the fighters, members of Moslem Brotherhood. It goes on to reach out and become one with another chain that includes the struggle of the Palestinians and Moslem Brotherhood in the 1948 war and the Jihad operations of the Moslem Brotherhood in 1968 and after.

Moreover, if the links have been distant from each other and if obstacles, placed by those who are the lackeys of Zionism in the way of the fighters obstructed the continuation of the struggle, the Islamic Resistance Movement aspires to the realisation of Allah's promise, no matter how long that should take. The Prophet, Allah bless him and grant him salvation, has said:

"The Day of Judgment will not come about until Moslems fight the Jews (killing the Jews), when the Jew will hide behind stones and trees. The stones and trees will say O Moslems, O Abdulla, there is a Jew behind me, come and kill him. Only the Gharkad tree, (evidently a certain kind of tree) would not do that because it is one of the trees of the Jews." (related by al-Bukhari and Moslem). . . .

Article Eight:

Allah is its target, the Prophet is its model, the Koran its constitution: Jihad is its path and death for the sake of Allah is the loftiest of its wishes. . . .

Incentives and Objectives:

Article Nine:

The Islamic Resistance Movement found itself at a time when Islam has disappeared from life. Thus rules shook, concepts were upset, values changed and evil people took control, oppression and darkness prevailed, cowards became like tigers: homelands were usurped, people were scattered and were caused to wander all over the world, the state of justice disappeared and the state of falsehood replaced it. Nothing remained in its right place. Thus, when Islam is absent from the arena, everything changes. From this state of affairs the incentives are drawn.

As for the objectives: They are the fighting against the false, defeating it and vanquishing it so that justice could prevail, homelands be retrieved and from its mosques would the voice of the mu'azen emerge declaring the establishment of the state of Islam, so that people and things would return each to their right places and Allah is our helper.

". . . and if Allah had not prevented men, the one by the other, verily the earth had been corrupted: but Allah is beneficient towards his creatures." (The Cow—verse 251).

Article Ten:

As the Islamic Resistance Movement paves its way, it will back the oppressed and support the wronged with all its might. It will spare no effort to bring about justice and defeat injustice, in word and deed, in this place and everywhere it can reach and have influence therein.

Strategies and Methods. . .

Article Thirteen:

Initiatives, and so-called peaceful solutions and international conferences, are in contradiction to the principles of the Islamic Resistance Movement. Abusing any part of Palestine is abuse directed against part of religion. Nationalism of the Islamic Resistance Movement is part of its religion. Its members have been fed on that. For the sake of hoisting the banner of Allah over their homeland they fight. "Allah will be prominent, but most people do not know."

Now and then the call goes out for the convening of an international conference to look for ways of solving the (Palestinian) question. Some accept, others reject the idea, for this or other reason, with one stipulation or more for consent to convening the conference and participating in it. Knowing the parties constituting the conference, their past and present attitudes toward Moslem problems, the Islamic Resistance Movement does not consider these conferences capable of realising the demands, restoring the rights or doing justice to the oppressed. These conferences are only ways of setting the infidels in the land of the Moslems as arbitraters. When did the infidels do justice to the believers?

"But the Jews will not be pleased with thee, neither the Christians, until thou follow their religion; say, The direction of Allah is the true direction. And verily if thou follow their desires, after the knowledge which hath been given thee, thou shalt find no patron or protector against Allah." (The Cow—verse 120).

There is no solution for the Palestinian question except through Jihad. Initiatives, proposals and international conferences are all a waste of time and vain endeavors. The Palestinian people know better than to consent to having their future, rights and fate toyed with. As in said in the honourable Hadith:

"The people of Syria are Allah's lash in His land. He wreaks His vengeance through them against whomsoever He wishes among His slaves. It is unthinkable that those who are double-faced among them should prosper over the faithful. They will certainly die out of grief and desperation.". . .

Article Thirty-One:

The Islamic Resistance Movement is a humanistic movement. It takes care of human rights and is guided by Islamic tolerance when dealing with the followers of other religions. It does not antagonize anyone of them except if it is antagonized by it or stands in its way to hamper its moves and waste its efforts.

Under the wing of Islam, it is possible for the followers of the three religions—Islam, Christianity and Judaism—to coexist in peace and quiet with each other. Peace and quiet would not be possible except under the wing of Islam. Past and present history are the best witness to that.

It is the duty of the followers of other religions to stop disputing the sovereignty of Islam in this region, because the day these followers should take over there will be nothing but carnage, displacement and terror. Everyone of them is at variance with his fellow-religionists, not to speak about followers of other religionists. Past and present history are full of examples to prove this fact.

"They will not fight against you in a body, except in fenced towns, or from behind walls. Their strength in war among themselves is great: thou thinkest them to be united; but their hearts are divided. This, because they are people who do not understand." (The Emigration—verse 14).

Islam confers upon everyone his legitimate rights. Islam prevents the incursion on other people's rights. The Zionist Nazi activities against our people will not last for long. "For the state of injustice lasts but one day, while the state of justice lasts till Doomsday."

"As to those who have not borne arms against you on account of religion, nor turned you out of your dwellings, Allah forbiddeth you not to deal kindly with them, and to behave justly towards them; for Allah loveth those who act justly." (The Tried—verse 8). . . .

Article Thirty-Two:

World Zionism, together with imperialistic powers, try through a studied plan and an intelligent strategy to remove one Arab state after another from the circle of struggle against Zionism, in order to have it finally face the Palestinian people only. Egypt was, to a great extent, removed from the circle of the struggle, through the treacherous Camp David Agreement. They are trying to draw other Arab countries into similar agreements and to bring them outside the circle of struggle.

The Islamic Resistance Movement calls on Arab and Islamic nations to take up the line of serious and persevering action to prevent the success of this horrendous plan, to warn the people of the danger emanating from leaving the circle of struggle against Zionism. Today it is Palestine, tomorrow it will be one country or another. The Zionist plan is limitless. After Palestine, the Zionists aspire to expand from the Nile to the Euphrates. When they will have digested the region they overtook, they will aspire to further expansion, and so on. Their plan is embodied in the Protocols of the Elders of Zion, and their present conduct is the best proof of what we are saying.

Leaving the circle of struggle with Zionism is high treason, and cursed be he who does that. "For whoso shall turn his back unto them on that day, unless he turneth aside to fight, or retreateth to another party of the faithful, shall draw on himself the indignation of Allah, and his abode shall be hell; an ill journey shall it be thither." (The Spoils—verse 16). There is no way out except by concentrating all powers and energies to face this Nazi, vicious Tatar invasion. The alternative is loss of one's country, the dispersion of citizens, the spread of vice on earth and the destruction of religious values.

Let every person know that he is responsible before Allah, for "the doer of the slightest good deed is rewarded in like, and the does of the slightest evil deed is also rewarded in like."

The Islamic Resistance Movement considers itself to be the spearhead of the circle of struggle with world Zionism and a step on the road. The Movement adds its efforts to the efforts of all those who are active in the Palestinian arena. Arab and Islamic Peoples should augment by further steps on their part; Islamic groupings all over the Arab world should also do the same, since all of these are the best-equipped for the future role in the fight with the warmongering Jews.

". . . and we have put enmity and hatred between them, until the day of resurrection. So often as they shall kindle a fire of war, Allah shall extinguish it; and they shall set their minds to act corruptly in the earth, but Allah loveth not the corrupt doers." (The Table—verse 64). . . .

Article Thirty-Six:

While paving its way, the Islamic Resistance Movement, emphasizes time and again to all the sons of our people, to the Arab and Islamic nations, that it does not seek personal fame, material gain, or social prominence. It does not aim to compete against any one from among our people, or take his place. Nothing of the sort at all. It will not act against any of the sons of Moslems or those who are peaceful towards it from among non-Moslems, be they here or anywhere else. It will only serve as a support for all groupings and organizations operating against the Zionist enemy and its lackeys.

The Islamic Resistance Movement adopts Islam as its way of life. Islam is its creed and religion. Whoever takes Islam as his way of life, be it an organization, a grouping, a country or any other body, the Islamic Resistance Movement considers itself as their soldiers and nothing more.

We ask Allah to show us the right course, to make us an example to others and to judge between us and our people with truth. " O Lord, do thou judge between us and our nation with truth; for thou art the best judge." (Al Araf—Verse 89).

The last of our prayers will be praise to Allah, the Master of the Universe.

Source: "Hamas Covenant 1988." Avalon Project at Yale Law School. Available online. URL: http://www.yale.edu/lawweb/avalon/mideast/hamas.htm. Accessed July 5, 2006. There are several different English translations available online. The reader may find it helpful to look at more than one translation, as the general tone and style of the writing are different from what most Western readers are accustomed to. One done by a research fellow at the Hebrew University in Jerusalem (http://www.ict.org.il/articles/h_cov.htm) has footnotes that may be helpful to the reader.

Hinduism

M. S. Golwalkar: "We Want Men with a Capital M" (1957) (excerpts)

M. S. Golwalkar, known as Guruji to followers of Hindutva, was the second head of the Rashtriya Swayamsevak Sangh. The following excerpts are taken from a speech he gave to a group of students in Bangalore on November 30, 1957. The speech is strongly nationalistic but lacks the note of hostility toward other faiths that came to characterize Hindutva after 1980.

Our workers say that Bangalore is a very important place, about which there is no doubt. That this is a great educational center is also true. Being an educational center, every one expects that this shall be one of the centers from which the, [sic] work of national upliftment is to get inspired and guided also. It is for this purpose that educational centers are to function. When our workers said that such young men who ought to be intelligent and have the powers of mind and thought well developed in them would be made to assemble, I succumbed to their pressure and have come here. . . .

The attitude of a beggar we need not have. Secondly, the attitude of swollen-headedness must also be eradicated. We must be idealists and realists too. Realists in the sense of understanding our own capabilities and limitations. We should have a happy confluence of both idealism and realism. Each one should examine himself and understand his capabilities. He should know what should be his standard of understanding, his qualities, and above all his character. Character should be developed both individually and from the national point of view. What is that character which is sound from both the national and individual points of view? I don't know whether one in a thousand knows this. . . .

Man is not meant to be confined to his little self alone, to his family alone. He wants a companion, he wants a family, he wants people. He is a social animal, they say. He cannot be confined to a small family. Therefore this should be broadened. Then, can we have the ideal of humanity? That is beyond our ken. But family is too small. Hence we get the perfect poise, the balance, the medium path when we serve the nation. I had once met a big lawyer in Agra. He said: "If I cannot think of Humanity then why should I not think of my own family only?" I replied "Our life and happiness were defeated and destroyed when we only thought of 'Brahma Satyam, Jaganmithya'. Similar fate overtook us when we were only interested in our narrow family life. Either talking to 'Brahma Satyam, Jaganmithya' or confining to family alone is not good. So our shastras have laid down that both 'Ativyapti' and 'Avyapti' must be shunned. We must have a balanced equilibrium of the mind. Hence the service to the Nation."

Then the question arises, 'What is the nation?' A nation requires a Motherland and a people with complete devotion to the land. The people in whom there is the common tradition, common ideal, common sense of danger, common aspirations, form the nation. In a simple word, this is Hindu Rashtra. This is our Motherland. We have been living here, we don't know since how long. The people in whom community of feelings, oneness of culture, oneness of interests, are found is known today as the Hindu. Others living here have their interests in conflict with this main current of life. How can those who have ideological conflicts, historical hostilities and diverse interests be brought together to build an integrated nation? Hence when we come to grips with the reality, the whole entity of national life comes up before us in the form of Hindu. The interest of the Hindu, therefore, is our National interest. . . .

Show me any other people in the world who have faced and lived up to the present day facing all calamities. Now we are hearing of Socialism. All this socialism is bound to be reduced to dust. It has no foundation. Show me a society, which has sustained so many calamities as ours and is still in existence. There is none. The so-called national socialism, international socialism i.e. Communism, are all bound to go down in course of time. Then what is that which stands as a beacon light for humanity? We have got such an immortal social order. It has stood as an invincible fortress to all outside attacks. We even now live on account of our cultural heritage. We should not forget this. Why should we have inferiority complex? To be a carbon copy of all others? Impossible.

So we begin with self. The real revolution must come from within. There should be a mental revolution. We must downright discard all that is foreign. Then, should we take nothing that comes from others? We take the food inside and not paint it on our body, digest it and turn it into our own body. Our body remains the same, becoming more strong. In the same manner if anything should be taken, it should be digested and made into our own body. But now we are taking all the things coming from outside at the cost of our own vitality. . . .

If then, as we have seen, the basic defect has been the absence of intense national sentiment and organised life, by concord and co-coordinated existence once again this great nation can be made to stand and maintain its position of dominance in the world—by the greatness of our life, with that eternal and immortal ideal in our life, with this intellectual revolution in our life. Let us all therefore come together and have a powerful national existence. The quality of imitation, looking at America or Russia, is that of an effeminate man. We want a 'Man' with a capital 'M'. We want a virile, masculine man. Now our people are feminine men. The masculinity, the great courage, the complete NARA is required. When NARAYANA, eternal knowledge [,] and NARA—eternal manliness—these come together it is all victory. Let us be strong on our own foundations, invincible and unshakable. Let us endeavour towards this ideal. That is my request to you all. I pray God for a very long life for every one of us in building up a strong co-coordinated national existence, which shall have the strength to face any calamity and stand unassailable in the world.

Source: "We Want Men with Capital 'M.'" SriGuruji.org. Available online. URL: http://www.shriguruji.org/index.php?option=com_content&task=view&id=47 &Itemid=84. Accessed July 5, 2006.

"Hindutva: The Great Nationalist Ideology" (undated)

The following undated document is posted on the official Web site of the Bharatiya Janata Party as a statement of its political philosophy. It is probably the best recent summary available in English of the beliefs and goals of adherents of Hindutva. The reader will note the strong undercurrent of hostility to Muslims.

In the history of the world, the Hindu awakening of the late twentieth century will go down as one of the most monumental events in the history of the world. Never before has such demand for change come from so many people. Never before has Bharat, the ancient word for the motherland of Hindus [, or] India, been confronted with such an impulse for change. This movement, Hindutva, is changing the very foundations of Bharat and Hindu society the world over.

Hindu society has an unquestionable and proud history of tolerance for other faiths and respect for diversity of spiritual experiences. This is reflected in the many different philosophies, religious sects, and religious leaders. The very foundation of this lies in the great Hindu heritage that is not based on any one book, teacher, or doctrine. In fact the pedestal of Hindu society stems from the great Vedic teachings Ekam Sat Viprah Bahudha Vadanti—Truth is One, Sages Call it by Many Names, and Vasudhaiva Kutumbakam—The Whole Universe is one Family. It is this philosophy which allowed the people of Hindusthan (land of the Hindus) to shelter the Jews who faced Roman persecution, the Zoroastrians who fled the Islamic sword and who are the proud Parsi community today, and the

Tibetan Buddhists who today face the communist secularism: persecution of religion.

During the era of Islamic invasions, what Will Durant called the bloodiest period in the history of mankind, many Hindus gallantly resisted, knowing full well that defeat would mean a choice of economic discrimination via the jaziya tax on non-Muslims, forced conversion, or death. It is no wonder that the residents of Chittor, and countless other people over the length and breadth of Bharat, from present-day Afghanistan to present-day Bangladesh, thought it better to die gloriously rather than face cold-blooded slaughter. Hindus never forgot the repeated destruction of the Somnath Temple, the massacre of Buddhists at Nalanda, or the pogroms of the Mughals.

Thus, the seeds of today's Hindu Jagriti, awakening, were created the very instance that an invader threatened the fabric of Hindu society which was religious tolerance. The vibrancy of Hindu society was noticeable at all times in that despite such barbarism from the Islamic hordes of central Asia and Turkey, Hindus never played with the same rules that Muslims did. The communist and Muslim intelligentsia, led by Nehruvian ideologists who are never short of distorted history, have been unable to show that any Hindu ruler ever matched the cruelty of even a "moderate" Muslim ruler.

It is these characteristics of Hindu society and the Muslim psyche that remain today. Hindus never lost their tolerance and willingness to change. However Muslims, led by the Islamic clergy and Islamic society's innate unwillingness to change, did not notice the scars that Hindus felt from the Indian past. It is admirable that Hindus never took advantage of the debt Muslims owed Hindus for their tolerance and non-vengefulness.

In modern times, Hindu Jagriti gained momentum when Muslims played the greatest abuse of Hindu tolerance: the demand for a separate state and the partition of India, a nation that had had a common history and culture for countless millenia. Thus, the Muslim minority voted for a separate state and the Hindus were forced to sub-divide their own land.

After partition in Pakistan, Muslim superiority was quickly asserted and the non-Muslim minorities were forced to flee due to the immense discrimination in the political and religious spheres. Again, Hindus did not respond to such an onslaught. Hindu majority India continued the Hindu ideals by remaining secular.

India even gave the Muslim minority gifts such as separate personal laws, special status to the only Muslim majority state—Kashmir, and other rights that are even unheard of in the bastion of democracy and freedom, the United States of America. Islamic law was given precedence over the national law in instances that came under Muslim personal law. The Constitution was changed when the courts, in the Shah Bano case, ruled that a secular nation must have one law, not separate religious laws. Islamic religious and educational institutions were given a policy of non-interference. The list goes on.

More painful for the Hindus was forced negation of Hindu history and factors that gave pride to Hindus. Hindu customs and traditions were mocked as remnants of a non-modern society, things that would have to go if India was to modernize like the west. The self-proclaimed guardians of India, the politicians of the Congress Party who called themselves secularists, forgot that it was the Hindu psyche that believed in secularism, it was the Hindu thought that had inspired the greatest intellectuals of the world such as Thoreau, Emerson, Tolstoy, Einstein, and others, and that it was Hindus, because there was no other land where Hindus were in a significant number to stand up in defence of Hindu society if and when the need arose, who were the most nationalistic people in India.

When Hindus realized that pseudo-secularism had reduced them to the role of an innocent bystander in the game of politics, they demanded a true secularism where every religious group would be treated the same and a government that would not take Hindu sentiments for granted. Hindutva awakened the Hindus to the new world order where nations represented the aspirations of people united in history, culture, philosophy, and heroes. Hindutva successfully took the Indian idol of Israel and made Hindus realize that their India could be just as great and could do the same for them also.

In a new era of global consciousness, Hindus realized that they had something to offer the world. There was something more than tolerance and universal unity. The ancient wisdom of sages through eternity also offered systems of thought, politics, music, language, dance, and education that could benefit the world.

There have been many changes in the thinking of Hindus, spearheaded over the course of a century by innumerable groups and leaders who made their own distinct contribution to Hindu society: Swami Vivekananda, Rabindranath Tagore, Gandhiji, Rashatriya Swayamsevak Sangh, Swami Chinmayananda, Maharishi Mahesh Yogi, International Society for Krishna Consciousness, Muni Susheel Kumarji, Vishwa Hindu Parishad, Bharatiya Janata Party, and others. Each in their own way increased pride in being a Hindu and simultaneously showed Hindus their greatest strengths and their worst weaknesses. This slowly shook the roots of Hindu society and prompted a rear-guard action by the ingrained interests: the old politicians, the Nehruvian intellectual community, and the appeased Muslim leadership.

The old foundation crumbled in the 1980s and 1990s when Hindus respectfully asked for the return of their most holy religious site, Ayodhya. This demand promptly put the 40-year old apparatus to work, and press releases were chunked out that spew the libelous venom which called those who represented the Hindu aspirations "militant" and "fundamentalist," stigmas which had heretofore found their proper place in the movements to establish Islamic law. Hindus were humble enough to ask for the restoration of an ancient temple built on the birthplace of Rama, and destroyed by Babar, a foreign invader. The vested interests were presented with the most secular of propositions: the creation of a monument to a national hero, a legend whose fame and respect stretched out of the borders of India into southeast Asia, and even into Muslim Indonesia. A hero who existed before there was anyone in India who considered himself separate from Hindu society. The 400-year old structure at one of the holiest sites of India had been worshipped as a temple by Hindus even though the Muslim general Mir Baqi had partially built a non-functioning mosque on it. It was very important that no Muslims, except those who were appeased in Indian politics, had heard of anything called Babri Masjid before the pseudo-secularist apparatus started the next to last campaign against the rising Hindu society. It was also important that no Muslim had offered prayers at the site for over 40 years.

Hindus hid their true anger, that their most important religious site still bore the marks of a cruel slavery that occurred so very recently in the time span of Hindu history. It was naturally expected in 1947 that freedom from the political and economic chains of Great Britain would mean that the systems and symbols that had enslaved India and caused its deterioration and poverty would be obliterated. Forty years after independence, Hindus realized that their freedom was yet to come.

So long as freedom to Jews meant that symbols of the Holocaust in Europe were condemned, so long as freedom to African-Americans meant that the symbols of racial discrimination were wiped out, and so long as freedom from imperialism to all people meant that they would have control of their own destinies, that they would have their own heroes, their own stories, and their own culture, then freedom to Hindus meant that they would have to condemn the Holocaust that Muslims reaped on them, the racial discrimination that the white man brought, and the economic imperialism that enriched Britain. Freedom for Hindus and Indians would have to mean that their heroes such as Ram, Krishna, Sivaji, the Cholas, Sankaracharya, and Tulsidas would be respected, that their own stories such as the Ramayana and the Mahabharata would be offered to humanity as examples of the brilliance of Hindu and Indian thinking, and that their own culture which included the Bhagavad Gita, the Vedas, the temples, the gods and goddesses, the art, the music, and the contributions in various fields, would be respected. Freedom meant that as the shackles of imperial dominance were lifted, the newly freed people would not simply absorb foreign ideas, they would share their own as well.

In India, something went wrong. The freedom from Britain was supposed to result in a two-way thinking that meant that non-Indian ideas would be accepted and that Indian ideas would be presented to the world. So long as the part of India giving to the world was suppressed, the freedom was only illusory and the aspirations of the freedom hungry would continue to rise in temperature.

The freedom could have been achieved if a temple to Rama was built and the symbol of foreign rule was moved to another site or demolished. The battle was never really for another temple. Another temple could have been built anywhere in India.

The humble and fair demand for RamaJanmabhoomi could have resulted in a freedom for India, freedom from the intellectual slavery that so dominated India. This freedom would have meant that all Indians regardless of religion, language, caste, sex, or color would openly show respect for the person that from ancient times was considered the greatest hero to people of Hindusthan. For the first time, Hindus had demanded something, and it was justifiable that a reasonable demand from an undemanding people would be realized. Imagine if the Muslim leadership had agreed to shift the site and build a temple in Ayodhya. How much Hindu-Muslim unity there would have been in India? India could then have used that goodwill to solve the major religious, caste, and economic issues facing the country.

But some of the vested interests in politics and in the Muslim community saw that such a change would mean that their work since 1947 would be overturned and that this new revolution would displace them. Rather than join forces and accept the rising tide, the oligarchy added fuel to the greatest movement in Indian history. One that on December 6, 1992 completely shattered the old and weak roots of Indian society and with it, the old political and intellectual structure. The destruction by the Kar Sevaks of the dilapidated symbol of foreign dominance was the last straw in a heightening of tensions by the government, and the comittant anger of more and more Hindus to rebuffs of their reasonable demands.

The ruthless last-ditch effort of the powers-that-be was the banning and suppression of the leaders of the Hindu Jagriti. The effort of the rulers reminds one of the strategy of all ill-fated rulers. Throughout history, when monumental upheavals have taken place, the threatened interests have resorted to drastic measures, which in-turn have hastened their own death.

Hindus are at last free. They control their destiny now and there is no power that can control them except their own tolerant ethos. India in turn is finally free. Having ignored its history, it has now come face to face with a repressed conscience. The destruction of the structure at Ayodhya was the release of the history that Indians had not fully come to terms with. Thousands of years of anger and shame, so diligently bottled up by these same interests, was released when the first piece of the so-called Babri Masjid was torn down.

It is a fundamental concept of Hindu Dharma that has won: righteousness. Truth won when Hindus, realizing that Truth could not be won through political or legal means, took the law into their own hands. Hindus have been divided politically and the laws have not acknowledged the quiet Hindu yearning for Hindu unity which has until recently taken a back seat to economic development and Muslim appeasement. Similarly, the freedom movement represented the supersedence of Indian unity over loyalty to the British Crown. In comparison to the freedom movement though, Hindutva involves many more people and represents the mental freedom that 1947 did not bring.

The future of Bharat is set. Hindutva is here to stay. It is up to the Muslims whether they will be included in the new nationalistic spirit of Bharat. It is up to the government and the Muslim leadership whether they wish to increase Hindu furor or work with the Hindu leadership to show that Muslims and the government will consider Hindu sentiments. The era of one-way compromise of Hindus is over, for from now on, secularism must mean that all parties must compromise.

Hindutva will not mean any Hindu theocracy or theology. However, it will mean that the guiding principles of Bharat will come from two of the great teachings of the Vedas, the ancient Hindu and Indian scriptures, which so boldly proclaimed—TRUTH IS ONE, SAGES CALL IT BY MANY NAMES—and—THE WHOLE UNIVERSE IS ONE FAMILY.

Source: "Hindutva: The Great Nationalist Ideology." Bharatiya Janata Party. Available online. URL: http://www.bjp.org/philo.htm. Accessed July 5, 2006.

PART III

Research Tools

6

How to Research Fundamentalism

GENERAL CONSIDERATIONS

Getting Started

When researching a large topic such as fundamentalism, it is best to focus the area of study as much as possible as quickly as possible. Although fundamentalism did not attract much attention from writers outside the field of American religious history until a few years ago, it has generated numerous popular as well as scholarly books and articles—particularly since the events of September 11, 2001. The amount of material available on the Internet as well as in printed books and newspaper archives is steadily increasing. In order to keep the area of research manageable, it is a good idea to be specific about the following points:

- The religion, denomination, or movement to be studied. If the religion in question is one of the three monotheistic faiths (Christianity, Judaism, or Islam), the researcher can narrow the field further and look at one specific church or branch of that religion. One way to focus the topic is to read an article about it in a general encyclopedia or an encyclopedia of religion. These resources are intended to provide a general overview of the subject and the main concepts or persons related to it. They will also suggest sources for further reading. If the researcher is interested in a specific person, a biographical dictionary or encyclopedia will often provide a short (usually up to two or three pages) article.
- The period of history under consideration, keeping in mind that fundamentalism is a 20th- and 21st-century development. In some cases World War I (1914–18) and World War II (1939–45) will serve as convenient historical markers for a "before-and-after" research project.

In the United States and western Europe, the 1960s are another useful historical turning point. More recently, 9/11 has become another watershed event.

- Specific features of interest in the group or movement: political, sociological, psychological, theological. If the group emphasizes political activism, what are its goals, leadership structure, and relationship to the government? If the group is interesting from a sociological or psychological perspective, who joins it and why? Does it attract people from certain social classes or age groups, or is it broadly based? How large is it in terms of the general population? How does it recruit new members? If the group defines itself theologically (by expecting members to accept specific doctrines or teachings), what are its sources of religious authority? Does it emphasize intellectual understanding more than emotional intensity? How does it spread its doctrines or instruct new members?

There are other questions that one can ask, but these may be useful in beginning to look for written resources, photographs, and other material.

Gathering Material

When gathering material, the researcher must consider how much and what types of documents are needed. A five-minute classroom talk will not need as much research as a 10- or 20-page paper. In addition, the historical period or date of the event, movement, or person of interest will indicate what types of documents will be most helpful. In general, the more recent the topic, the more current the sources will need to be. An information time line may be useful:

- Immediate information about developing situations (minutes to hours old): the Internet
- One day to one week: the Internet and general newspapers; some weekly news magazines
- One month: popular magazines, including popular religious periodicals
- Several months or more: scholarly journals
- A year or more: encyclopedias and similar reference sources; printed books

In general, a topic that would come under the heading of current events requires recent materials that reflect current perspectives on the subject, whereas a topic of a historical nature will require a variety of resources from different time periods. For example, someone researching recent episodes of Muslim fundamentalists attacking bars or liquor stores will begin with Internet news sources, newspapers, and news magazines, whereas someone studying the Prohibition era in American history will consult encyclopedia articles about it, perhaps a biographical dictionary for a brief article about Frances Willard or Billy Sunday, general histories of the 1920s, histories of American religion in the 20th century, and articles about Prohibition in scholarly journals. The books and journal articles may be chosen from different time periods as a way of getting different perspectives on Prohibition. For example, people writing in the 1940s, about a decade after Prohibition had been repealed, looked at the period differently from writers in the 1970s, who often compared Prohibition to current attempts to control marijuana and other drugs. People writing in the early 2000s have still another perspective, shaped by two decades of medical research into alcohol and drug addiction.

The reader should note that books, encyclopedias, and scholarly journals are often available on the Internet. Many school and public libraries subscribe to such database services as American National Biography, published by Oxford University Press, or InfoTrac, published by Thomson Gale. InfoTrac is a collection of databases that includes such specific resources as the World Biographical Information System, History Resource Center, Declassified Documents Reference System, National Newspaper Index, Biography Resource Center, and others that are useful in researching topics related to fundamentalism.

Researchers interested in the sacred books of a specific religion or denomination can usually find such documents in their entirety on the Internet in at least one English version. Below are listed some specific URLs.

CHRISTIANITY

The Holy Bible is available in full online in a number of different English translations:

Douai-Rheims (1582). URL: http://www.drbo.org/. This was the standard English translation used by Roman Catholics before the Second Vatican Council.

King James Version (1611). URL: http://www.bartleby.com/108/ (each chapter is in a separate file) or http://etext.lib.virginia.edu/kjv.browse.html.

Scofield Reference Bible (1917 edition). URL: http://www.biblebelievers.com/scofield_reference_bible/index.html or http://bible.crosswalk.com/Commentaries/ScofieldReferenceNotes/.

Revised Standard Version (1952). URL: http://etext.lib.virginia.edu/rsv.browse.html. New Revised Standard Version (1989). URL: http://www.devotions.net/bible/00bible.htm.

HINDUISM

The Vedas: URL: http://www.sacred-texts.com/hin/ or http://www.comparative-religion.com/hinduism/vedas/. The former offers the 1896 and 1914 translations by Ralph Griffith and A. B. Keith, as well as the original Sanskrit texts.

ISLAM

The Qur'an: URL: http://www.hti.umich.edu/k/koran/ or http://etext.lib.virginia.edu/koran.html. Both of these are the M. H. Shakir translation.

JUDAISM

The Hebrew Bible (Tanakh): URL: http://www.jewishvirtuallibrary.org/jsource/Bible/jpstoc.html or http://www.mechon-mamre.org/p/pt/pt0.htm. The first is the 1917 English translation by the Jewish Publication Society; the second is a Hebrew-English version of the Masoretic text and the JPS 1917 translation.

MORMONISM

The Church of Jesus Christ of Latter-day Saints has the complete texts of the *Book of Mormon, Doctrine and Covenants,* and *Pearl of Great Price* on its Web site: URL: http://scriptures.lds.org/contents.

Evaluating Documents

Evaluating materials once they have been gathered is a critical step in researching topics related to fundamentalism. This task is not always easy, but with practice and experience, a careful reader can usually decide whether a document is reliable or whether its source is trustworthy.

DOCUMENT SOURCE

The first consideration is the document's source. Does it come from inside or outside the group being studied? If it is an internal document, is it used in worship (such as a hymn, a prayer, a liturgy, a sermon, a passage from a sacred book) or is it an official history of the group, statement of faith, papal encyclical, or similar public document? In general, hymns, prayers, chants, and portions of a liturgy are devotional in character; they should not be read in the same way as formal statements of faith or scholarly theological works. If a document comes from outside the group being studied, is it intended for general readers (such as reports in a newspaper, weekly news magazine, or posted on an Internet site) or is it written for an academic audience? If it is written for educated readers, is it intended for those with a general interest in the subject or is it written for experts with specialized training or background information? As a rule, academic resources are usually more trustworthy with regard to basic facts (full names and titles of persons, dates and locations of events, correct spelling of foreign words, etc.) than reports in the mass media.

DATE OF PUBLICATION

The date of publication is an important item of information in evaluating the completeness or currency of the information it contains. If the topic being researched concerns recent events, newspaper and Internet reports should be arranged in order of the date of publication or posting. The reason for this precaution is that first reports—particularly of tragic or horrifying events—are often inaccurate in some of their details. The first analyses or interpretations of the event are also often incorrect. One example of this problem is the Oklahoma City bombing of April 1995. Even though Timothy McVeigh was caught within an hour of the attack, the first news reports speculated that the explosion had been caused by Arab terrorists. Precisely because fundamentalism is an emotion-laden subject for many people, it is important to make sure that the basic facts of any current event are stated as accurately as possible in a research study. For this reason it is a good idea to gather news reports from more than one newspaper or communications service (such as Reuters or the Associated Press).

If the topic is historical, the date of publication may shed some light on the author's perspective or analysis. For example, books on terrorism written after September 2001 typically contain more information about religious fundamentalism than those written before that date. In addition, books or journal articles written before the 1990s generally speak of fundamentalism as belonging to the past, whereas those written after the reemergence of fundamentalist movements are more likely to discuss it as a present concern.

TONE

Tone refers to the style or manner in which a document is written. It is often necessary to ask questions in evaluating the tone of a document related to fundamentalism. If the material is used in worship, is it intended to instruct the worshipper or arouse religious feelings? If it is intended to teach, is it concerned with positive teachings of the religion or with drawing lines between the group and outsiders? Is it judgmental or hostile? Does it contain conspiracy theories or emphasize the importance of secrecy? If the document is intended to arouse feelings, what emotions does it bring to the surface? Does it move the worshipper to love and trust God and the neighbor? To be fearful and anxious about the future? To lash out in anger at outsiders? The same question of tone can be asked of official statements of faith or histories of the group written by its members. Are they straightforward and matter-of-fact in setting out the group's beliefs (or its history), or do they seem intended to convert rather than inform the reader?

Tone is also an important consideration in evaluating documents that originate outside a group, particularly with a subject like fundamentalism. As was mentioned in Part I, American fundamentalists were regarded for many years as unworthy of serious attention, and the term *fundamentalist* was all too often used carelessly to make fun of or attack any religious conservative. Newspaper editorials or opinions written by columnists about fundamentalism, for example, are usually quite different in tone from news reports because they are intended to persuade the reader to agree with the editor or columnist's viewpoint.

Tone also covers matters such as formality of language. In general, objective descriptions of a movement, person, or event are more likely to be written in formal English than in a casual or chatty manner. Scholarly books or journals are typically written in a more formal tone than news reports or popular magazines, which have more freedom to use current slang or colloquial expressions.

RELIABILITY

Reliability refers to the integrity or dependability of the source in question. In some instances, as in the case of Mark Hofmann mentioned in Part I, documents turn out to be forgeries. Sometimes, of course, newly discovered documents are sometimes labeled as forgeries by people who are uncomfortable with their contents. For example, when the Dead Sea scrolls were discovered in the late 1940s, some of them contained versions of some Bible verses that differed from those in the manuscripts used by the translators of the King James Bible. As a result, some American fundamentalists claimed that the Dead Sea scrolls were forgeries sold to Western scholars to discredit Christianity. An electronic version of forgery that sometimes occurs on the Internet is the planting of a fake document on a Web site.

The most common problem that a beginning researcher confronts in studying fundamentalism, however, is *bias.* Bias refers to a prejudice or tendency of mind that prevents a person from making an objective or impartial judgment. In some cases, bias is the result of government or religious censorship. For example, the government of India in the late 1990s ordered history textbooks used in schools to be rewritten to advance the theories of Hindu nationalists. Another example is the withdrawing of a book by an American scholar from publication in India in 2004 because some fundamentalists were upset by his study of a 17th-century ruler they regard as a hero. In other cases, however, bias results from the writer's own prejudices or blind spots. For example, the sharp division between religious and secular Israelis, which is reinforced by the country's parallel educational systems, means that a book on Jewish fundamentalism by a secular Israeli writer, or a book on Israeli secularism by a fundamentalist, may be biased in its selection of material for discussion. One way to check for bias is to gather materials from sources on opposite sides of the issue as well as from different historical periods.

Another problem related to reliability concerns news reports about current events. Most reporters are conscientious professionals who do their best to convey accurate information about breaking news in a straightforward and timely fashion. News reports, however, are sometimes misleading because reporters are not experts on every subject they must cover in the course of their work. In addition, they are usually under pressure to file stories within a very short period of time. With respect to religion in particular, a reporter who is not well acquainted with the faith represented in a news story may not understand the significance of certain aspects of the story or may interpret them in terms that are more familiar to him or her but are not accurate. A specific example is the tendency to equate "Arab" with "Muslim." There were a number of news stories filed in the fall of 2003 about the bombing of a foreign workers' compound in Saudi Arabia and a restaurant in Israel in which reporters assumed that the Lebanese workers in the compound and the Arab co-owner of the restaurant were Muslims because of their ethnicity. The news commentators then asked why the terrorists who planted the bombs were targeting "fellow Muslims." In fact, all of the victims were Lebanese and Arab Christians who had been targeted because of their religion. While this type of misunderstanding should not be confused with intentional bias or slanting of a news report, it does mean that readers should not assume that current news reports, whether online or in print, are always completely reliable.

Special Concerns

FOREIGN LANGUAGES

There are a few special problems related to researching fundamentalism beyond English-speaking Protestantism that should be mentioned. The first concerns translations. Readers who are interested in topics related to Roman Catholicism, Judaism, Islam, or Hinduism must depend on accurate translations if they cannot read Latin, Hebrew, Arabic, Urdu, Hindi, or Sanskrit. Accuracy and clarity are not usually issues with translations of Roman

Catholic or Jewish documents, as both faiths have a long tradition of biblical scholarship and are relatively familiar to readers in North America. In the case of Islam and Hinduism, however, it is a good idea to read a specific document in more than one translation if possible—partly because these religions are less familiar to most Westerners and partly because their vocabulary and concepts can often be translated in more than one way.

REJECTION OF OBJECTIVITY AS A VALUE

A more pressing problem, however, is that political fundamentalist movements in India and in Muslim countries disagree with the very notion of objectivity or impartiality because they see it as a "Western" attack on their religious faith. Printed materials or Web sites produced by these movements or organizations are often quite frank about urging their point of view on readers and make no attempt to follow conventional standards of objectivity. It is best to use such materials with care and to check their contents against information gathered from encyclopedias of religion or similar reference books.

Rejection of objectivity is one reason why open-source encyclopedias on the Internet—Wikipedia being the best-known example—should be consulted sparingly if the researcher is studying Muslim or Hindu fundamentalisms. Although many observers have noted that Wikipedia articles in general vary widely in quality, problems of bias are particularly common in articles dealing with Islam, Hinduism, or political groups related to them. Since anyone can edit Wikipedia articles, it is not unusual to find an article on a topic related to Islam or Hinduism rewritten literally overnight, often by someone whose English is not the best. Some biographies of religious leaders or holy people have a devotional or preachy quality that is out of place in a reference source. Although articles that are questioned in regard to objectivity or considered unsatisfactory for other reasons are often identified as such by an icon and accompanying comment, the feedback and correction process can be quite slow.

MEMBERSHIP STATISTICS

A third problem in studying fundamentalism is interpreting membership statistics. One method of determining size comes from official denominational or organizational statistics. The difficulty here is that different religious groups count members in different ways. Some count only those who attend services on a regular basis or who have completed a formal process of initiation (adult baptism, confirmation, First Communion, bar/bas mitzvah, etc.), while others count anyone who has ever been baptized as an infant or attended services as a child.

Other sources of religious membership statistics include government censuses or polls and surveys. These two types of source rely on self-identification; that is, the person describes or acknowledges their religious affiliation to the census taker or the survey worker. These sources are not always reliable because some countries do not ask citizens about religion. In addition, a census taken every 10 years may not be helpful in identifying recent membership trends. The accuracy of polls and surveys depends on the size of the sample. In particular, polls often under-report the membership of small religious groups because they may not take a large enough sample of the general population to obtain accurate statistics.

The last method for estimating the size of a religious group is indirect. Indirect methods are used with groups that maintain a high level of secrecy, such as most Christian Identity groups. These indirect methods include magazine circulation figures or an estimate of the number of people who attend the group's conferences or other public events.

In general, when comparing sizes of different religious bodies, it is best to obtain figures that were obtained in the same way from each group in the comparison. If comparable figures cannot be gathered, the researcher should note the method of collection for each group.

BIBLIOGRAPHIC RESOURCES

Library of Congress

For researchers interested in historical topics related to fundamentalism, the Library of Congress Online Catalog (http://catalog.loc.gov/) is a good place to begin. The online catalog has a page of frequently asked questions (FAQs) and another page of tips for basic or guided searching that are useful for beginner researchers. The basic search page allows searching under title, author, keyword, and subject heading. *Subject heading* refers to the library's system for indexing books and other materials in their holdings by topic. The Library of Congress Subject Heading (LCSH) system is used by most other large libraries in the United States. LCSH headings are broken down into subheadings by geographical area, historical period, literary category, and others. For example, using *fundamentalism* in the "subject browse" function yields 318 LCSH subheadings, including Fundamentalism—Case studies, Fundamentalism—Economic aspects, Fundamentalism—Fiction, and many others. Searching under the subhead "Case studies" yields two specific book titles. Reference librarians in most school and public libraries are usually available to help researchers with specific questions about the LCSH system.

Institutional Libraries

Institutional libraries are good places to look for materials on fundamentalism that may not be available in general public libraries. Some large university libraries have online catalogs that can be consulted by off-campus researchers. The libraries of theological seminaries or research institutions often have large collections of books on fundamentalism. In some cases, researchers can obtain specific titles through an interlibrary loan or request photocopies of documents, although there is usually a per-page charge for photocopied materials as well as a time delay.

Special Collections

There are some American libraries affiliated with conservative, fundamentalist, or evangelical churches or educational institutions that have special collections of congregational histories, personal papers, videotapes, oral histories, or similar materials related to the history of conservative religious movements in the United States. The J. S. Mack Library at Bob Jones University (http://www.bju.edu/library/home.html), the Southern Baptist Historical Library and Archives (http://www.sbhla.org/info.htm), the Concordia Historical Institute of the Lutheran Church–Missouri Synod (http://chi.lcms.org/), the Cushwa Center for the Study of American Catholicism at the University of Notre Dame (http://www.nd.edu/~cushwa/), and the Institute for the Study of American Evangelicals at Wheaton College (http://www.wheaton.edu/isae/) are all open to researchers interested in their special collections. Again, many of these libraries will send photocopies of specific materials to researchers who live at a distance.

Periodicals

Religious periodicals can be very helpful to researchers studying recent events or new movements related to fundamentalism. Those that have been in publication for long periods of time (50 years or longer) can also be useful in tracing the development of fundamentalist, evangelical, or conservative religious movements over a specific time span. Theological seminary libraries often have archives of religious periodicals; in addition, some of these journals are available online.

The reader should note, however, that religious periodicals range from popular monthly magazines intended for a general audience to highly specialized academic journals. The following broad outline of periodical types may be useful in narrowing the search.

- Denominational magazines intended for the membership of a specific church. These often resemble popular weekly news magazines in format. They are printed on glossy paper, usually with numerous photographs. Articles are generally written in a journalistic rather than academic style; they are signed but do not carry footnotes or bibliography. Examples include *U.S. Catholic, Presbyterians Today, The Lutheran,* and *United Church News.*
- Interdenominational journals for the educated laity. These carry editorials and commentaries on current events as well as news items from a range of denominations or faith groups. The best-known examples in this category are *Christian Century,* which represents the outlook of the mainline churches, and *Christianity Today* (*CT*), which is evangelical Protestant. *CT* is a good source of current news items about fundamentalist groups.
- Professional journals for clergy and church musicians. These periodicals resemble academic journals in writing style and format; articles are usually peer reviewed and include bibliographies and footnotes. Some deal with general matters of church administration and leadership, such as *Clergy Journal* (mainline Protestant), *Ministry and Liturgy* (Roman Catholic), or *Leadership* (Protestant evangelical). Others are devoted to specific areas of ministry, such as preaching (*Homiletic, Pulpit Helps, The African American Pulpit*), counseling (*Journal of Pastoral Theology, American Journal of Pastoral Counseling*), or Christian education (*Christian Educators Journal, Journal of Christian Education and Information Technology*). Periodicals in this category can be helpful to researchers interested in the worship life of fundamentalist, evangelical, and traditionalist Roman Catholic groups. Journals of pastoral counseling are good places to look for case studies of former fundamentalists who have joined more liberal churches.
- Scholarly journals. These are usually published on a quarterly or semiannual basis. Articles are peer reviewed and typically have extensive footnotes and bibliographies, which can be useful to researchers looking for additional resources. Journals of this type can be useful for researching topics in the psychology, social background, or political activity of fundamentalists, as well as the history and beliefs of fundamentalist groups.

The American Theological Libraries Association (ATLA) Religion Database includes three major electronic indexes to help researchers: Religion Index One (RIO), which covers more than 1,400 periodicals; Religion Index

Two (RIT), which covers multi-author publications; and the Index to Book Reviews in Religion (IBRR). Most university or theological seminary libraries will have this database or the print editions of RIO, RIT, and IBRR.

INTERNET RESOURCES

Search Engines

The Internet can be used to gather material directly as well as to carry out online searches of library collections or databases. Typing keywords or subject headings into the search function is one way to start. If the researcher is looking for a specific event or a specific time period in history, he or she can add dates to the string. Typing "American Protestant fundamentalism before 1920" will yield more useful results than typing just "fundamentalism."

There are several popular search engines, including Google, Yahoo!, Ask.com, MSN Search, AltaVista, and AOL Search. Each uses its own algorithm (a sequence of steps used to program the search) so that different search engines may locate different sets of Web documents from the same keyword search. Some researchers like to use so-called metacrawlers or metasearch engines, which are programs that relay keywords to several search engines at once and then display the combined results on one screen. For example, Dogpile sends keyword searches to Google, MSN Search, Ask.com, and Yahoo! Search. Other recommended metasearch engines are Mamma and MetaCrawler.

A site that may be useful to researchers who are new to the Internet is Search Engine Watch, which has a portion of its site devoted to Web searching tips (http://searchenginewatch.com/facts/). The page includes links to pages on Boolean searching, search engine tutorials, a glossary of terms related to search engines, and other useful features.

Gateway Sites

Gateway sites are Web pages that contain links to more specific pages about an institution or topic. Some gateway sites that are particularly useful to researchers studying fundamentalism are the following:

- Religious Movements Homepage Project (http://religiousmovements.lib.virginia.edu/) was begun by a professor at the University of Virginia in the early 1990s. It has since expanded under a new editor to become a worldwide resource for information on new religious movements (NRMs) and established religions. The site contains detailed profiles of more than 200 groups, each with a bibliography for suggested further reading. The site also contains essays on cult controversies, as well as other essays and teaching resources.

- Adherents (http://www.adherents.com/) is a general religion site that specializes in membership statistics and religious geography. As of early 2006, the site has membership figures for more than 4,200 religions, denominations, sects, faith groups, and NRMs. It also has lists of famous or influential people belonging to more than 100 religions and faith groups. Researchers can search the site by geographical location or by the name of the religious group to answer such questions as the number of Roman Catholics living in New Jersey or the number of different religions represented in India.
- The Wabash Center Internet Guide (http://www.atla.com/wabash/front.htm) is a selective, annotated guide to electronic resources in theology and religion. It classifies resources by topic, by geographical area, by historical period, and by type of material (journals, books, online course syllabi, reference materials, liturgical resources, texts, images, etc.) It also contains links to centers and institutes, professional societies in the field of religion, and the official Web sites of various religious bodies. Lastly, the guide includes a section on available Internet resources and an introduction to conducting online searches.

Institutional Sites

RELIGIOUS

Religious institutional sites are often useful in gathering information about a faith group's beliefs and practices. Many official denominational Web sites post a statement of belief or list of doctrinal authorities, although some, such as the Church of God of Prophecy, may place such information in the form of a mission statement. Some have short videos with brief descriptions of their beliefs and worship practices.

Colleges and universities related to fundamentalist or evangelical groups usually post statements about codes of behavior and lifestyle issues as well as beliefs that faculty and students are expected to hold on the official Web site. For example, Bob Jones University has a page on "Student Expectations" that summarizes the school's intention to "promote holy living by removing as much as possible the influences of worldliness and evil." Similarly, the Web sites of theological seminaries usually include basic information about the school's denominational affiliation (if any) and its theological orientation (liberal, mainline, conservative confessional, evangelical, fundamentalist, etc.).

Some of the larger church bodies maintain Web sites with complete texts of their sacred books or official documents. The Web site of the Church of Jesus Christ of Latter-day Saints has links to the full texts of the *Book of Mormon, Doctrine and Covenants,* and *Pearl of Great Price,* as mentioned earlier. The official Vatican Web site (http://www.vatican.va/) has the complete texts of all the documents of the Second Vatican Council as well as papal encyclicals, apostolic letters, and other decrees. They are available in French, German, Spanish, and other languages, in addition to English.

POLITICAL AND GOVERNMENT-RELATED

Researchers looking for information about religious freedom, state churches, or state religions in other countries may wish to begin by looking at a country's constitution or other laws concerning religion. Most nations around the world have the texts of their constitutions posted on their official sites. Another source of basic information that is slightly dated as of the early 2000s is the series of Country Studies that were commissioned by the Department of the Army and published by the Federal Research Division of the Library of Congress. They can be consulted on the Country Studies Web site (http://lcweb2.loc.gov/frd/cs/cshome.html). The Country Studies include one- or two-page summaries of religious life in each country, as well as information about the government, political parties, geography, climate, etc.

For historical documents related to the United States, the Avalon Project of the Yale Law School (http://www.yale.edu/lawweb/avalon/avalon.htm) is an excellent resource. The full texts of colonial charters and related documents, diplomatic treaties, presidential addresses and annual messages, congressional resolutions, the Constitution, the *Federalist Papers,* state constitutions after 1776, and many other collections related to history, law, and diplomacy are available on this site. It also offers a chronology of American history.

Legal cases in the United States can be searched online at FindLaw (http://lp.findlaw.com/). Supreme Court cases are available at the Legal Information Institute Web site (http://supct.law.cornell.edu/supct/index.html). Specific cases can be searched according to the names of the parties involved or according to the volume number, court, report number, and year assigned to the case.

Finally, the Federal Bureau of Investigation Web site (http://www.fbi.gov/homepage.htm) is a helpful resource for researching terrorist groups or specific incidents involving terrorism.

Online Booksellers

Online booksellers, such as Amazon, Barnes and Noble, and Borders, have search functions that can be used to identify and locate books related to a research topic that may not appear in library catalog searches. Amazon and Barnes and Noble also offer used books for sale at lower prices through vendors who are registered with them.

Blogs

Web logs, or blogs for short, are an evolving form of online communication that can be helpful in researching some topics related to fundamentalism. Blogs began as online diaries posted by individuals but have taken new forms since the early 2000s. There are now group blogs, blogs for people in specific professions, and editorial or opinion blogs associated with online periodicals. For example, Michael Barone hosts the Barone Blog at *U.S. News and World Report*'s online edition, and Richard John Neuhaus and Joseph Bottum blog at *First Things,* a journal devoted to religion and politics. Readers interested in issues related to religious journalism may wish to visit GetReligion, a group blog hosted by five journalists who are professional religion reporters. The blog takes its name from a quote by William Schneider, a political analyst for CNN, who once said that "The press is one of the most secular institutions in American society. It just doesn't get religion or any idea that flows from religious conviction."

Blogs can be useful sources of opinion about current events related to conservative religious groups, particularly for researchers looking for a range or variety of reactions. In addition, they are a good source of a specific type of document that is closely associated with fundamentalism—the conversion narrative. Conversion narratives are highly individualized accounts of a person's faith journey from unbelief to being "born again" or having a comparable change of heart. Fundamentalist churches that expect potential members to undergo a conversion experience before admitting them to full membership are not, however, the only groups that produce conversion narratives. Some evangelicals or members of mainline churches also blog about conversion experiences from time to time. There is also a subcategory of deconversion narratives, in which people who have left fundamentalist Christian groups or fundamentalist Islam tell about their movement from one religion to another or from faith to agnosticism or atheism.

7

Facts and Figures

INTRODUCTION

PERCENTAGE OF WORLD POPULATION FOR MAJOR RELIGIONS

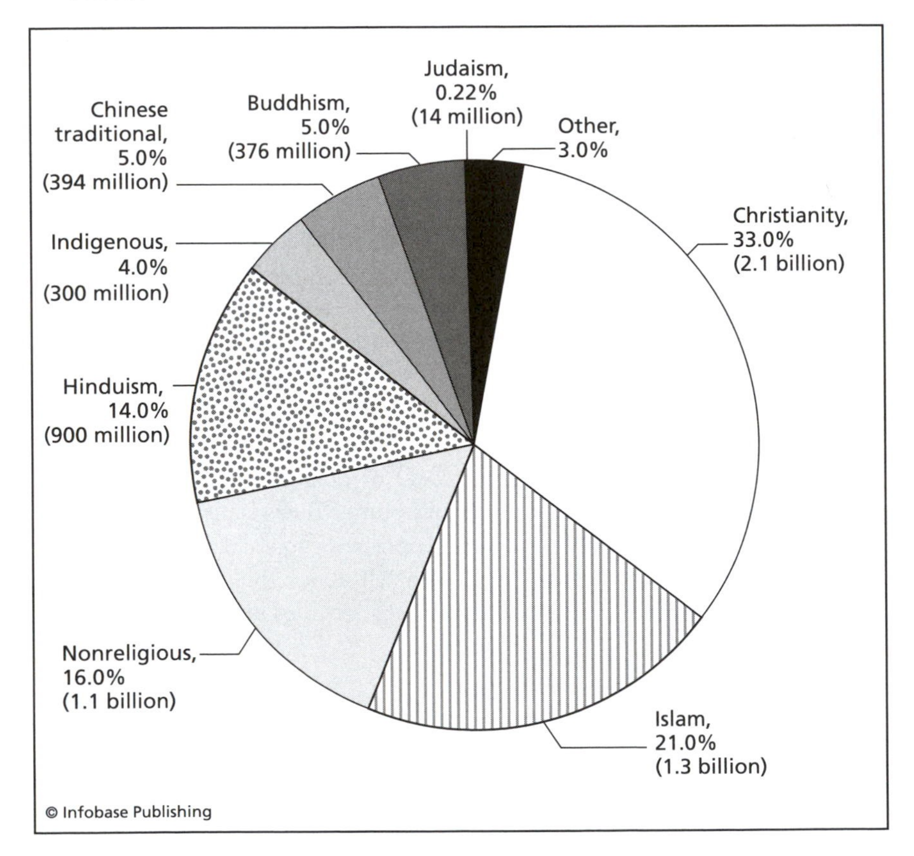

FOCUS ON THE UNITED STATES

ROUTE OF MORMON MIGRATION, 1830–1847

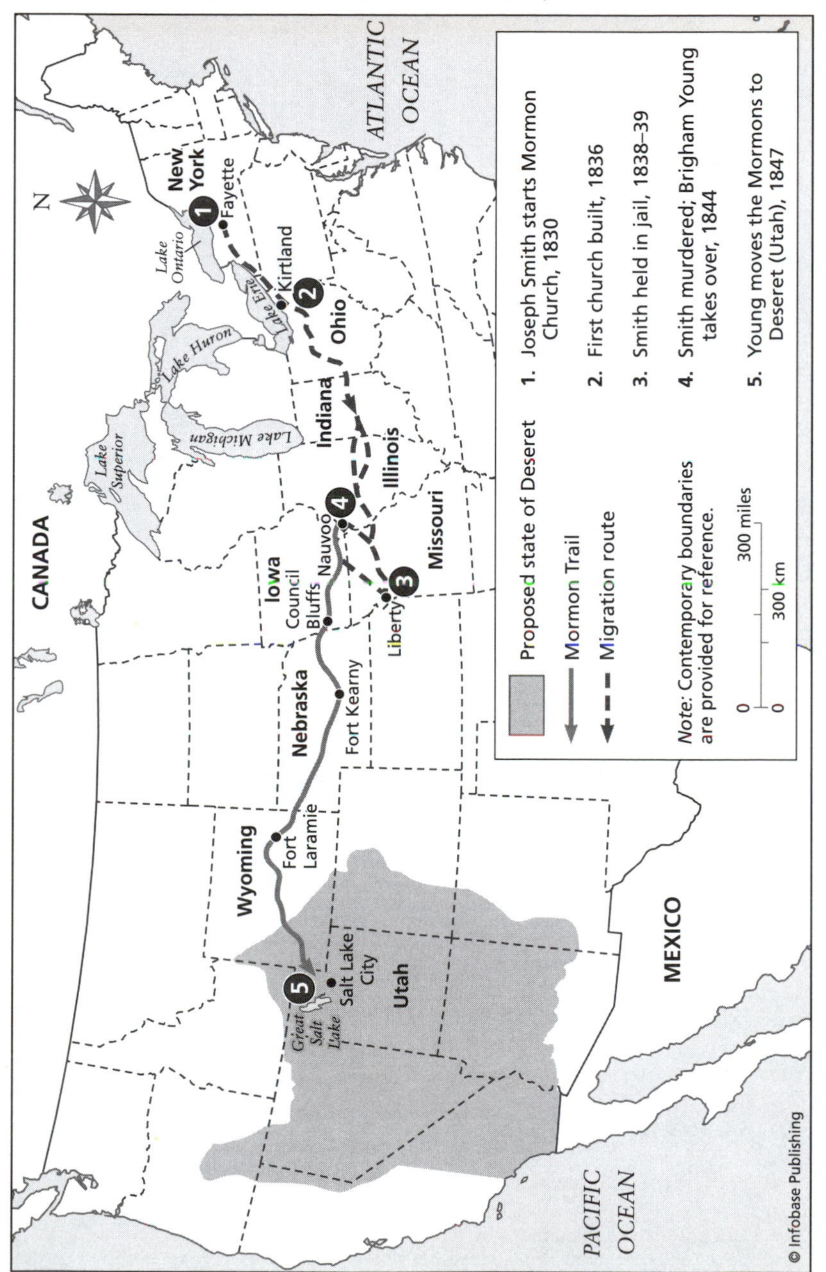

Religious Groups in the United States

BRITISH COLONIES, 1750

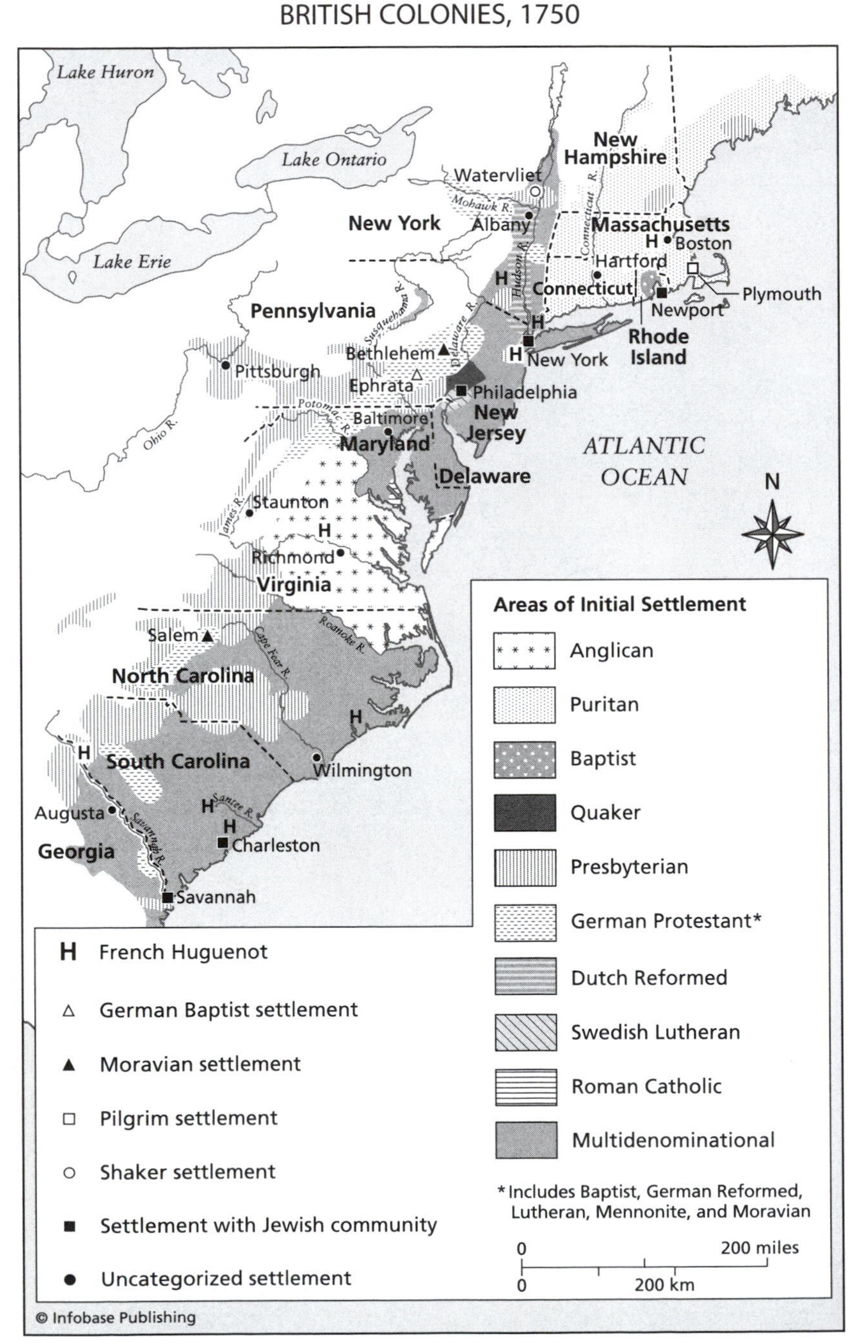

ON THE EVE OF THE CIVIL WAR, 1860

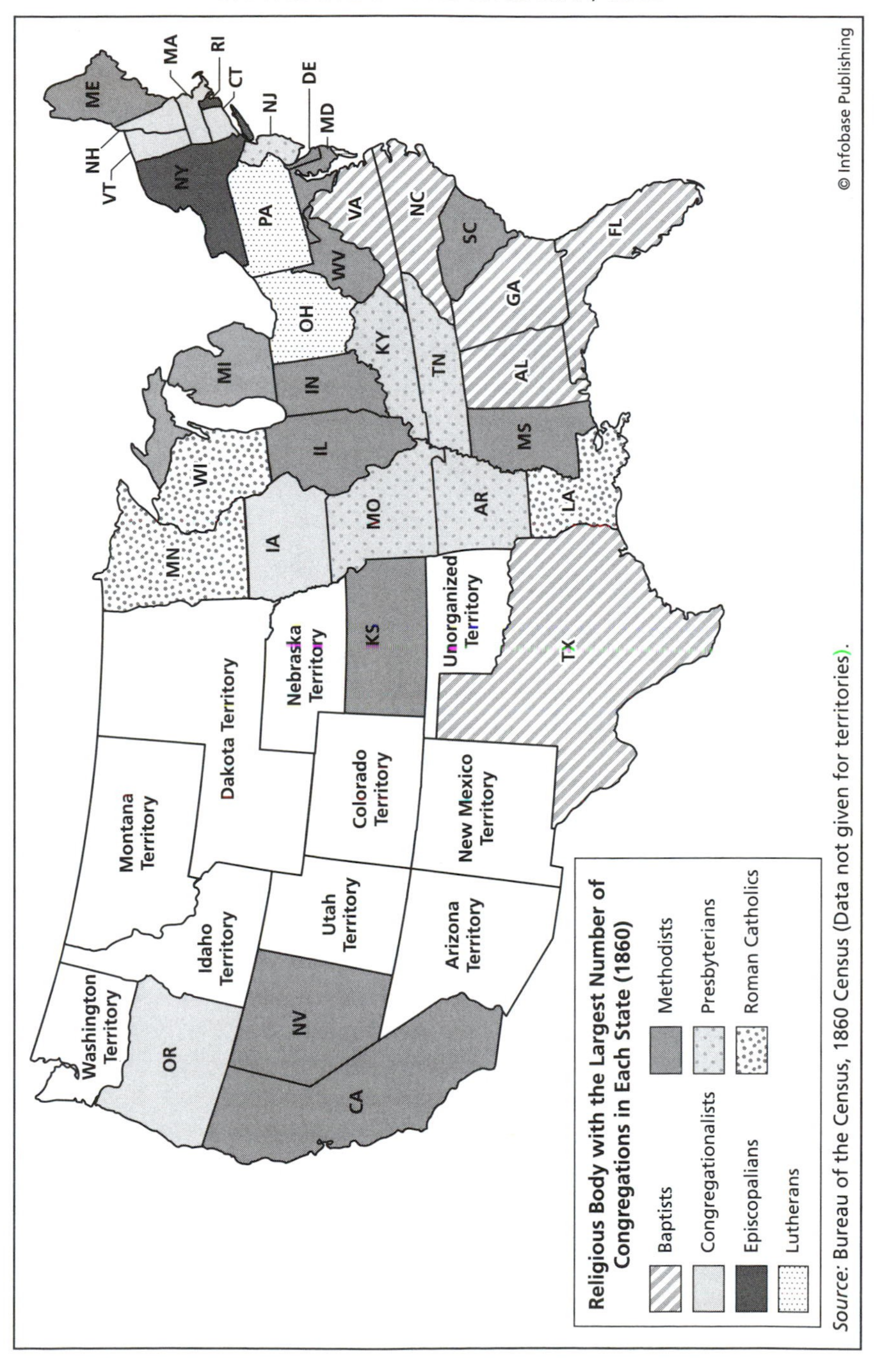

Source: Bureau of the Census, 1860 Census (Data not given for territories).

CONGREGATIONS, 2000

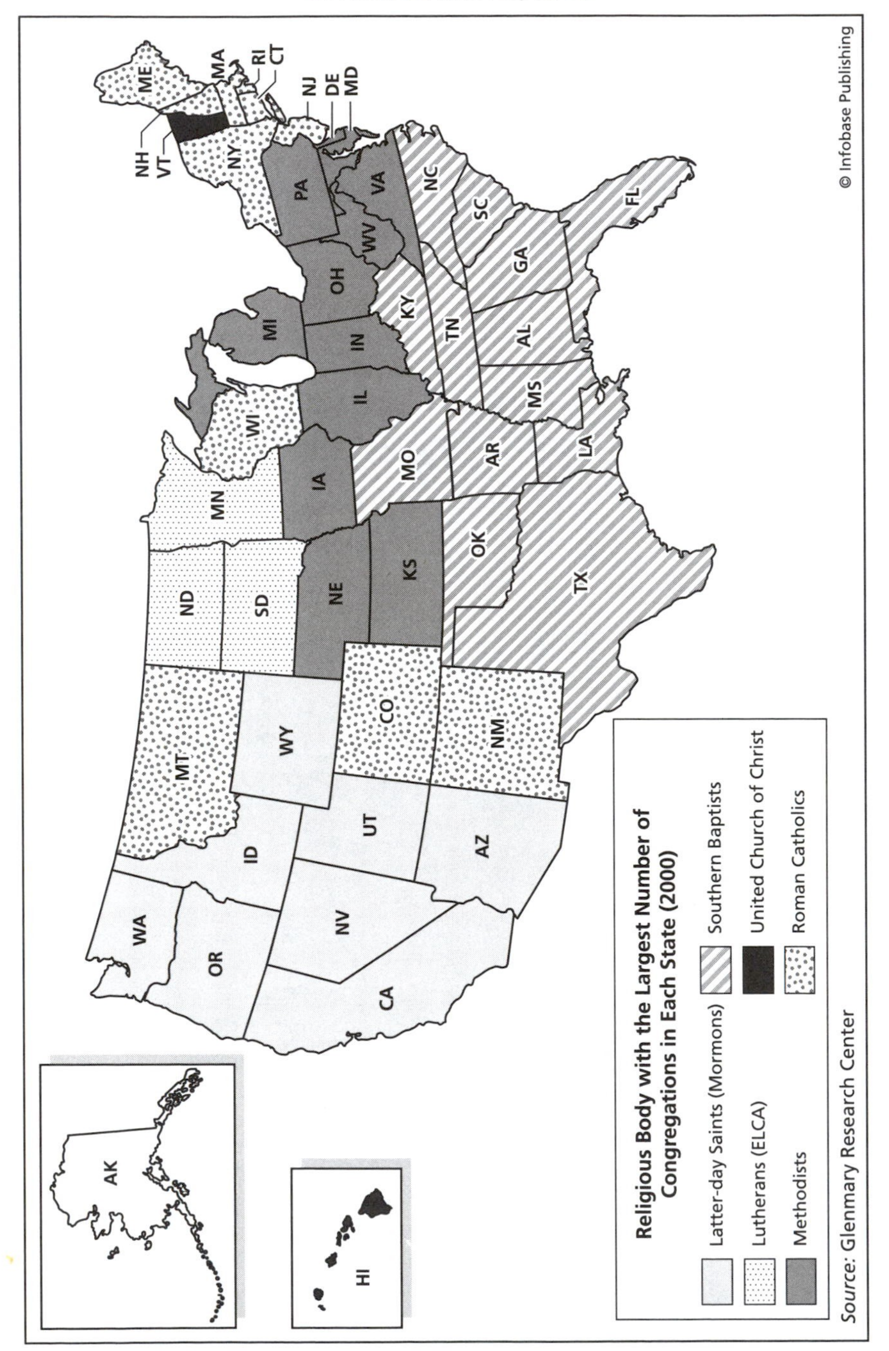

MEMBERS, 2000

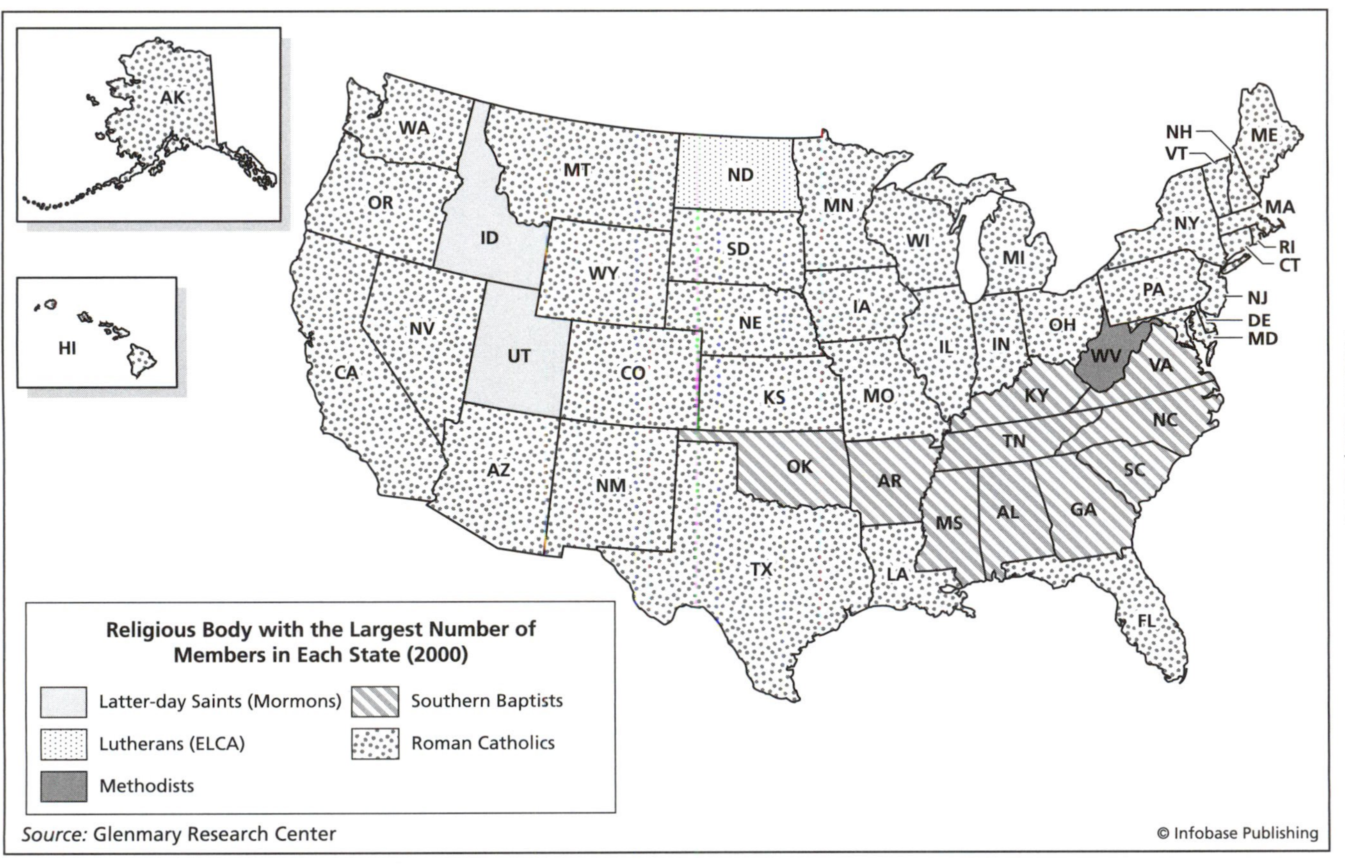

PERCENTAGE OF U.S. POPULATION FOR MAJOR RELIGIONS

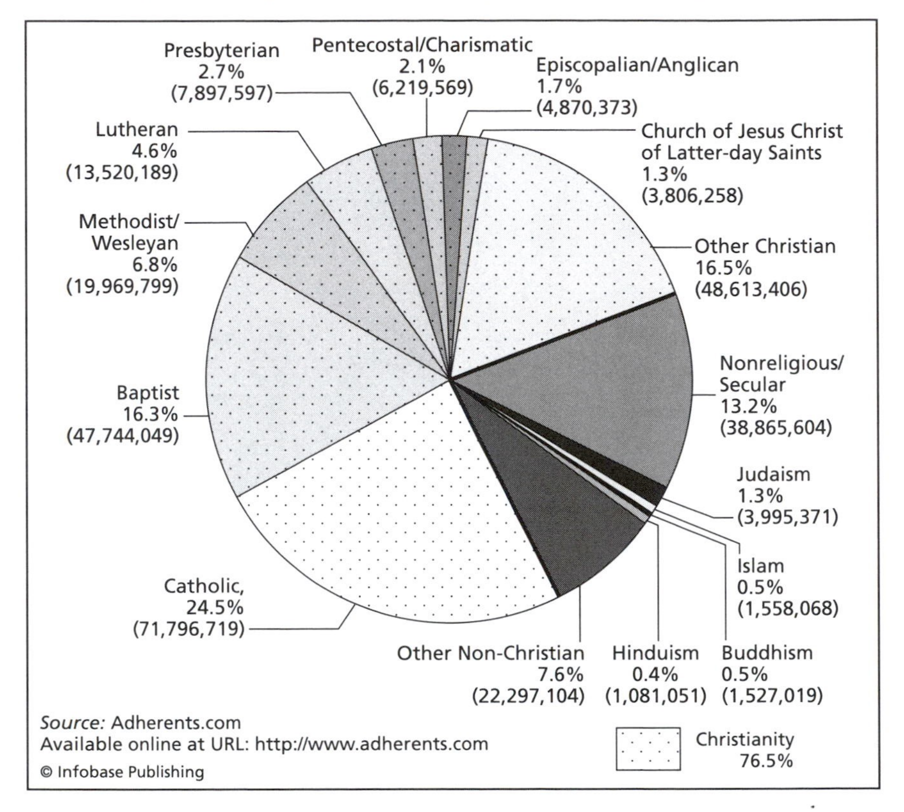

Source: Adherents.com
Available online at URL: http://www.adherents.com

GLOBAL PERSPECTIVES

ESTIMATED POPULATION FIGURES
FOR SELECTED FUNDAMENTALIST GROUPS

GROUP	NUMBER OF MEMBERS
Fundamentalist Protestants	
Southern Baptist Convention	16,400,000 (U.S.)
Lutheran Church–Missouri Synod	2,700,000 (U.S.)
Orthodox Presbyterian Church	20,000 (U.S.)
Church of God of Prophecy	400,000 (U.S.)
Snake-handling groups	6,000 (southern U.S.)
Fundamentalist Mormons	30,000–100,000 (U.S., Canada, and Mexico)
Christian Identity groups	50,000 (U.S.)
Church of Jesus Christ Christian (Aryan Nations)	unknown as of 2006; estimated at 500 (U.S.)
Kingdom Identity Ministries	unknown as of 2006; estimated at 250 (U.S.)
Traditionalist Roman Catholics	
Society of St. Pius X	150,000 (worldwide); 15,000 (U.S.)
Society of St. Pius V	2,000 (U.S.)
Opus Dei	80,000 (worldwide)
Haredi Jews	250,000 (Israel)
Gush Emunim	20,000 (Israel)
Hindutva	unknown
Rashtriya Swaramsevak Sangh	22,500,000 (India)
Muslim fundamentalist groups	500,000–5,000,000 (worldwide)
Hamas	1,000 (military wing)
Jamaat-e-Islami	5,000,000 (Pakistan/Bangladesh)
Muslim Brotherhood	500,000 (worldwide)

ISRAELI DISENGAGEMENT, AUGUST 2005

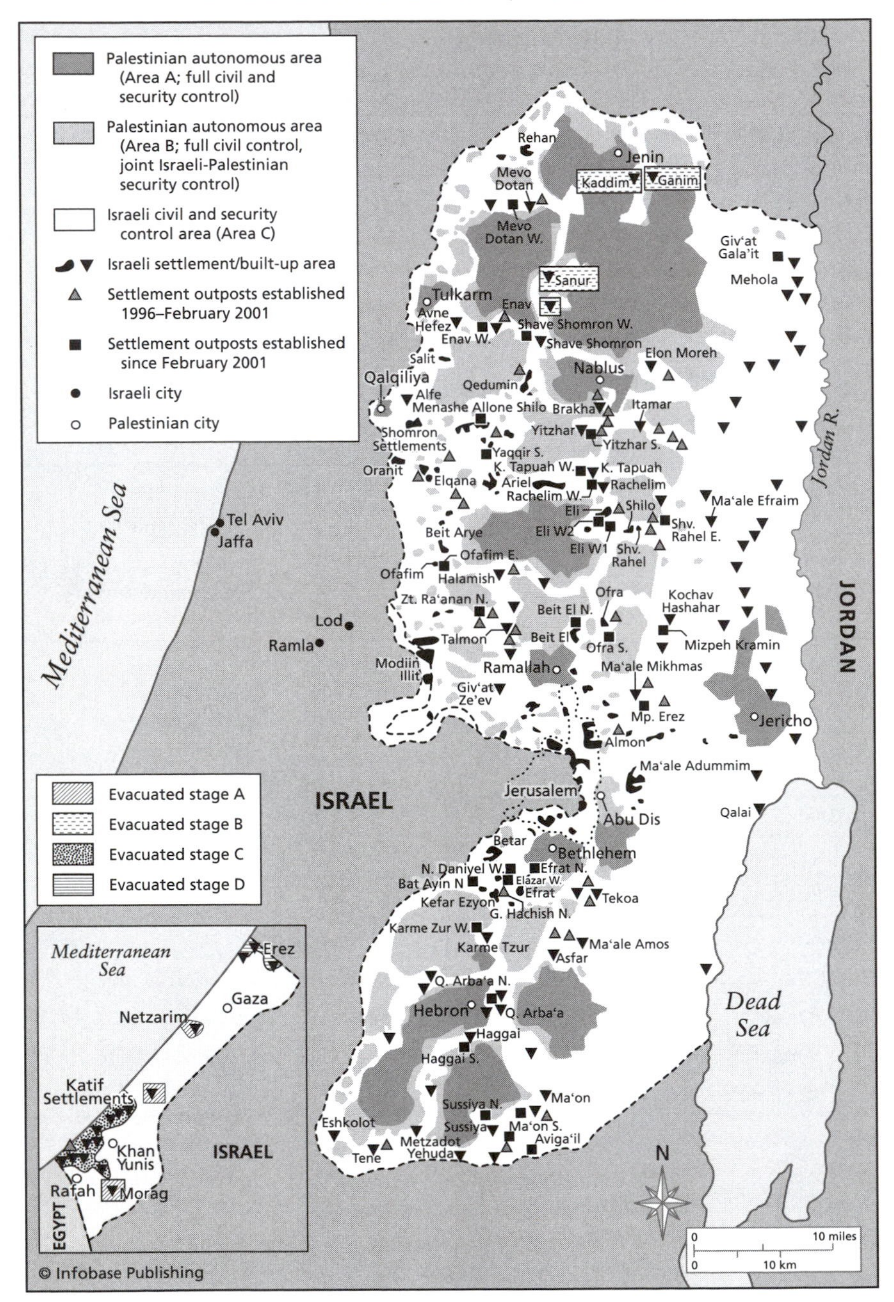

ROUTE OF ISRAELI SECURITY FENCE (FEBRUARY 20, 2005)

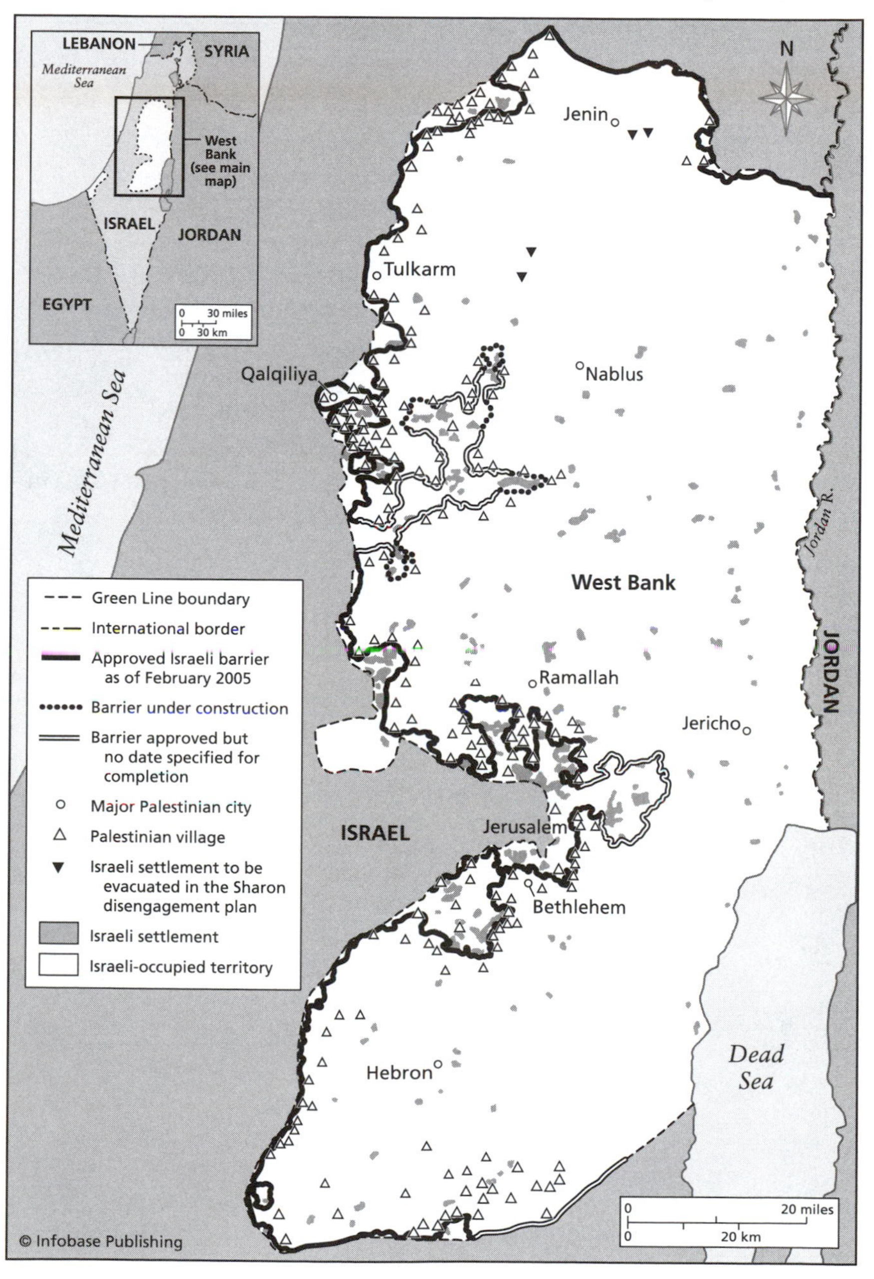

MODERN INDIA

8

Key Players A to Z

PAUL AULAGNIER (1943–) Roman Catholic priest and former assistant to Archbishop Marcel LEFEBVRE. The first French seminarian to be ordained into the Society of St. Pius X (SSPX), Aulagnier was close to Lefebvre until his death and was one of the strongest supporters of Lefebvre's consecration of four bishops in 1988. He served for three years as a professor at Lefebvre's seminary in Ecône, Switzerland, and for 18 years (1976–94) as the superior of the French district of the SSPX. In 2001, Aulagnier was transferred to Brussels, and in 2002, to Quebec. By this time, he had become an outspoken advocate of reconciliation with Rome and was no longer in favor with other leaders of the SSPX. Aulagnier was expelled from the society in 2003.

BENEDICT XVI (JOSEF RATZINGER, 1927–) Roman Catholic theologian, pope, archbishop, and cardinal. Born in Bavaria, he was the third and youngest child of a police officer and a domestic. Drafted into the German army in 1944, he was briefly held in an American prisoner-of-war camp in 1945. He and his older brother then entered seminary and were ordained to the priesthood in 1951. In 1957, he completed his doctoral studies and began a distinguished career as a university professor at the Universities of Bonn, Tübingen, and Regensburg. He became archbishop of Munich in March 1977 and was made a cardinal by Pope PAUL VI in May 1977. In addition to his other duties in the 1980s, he served as Pope John Paul II's representative in a series of negotiations with Archbishop Marcel LEFEBVRE. Since his election as Pope Benedict XVI in April 2005, he has met with Bernard FELLAY, the current superior general of the Society of St. Pius X, and appears to be following John Paul II's attempts to win back the schismatic group to the mainstream church.

DAYANANDA SARASVATI (1824–1883) Hindu religious teacher and reformer. Dayananda was born into a high-caste Brahman family in Gujarat on the western coast of India. His family was devoted to the god Shiva, but Sarasvati became disillusioned with the traditional rituals associated with Shiva's cult as a teenager. In 1846, he left his family to live the life of an ascetic holy man and took a formal vow of renunciation in 1847. For the next 13 years, he wandered around India until he found a teacher whose beliefs were similar to his own developing views. Dayananda had decided that the Hindu gods and goddesses worshipped by most Indians were imaginary; the true God was invisible and had been worshipped by the sages who wrote the Vedas. In addition to rediscovering what he understood to be the central holy books of Hinduism, Swami Dayananda thought he had recovered the pure forms of true ritual worship. In 1875, he founded the Arya Samaj in Mumbai (Bombay) to preserve and promote the religious heritage of the Vedas. Unlike earlier Hindu reform movements, his was intended for people at all levels of society and not just for the educated elite. He was also involved in the Indian independence movement.

JONATHAN EDWARDS (1703–1758) Congregational minister, missionary to Native Americans, and college president. Edwards was born in a parsonage, his father Timothy being the minister of the Congregational church in East Windsor, Connecticut. After completing a master's degree at Yale in 1722, Edwards served as an apprentice minister under his mother's father, Rev. Solomon Stoddard, in Northampton, Massachusetts. In 1729, Edwards succeeded his grandfather as the senior pastor of the Northampton congregation. Edwards's preaching sparked a revival in his congregation in 1734 that is usually considered the beginning of the Great Awakening. Unlike George WHITEFIELD's preaching style, Edwards's manner in the pulpit was not theatrical; his listeners were convinced by his orderly presentation and his own depth of conviction rather than by gestures or a loud voice. In 1750, Edwards was asked to leave the congregation in Northampton; he went to Stockbridge, Massachusetts (at that time a frontier settlement), where he preached to Native Americans living nearby and tried to protect them from mistreatment at the hands of white settlers and colonial officials. During his years in Stockbridge, Edwards wrote some of his best-known theological treatises, including *Freedom of the Will* (1754). In 1757, Edwards was chosen as the first president of what is now Princeton University. He served only a few months before dying in 1758 from complications of a botched smallpox vaccination. Edwards is generally considered the greatest theologian in the history of American Christianity.

JERRY LAMON FALWELL (1933–) Independent Baptist pastor, televangelist, and conservative political activist. Falwell and his fraternal twin brother were born in Lynchburg, Virginia, in 1933. His father was an agnostic who ran an illegal whiskey distillery during Prohibition. Falwell had a conversion experience as a teenager and prepared for the ministry at Bible Baptist College in Springfield, Missouri. Returning to Virginia, he founded the Thomas Road Baptist Church in 1956 with 35 charter members; the church now has a membership of more than 20,000. As the church grew, Falwell decided to start a kindergarten–graduate school system of Christian education. Lynchburg Christian Academy was opened in 1967 and Liberty University in 1971. The university had a student body of 10,000 as of early 2006. Falwell became a national figure when he started the Moral Majority, a conservative political action group, in 1979. Although the organization was disbanded in 1989, Falwell is still considered a major spokesperson for conservative Protestant views.

BERNARD FELLAY (1959–) Superior general of the Society of St. Pius X (SSPX). Fellay was born in Sierre, Switzerland, and graduated from Archbishop Marcel LEFEBVRE's seminary in Ecône. Ordained to the priesthood by Lefebvre in 1982, he was one of four bishops consecrated in 1988 and incurred automatic excommunication for his disobedience to Pope John Paul's apostolic letter "Ecclesia Dei." Fellay is the present superior general of the SSPX, having succeeded Father Franz Schmidberger in July 1994. Under Fellay, the SSPX has lost a large number of its members, some choosing to reconcile with Rome, others joining sedevacantist groups, and a few working completely on their own. The loss of membership has been attributed to the SSPX's increasingly hard-line stand and Fellay's recent expulsion of several priests without judicial process for disagreeing with the society's governing council, as well as attempts by the SSPX to claim jurisdiction over marriage matters that are usually handled in Rome.

HARRY EMERSON FOSDICK (1878–1969) Liberal Northern Baptist clergyman and writer. Fosdick was born in Buffalo, New York, and graduated from Colgate University and Union Theological Seminary. He was ordained into the Baptist ministry in 1903. Although he had had a "born again" experience at the age of seven, Fosdick rejected both fundamentalism and Calvinism by the time he was an adolescent. He had a nervous breakdown during his seminary years. From 1918 to 1923, Fosdick served as the minister of First Presbyterian Church in New York City, where his prominence earned him the opposition of such conservatives as J. Gresham MACHEN and William Jennings Bryan. In 1922, he attracted national attention with his sermon "Shall the Fundamentalists Win?" The resultant controversy eventually forced Fosdick to resign his pulpit; however, he had also gained the support of John D. Rockefeller (at that time the wealthiest individual in the United

States), who built Riverside Church in Manhattan to provide Fosdick with a new church home. Fosdick, however, was not simply antifundamentalist. He was capable of criticizing liberal Protestantism for its uncritical embrace of secular culture; in 1935, he shocked colleagues by preaching a sermon called "The Church Must Go beyond Modernism." In his later years, he did a considerable amount of pastoral counseling, his concern for his parishioners stemming from his own early experience with emotional collapse.

BARUCH GOLDSTEIN (1956–1994) American/Israeli physician and terrorist. Goldstein was born into an Orthodox Jewish family in Brooklyn, New York. He attended a religious day school and graduated from Yeshiva University and Albert Einstein Medical School. He joined Meir KAHANE's Jewish Defense League in the United Sates and eventually made aliyah (immigrated to Israel) in 1982. He served in the Israeli Defense Force (IDF) as a physician, where he became notorious for refusing to treat non-Jews, even those who were in the IDF. Goldstein lived in Kiryat Arba, the settlement outside of Hebron founded by Moshe LEVINGER. On February 25, 1994, Goldstein went into the Cave of the Patriarchs in Hebron, where he fired more than 100 shots into a crowd of Muslims at morning prayer. He killed 29 worshippers and injured 125 others. After being subdued with a fire extinguisher, Goldstein was beaten to death by the survivors. It is thought that he was motivated by the desire to avenge the 1990 assassination of Kahane as well as by feelings of humiliation related to the secular Israeli state's apparent unwillingness to protect Jewish settlers from harassment by Palestinians. Although most Israelis were shocked by Goldstein's act of mass murder, his grave has become a holy site for members of radical right-wing groups.

MADHAV SADASHIV GOLWALKAR (1906–1973) Indian nationalist and head of the Rashtriya Swayamsevak Sangh (RSS). Golwarkar was born in Nagpur into a middle-class family; his father was a postal clerk and later a schoolteacher. Golwarkar eventually became a professor of zoology in 1930 but gave up the field to study law in 1933. By this time, he had joined the RSS, a right-wing Hindutva nationalist organization. He became its leader when K. B. HEDGEWAR died in 1940. Golwarkar's most important book, *We, or Our Nationhood Defined,* was published in 1939. The attitudes toward Christians and Muslims expressed in the book became controversial after World War II, when Golwalkar's praise for Hitler's persecution of the Jews proved to be embarrassing to the RSS. In 1948, Golwalkar was arrested after the assassination of Mohandas Gandhi on suspicion of involvement in the conspiracy but was released in August. He was instrumental in founding the Vishwa Hindu Parishad (VHP), or World Hindu Council, in 1964. Golwarkar was diagnosed with cancer in 1969 and died in 1973.

WILLIAM FRANKLIN GRAHAM, JR. (BILLY GRAHAM, 1918–) American Protestant evangelist. Born into a Presbyterian family in Charlotte, North Carolina, Graham became a Southern Baptist in high school. He attended Bob Jones University but found it too fundamentalist; he eventually graduated from Wheaton College in 1943. He joined Youth for Christ after graduation, becoming one of its field representatives in 1945. In 1949, he became a traveling evangelist, serving at the same time as president of Northwestern College in Minnesota until 1952. He founded the Billy Graham Evangelistic Association (BGEA) in 1950. The BGEA publishes *Decision* magazine and broadcasts a weekly radio program called *Hour of Decision.* Graham is said to have preached to more people in live audiences (more than 210 million) than anyone else in history. Diagnosed with Parkinson's disease in 1990, he began his last North American crusade in June 2005 in New York City. He has been honored by the George Washington Carver Memorial Institute for his contributions to race relations and by the Anti-Defamation League of B'nai B'rith for his advocacy of better relationships between Christians and Jews. He has also been criticized by some Protestant fundamentalists for his personal friendship with Pope John Paul II.

KESHAVA BALIRAM HEDGEWAR (1889–1940) Indian nationalist leader and founder of the Rashtriya Swayamsevak Sangh (RSS). Hedgewar received a privileged English-language education as a youth. He attended medical school in Calcutta and became involved in the Indian independence movement. He served a year in prison for his revolutionary activities in 1921. He then joined the Hindu Mahasabha in Nagpur in 1923, where he came under the influence of Vinayak SAVARKAR. Although Hedgewar agreed with the ideology of Hindutva, he did not think the Hindus needed a political party but rather an organization that would instruct members in communal discipline and traditional Hindu beliefs. He differed from DAYANANDA SARASVATI in regarding Shivaji, a 17th-century Indian warrior hero, as a central ideal rather than the Vedas. Hedgewar began to recruit high-caste youth in Nagpur to form the first *shakha* (branch) of the RSS in 1925. He continued to work with the RSS until his death from typhoid fever 15 years later.

MEIR KAHANE (1932–1990) American/Israeli Orthodox rabbi and radical right-wing political leader. Kahane was born in Brooklyn, New York, the son of a rabbi who had emigrated from Poland to the United States. Kahane himself was ordained to the rabbinate in Brooklyn and served several Orthodox congregations in the 1960s. He eventually completed a degree in international law from New York University and worked as an undercover agent for the Federal Bureau of Investigation (FBI). In 1968, he founded the Jewish Defense League (JDL), supposedly in response to anti-Semitic threats that had been made by the Black Panthers. When the JDL began to participate in terrorist activities in the 1970s, Kahane was pressured by the police and decided to move to Israel in 1971. There he founded Kach ("only thus" in Hebrew), a right-wing political party that was eventually condemned as racist by the Israeli Knesset (parliament) and as a foreign terrorist organization by the U.S. State Department. Kahane was assassinated in Manhattan by an Arab terrorist in 1990; his son and daughter-in-law were assassinated in Israel in 2000.

CLARENCE JAMES KELLY (1941–) Roman Catholic bishop and superior of the Society of St. Pius V (SSPV). Kelly studied for the priesthood at the international seminary founded by Archbishop Marcel LEFEBVRE in Ecône, Switzerland. He was ordained to the priesthood by Lefebvre on April 13, 1973, and remained within the Society of St. Pius X (SSPX) until 1983. At that time the archbishop expelled him from the society along with eight other priests for disagreements over the validity of the 1962 Roman Missal and the legitimacy of the popes elected since the death of Pius XII. At the time of his expulsion, Kelly was the superior of the Northeast USA District of the SSPX. He and the other eight priests formed the SSPV; four of the eight withdrew after a few years to form their own sedevacantist groups. Kelly was consecrated a bishop on October 19, 1993, by Alfredo José Méndez-González, the retired bishop of Arecibo in Puerto Rico. The consecration was not made public, however, until a few days after Méndez-Gonzáalez's death in 1995. Because of the delayed announcement, some observers question whether the ceremony ever took place. The SSPV is presently headquartered at Oyster Bay Cove in New York.

ABRAHAM ISAAC KOOK (1864–1935) First Ashkenazic chief rabbi of Palestine, first leader of the religious Zionist movement, and founder of the Mercaz Harav yeshiva. Kook was born in what is now Latvia and became a rabbi at the age of 23. Between 1901 and 1904, he published several articles on the worldview that eventually became religious Zionism. In 1904, he moved to Palestine to take the position of rabbi in the city of Jaffa, where he became acquainted with the secular Zionists in the nearby agricultural settlement. Kook returned to Europe, where he was trapped by the outbreak of World War I. During his forced stay in London, he became involved in the planning that led to the Balfour Declaration of 1917, which promised the Jews a homeland in what is now Israel. He returned to Palestine after the war ended in 1918 and was appointed the mandate's first chief rabbi in 1921. In 1924 he founded the Mercaz Harav yeshiva, which trained most of the early leaders of Gush Emunim in the 1940s and 1950s. Kook was best known for his work in building alliances between religious Zionism and secular Zionism on the one hand and the ultra-orthodox *haredim* on the other.

ZVI YEHUDA KOOK (1891–1982) Son of Abraham Isaac Kook and the spiritual leader of Gush Emunim. He is sometimes called the "prophet of Greater Israel" for his role in inspiring the settler movement in the territories. Kook was born in Zaumel, Lithuania, where his father was then serving as rabbi. He immigrated with his parents to Palestine in 1904. As he grew older, Kook assisted his father as rabbi and began to edit and publish his writings. In order to find time for his own studies, he went to Europe but, like his father, was unable to return to Palestine until after World War I; he eventually joined his father in London. He married the daughter of a Warsaw rabbi in 1922 and returned to the mandate a year later. Kook was active in bringing many Russian Jews to Israel between 1929 and 1933. In 1952, he succeeded Rabbi Yaakov Charlop as the head of the Mercaz Harav yeshiva in Jerusalem, a position he kept until his death 30 years later. Kook enlarged the yeshiva and transformed it into a rigorous modern educational institution.

MARCEL-FRANÇOIS LEFEBVRE (1905–1991) Roman Catholic archbishop and founder of the Society of St. Pius X (SSPX), a schismatic group of ultratraditionalist Roman Catholics. Born in Tourcoing, France, Lefebvre was raised in a devout Roman Catholic household and felt called to the priesthood at an early age. He was ordained a Spiritan (Holy Ghost) missionary and sent to French-speaking West Africa, where he became the first archbishop of Dakar, Senegal. Under Pope Pius XII, Lefebvre became the papal legate to French-speaking Africa and superior general of the Spiritan missionaries. He was invited by Pope John XXIII to be a member of the preparatory commission for the Second Vatican Council in 1962 and retired in Rome shortly after the end of the council in 1965. He came out of retirement in 1969 at the request of several young men studying for the priesthood within the French seminary system who were upset by extreme forms of modernization that went further than the council's recommendations. Lefebvre founded a house of studies in 1969 that evolved into his international seminary in Ecône, Switzerland, and the SSPX. In 1988, Lefebvre was excommunicated for schism after consecrating four bishops contrary to Pope John Paul II's warning. He was never reconciled to the church. Lefebvre died of cancer in Martigny, Switzerland, in 1991.

MOSHE LEVINGER (1942–) Controversial rabbi, leader of the Jewish fundamentalist group Gush Emunim (GE), and the first modern-day Jewish settler in Hebron, Israel. Levinger is regarded by those outside his movement as a troublemaker and demagogue, and as a source of inspiration by the most radical members of GE. Levinger led his followers in 1968 to build the settlement at Kiryat Arba, just outside Hebron. In 1988, Levinger served 13 weeks in prison for the murder of a Palestinian owner of a shoe store. He told police that he was defending himself from a group of teenagers throwing stones. Levinger's son Menashe was arrested in May 2002 for suspected involvement in a plot to blow up an Arab hospital and girls' school in Jerusalem.

JOHN GRESHAM MACHEN (1881–1938) Conservative Presbyterian minister, professor of the New Testament, and systematic theologian. Machen was born into a well-to-do, well-educated Baltimore family. He inherited enough money from his grandfather and father to make him independently wealthy by the standards of the early 1900s. He graduated from Johns Hopkins University and Princeton Seminary. He then studied for a year in Germany (1905–06) and almost became a theological modernist under the influence of Wilhelm Herrmann, a systematic theologian who taught at the University of Marburg. Returning to Princeton in 1906, Machen taught the New Testament until he left the school to found Westminster Theological Seminary in 1929. Although he was embroiled in the modernist-fundamentalist controversy within the Presbyterian Church for two decades, he refused to call himself a fundamentalist, preferring instead to be known as "an adherent of the Reformed faith." Machen was stripped of his ordination in 1935 by the Presbyterian Church; he then led the formation of the Orthodox Presbyterian Church in 1936. Machen died in North Dakota of pneumonia on New Year's Day, 1937; he had traveled there in subzero temperatures at the request of a friend. Machen was one of the most scholarly theological conservatives of the early 20th century; his work was distinctive for its critical assessment of the larger cultural issues that had produced modernism.

ABUL ALA MAWDUDI (1903–1979) Journalist, scholar, and one of the founders of political Islam. Mawdudi was born in Aurangabad, India, the youngest son of a lawyer. He was educated at home and the Madrasah Furqaniyah, a high school that offered a traditional Islamic education. In 1918, he took a job as a journalist to support himself when his father died. From 1921 to 1923, he served as editor of a Muslim newspaper in Delhi. He participated in the Khilafat movement, an organization of Muslim Indians dedicated to Indian independence from Britain. Mawdudi also began to publish books and helped to found an Islamic study center in Pathankot. In 1941, he founded Jamaat-e-Islami, a movement to promote political Islam in India; he served as its president from its foundation until 1972. Mawdudi was initially opposed to the partition of India in 1947 but moved to Pakistan when that country became an independent state. His primary political goal was to make Sunni Islam the supreme organizing principle of society; he was strongly opposed to secular nationalism and feminism. His political philosophy has been critiqued by some Muslim clerics as well as by secular Pakistani nationalists.

CARL MCINTIRE (1906–2002) American fundamentalist Presbyterian minister and founder of the American Council of Christian Churches (ACCC). McIntire was the son of a Presbyterian minister in Michigan who was hospitalized for a nervous breakdown in 1912. McIntire's mother divorced his father and moved with her sons to Oklahoma, where she took a position as dean of women at a state teachers' college. McIntire graduated from Park College in Missouri and went to Princeton Seminary for one year, leaving in 1929 when J. Gresham MACHEN left Princeton to found Westminster Theological Seminary. He graduated from Westminster in 1931 and became a founding member of the Orthodox Presbyterian Church (OPC) in 1936. By the end of 1937, however, McIntire left the OPC to found the fundamentalist Bible Presbyterian Church, taking 12 other clergy with him. In 1937, McIntire established his own theological seminary, and in 1941, he started the ACCC. He was also a radio preacher; at the height of his popularity in the 1960s his *Twentieth Century Reformation Hour* reached an audience of millions. McIntire was an opponent of the ecumenical movement, communism, and theological modernism. He quarreled with many other religious leaders in the course of his career, including Billy GRAHAM, Martin Luther King, Jr., and his former coworker Francis SCHAEFFER.

GIOVANNI CARDINAL MONTINI *See* PAUL VI.

DWIGHT LYMAN MOODY (1837–1899) American Protestant evangelist and founder of Moody Bible Institute in Chicago. Born in Northfield, Massachusetts, Moody went to Boston to work for an uncle in the shoe business while he was still a teenager. He had always been devout, but after a conversion experience in 1854, he became interested in the Sunday School movement. Moody continued to be a Sunday School worker after he moved to Chicago in 1856. He was doing so well in the shoe business that his new employer sent him out as a commercial traveler, but after the Civil War began, Moody decided to give up secular employment for full-time evangelistic work. As a member of the wartime Christian Commission, Moody visited prisoner-of-war camps for Confederate soldiers in the Chicago area, handing out pocket-sized Bibles and holding revival meetings. After the war, he traveled to England to study British methods of evangelism and to hear the famous preacher Charles Spurgeon. Moody himself began to preach in Scotland and Ireland as well as England, drawing crowds as large as 20,000.

He drew similarly large crowds after returning to the United States; President Ulysses S. Grant attended one of Moody's services in 1876. Moody was invited to preach at the Chicago World's Fair in 1893. He died in 1899 after a series of heart attacks. Moody's evangelistic style is noteworthy because there was nothing sensationalistic or flamboyant about his preaching. He was not attracted to controversy with liberal clergy, and he strove to be "homey" and sincere rather than entertaining or provocative.

PAUL VI (GIOVANNI MONTINI, 1897–1978) Roman Catholic pope, archbishop, and cardinal. Born in the Italian province of Brescia, he was ordained to the priesthood in 1920 and completed graduate studies at the University of Rome. During World War II, he was involved in raising money to assist European Jews in fleeing the Continent. In 1953, he became archbishop of Milan and was made a cardinal by Pope John XXIII. Montini presided over the majority of the sessions of the Second Vatican Council and oversaw the implementation of its decrees. Elected to the papacy when John XXIII died of cancer in 1963, Montini's pontificate was overshadowed by controversy over his reaffirmation of priestly celibacy and the church's traditional ban on artificial contraception.

PIUS X (GIUSEPPE SARTO, 1835–1914) Roman Catholic archbishop, cardinal, and pope. He was born into a poor family in a small town near Venice, Italy. Ordained to the priesthood in 1858, he served as a seminary professor from 1880 to 1884 and then became bishop of Mantua. In 1893, he was made a cardinal. He became patriarch of Venice in 1896 and was elected to the papacy after the death of Pope Leo XIII in 1903, taking the title of Pius X. His pontificate was one of the most controversial of the modern era; he reversed Leo XIII's relatively open approach toward secular governments, refusing to meet with the president of France during a state visit in 1904. He also offended the heads of state of Portugal, Poland, Great Britain, and Russia. Pius X was known for restoring Gregorian chant to the liturgy and for beginning the process of codifying Roman Catholic canon law. The completed code, known as the Pio-Benedictine Code, was finally published in 1917 during the pontificate of Benedict XV. Pius X is best known, however, for his attack on theological modernism; he issued a decree in July 1907 ("Lamentabili sane exitu") condemning 65 modernist propositions about the divinity of Christ, the nature of the church and the sacraments, biblical exegesis, and similar subjects. He also required all clergy to take a formal oath against modernism. Pius X died in August 1914, just before the outbreak of World War I. He was canonized in 1954 by Pius XII, the first pope to be declared a saint since the 16th century.

SAYYID QUTB (1906–1966) Egyptian intellectual, writer, and leader of the Muslim Brotherhood. He is best known for his work *Fi zilal al-Qur'an* (*In the Shade of the Qur'an*), which was published between 1954 and 1964. Qutb received a Western education in Cairo between 1929 and 1933; he studied for a master's degree in education in Colorado between 1948 and 1950. He began his career by writing novels and working for the Egyptian Ministry of Education. Qutb turned to radical Islamism after his return to Egypt in 1950, partly as a result of his dislike of the United States and partly due to his disillusionment with President Gamal Abdel Nasser's brand of Egyptian nationalism. Qutb, who had become a publicist for the Muslim Brotherhood, was jailed after the attempt on Nasser's life in 1954. In prison, he wrote his commentary on the Qur'an and a manifesto of political Islam translated into English as *Milestones.* Among other things, he justified violent jihad and advocated the establishment of an Islamic theocracy in Egypt. He was released from prison briefly in 1964, rearrested in 1965, and hanged for plotting to overthrow the state in 1966.

ABDEL AZIZ RANTISI (1947–2004) Pediatrician, political activist, and cofounder of Hamas. Rantisi was born in Yubna, a village close to the city of Jaffa in Israel. His family moved to the Gaza Strip after the 1948 Arab-Israeli War. Rantisi graduated from medical school in Alexandria, Egypt, and qualified to practice as a pediatrician. While in Alexandria, he joined the Muslim Brotherhood. He returned to Gaza in 1976, where he married and had six children. In 1987, he organized Hamas together with Sheikh Ahmed YASSIN. A follower of Abul Ala MAWDUDI's brand of Islamic fundamentalism, Rantisi was arrested several times by the Palestinian Authority for his criticisms of Yassir Arafat. After Yassin was released from prison in 1997, Rantisi worked closely with him to reorganize Hamas and recruit new members. He shared Yassin's unrelenting opposition to any kind of compromise with Israel. He became the political head of Hamas after Salah Shehada was killed in 2002. Rantisi became the spiritual leader of Hamas after Yassin was killed by an Israeli missile in March 2004. His leadership lasted only a month, as he himself was killed in the same way in April 2004.

JOSEF CARDINAL RATZINGER *See* BENEDICT XVI.

GIUSEPPE CARDINAL SARTO *See* PIUS X.

VINAYAK DAMODAR SAVARKAR (1883–1966) Indian freedom fighter, nationalist leader, and creator of the concept of Hindutva, or "Hinduness." Orphaned by the time he was 16, Savarkar completed his college-level studies in India. He won a scholarship to study law in London, where he moved in June

1906. There, he founded the Free India Society and published his first book, *The Indian War of Independence, 1857,* in 1908. The book, which was militantly anti-British, was banned by British authorities but was smuggled into India nonetheless. Savarkar was captured in Paris for his part in a conspiracy to kill British officials and taken back to India, where he was sentenced to 50 years in prison. While in jail, he wrote *Hindutva,* which set out his strongly anti-Muslim view of Hindu nationalism. Released from jail in 1924, Savarkar joined the Hindu Mahasabha and served as its president for seven years. He was arrested on suspicion of involvement in Mohandas Gandhi's assassination in 1948 but was released for lack of evidence. His last book, a history of India published in 1966, presented the Muslims as the most important of a long string of invaders that the Hindus had successfully vanquished.

FRANCIS AUGUST SCHAEFFER (1912–1984) Presbyterian minister, cultural critic, and founder of L'Abri Fellowship. Schaeffer was born and reared in Germantown, a suburb of Philadelphia. Originally an agnostic, he had a conversion experience in 1930 after reading the Bible. He graduated from Faith Theological Seminary in 1938. He served several parishes in Pennsylvania and Missouri and then worked with Carl McIntire in the American Council of Christian Churches (ACCC), touring Europe after World War II to see where the need for evangelism was greatest. He decided to move permanently to Switzerland in 1948 to work with youth. In 1955, he opened his home in Huemoz to young people searching for answers to the general crisis of Western culture. He called the house L'Abri (the shelter); by the 1960s, he had thousands of visitors annually. Schaeffer began to publish books about real-world problems, such as *Escape from Reason* and *The God Who Is There.* After the *Roe v. Wade* decision, Schaeffer coauthored a book with C. Everett Koop, the former U.S. surgeon general, about abortion and end-of-life issues. Schaeffer died of cancer in 1984. Although he is sometimes regarded as a founding theoretician of Christian reconstructionism because he inspired a number of Protestant evangelicals and fundamentalists to return to political activism, Schaeffer did not go as far as some of his disciples have suggested. In particular, he was more interested in the arts and their influence on modern society than most leaders of the Christian Right have been. Schaeffer's son Frank became a successful author and film director; he has left the strict Calvinism of his upbringing to enter the Eastern Orthodox Church.

THERESA MARIE (TERRI) SCHIAVO (1963–2005) An insurance claims clerk from Florida whose medical condition led to a court battle between her parents and her husband over her treatment, particularly the feeding tube that was keeping her alive. Randall Terry and other pro-life activists joined the legal battle on the side of Terri's parents, who did not want the feeding tube removed.

WILLIAM JOSEPH SEYMOUR (1870–1922) African-American minister and founder of the worldwide Pentecostal movement. Seymour was born in Centerville, Louisiana, the son of freed slaves who reared him in the Baptist tradition. He moved to Cincinnati, Ohio, as a young man and came into contact with the Holiness movement through Martin Wells Knapp's congregation and Daniel S. Warner's Church of God Reformation movement, otherwise known as the Evening Light Saints because the members thought they were living in the twilight of human history just before the Second Coming of Christ. Seymour left Cincinnati for Houston, Texas, where he attended a Holiness church led by a woman minister, Lucy F. Farrow. Seymour began to preach while in Houston, and his sermons impressed a visitor from Los Angeles whose church needed a pastor. Seymour was removed from this first pastorate in Los Angeles for teaching that the gift of speaking in tongues is proof of baptism in the Holy Spirit. He found a rundown building on Azusa Street and began to preach there; the result was a revival that lasted from 1906 to 1909. Seymour was ahead of his time in rejecting not only racial barriers but also limitations on the leadership of women. Most contemporary forms of Pentecostalism and the charismatic movement as well as the Assemblies of God congregations can be traced to the Azusa Street revival. Seymour died of a heart attack in 1922.

JOSEPH SMITH, JR. (1805–1844) The principal founder and first prophet of the Church of Jesus Christ of Latter-day Saints. Smith was born in Vermont but grew up in Palmyra, New York, where his family had moved after several years of crop failures. He began to have religious visions when he was 14. In 1823, he reported that he had been visited by the angel Moroni, who directed him to dig up some gold plates from a hillside near Palmyra, which he was not allowed to receive and translate until 1827. By 1829, Smith had attracted several followers who claimed that John the Baptist and the apostles Peter, James, and John had appeared to them and ordained them to the priesthood in order to restore the true church of Jesus Christ. In 1830, Smith published the *Book of Mormon* and founded the first Mormon congregation. From 1830 to 1844, Smith and his growing number of followers moved from Ohio to Missouri to Illinois to escape the growing hostility of outsiders who disapproved of polygamy, which Smith had begun to practice in 1833. In February 1844, Smith announced his candidacy for the presidency of the United States with Sidney Rigdon as his running mate. Smith was placed in jail in Carthage, Illinois, for his own safety in June 1844 and killed there by an angry mob on June 27.

WILLIAM ASHLEY SUNDAY (BILLY SUNDAY, 1862–1935) American fundamentalist preacher and revivalist. Sunday grew up in Bina, Iowa, the son of a Civil War widow. His early life was marked by poverty; at one point, he worked as a stable boy for a local colonel who took him in and enabled him to attend high school. Sunday left before graduating and became a professional baseball player for the Chicago White Stockings, the Pittsburgh Alleghenies, and the Philadelphia Phillies. In 1887, Sunday had a "born again" experience at a revival meeting he attended after a night of drinking with his teammates. In 1891, he quit baseball altogether and accompanied J. Wilbur Chapman, another evangelist, before beginning a solo ministry in 1896. He was ordained in the Presbyterian Church in 1903. Unlike Jonathan EDWARDS and Dwight L. MOODY, Sunday was famous for a highly emotional, fiery, and occasionally entertaining pulpit style. He preached in his shirtsleeves (unheard of at the time) and frequently drew on his former career to race around the stage at his revivals, gesture like an umpire, and use sports slang in his sermons. He was also one of the first revivalists to make use of radio, then a new medium. Sunday was best known for his sermons on the evils of alcohol and is considered by some historians to be a major influence on the temperance movement that led to Prohibition in 1919. He was awarded an honorary Doctor of Divinity by Bob Jones University in 1935.

WESLEY SWIFT (1913–1970) Methodist minister, kleagle (recruiter) of the Ku Klux Klan, and founder of the Church of Jesus Christ–Christian, a Christian Identity group. Swift was a follower of Gerald L. K. Smith, the Disciples of Christ minister who founded the Christian Defense League in the 1930s. Swift helped Smith in editing the league's official journal, *The Cross and the Flag.* He is credited with adding the ideas of British Israelism to Smith's anti-Semitic conspiracy theories, thus becoming one of the leaders of the Christian Identity movement. In 1946, Swift founded the Church of Jesus Christ–Christian at the Aryan Nations compound he established at Hayden Lake, Idaho. He was among the first in the Christian Identity movement to encourage the development of paramilitary organizations within the movement and to urge it to accomplish its goals by militant rather than merely journalistic means. In the early 1960s, Swift worked together with William Potter Gale to form a racist paramilitary group called the California Rangers; the two men split after a violent argument in December 1963. Swift's ministry was continued after his death in 1970 by his wife, Lorraine Swift, and Richard Butler. In 2001, the Hayden Lake compound was sold to meet the costs of a civil lawsuit brought by Victoria and Jason Keenan after the Keenans were attacked and injured by Aryan Nations guards.

RANDALL TERRY (1959–) American political and religious activist and founder of Operation Rescue of the anti-abortion movement. Terry, who grew up in upstate New York, led his first Operation Rescue blockade of an abortion clinic in fall 1987. Terry describes himself as a militant fundamentalist influenced by Francis SCHAEFFER's concept of Christian civil disobedience, although he has repeatedly denied any connection with dominionism or Christian reconstructionism. James C. Kopp, who murdered an abortion provider in Buffalo, New York, in 1998, reportedly accompanied Terry on Operation Rescue protests in 1988. In addition to Operation Rescue, Terry has been involved in the antigay movement; he disowned his son who came out in 2004. His most recent appearance in the news media was as a spokesman for Terri SCHIAVO's parents in March 2005. In 2000, Terry was censured by his home congregation in Binghamton, New York, for divorcing his wife of 20 years and for a series of extramarital liaisons with single as well as married women.

GEORGE WHITEFIELD (1714–1770) Anglican priest, traveling evangelist, and one of the leaders of the Great Awakening. Born in Gloucester, England, Whitefield was educated at Pembroke College, Oxford, where he met John and Charles Wesley. Ordained in the Church of England by the bishop of Gloucester in 1736, Whitefield made his first voyage to the American colonies in 1738, preaching primarily in Savannah, Georgia, where he established the Bethesda Orphanage, which still exists. He made seven voyages to America in total as well as 15 trips to Scotland, two to Ireland, and one to Bermuda. It is estimated that he preached more than 18,000 formal sermons in the course of his life and probably 12,000 additional informal presentations. Unlike Jonathan EDWARDS, Whitefield had a powerful voice that carried for a considerable distance when he preached in the open air. He was famous for preaching without notes, which was an innovation at the time, and for stirring the emotions of his listeners. His democratic speaking style made him particularly appealing to colonial American audiences, and his skill in using newspapers to generate favorable publicity for his preaching tours made him one of the most widely recognized individuals in North America before the Revolution. He died of asthma in Newburyport, Massachusetts, in 1770, and was buried beneath the pulpit of the Old South First Presbyterian Church.

SHEIKH AHMED YASSIN (1937?–2004) Member of the Muslim Brotherhood and cofounder of Hamas. Born near Ashkelon in the British Mandate of Palestine, Yassin was educated at Al-Azhar University in Cairo, Egypt. There, he joined the Muslim Brotherhood, an organization that opposed the growing secularism of Egyptian society. Confined to a wheelchair as the result of a gymnastics accident in his youth, Yassin nonetheless married and fathered 12 children. Returning to Gaza, Yassin was employed for some years as a schoolteacher and community worker. After the foundation of Hamas in 1987, Yassin authorized the killing of Palestinians suspected of collaborating with Israel. He also ordered the kidnapping and murder of Israeli soldiers. Arrested by the Israelis in May 1989, Yassin was kept in prison until 1997, when he was released in exchange for two Mossad agents held in Jordan. Yassin was opposed to any kind of peace process with Israel and favored the use of suicide bombers as a terrorist tactic. He was killed in March 2004 by a missile strike from an Israeli helicopter gunship.

BRIGHAM YOUNG (1801–1877) Second president of the Church of Jesus Christ of Latter-day Saints. Young was born in rural Vermont and joined the Methodist Church in 1823. He became interested in Mormonism after the publication of the *Book of Mormon* in 1830. Young helped to establish the Mormon settlement at Nauvoo, Illinois, in the early 1840s and became the de facto president of the Mormon church during the period of confusion after Joseph SMITH was murdered by a mob of vigilantes in 1844. In 1846, Young decided, after repeated conflicts between the Mormons and their neighbors in the Middle West, to relocate the entire group in Utah, which was then part of Mexico. The group finally arrived in the Salt Lake Valley in July 1847. He is sometimes called the "American Moses" for his leadership of the early Mormon pioneers. Although Young was not the governor of Utah Territory, he wielded enough political power that Abraham Lincoln dealt with him rather than with the governor during the laying of the transcontinental telegraph wire. Young is still a controversial figure because of his doctrine of blood atonement; his possible involvement in the Mountain Meadows massacre of 1857, when 120 members of a non-Mormon wagon train were ambushed near Cedar City, Utah; and his open practice of polygamy. Young married at least 50 wives, possibly as many as 52, and had 57 known children. Young's example is cited by contemporary fundamentalist Mormons as justification for their own practice of plural marriage.

9

Organizations and Agencies

This chapter provides contact information for various types of groups related to the study of religious fundamentalism. They include civil liberties organizations and research centers; religious groups that are considered fundamentalist, evangelical, or traditionalist; political action groups or parties; and national or international commissions on religious freedom. The lists are arranged alphabetically.

ACCREDITING, CIVIL LIBERTIES, AND RESEARCH ORGANIZATIONS

American-Arab Anti-Discrimination Committee (ADC)
URL: http://www.adc.org
1732 Wisconsin Avenue NW
Washington, DC 20007
Phone: (202) 244-2990
Fax: (202) 244-7968

The ADC describes itself as "a grassroots civil rights organization that welcomes people of all backgrounds, faiths and ethnicities as members." Founded in 1980 by a former U.S. senator from South Dakota, James Abourezk, who was the first Arab American to serve in the Senate, the ADC states as its primary goals "protecting civil rights and advocating a balanced Mideast policy." The organization's West Coast headquarters were bombed by the Jewish Defense League in October 1985; the explosion killed the office's director, Alex Odeh. The ADC states that as of 2006, 3 million Americans—three-quarters of whom are Christians—can trace their ancestry to Arab countries.

Association of Theological Schools (ATS)
URL: http://www.ats.edu

10 Summit Park Drive
Pittsburgh, PA 15275-1103
Phone: (412) 788-6505
Fax: (412) 788-6510

The ATS is the body responsible for accrediting institutions in the United States and Canada offering postgraduate (masters' and doctoral) degrees in theology and ministry. It is recognized by the U.S. Department of Education and the nongovernmental Council for Higher Education Accreditation. As of 2006, 251 schools of theology, both free-standing seminaries and those affiliated with colleges or universities, have been accredited or pre-accredited by the ATS. Fifty-eight seminaries are Roman Catholic or Eastern Orthodox denominational schools; the remaining 193 are either interdenominational or affiliated with one of the Protestant churches. At a minimum, 30 to 35 of these schools can be categorized as evangelical or conservative, with seven belonging to denominations usually considered fundamentalist.

Center for Millennial Studies (CMS)
URL: http://www.mille.org
Boston University
704 Commonwealth Avenue
Suite 205
Boston, MA 02215
Phone: (617) 358-0226
Fax: (617) 358-0225

The CMS was founded in the 1990s, in part to collect the apocalyptic literature that was expected to appear as the year 2000 approached. The center also studies and analyzes millenarian groups and their ideas in order to understand movements of this type and the changes they undergo when their expectations of the fulfillment of prophecy are disappointed. Some historical research into previous periods of millenarian speculation is also done at the CMS. In addition, the center offers its analyses of current movements to the media, researchers, policy makers, and others who are looking for impartial as well as timely information about millenarian groups and their leaders.

Center for Religious Freedom
URL: http://www.freedomhouse.org/religion
Freedom House
1319 18th Street NW
Washington, DC 20036

Phone: (202) 296-5101
Fax: (202) 296-5078

The Center for Religious Freedom is a self-supporting division of Freedom House, an organization founded in 1941 by Eleanor Roosevelt and Wendell Willkie to oppose fascism and communism in Europe. The center itself began in 1986 and presently advocates on behalf of all religious minorities persecuted anywhere in the world, including Muslim dissidents as well as Jews and Christians. It conducts field investigations and issues periodic reports to the media, Congress, the State Department, and the executive branch of the U.S. government.

Cushwa Center for the Study of American Catholicism
URL: http://www.nd.edu/~cushwa/
University of Notre Dame
1135 Flanner Hall
Notre Dame, IN 46556-5611
Phone: (574) 631-5441
Fax: (574) 631-8471

The Cushwa Center, which was opened in 1975, is considered the leading institution for researching the history of Roman Catholicism in the United States. The center has sponsored studies of the growth of Hispanic Catholicism in the United States, the history of American Catholic parish life, the history of Irish Catholics in America, the impact of the Second Vatican Council on American Catholicism, and the role of women in religious history. It publishes a newsletter twice a year.

Fellowship of Catholic Scholars
URL: http://www.catholicscholars.org
Phone: (734) 827-8043

The Fellowship of Catholic Scholars was formed in 1977 by a group of scholars who felt alienated both from the secularism of the institutions in which they were teaching and the hostility expressed by many Catholic intellectuals in the late 1970s toward the church's magisterium (teaching authority). The fellowship accepts the teachings of the Second Vatican Council. It states as one of its purposes to consider the questions raised by contemporary thought with courage and honesty. As of early 2006, it had branches in Ireland, Canada, and Australia. Its president is Dr. Bernard Dobranski.

Foundation for Ancient Research and Mormon Studies (FARMS)
URL: http://farms.byu.edu
P.O. Box 7113
University Station
Provo, UT 84602
Phone: (801) 422-9229
Fax: (801) 422-0040

Established in 1979 as a private research institute, FARMS was moved to the campus of Brigham Young University in 1997. It focuses on scholarly work related to Mormon scriptures and on some subjects connected with the Middle East and Mesoamerica. The foundation states that it "views the Bible and the *Book of Mormon,* as well as other scripture such as the Book of Abraham and the Book of Moses, as authentic, historical texts." It publishes some periodicals intended for Mormon readers but also works with Mormon scholars "to get the results of their research published by various university presses aimed at academic audiences." FARMS is particularly concerned with refuting the historical work of D. Michael Quinn and others who have been excommunicated by the Church of Jesus Christ of Latter-day Saints.

Hartford Institute for Religion Research (HIRR)
URL: http://hirr.hartsem.edu
Hartford Seminary
77 Sherman Street
Hartford, CT 06105-2260
Phone: (860) 509-9543
Fax: (860) 509-9551

HIRR is an excellent resource for anyone interested in studying specific congregations, whether in fundamentalist or non-fundamentalist traditions, as well as denominations. The various researchers associated with the institute specialize in such subjects as national religious trends, immigrant and racial or ethnic groups within religious institutions, and congregational renewal and growth within urban settings. The HIRR Web site includes links to online resources in the field of sociology of religion.

Institute for Counter-Terrorism (ICT)
URL: http://www.ict.org.il
Interdisciplinary Center Herzlia
P.O. Box 167

Herzlia, 46150
Israel
Fax: (972-9) 951-3073

The ICT is an Israeli research institute and think tank for developing better public policy responses to international terrorism. It describes itself as solutions-oriented and concerned with affecting policy at the highest levels, although it also offers recommendations for specific situations. It hosts educational conferences and offers an executive certification program in security issues as well as maintaining an extensive database and publishing articles on specific terrorist attacks and threats. The Web site has a number of online articles, news reports, research reports, editorial commentary, and psychological profiles of terrorists and terrorist groups.

Jerusalem Center for Public Affairs (JCPA)
URL: http://www.jcpa.org
Beit Milken, 13 Tel Hai Street
Jerusalem 92107
Israel
Phone: (972-2) 561-9281
Fax: (972-2) 561-9112

The JCPA is an independent nonprofit institution for policy research related to Israel's security and political concerns. It publishes the *Jewish Political Studies Review* as well as newsletters, interviews with prominent political leaders, and such online publications as *Jerusalem Issue Briefs* and *Israel Campus Beat.* In recent years, the center has turned its attention to the resurgence of anti-Semitism in many countries around the world and to studies of the changing relationships between evangelical Christians and Jews. The site is available in Hebrew and English.

Mormon History Association (MHA)
URL: http://www.mhahome.org
581 South 630 East
Orem, UT 84097
Phone: (801) 224-0241
Fax: (801) 224-5684

The MHA was founded in 1965 by Leonard Arrington, a noted Mormon scholar who served as the official denominational church historian from 1972 to 1982. The MHA is an independent nonprofit organization open to all persons interested in the Mormon past, "irrespective of religious affiliation, academic training, or world location." It sponsors conferences and publishes the *Journal of Mormon History,* which began publication in 1974. The MHA is affiliated with the American Historical Association and the Western History Association.

Office of the High Commissioner for Human Rights (OHCHR)
URL: http://www.unhchr.ch
United Nations Office at Geneva
1211 Geneva 10
Switzerland
Phone: (41-22) 917-9000
Fax: (41-22) 917-9022

The OHCHR is a department within the United Nations (UN). Its mission is to promote and protect the full enjoyment, by all people in all member nations, of all human rights recognized in the Charter of the United Nations and in international human rights treaties and agreements. It also has a mandate to prevent human rights violations, including violations of religious freedom. The priorities of the OHCHR are set by the UN's General Assembly.

Ontario Consultants on Religious Tolerance (OCRT)
URL: http://www.religioustolerance.org
Box 27026
Kingston, ON K7M 8W5
Canada
Fax: (613) 547-9015

The OCRT is a group of volunteers from different religious traditions who maintain a Web site intended to provide accurate information about religious groups and expose frauds or false information. The group also seeks to provide a forum for debating "hot" issues (abortion, euthanasia, plural marriage, etc.) and "to present, compare and contrast *all* sides to each issue." They state that their postings are reviewed by persons familiar with the subject who represent different points of view. Their view on religion in general is as follows: "We believe that most religions have a generally positive influence on their followers and on society. Of all of the faith groups that we have studied, only a handful of destructive cults have had an overall negative effect. We do not believe that all religions and spiritual paths are the same, or that all are equally good, or that all are equally valid." The group no longer posts a telephone number in its contact information because of death threats.

Pluralism Project
URL: http://www.pluralism.org/about/index.php

1531 Cambridge Street
Cambridge, MA 02139
Phone: (617) 496-2481
Fax: (617) 496-2428

The Pluralism Project is a research project that has been associated with Harvard University and funded by the Ford and Rockefeller Foundations since the mid-1990s. It studies the impact of the new religious diversity in the United States on public life, particularly in communities where the change has been most noticeable, and the implications of this diversity for law and public policy. It also examines the new religious groups themselves, the response of Christian and Jewish groups to them, and the development of interfaith networks. The project publishes the *Directory of U.S. Religious Centers.*

Project Muslims in American Public Square (Project MAPS)
URL: http://www.projectmaps.com
Center for Muslim-Christian Understanding
Georgetown University
37th and O Streets NW
Washington, DC 20057
Phone: (202) 687-0291
Fax: (202) 687-6001

Project MAPS is one of the three Initiatives for Religious Communities funded by the Pew Foundation. It is situated on the campus of Georgetown University in the Center for Muslim-Christian Understanding, which was founded in 1993 as part of the Edmund A. Walsh School of Foreign Service. Project MAPS is in the process of publishing a two-volume set of scholarly papers on "the participation, contribution and role of the Muslim community in American civic life," as well as conducting a two-stage survey of U.S. Muslim mosques and leaders. The project has also sponsored workshops, focus groups, and conferences around the country. It has a Web site and a newsletter.

Sunstone Education Foundation
URL: http://www.sunstoneonline.com
343 North 300 West
Salt Lake City, UT 84103
Phone: (801) 355-5926

The Sunstone Education Foundation was started in 1974 by a group of Mormon graduate students at Brigham Young University who were interested in exchanging their ideas and religious experiences. The foundation has no official ties to the Church of Jesus Christ of Latter-day Saints. Sunstone regards its mission as the sponsorship of open forums on Mormon thought and experience, including art, humor, and short fiction, as well as Mormon history and theology. Many of its early members and participants were regarded with suspicion and disciplined by Mormon authorities. Six authors in academic positions of various types were excommunicated or disfellowshipped by Mormon authorities in September 1993. Sunstone began as a student magazine and gradually expanded to host an annual four-day symposium of panels and workshops in Salt Lake City that draws more than a thousand participants.

Temple Institute
URL: http://www.templeinstitute.org
P.O. Box 31876
Jerusalem
Israel
Phone: (972-2) 626-4545
Fax: (972-2) 627-4529

The Temple Institute describes itself as a nonprofit religious and educational foundation located in the Old City of Jerusalem. Its long-term goal is the rebuilding of the Temple; its immediate focus is research, restoration, and construction of the sacred vessels for service in the Temple. At present, the institute has completed the musical instruments used by the Levitical choir, the altar of incense, the menorah, and other items. Its present project is the reconstruction of the vestments worn by the high priest. The founder of the institute is a rabbi who served in the paratrooper brigade that secured the Temple Mount during the Six-Day War in 1967.

United States Commission on International Religious Freedom (USCIRF)
URL: http://www.uscirf.gov/home.html
800 North Capitol Street NW
Suite 790
Washington, DC 20002
Phone: (202) 523-3240
Fax: (202) 523-5020

USCIRF was established in 1998, when the International Religious Freedom Act (IRFA) became law. The commission will expire in September 2011, although the Office of International Religious Freedom within the State Department that was also set up by IRFA will continue. USCIRF issues a report each May on selected "countries of particular concern" (CPCs) regarded as violators of religious freedom. There are nine commissioners, who serve two-year terms and may be reappointed. Three are selected by the president, four by the leaders of the party not in the White House, and two by the congressional leaders of the president's party. The commissioners are chosen on the basis of their expertise in human rights issues, not because they represent specific religions. USCIRF's authority is limited to monitoring religious matters in other countries and making policy recommendations. It does not have the power to impose sanctions of any kind.

EVANGELICAL ORGANIZATIONS

Campus Crusade for Christ International (CCCI)
URL: http://www.ccci.org
100 Lake Hart Drive
Orlando, FL 32832
Phone: (407) 826-2000

CCCI was founded by Bill Bright in 1951 as an evangelical fellowship group for college students. It has since branched out into films, publications, and other ministries not directly connected with undergraduate outreach. CCCI is reportedly the largest evangelical organization in the United States, reaching professional athletes, military personnel, and prisoners, as well as institutions of higher education. As of 2006, it had more than 26,000 full-time staff members working in 191 different countries.

Fuller Theological Seminary
URL: http://www.fuller.edu
135 North Oakland Avenue
Pasadena, CA 91182
Phone: (800) 2-FULLER; (626) 584-5498

Fuller Theological Seminary, which was founded in 1947, has become the flagship theological school for American evangelicals. It was named for Henry Fuller, a devout layman and generous supporter of overseas missions. One of the largest seminaries in the United States, Fuller is also one of the most diverse and academically demanding. Its present student body is drawn from 67 countries and 108 denominations. In addition to the standard degree programs for parish ministry, Fuller offers Ph.D. and D.Min. graduate programs, including doctoral programs in clinical psychology and marriage and family counseling. The school has also pioneered a graduate course in intercultural studies, extension courses for laypeople, and a special D.Min. program for Korean-American and Korean pastors.

InterVarsity Christian Fellowship (IVCF)
URL: http://www.intervarsity.org
6400 Schroeder Road
P.O. Box 7895
Madison, WI 53707
Phone: (608) 274-9001
Fax: (608) 274-7882

The older of the two major evangelical parachurch organizations for college students and faculty, IVCF sponsors urban mission projects and multiethnic ministries, as well as campus Bible study groups and a fellowship group for nursing students. It also has a publishing house that produces books on topics of interest to students, including such subjects as postmodernism, ecology, and political involvement, as well as theology and philosophy. IVCF has about 800 undergraduate campus fellowship groups and 141 graduate student/faculty groups on 565 campuses around the United States. It is a member of the International Fellowship of Evangelical Students, a global network of campus ministries headquartered in the United Kingdom.

National Association of Evangelicals (NAE)
URL: http://www.nae.net
Governmental Affairs Office
701 G Street SW
Washington, DC 20024
Phone: (202) 789-1011

The NAE was founded in 1942 as an umbrella organization for various non-fundamentalist Protestant evangelical bodies. As of 2006, the NAE represented 52 member denominations with a total of 30 million members. The NAE is a politically active group, "aggressively and proactively seeking to weigh in on contemporary concerns. . . and provide the media and others with the evangelical Christian perspective." It is not, however, separatist, allowing its member churches to have dual memberships in the National Council of Churches.

Wheaton College
URL: http://www.wheaton.edu
501 College Avenue
Wheaton, IL 60187
Phone: (630) 752-5000

Wheaton is generally considered the most academically selective evangelical college in the United States. It is interdenominational rather than affiliated with a specific church body. The school's Billy Graham Center could be described as a think tank for training the next generation of evangelists to work in rapidly changing cultures around the globe. It also has the Institute for the Study of American Evangelicals (ISAE), founded in 1982 to support research on the history on evangelical Christianity in North America. The ISAE publishes a 12-page *Evangelical Studies Bulletin* four times a year. Papers from ISAE's most recent research projects, on the confessional traditions in American religious life and on the changing face of American evangelicalism, are available on request.

FUNDAMENTALIST AND TRADITIONALIST ORGANIZATIONS

American Council of Christian Churches (ACCC)
URL: http://www.amcouncilcc.org
P.O. Box 5455
Bethlehem, PA 18015
Phone: (610) 865-3009
Fax: (610) 865-3033

The ACCC is an interdenominational association of separatist fundamentalist churches founded in 1941 by Carl McIntire to counter the liberalism of the Federal Council of Churches (the forerunner of the present National Council of Churches). Unlike the National Association of Evangelicals, the ACCC is a militantly separatist organization. As of 2006, it had seven denominations as members; its current president is Dr. John McKnight.

Aryan Nations World Headquarters
URL: http://www.twelvearyannations.com/
P.O. Box 151
Lincoln, AL 35096
Phone: (205) 616-6497

Aryan Nations
URL: http://aryan-nations.org
P.O. Box 719
Lexington, SC 29071
Phone: (803) 233-6601

Aryan Nations, which is part of the Christian Identity movement, was the political wing of Wesley Swift's Church of Jesus Christ–Christian during the years that the church owned a compound in Hayden Lake, Idaho. After the compound was sold to pay off a civil lawsuit, the movement split and formed groups in Alabama and South Carolina, respectively. The Alabama group has been led by a group of three men since the death of Richard Butler in 2004. They distribute their own white power music under the label of Aryan Nations Records; their first release is called *The Battleaxe Compilation: 27 Anthems of Resolution.* Their Web site maintains an archive of Butler's writings and a photo album. The South Carolina group maintains that securing an Aryan homeland must now be a secondary goal. They define their new primary goal as an anti-Semitic "Aryan Jihad": "It is our intention to see Judaic-influenced society and governmental infrastructures to be pushed into a state of perpetual revolution. . . . [We wish] to redress the imbalance caused by the Jew and their hubristic sycophants and restore this earth to a state of cosmic harmony."

Arya Pratinidhi Sabha America (Congress of Arya Samajs in North America)
URL: http://www.aryasamaj.com/
c/o Ved Niketan
5450 Daniels Drive
Troy, MI 40898
Phone: (248) 879-2531

Like its parent organization in India, the Congress of Arya Samajs in the United States and Canada is dedicated to purifying Hindu faith and practice on the basis of the Vedas, the earliest Hindu sacred texts. Arya Samaj has a list of 10 principles that summarize its central beliefs. According to the editor of its newsletter, there are chapters in most large cities in North America. The organization sponsors an annual *sammalan,* or meeting; it also began a weekly radio program in 2005. It maintains an academic program for training and credentialing persons who are seeking ordination as Vedic *purohits,* or priests.

Bob Jones University (BJU)
URL: http://www.bju.edu
1700 Wade Hampton Boulevard
Greenville, SC 29614
Phone: (864) 242-5100

BJU is one of the best-known educational institutions associated with fundamentalism. Founded in 1927 by the evangelist Bob Jones, Sr., BJU describes itself as "the citadel of biblical Christianity for its adherence to the Bible as mankind's only source of faith and Christian practice." The school's J. S. Mack Library has a special collection known as the Fundamentalism File. Begun in 1978, the file collects non-book items (mostly periodical articles) on subjects of religious interest. As of 2006, the file had 100,000 articles listed under 5,000 subject headings. Some research reports produced from documents in the file are available online (URL: http://www.bju.edu/library/collections/fund_file/filerpts.html). Visitors are not required to obtain any special permission to use the file; out-of-town researchers may request copies of documents to be mailed to them (for a fee).

Catholics United for the Faith (CUF)
URL: http://www.cuf.org
827 North Fourth Street
Steubenville, OH 43952
Phone: (800) 693-2484

CUF was established in 1968 by a layman named H. Lyman Stebbins in order to defend the teachings of the Roman Catholic Church in accordance with the principles set forth by the Second Vatican Council. CUF is not sponsored or directed by clergy; it is organized as a private association of laypeople and incorporated as a nonprofit organization registered in Ohio. It publishes a bimonthly magazine called *Lay Witness.* As of 2006, there were about 80 CUF chapters in 30 states.

Chalcedon Foundation
URL: http://www.chalcedon.edu
P.O. Box 158
Vallecito, CA 95251
Phone: (209) 736-4365
Fax: (209) 736-0536

According to its Web site, the Chalcedon Foundation is a "non-profit Christian educational organization devoted to research, publishing, and promoting Christian reconstruction in all areas of life." Founded by Rousas J. Rushdoony in 1965, the foundation seeks to bring about social change through "regeneration and obedience by the people of God." The organization's credo is an attempt to respond to its critics and state positively what its members believe about the role of the Christian as citizen: "Our objective . . . in supporting

Christian political involvement is to *scale down* the massive state in Western democracies, reducing it to its Biblical limits. We do not believe in political salvation of any kind." The Web site includes a new blog as well as online articles and position papers.

Full Gospel Business Men's Fellowship International (FGBMFI)
URL: http://www.fgbmfi.org
27 Spectrum Pointe Drive
Suite 312
Lake Forest, CA 92630
Phone: (949) 461-0100
Fax: (949) 609-0344

FGBMFI was started in Los Angeles in 1952 by a California dairyman named Demos Shakarian. It now has members in 132 countries. Members meet at mealtimes for outreach, fellowship, and ministry to one another. The fellowship sees itself as the fulfillment of prophetic messages given over a period of time beginning in 1855 and confirmed by a vision given to Shakarian. The group's doctrinal statement includes the following affirmation about the Scriptures: "We believe in the Bible, in its entirety, to be the inspired Word of God and the only infallible rule of faith and conduct."

Hindu University of America
URL: http://www.hindu-university.edu/
113 North Econlockhatchee Trail
Orlando, FL 32825-3732
Phone: (407) 275-0013

The Hindu University of America was incorporated in 1989 and began offering courses in 1993. It moved to its present location outside Orlando, Florida, on September 8, 2001. Its stated mission is to "provide for learning, research, community service, and training in a broad spectrum of topics related to the Vedic/Hindu culture including religions, philosophies, sciences, practices and other related areas." As of early 2006, it offered correspondence courses as well as classroom instruction for students preparing for a religious vocation. The university offers master's and doctoral programs in Hindu studies, with concentrations in Hindu philosophy, music, Hindu/Vedic astrology, yoga philosophies and meditation, and Ayurvedic sciences. All instruction is in English. It expects to introduce an undergraduate program within the next few years.

IFCA International
URL: http://www.ifca.org

P.O. Box 810
Grandville, MI 49468
Phone: (800) 347-1840
Fax: (616) 531-1814

IFCA began in 1930 as the Independent Fundamental Churches of America, an association of "Bible believing" fundamentalist congregations not affiliated with larger denominations. The association changed its name for two reasons: Its member congregations came to include some outside the United States, and it recognized that the term *fundamental* conveyed a strongly negative impression to others. As its Web site states, "It carried all the ideas associated with radical 'fundamentalists' (hate, snake handling, etc.)." The name change, however, does not reflect any alteration in the group's historic commitment to "the 'fundamentals' of the faith as taught in God's inspired word." IFCA presently describes itself as "an ethnically blended fellowship of men and churches, reflecting the diversity of the Body of Christ, who are committed to working together in Biblical ministry worldwide."

International Seminary of Saint Pius X
URL: http://wwgb.seminaire-econe.com
Ecône
CH–1908 Riddes
Switzerland
Phone: (41-27) 305-1080
Fax: (41-27) 744-3319

The International Seminary of St. Pius X is the main extreme traditionalist institution for the training of priests founded by Archbishop Marcel Lefebvre in 1971. According to its Web site, it has a student body of about 100 as of early 2006, including students from France, Switzerland, Italy, the United Kingdom, Australia, India, New Zealand, and the United States. The course of studies is five years in length; the total period of spiritual formation is six years. The average age of the students is 24. Candidates for entry must have the equivalent of the French *baccalauréat,* the Swiss *maturité,* or two English A-levels. Instruction is in French; knowledge of Latin is not required for entry, but the students must complete three years of intensive instruction in Latin. The current rector of the seminary is Father Benoît de Jorna.

Jewish Defense League (JDL) (United States)
URL: http://www.jewishdefenseleague.org/

P.O. Box 480370
Los Angeles, CA 90048
Phone: (818) 980-8535
Fax: (781) 634-0338

Jewish Defense League (Israel)
URL: http://www.jdl.org.il/

The JDL is a right-wing Jewish activist organization founded in New York City in 1968 by Rabbi Meir Kahane to protect Orthodox Jewish people and property from anti-Semitic attacks by the Black Panthers and teenage minority gang members. The JDL has been controversial almost from its beginning, having been described in an FBI report from 2000 as "violent" and "extremist." The JDL was credited with 40 to 50 terrorist attacks, mostly bombings, in the period from 1968 to 1987. The group split into factions following Kahane's assassination in 1990. It was further disrupted by the imprisonment and deaths in prison of Irving Rubin, the JDL's international chairman (he died following a fall in 2002, ruled a suicide), and Earl Krugel (killed by other prison inmates in Arizona in 2005). The two had been convicted in December 2001 of conspiracy to commit acts of terrorism. In October 2004, the JDL split into a faction in California led by Rubin's widow, Shelley Rubin, and a group in Israel led by Ian Sigel.

Kahane Movement
URL: http://www.kahane.org
1312 Avenue M
Suite 2332
Brooklyn, NY 11230
Phone: (718) 670-3771

The Kahane Movement is a small remnant of the radical Kach and Kahane Chai organizations. It maintains a Web site and forum; publishes Meir Kahane's writings on the Internet, also offering some in video and audiotape format; and links readers to news and right-wing commentary from Israel. The Web site also contains a photo archive and a brief history of Kahane and his son Binyamin.

Kingdom Identity Ministries
URL: http://www.kingidentity.com
P.O. Box 1021
Harrison, AR 72602
Phone: (870) 741-1119
Kingdom Identity Ministries describes itself on its Web site as a "*Politically Incorrect* Christian Identity outreach ministry to God's chosen race (true

Israel, the White, European peoples)." The group offers print publications, videos, audiotapes, an American Institute of Theology Bible correspondence course, radio broadcasts, a prison ministry, and a catalog of items for children. It promises that "the Elect Remnant, Christian Patriots, Nationalists, Reconstructionists, Racialists, and all seeking a higher level of understanding will learn Biblical solutions to personal and national problems, and be given keys to unlock hidden truth." It appears to regard itself as a successor group to Wesley Swift's Church of Jesus Christ–Christian.

Lutheran Church–Missouri Synod (LCMS)
URL: http://lcms.org
1333 South Kirkwood Road
St. Louis, MO 63122-7295
Phone: (888) THE-LCMS; (314) 965-9000
Fax: (314) 996-1016

The second-largest Lutheran body in the United States, the Missouri Synod was founded in 1847 by a group of 12 pastors who had emigrated from Germany to avoid a forced merger with a Reformed church. As a result of this experience in its homeland, the LCMS has always placed a heavy emphasis on faithfulness to the Lutheran Confessions as well as the Scriptures. It maintains the largest network of non–Roman Catholic parochial schools in the United States as well as the oldest religious radio station in the world, KFUO in St. Louis. It is a separatist denomination; LCMS has never joined the Lutheran World Federation, the National Council of Churches, or the World Council of Churches.

Mercaz Harav (Yeshivat Mercaz HaRav Kook)
URL: http://www.mercazharav.org
12 Ben Dor Street
P.O. Box 5010
Jerusalem 91050
Israel
Phone: (972-2) 652-4793; (972-2) 652-4821
Fax: (972-2) 654-0356

Mercaz Harav is a yeshiva (academy for the study of Torah) established in Jerusalem by Rabbi Abraham Isaac Kook in 1924. Its graduates formed the nucleus of Gush Emunim (GE) in the early 1970s. As of early 2006, it had a total enrollment of about 700 students (males only), which makes it one of the largest yeshivot in Israel. The teaching staff is currently headed by Abraham Shapiro, a former chief rabbi of Israel. All instruction is in Hebrew. Mercaz Harav reflects GE's fusion of religion and nationalism by describing itself as "Israel's National Yeshiva": "It was here that the spiritual significance of [Israeli] Independence Day and Jerusalem Day receive their full emphasis, to become holidays of national thanksgiving celebrated in their full glory, by Israel's great Torah sages together with the heads of the state and its leaders."

Moody Bible Institute (MBI)
URL: http://www.moody.edu
820 North LaSalle Boulevard
Chicago, IL 60610
Phone: (800) DLMOODY; (312) 329-4000

MBI defines its purpose as educating and equipping persons for ministries that "educate, edify, and evangelize." Its Doctrinal Statement describes the Bible as "a divine revelation, the original autographs of which were verbally inspired by the Holy Spirit." MBI has offered undergraduate and graduate courses since its foundation in 1886 and now offers distance learning online as well. Its latest degree program is a bachelor's degree in mission aviation, offered in conjunction with Spokane Community College. MBI also operates about 10 radio stations and two publishing houses.

Muslim Brotherhood (Ikhwan)
URL: http://www.ikhwanweb.com

The Muslim Brotherhood was started in Egypt by Hassan al-Banna in 1928 as a charitable and social reform movement. Egypt is still considered its center, although the Muslim Brotherhood has branches in such countries as Syria, Jordan, Kurdistan, Iraq, and Saudi Arabia. Hamas is the name of its Palestinian branch. After the Egyptian government declared the Muslim Brotherhood illegal following the 1954 assassination attempt on President Nasser, the Brotherhood became the major source of political opposition to the established regimes in several Arab countries. Its leaders are still subjected to occasional mass arrests. The Muslim Brotherhood has only one official English-language Web site, Ikhwanweb, which is headquartered in London. The only contact information given is a set of e-mail addresses.

Religious Zionists of America (RZA)
URL: http://www.rza.org
Seven Penn Plaza
Suite 205
New York, NY 10001
Phone: (212) 465-9234
Fax: (212) 465-9246

The RZA is the American branch of the World Mizrachi Organization, an umbrella group of religious Zionist movements around the world. The RZA describes itself as "an ideological and educational organization" intended to strengthen the commitment of American Jews to religious Zionism. It combines religious and nationalistic interests, dedicating itself to "the preservation of Jewish political freedom" as well as enhancing Jewish religious life in Israel. It sponsors adult educational programs, a network of summer camps for young people, and a curriculum on religious Zionism for use in Jewish day schools. The RZA also promotes aliyah (immigration to Israel) and the use of Hebrew in daily life.

The Remnant
URL: http://www.remnantnewspaper.com
P.O. Box 1117
Forest Lake, MN 55025
Phone: (651) 204-0145
Fax: (651) 204-6421

The Remnant is a traditionalist Roman Catholic newsletter that has published issues every two weeks since 1967. Objecting to many of the changes in worship and other church practices that followed the Second Vatican Council, the writers and publishers of the newsletter nonetheless consider themselves the "loyal opposition": "*The Remnant* fights the revolutionaries in the Church from within the Church. It is opposed to Modernism, Papolatry (the worship of the Pope), phony ecumenism and anything else which compromises the traditional Catholic Faith—but it labors for a restoration of the old Faith, and not for the foundation of a new 'traditional' church."

Revava
URL: http://www.revava.org
P.O. Box 960121
143 Doughty Boulevard
Inwood, NY 11096
Phone: (212) 561-5924

Revava is a Jewish grassroots organization with ties to religious Zionism whose stated purpose is to restore "self-esteem" to the nation of Israel "by restoring Jewish national pride and values." Revava supports the settlement movement and is presently helping persons displaced by the Israeli government's withdrawal from the settlements. In addition, the group is conducting a "Revava to the Temple Mount" campaign to bring 10,000 Jews to the Temple Mount in a condition of ritual purity.

Society of Saint Pius V (SSPV)
URL: http://www.sspv.net
St. Pius V Church
Eight Pond Place
Oyster Bay Cove, NY 11771
Phone: (516) 922-5430

The SSPV, which represents a group of sedevacantist priests expelled from the Society of St. Pius X in 1983, describes itself as "an organization of traditional Catholic priests dedicated to the preservation of the traditional Latin Mass." They believe that the changes in the liturgy implemented after the Second Vatican Council "compromise the true Catholic Religion" and do not convey the faith defined by Jesus Christ and committed to the Apostles. The society maintains a seminary in Round Top, New York, known as Immaculate Heart Seminary. Its membership has been decreased since 1997 by further splits within the extreme traditionalist movement. Its present superior general is Bishop Clarence Kelly, consecrated in 1993 by a retired bishop from Puerto Rico. The SSPV is named for Pope Pius V (1504–72), pope from 1566 to 1572. He was involved with the Inquisition and staunchly opposed to the Reformation. Pius V was canonized by Pope Clement XI in 1712.

Society of Saint Pius X (SSPX), United States of America District
URL: http://www.sspx.org
Regina Coeli House
2918 Tracy Avenue
Kansas City, MO 64109
Phone: (816) 753-0073
Fax: (816) 753-3560

The SSPX was founded by Archbishop Marcel Lefebvre in Switzerland in 1969 as a society for the spiritual formation of Roman Catholic priests. It was recognized by the bishop of Lausanne, Geneva, and Fribourg in 1970. In 1995, the society had four bishops and 360 priests in 27 countries as members. The Third Order, intended for laypeople "thirsting for perfection" while living in the world, requires a commitment to regular morning and evening prayer, daily attendance at Mass, confession once a month, and a retreat every two years. The SSPX maintains a publication house and 25 parochial schools in the United States.

Southern Baptist Convention (SBC)
URL: http://www.sbc.net/default.asp
Office of Convention Relations

Southern Baptist Convention Building
901 Commerce Street
Nashville, TN 37203-3699
Phone: (615) 244-2355

The SBC is the largest group of American Christians usually identified as fundamentalist and the second-largest group overall, Roman Catholics being the largest. It has more churches than any other religious group in the United States—more than 37,000 as of the early 2000s. The term *convention* refers both to the name of the denomination and its annual meeting. The church maintains a center for scholarly research into Baptist history known as the Southern Baptist Historical Library and Archives (SBHLA). The library is housed within the denomination's Convention Building and may be contacted by telephone at (615) 244-0344.

Temple Mount and Eretz Yisrael Faithful Movement
URL: http://www.templemountfaithful.org
P.O. Box 18325
Yohanan Harkanos #4
Jerusalem
Israel
Phone: (972-2) 625-1112
Fax: (972-2) 625-1113

The movement states that its first long-term objective is liberating the Temple Mount from Islamic occupation and removing the "pagan shrines," which can be "transferred to and rebuilt at Mecca." It then proposes to reconsecrate the Mount and build the Third Temple as "a house of prayer for the people of Israel and all nations." The movement is opposed to "false peace talks" and supports the settlements in Judea, Samaria, and the Golan Heights. "No one is allowed to break the Word and the Will of G-d by commanding the settlers to leave." The organization's immediate goals are educating the people of Israel about the importance of the Temple Mount and the boundaries of the land of Israel through publications, youth clubs, and the purchase of a house to serve as a conference center.

World Apostolate of Fatima, U.S.A.
Blue Army of Our Lady of Fatima
URL: http://www.wafusa.org
Blue Army Shrine
P.O. Box 976
Washington, NJ 07882

Phone: (908) 698-1701
Retreat Center: (908) 689-7330

The Blue Army is the American branch of a worldwide movement of Roman Catholics dedicated to spreading the message of Fátima, where the Virgin Mary is said to have appeared to three Portuguese children in 1917. The Blue Army Shrine, located in Asbury, New Jersey, was completed in 1978 and draws 50,000 visitors each year.

World Mizrachi Movement
URL: http://www.mizrachi.org
54 King George Street
P.O. Box 7720
Jerusalem 91074
Israel
Phone: (972-2) 620-9000
Fax: (972-2) 625-7418

Mizrachi is the Hebrew acronym for Merkaz Ruchani, which means "religious center." It is a religious Zionist movement founded in 1902. It joined with two other religious Zionist groups to found the National Religious Party (NRP) of Israel in 1956. The World Mizrachi Movement has branches in 37 countries around the world. Its youth movement, Bnei Akiva, was founded in 1929 and is the largest religious youth group in Israel.

POLITICAL GROUPS AND COMMISSIONS

Bharatiya Janata Party (BJP)
URL: http://www.bjp.org/
Central Office
11, Ashoka Road
New Delhi 110 001
India

The BJP is the Indian nationalist party most closely associated with the ideology of Hindutva. Its Web site has a page devoted to "BJP Philosophy: Hindutva" and a set of articles with the following disclaimer: "Hindutva or Cultural Nationalism presents the BJP's conception of Indian nationhood, as explained in the following set of articles. It must be noted that Hindutva is a nationalist, and not a religious or theocratic, concept." Given that one of the articles on the page maintains that Christianity and Islam are to blame for religious intolerance in India, the reader may wish to question the disclaimer.

Christian Coalition of America (CCA)
URL: http://www.cc.org
P.O. Box 37030
Washington, DC 20013-7030
Phone: (202) 479-6900
Fax: (202) 479-4260

The CCA is a political advocacy group of conservative Christians ranging from fundamentalists and Pentecostals to Roman Catholics and members of mainline Protestant churches. It describes itself as an "active conservative grassroots political organization . . . offer[ing] people of faith the vehicle to be actively involved in shaping their government." Its initial funding came from Pat Robertson's failed 1988 campaign for the presidency. Originally based in the Chesapeake Bay area, it moved its offices to Washington in 2000. The CCA obtained tax-exempt status from the IRS in 2005 after several years of disputes, even though it distributes voter guides directly in churches.

Jamaat-e-Islami Pakistan
URL: http://www.jamaat.org/
Mansoorah, Multan Road
Lahore
Pakistan
Phone: (92-42) 541-9520–4; (92-42) 543-2391–5
Fax: (92-42) 543-7950

Jamaat-e-Islami is the organization that was founded by Abul Ala Mawdudi in 1941. It describes itself as a "religiopolitical organization" with particular appeal to "the intelligentsia and youth of the South-Asian sub-continent and the world." Like the Muslim Brotherhood, the Jamaat regards Islam as a comprehensive way of life covering all human activities and not just a set of pious practices limited to "religion." The Web site contains an English translation of the organization's constitution as well as profiles of the current leadership, a biography of Mawdudi, and some basic facts about Jamaat. The English text is not always easy to read because of grammatical difficulties, however.

National Religious Party (NRP; Mafdal)
URL: http://www.mafdal.org.il/?sid=27

The NRP (known in Israel as Mafdal) was created in 1956 by the merger of two smaller religious Zionist groups. Originally a centrist party, it turned toward the right after the Six Days' War of 1967 and became associated with Gush Emunim. As of the early 2000s, it was strictly a right-wing party, devoted to Israel's security and enhancing the country's Jewish identity. The NRP is not, however, interested in establishing a theocracy; it wants to preserve Israel's democratic structure. It supports the country's religious schools and the settlement movement and is opposed to giving over any part of Israel's present territory to a foreign power.

National Right to Life Committee (NRLC)
URL: http://www.nrlc.org
512 10th Street NW
Washington, DC 20004
Phone: (202) 626-8800

The NRLC was founded in 1973 as a response to *Roe v. Wade.* It began as a pro-life organization that opposed unrestricted abortion but has since extended its concerns to euthanasia, living wills, cloning, and the use of newborns for nontherapeutic scientific experimentation. Although the group is supported by many pro-life Roman Catholics, it is officially nonpartisan and nonsectarian. Its board of directors has representatives from each of the 50 states plus three "at large" members. The NRLC publishes a monthly newsletter and supports an educational trust fund. The committee does not have an official position "on issues such as contraception, sex education, capital punishment, and national defense."

Palestinian Information Center (PIC)
URL: http://www.palestine-info.co.uk/am/publish/index.shtml

The PIC serves as the official English-language Web site for Hamas's point of view about trends and events in the Middle East. It is based in the United Kingdom but provides no other contact information or an "about" page to introduce the site to readers. The Web site offers analyses of current events as well as news reports but makes no pretense of objectivity or impartiality. The articles and reports are unsigned, which makes authorship difficult to trace or evaluate, and the English is not always easy to read. There is also no e-mail function for leaving questions or feedback for the unnamed editor and contributors.

10

Annotated Bibliography

This annotated bibliography on fundamentalism is divided into the following broad subject areas:

General Intellectual and Religious History

American Religious History

Social-Scientific Analysis of Fundamentalism

Roman Catholic Traditionalism

Judaism

Islam

Hinduism

Each of these areas is subdivided into three subsections: Books (and Book Chapters), Print Articles, and Web Documents.

GENERAL INTELLECTUAL AND RELIGIOUS HISTORY

Books

Almond, Gabriel, R. Scott Appleby, and Emmanuel Sivan. *Strong Religion: The Rise of Fundamentalisms around the World.* Chicago: University of Chicago Press, 2003. This book is a follow-up to the scholarly six-volume series on fundamentalisms sponsored by the American Academy of Arts and Sciences and published by the University of Chicago Press. It was published after the events of September 11, 2001, and is in part a response to them. It is divided into six chapters that discuss fundamentalism as an enclave culture, attempt to construct categories for classifying different fundamentalist movements, discuss the various strategies that fundamentalists use to further their causes, and offer a prediction of the future of these movements. The book is written at a high level of scholarship and is difficult reading for those without an academic background in the social sciences. It does, however, advance the discussion of fundamentalist groups by offering a model that can be tested as the development of these groups continues to unfold.

Armstrong, Karen. *The Battle for God: A History of Fundamentalism.* New York: Ballantine Books, 2001. Published before the events of September 11, 2001, Armstrong's book has since been reissued with a new preface written as a commentary on the tragedy. Armstrong limits her comparative study to fundamentalist movements within Christianity, Judaism, and Islam, as she appears to think that the similarities among these three Western faiths are more significant than the differences in their responses to modernity.

———. *Jerusalem: One City, Three Faiths.* New York: Alfred A. Knopf, 1996. This book is a highly readable and useful account of the history of the city of Jerusalem and the country of which it is the capital. Armstrong begins with the earliest archaeological records of human settlement in Jerusalem and ends with the late-20th-century divided city. The early chapters on Jerusalem in the ancient world and the medieval period are a helpful historical overview for readers who are not familiar with those eras of history. The book also is plentifully illustrated with line drawings, maps, and photographs.

Bruce, Steve. *Fundamentalism.* Malden, Mass.: Blackwell Publishers, 2000. The author wrote this book after participating in the five-volume Fundamentalism Project undertaken by the University of Chicago in the early 1990s. A professor at the University of Aberdeen, he presents a brief, yet helpful and clearly written introduction to the subject. Bruce's basic thesis is that societies cannot modernize in a partial way; they must accept the whole "package" of modernity or none of it; and as a result, "Fundamentalism in the West has no chance of winning."

———. *God Is Dead: Secularization in the West.* Malden, Mass.: Blackwell Publishers, 2002. *God Is Dead* is a restatement of the author's basic argument—that the revival of fundamentalist religion in many parts of the world does not disprove the secularization theory. This is a lengthier and more detailed study than *Fundamentalism.* Several American reviewers of this book have taken issue with Bruce's picture of religion in the United States, maintaining that he is too eager to fit it into his overall gloomy view of the prospects of organized religion in the West.

Juergensmeyer, Mark. *Terror in the Mind of God: The Global Rise of Religious Violence.* 3d ed. Berkeley: University of California Press, 2003. Juergensmeyer's book is an attempt to understand religious terrorism "from the inside," that is, by interviewing terrorists representing a variety of religious traditions and investigating their cultural environments. The case studies are informative and helpful illustrations of the common threads linking terrorist acts even though the religions used to justify them are diverse. The book includes chapters on American opponents of abortion, the settlers' movement in Israel, Sikh fundamentalists in India, Hamas and the World Trade Center bombing in 1993, and the Aum Shinrikyō attack on the Tokyo subway system in 1995. Juergensmeyer's analysis of terrorist violence as a reaction to specifically male fears of loss of identity and loss of control is persuasive, at least in its broad outlines. The photographs in the center of the book are chilling.

McGrath, Alister. *The Twilight of Atheism.* New York: Doubleday, 2004. McGrath's book is an expanded version of a speech he gave at a 2002 debate in the Oxford

Union about the decline of atheism in the postmodern period. McGrath's suggestion that the Protestant Reformation was a major reason for the emergence of atheism within western Europe because it broke the connection between the sacred and the secular—"an erosion of any sense of direct encounter with the divine"—is an interesting subject for debate.

Niebuhr, H. Richard. *Christ and Culture.* New York: Harper & Row, 1951. Niebuhr's typology of the five different ways that Christians have engaged their surrounding culture (Christ against culture, the Christ of culture, Christ above culture, Christ and culture in paradox, and Christ the transformer of culture) has become a classic and is still a useful framework for discussing such trends in religion as the resurgence of fundamentalism. Although some of Niebuhr's selections of case studies for his five types have been criticized since *Christ and Culture* was first published, the book is still a helpful introduction to the history of Christian thought for general readers.

Rieff, Philip. *The Triumph of the Therapeutic: Uses of Faith after Freud.* New York: Harper & Row, 1966. Readers who are interested in the impact of psychoanalysis (and other schools of psychotherapy) on Western culture in general and religion in particular will find Rieff's analyses of Freud, Jung, Reich, and others stimulating and provocative. The author's basic thesis is that psychotherapy has become a substitute for religion for many moderns and a synthetic religion for others. Because of its individualistic presuppositions, however, the "triumph of the therapeutic" has led to a weakening of the communal dimension of Western culture.

Sennett, Richard. *The Fall of Public Man.* New York: Vintage Books, 1978. Although Sennett does not deal directly with the topic of religious fundamentalism, his historical analysis of the decline of public life and the rise of the cult of personality is quite relevant to such aspects of contemporary fundamentalism as televangelism and the use of the mass media. Sennett's discussion of the modern fascination with charismatic politicians in the last quarter of the book could easily be applied to many religious leaders as well.

Taylor, Charles. *Sources of the Self: The Making of the Modern Identity.* Cambridge, Mass.: Harvard University Press, 1989. Taylor's book is a long, detailed, and intellectually demanding history of the definition of personhood in Western culture. Taylor is committed to the value of Western moral thought, particularly to its defense of what he calls "the affirmation of ordinary life" and its respect for human dignity. Among other strands of Western thought, Taylor examines the role of the biblical religions in shaping the intellectual tradition of the West.

Print Articles

Armstrong, Karen. "Cries of Rage and Frustration." *New Statesman* 130 (September 24, 2001): 17. Armstrong's article is an expansion of a point she made in her earlier book on fundamentalism, namely that this form of religious belief is a response to fears of total annihilation by the forces of modernity.

Davie, Grace. "Prospects for Religion in the Modern World." *Ecumenical Review* 52 (October 2000): 455–464. Davie's work is, among other things, an attempt to answer Steve Bruce's view that the process of secularization is universal and irreversible. She points to religious developments in Latin America and Africa as evidence that the European model of secularization cannot be applied to other parts of the world and that Europe in fact may be atypical in its secularism.

Huff, Peter A. "The Challenge of Fundamentalism for Interreligious Dialogue." *Cross Currents* (Spring–Summer 2000): 94–100. This article is based on a paper that the author presented at the Parliament of the World's Religions in Cape Town, South Africa, in December 1999. Huff argues that participants in interfaith conversations need the fundamentalist perspective on the limitations of modernity and adds that fundamentalism may prove to be the religious phenomenon of the 21st century.

Keddie, Nikki R. "Secularism and Its Discontents." *Daedalus* 132 (Summer 2003): 14–30. Keddie's article is a good short summary, first of the history of the term *secularization,* and second of the revivals of fundamentalist religion in various parts of the world. She offers a number of examples that support her main points: "Secularization around the world has been a far longer, more difficult, and more partial process than is usually assumed. . . . in both the West and the East, the difficulties of establishing stable secular regimes have often been underestimated." Her other conclusion is that "the Western path to secularism, and indeed the Western definition of secularism, may not be fully applicable in all parts of the world, because of religious differences and the complex impact of Western colonialism."

Rosin, Hanna. "Beyond Belief: The Real Religious Divide in the United States Isn't between the Churched and the Unchurched. It's between Different Types of Believers." *Atlantic Monthly* 295 (January–February 2005): 117–120. Rosin's account is a journalist's assessment of the recent alliance in the United States between conservative Roman Catholics and Protestant evangelicals and the way in which the 2004 presidential election demonstrated the growing strength of that alliance.

Volf, Miroslav. "Floating Along?" *Christian Century* 117 (April 5, 2000): 398. The author takes a feature article on a conservative Christian family from the *New York Times Sunday Magazine* (February 27, 2000) as the starting point for observations about the inability of non-fundamentalist believers to create alternatives to secular consumer culture.

Web Documents

Berger, Peter L. "Protestantism and the Quest for Certainty." *Christian Century* (August 26, 1998): 782–796. Available online. URL: http://www.religion-online.org/showarticle.asp?title=239. Accessed December 1, 2005. Berger tackles the matter of his early work on secularization and why he "made one big mistake" when he originally argued that modernization inevitably leads to a decline in religious faith and activity. He also offers some interesting insights on the possibility of living gracefully and faithfully with theological uncertainty in a pluralistic world.

———. "Reflections of an Ecclesiastical Expatriate." *Christian Century* (October 24, 1990): 964–969. Available online. URL: http://www.religion-online.org/show

article.asp?title=232. Accessed December 1, 2005. Berger's article is an autobiographical account of the way in which his denomination (mainstream Lutheran) changed from the time he arrived in the United States as an immigrant from Germany to the early 1990s. His assessment of the changes in the American middle class—specifically, the way in which the middle class has divided into a "new class" of knowledge experts and an older business class—as a major reason for the membership losses in the mainstream Protestant churches is still persuasive.

Davies, Christie. "The Death of Religion and the Fall of Respectable Britain." *New Criterion* 23 (Summer 2004). Available online. URL: http://www.newcriterion.com/archive/22/sum04/davies.htm. Accessed December 6, 2005. The author offers a different perspective on the material analyzed in Steve Bruce's books. She also contrasts the current state of religion in Great Britain with that in the United States.

Episcopo, Joanne. "Spanish Police Foil Mass Suicide." BBC News, January 8, 1998. Available online. URL: http://news.bbc.co.uk/1/hi/despatches/45794.stm. Accessed November 8, 2005. This is a news report on a planned mass suicide on Tenerife in the Canary Islands that was prevented when local police arrested the leader, a German psychologist. Most of the 31 members of the cult were from Germany.

Hitchcock, James. "Supremely Modern Liberals: The Unhappy and Abusive Marriage of Liberalism and Modernism." *Touchstone* 17 (May 2004). Available online. URL: http://www.touchstonemag.com/docs/issues/17.4docs/17-04-021.html. Accessed November 20, 2005. The author attempts to trace the current combination of political and religious polarization in American culture to modernism.

Huntington, Samuel P. "The Clash of Civilizations." Alamut. Available online. URL: http://www.alamut.com/subj/economics/misc/clash.html. Accessed December 18, 2005. Originally published in *Foreign Affairs* 72 (Summer 1993), this article has become extremely influential since its first appearance. Huntington's basic thesis is that conflicts among nations in the 21st century will not involve political ideologies but rather cultural differences: "The great divisions among humankind and the dominating source of conflict will be cultural. Nation states will remain the most powerful actors in world affairs, but the principal conflicts of global politics will occur between nations and groups of different civilizations. The clash of civilizations will dominate global politics. The fault lines between civilizations will be the battle lines of the future." Huntington bases his thesis on the following points: Differences between civilizations are basic rather than superficial; the world is becoming smaller, making people more aware of the differences between civilizations; economic globalization has weakened the nation-state as a source of identity; and cultural differences—which include religious differences—are more difficult to change than economic or political ones. The central section of Huntington's essay deals with the specific clash between the West and Islam. Huntington concludes with the expectation that "there will be no universal civilization, but instead a world of different civilizations, each of which will have to learn to coexist with the others."

James, William. *The Varieties of Religious Experience.* Electronic Text Center, University of Virginia Library. Available online. URL: http://etext.lib.virginia.edu/toc/modeng/public/JamVari.html. Accessed January 14, 2006. First published as a book in 1902, the chapters were originally delivered as the Gifford Lectures at the University of Edinburgh in 1901 and 1902. *Varieties* was recognized from its first appearance in print as a landmark in the psychology of religion. James had been trained as a physician but never practiced medicine because of repeated episodes of depression and what would now be called panic attacks. He became a professor of philosophy and psychology at Harvard, where he was regarded as a first-rate teacher. What strikes the contemporary reader more than a century after James's lectures were first delivered is his high regard for the persons whose narratives form the core of the book. In an age when many intellectuals openly scoffed at the possibility of reconciling science and religion, James made a case for personal experience as a legitimate support for religious belief. Readers interested in the history of fundamentalism will want to read the conversion narratives in Lectures IX and X.

AMERICAN RELIGIOUS HISTORY

Books and Book Chapters

Ahlstrom, Sydney. *A Religious History of the American People.* New Haven, Conn.: Yale University Press, 1972. Ahlstrom's history, which won the National Book Award for 1973, has been used as a basic introduction to American church history at the seminary level. Although it ends with the 1970s, it is still a useful guide to earlier periods in the religious history of the United States. The book is quite long—more than 1,100 pages—but has an index that allows readers looking for an overview of a specific person or topic to quickly find that information. The book is also noteworthy for its extensive coverage of the black churches and nontraditional faith groups, topics that were often overlooked by previous generations of church historians. In addition, Ahlstrom begins the book with a section on the European roots of American Christianity, thus giving the reader some background and perspective on the later periods.

Ammermann, Nancy T. "North American Protestant Fundamentalism." In Martin E. Marty and R. Scott Appleby, eds. *Fundamentalisms Observed.* Chicago and London: University of Chicago Press, 1991. As chapter 1, Ammermann's outline of the historical development of American fundamentalism opens the first volume of the five-volume Fundamentalism Project series. This ambitious scholarly undertaking was sponsored by the American Academy of Arts and Sciences. It published five thick volumes of essays on various aspects of fundamentalist groups within the major religions of the world between 1991 and 2004. The essay-chapters in these volumes are challenging material; they assume that the reader is seriously interested in the subject and has some background in history or one of the social sciences. The series editors have been criticized, however, for excluding writers who still consider themselves fundamentalists. With these limitations in mind, readers who want to learn more about a specific fundamentalist group or movement will find these volumes a rich resource.

Bainton, Roland H. *Yale and the Ministry: A History of Education for the Christian Ministry at Yale from the Founding in 1701.* Rev. ed. San Francisco: Harper & Row, 1985. The author examines the evolution of the ministry in the mainline Protestant churches from the Great Awakening through the early 1950s through the lens of one university-related school of theology. The 1985 epilogue by Leander Keck discusses the impact of evangelicalism and fundamentalism on ministerial students, as well as the changes in American Roman Catholicism since the Second Vatican Council.

Bellah, Robert N., et al. *Habits of the Heart: Individualism and Commitment in American Life.* New York: Harper & Row, 1985. Bellah's book provoked considerable discussion at the time of its publication. Taking the book's title from a phrase used by Alexis de Tocqueville, Bellah and his coauthors examine the ways in which social institutions in the United States may help to limit and restrain the destructiveness of uninhibited individualism. He states in the introduction that "this individualism may have grown cancerous . . . that it may be threatening the survival of freedom itself." In chapter 2, he traces four strands of thought that he regards as having shaped the American character—biblical religion, the republican ideal of government, utilitarianism, and expressive individualism. Chapter 9 discusses the historic as well as the contemporary role of religion in American life. Bellah expresses concern about the impact of excessive individualism on American religious communities: "Absolute independence is a false ideal. It delivers not the autonomy it promises but loneliness and vulnerability instead. . . . the church idea reminds us that authority need not be external and oppressive."

Booth, Wayne C. "The Rhetoric of Fundamentalist Conversion Narratives." In Martin E. Marty and R. Scott Appleby, eds. *Fundamentalisms Comprehended.* Chicago and London: University of Chicago Press, 1995. Booth, who died in October 2005, was a literary critic who had been a Mormon fundamentalist in the 1940s. In this essay, chapter 15, he studies people's accounts of their conversion experiences from a literary perspective. Booth notes the following qualities: a sharp division between the "before" and "after" portions of the person's life, rapid changes in the person's character over time, an emphasis on the beneficial effects of conversion, and a strong overall moral message with no loose ends. Another important point that Booth makes is that fundamentalists in general prefer conversion narratives to scholarly arguments about doctrine or sacred texts in spreading their message.

Carter, Paul A. *The Spiritual Crisis of the Gilded Age.* De Kalb: Northern Illinois University Press, 1971. This is a readable and fascinating study of a period of American history (from the end of the Civil War to the turn of the 20th century) that is often skimmed over in standard textbooks. Carter divides his material into chapters by topic, such as the impact of Darwinism on American Christianity, the trial of Henry Ward Beecher, the crisis within American Catholicism, the spread of agnosticism and atheism, and the country's first encounter with Asian religions. Although the book is not a history of fundamentalism as such, it provides some context for understanding the emergence of fundamentalism in this time period. The illustrations are also informative.

Deck, Allan Figueroa. "'A Pox on Both Your Houses': A View of Catholic Conservative-Liberal Polarities from the Hispanic Margin." In Mary Jo Weaver and R. Scott Appleby, eds. *Being Right: Conservative Catholics in America.* Bloomington: Indiana University Press, 1995. Deck's chapter, chapter 4, is a healthy reminder that the arguments among liberals, traditionalists, and ultratraditionalists within American Catholicism largely concern white North Americans. Hispanic believers constitute between 35 and 38 percent of Roman Catholic parishioners in the United States but are often overlooked because of their internal diversity. They vary in terms of national origin and also in level of assimilation. Deck believes that the different sense of tradition in Hispanic Catholicism, which is less academic and doctrine-centered, may offer a way out of the present polarization of the American church.

Garvey, John H. "Fundamentalism and American Law." In Martin E. Marty and R. Scott Appleby, eds. *Fundamentalisms and the State: Remaking Politics, Economies, and Militance.* Chicago and London: University of Chicago Press, 1993. This essay, chapter 3, is not a particularly profound overview, but it does give the reader a basic introduction to the complexity of the relations between fundamentalists and American constitutional law. The author shows that contemporary fundamentalism should not be oversimplified as nothing more than a wish to return to the Puritan past.

Hitchcock, James. *The Decline and Fall of Radical Catholicism.* New York: Herder & Herder, 1971. At the time that Hitchcock wrote this book, he still considered himself a liberal Roman Catholic. There have been a number of changes in the American Catholic Church since the book was published, but it still offers a time-specific perspective on the turmoil in the church following the Second Vatican Council. Hitchcock's analysis has much in common with Peter Berger's "new class" theory—that is, that the religious quarrels among Roman Catholics in the late 1960s represented a clash between a "new class" of highly educated professionals (including priests and nuns) and an older generation of conservative laypeople.

Kelley, Dean M. *Why Conservative Churches Are Growing: A Study in Sociology of Religion.* New York: Harper & Row, 1972. Kelley's book ignited considerable controversy when it first appeared in the early 1970s, particularly because it was written by an "insider"—in this case, an ordained Methodist minister who served for many years as the religious liberties counselor with the National Council of Churches. Kelley, who died in 1997, testified before Congress on such controversial groups as the Branch Davidians and the Church of Scientology. Although Kelley's conclusions about the growth of conservative churches was disquieting news to many liberal church members, the book has remained a classic because the trends Kelley outlined in the 1970s have continued uninterrupted into the early 21st century.

Krakauer, Jon. *Under the Banner of Heaven: A Story of Violent Faith.* New York: Anchor Books, 2004. Well known for his books on mountain climbing—particularly the disaster on Mount Everest in 1996—Krakauer has written an account of the murders of a woman and her daughter committed by Mormon fundamentalists. Although the author is a journalist rather than a professional historian, he spent three years researching Mormon history and culture prior to writing this account.

Lasch, Christopher. *The Revolt of the Elites and the Betrayal of Democracy.* New York and London: W. W. Norton, 1995. Lasch's basic point throughout this book is that class divisions have intensified in the United States over the course of the past several decades, and religion is one area in which the division is most evident: "The elites' attitude toward religion ranges from indifference to active hostility. It rests on a caricature of religious fundamentalism." Lasch goes on to state that this attitude is based on a fundamental misunderstanding of religion—namely, that it is "a source of intellectual and emotional security, not a challenge to complacency and pride. . . . What makes the modern temper modern, then, is not that we have lost our childish sense of dependence but that the normal rebellion *against* dependence is more pervasive than it used to be."

Lawrence, Bruce B. "American-Style Protestant Fundamentalists." In Bruce B. Lawrence. *Defenders of God: The Fundamentalist Revolt against the Modern Age.* San Francisco: Harper & Row, 1989. Lawrence focuses on the warfare between science and religion in his account of American fundamentalism. Chapter 7 discusses Darwin's theory of evolution and creation science at length, providing thumbnail sketches of fundamentalist thinkers who are generally passed over in other histories. It is less satisfactory, however, in its treatment of fundamentalist organizations and does not deal at all with the political reemergence of fundamentalists after World War II.

Marsden, George M. *Fundamentalism and American Culture: The Shaping of Twentieth-Century Evangelicalism, 1870–1925.* Oxford: Oxford University Press, 1980. This is a detailed history of fundamentalism in the United States by a well-known church historian. Marsden maintains that the intellectual concerns of American fundamentalism must be taken seriously, as well as the social, political, and demographic trends that contributed to its emergence. The book also contains a number of reproductions of the cartoons and line drawings that were used to illustrate fundamentalist pamphlets and newspapers of the period.

———. *Understanding Fundamentalism and Evangelicalism.* Grand Rapids, Mich.: William B. Eerdmans Publishing, 1991. This book is a broad overview of the movements that the author treats in much greater detail in *Fundamentalism and American Culture.* Marsden, who is generally considered the leading scholar in this field as of the early 2000s, traces the emergence of contemporary Protestant evangelicalism to the split that developed in the 1930s and 1940s between separatist fundamentalists and moderates who were willing to work with members of mainline churches.

Naifeh, Steven, and Gregory White Smith. *The Mormon Murders: A True Story of Greed, Forgery, Deceit, and Death.* New York: St. Martin's Press, 1988. This book is an account of the Mark Hofmann murder case of October 1985. In addition to explaining the legal and forensic aspects of the investigation of a domestic terrorist bombing, the authors provide a thorough account of the structure of the Mormon church and its attitude toward historical scholarship. This background helps the reader understand why Hofmann's forged documents were so upsetting to the Mormon hierarchy and how he planned to use them to destroy the church.

Quinn, D. Michael. "Plural Marriage and Mormon Fundamentalism." In Martin E. Marty and R. Scott Appleby, eds. *Fundamentalisms and Society.* Chicago and London: University of Chicago Press, 1993. Part of Quinn's task in chapter 10 is to correct what he regards as unfair stereotypes of Mormon fundamentalists—that they are all either practicing polygamists or "sectarian murderers." He also maintains that population figures given by the media for this subset of Mormons are about a third too high. Quinn then provides a historical outline of the mainstream Mormon church's changing attitudes toward polygamy plus a detailed look at four fundamentalist communities and a fifth group that he calls "the independents." He concludes that Mormon polygamists have helped by "participating with all other nonmonogamous households in a domino effect that has altered judicial and social realities of the nation as a whole." Ironically, Quinn was one of six academics and intellectuals excommunicated by the Church of Jesus Christ of Latter-day Saints the same year this chapter appeared in print.

Rose, Susan. "Christian Fundamentalism and Education in the United States." In Martin E. Marty and R. Scott Appleby, eds. *Fundamentalisms and Society.* Chicago and London: University of Chicago Press, 1993. Rose's essay, chapter 16, is partly a historical account of the development of a fundamentalist and evangelical education movement in the United States since the 1970s and partly an examination of the types of approaches used: homeschooling, the establishment of private Christian schools, and battles over textbooks and curricula in public schools.

Schulze, Quentin. "The Two Faces of Fundamentalist Higher Education." In Martin E. Marty and R. Scott Appleby, eds. *Fundamentalisms and Society.* Chicago and London: University of Chicago Press, 1993. Schulze maintains in chapter 17 that fundamentalists have had relatively little impact on American higher education because they catered primarily to a small group of separatist denominations. He calls attention, however, to recent changes in evangelical higher education, particularly its new concern for academic respectability: "The strident militancy and intolerance of earlier fundamentalism has given way to a remarkably open-minded attitude toward learning, teaching, and education at the college and university levels." He believes that the movement has shifted its focus toward transforming the world rather than rejecting it. Schulze takes a detailed look at three fundamentalist institutions: Bob Jones University, Liberty University, and Regent University.

Singular, Stephen. *Talked to Death: The Murder of Alan Berg and the Rise of the Neo-Nazis.* New York: Berkley Books, 1987. This is a fast-paced and readable history of the development of a major Christian Identity group through the mid-1980s, as well as an account of a murder investigation. The "Declaration of War" reproduced on pages 236 to 242 is a disturbing reflection of the mindset of Christian Identity members.

Annotated Bibliography

Print Articles

"Ex-Church Members Establish a Group." *New York Times,* February 19, 1986, p. C7. A brief news report about Richard Yao and the founding of Fundamentalists Anonymous.

Hollandsworth, Skip. "Sects with Strangers: An Offshoot of the Mormon Church That's Big on Polygamy Has Set Up Shop in West Texas." *Texas Monthly* 32 (November 2004), 60–64. According to the author, much of the anxiety felt by townspeople in the vicinity of a new Mormon polygamous community is related to fears of another disaster like Waco.

Marshall, Paul. "Fundamentalists and Other Fun People: To Know Them Is Not to Despise Them." *Weekly Standard* 10 (November 22, 2004): 16–18. The author, an investigative analyst of religious repression, makes a plea for restraint from the mass media in the "mindless stereotyping" of American fundamentalists.

McClay, Wilfrid M. "The Soul of a Nation." *Public Interest* 155 (Spring 2004): 4–19. The author interprets the general public's response to 9/11 as a revitalization of American civil religion, which he defines as "that strain of American piety that bestows many of the elements of religious sentiment and faith upon the fundamental political and social institutions of the United States." Against both religious separatists and radical secularists, McClay argues that civil religion is not a bad thing insofar as it allows believers and nonbelievers in a pluralistic society to live together with the help of "a second language of piety, one that extends their other commitments without undermining them."

Mittleman, Alan. "Jews in Multicultural America." *First Things* 68 (December 1996): 14–17. Mittleman discusses the difference between cultural pluralism and multiculturalism in terms of recent changes in the various Jewish communities in the United States. Mittleman notes that the sectarian wing of Orthodox Judaism, which is opposed to modernization, is growing faster and appears to be more vital than the moderate Orthodox wing.

Noll, Mark. "The Evangelical Mind Today." *First Things* 146 (October 2004): 34–39. Noll, a professor of history at Wheaton College, wrote this article as an update to his 1994 book, *The Scandal of the Evangelical Mind,* which caused a furor in conservative Protestant academic circles because of its harsh criticism of evangelicals' intellectual weaknesses. Noll described these weaknesses as populism, an insistence on immediate results, antitraditionalism, and a tendency toward dualistic thinking. In his update, Noll maintains that he now sees signs of hope, "signs of life on the ground," and more "possibilities than problems." He attributes "improved evangelical use of the mind" to closer relationships with Roman Catholics over the last 10 years, among other factors.

Phillips, Rick. "Can Rising Rates of Church Participation Be a Consequence of Secularization?" *Sociology of Religion* 65 (Summer 2004): 139–153. Phillips uses so-called neosecularization theory to explain rising rates of church participation among Mormons in Utah in the 20th century and among 19th-century New England Protestants during the Second Great Awakening.

Woodberry, Robert D., and Christian S. Smith. "Fundamentalism et al. Conservative Protestants in America." *Annual Review of Sociology* 24 (1998): 25–56. This article is a useful historical survey of the various subtypes of conservative American Protestants and makes careful distinctions among fundamentalists, evangelicals, charismatics, and Pentecostals. The discussion of regional variations in the United States is particularly helpful.

Web Documents

Ambrose, Jay. "Guns in the Basements." *Washington Times,* April 17, 2005. Available online. URL: http://www.washtimes.com/commentary/20050416-111827-1199r.htm. Accessed November 22, 2005. The author compares prejudice among liberal opinion-shapers against Protestant evangelicals to the anti-Catholic sentiments expressed in 1960, when John F. Kennedy ran for the presidency.

Bellah, Robert N. "Civil Religion in America." Hartford Institute for Religious Research. Available online. URL: http://hirr.hartsem.edu/Bellah/articles_5.htm. Accessed January 11, 2006. This essay, published in *Daedalus* 96 (Winter 1967), is preceded by a note that Bellah attached to a reprinting of it in 1968 after he had been accused of advocating "an idolatrous worship of the American nation." He states that he is rather seeking "within the civil religious tradition for those critical principles which undercut the ever-present danger of national self-idolization." Written only a few years after the assassination of John F. Kennedy, the essay begins with Kennedy's inaugural address and anchors it in the religious principles of the founding fathers. Bellah then explores the impact of the Civil War on American civil religion and moves to what he considers the "third great trial" of the United States as a nation: "This is the problem of responsible action in a revolutionary world, a world seeking to attain many of the things, material and spiritual, that we have already attained." Bellah's words still apply, nearly 40 years after they were first written.

Kelley, Dean M. "Waco: A Massacre and Its Aftermath." *First Things* 53 (May 1995). Available online. URL: http://www.firstthings.com/ftissues/ft9505/articles/kelley.html. Accessed December 31, 2005. This article, written by the author of *Why Conservative Churches Are Growing,* begins with the early history of the Branch Davidian movement and the man who renamed himself David Koresh. He describes Koresh's apocalyptic worldview and the attempts of two mediators to talk with him within this frame of reference. Kelley argues that the tragedy of Waco was in large part due to the government agencies' refusal to listen to the suggestions made by experts in religion about defusing the standoff. The FBI in particular insisted on regarding the Branch Davidian compound as a hostage-rescue situation rather than "reality," which Kelley defines as "a band of adults voluntarily and devotedly following a visionary they thought touched by the finger of God."

Lattin, Don. "The End to Innocent Acceptance of Sects." Rick A. Ross Institute of New Jersey. Available online. URL: http://www.rickross.com/reference/jonestown/jonestown5.html. Accessed November 15, 2005. Lattin makes use of the 20th anniversary of the Jonestown tragedy to reflect on the emergence of a number of violent religious sects in the 1990s. It was published in the *San Francisco Chronicle,* November 13, 1998.

Noll, Mark A. "The Lutheran Difference." *First Things* 20 (February 1992). Available online. URL: http://www.firstthings.com/ftissues/ft9202/articles/noll.html. Accessed January 10, 2006. Mark Noll, an evangelical professor of church history at Wheaton College, offers an outsider's perspective on American Lutheranism and its European roots. Readers who are unfamiliar with this form of conservative Christianity will find Noll's article informative and enjoyable to read.

Piper, John. "J. Gresham Machen's Response to Modernism." Desiring God. Available online. URL: http://www.desiringgod.org/Resource/Library/Biographies/1464_J_Gresham_Machens_Response_to_Modernism/. Accessed January 9, 2006. This is a fairly lengthy and analytical biography of Machen, a figure who should be better known but is often categorized as a "fundamentalist" even though he refused to accept the term. Piper points out in this paper given at a conference for pastors, January 26, 1993, that Machen criticized the fundamentalists of the 1920s for their lack of a historical perspective, their suspicion of scholarship, their unconcern about precise formulations of Christian doctrine, their one-sided otherworldliness and refusal to transform the popular culture they rejected, and their perfectionistic obsession with such habits as smoking. Piper also has some insightful comments toward the end of his presentation about Machen's flaws as well as his virtues.

Schrag, Carl. "American Jews and Evangelical Christians: Anatomy of a Changing Relationship." *Jewish Political Studies Review* 17 (Spring 2005). Available online. URL: http://www.jcpa.org/cjc/cjc-schrag-s05.htm. Accessed October 22, 2005. The author begins with the observation that American Jews' long-standing opposition to building political coalitions with Protestant evangelicals is slowly changing because of the increasing isolation of Israel among world powers. He then notes that Jewish groups are so used to forming alliances with liberals that "the challenge of working with conservatives catches them unprepared." In addition, many Jews are still concerned about the possibility that Christian evangelicals will use coalition building as an opening for proselytizing. The author concludes, however, that the size of the evangelical voting bloc as well as Israel's present difficult situation make it nearly inevitable "that increasing numbers of pro-Israeli Jews will reach the conclusion that Israel's interests will be served by a cautious embrace of these millions of supporters."

Smith, Tom W., and Seokho Kim. "The Vanishing Protestant Majority." NORC/University of Chicago, GSS Social Change Report No. 49, July 2004. Available online. URL: http://www.norc.uchicago.edu/issues/PROTSGO8.pdf. Accessed November 16, 2005. This is a highly technical report with masses of tables and statistics, but it demonstrates the accuracy of Dean Kelley's prediction regarding the ongoing decline of mainline Protestantism within the religiously active portion of the American population. According to the authors, mainline Protestants presently represent less than half of all Americans for the first time in the history of the nation.

Tanner, Jerald, and Sandra Tanner. "Mormon Blood Atonement: Fact or Fantasy?" *Salt Lake City Messenger* 92, (April 1997). Available online. URL: http://www.xmission.com/~country/reason/blood.htm. Accessed November 16, 2005. The Tanners established the Lighthouse Ministry and began publishing the *Salt Lake City Messenger* in 1983 after leaving the Church of Jesus Christ of Latter-day Saints. Sandra is a great-great-granddaughter of Brigham Young who became disillusioned with Mormonism after studying her ancestor's writings. The Tanners have published numerous books on Mormon history and doctrine. This article explains the Mormon doctrine of blood atonement and illustrates it with quotations from Young's sermons.

"University Cancels Class on Creationism." *New York Times,* December 1, 2005. Available online. URL: http://www.nytimes.com/aponline/national/AP-Creationism Class.htm. A brief news report on a controversy at the University of Kansas that resulted in the cancellation of a course debunking creationism when the professor offering the course sent some e-mails containing rude comments about "fundies" to potential students.

Willimon, William H. "Mixing Religion and Politics." North Alabama Conference of the United Methodist Church. Available online. URL: http://www.northalaba maumc.org/Willimon/willimon051024.html. Accessed October 27, 2005. The text of the article was originally delivered as a talk to the Rotary Club of Birmingham, Alabama. Willimon, former dean of the college chapel at Duke University and presently a bishop in the United Methodist Church, comments on the lengthy history of mixing politics with religion in America, among Jews as well as Christians.

Windmueller, Steven. "Are American Jews Becoming Republican? Insights into Jewish Political Behavior." *Jerusalem Viewpoints* 509 (December 15, 2003). Available online. URL: http://www.jcpa.org/jl/vp509.htm. Accessed November 3, 2005. This article is particularly interesting because it contains a historical analysis of Jewish voting patterns in the United States from George Washington's first administration to 2002, as well as the author's opinions about current political trends.

SOCIAL-SCIENTIFIC ANALYSIS OF FUNDAMENTALISM

Books and Book Chapters

Adorno, Theodor, and Max Horkheimer. *The Authoritarian Personality.* New York: Harper & Row, 1950. Adorno and Horkheimer's book grew out of experiments in human psychology at the University of California at Berkeley in the late 1940s. Using Freud's theories of the stages of early human development, the authors attempted to explain the appearance of fascist or antidemocratic beliefs in adults as the result of childhood experiences with bullying or domineering fathers. They then developed various psychological tests to evaluate subjects for anti-Semitism, ethnocentrism, and political or economic conservatism. The authors' theory has been criticized on several grounds, including its failure to account for differences in social class and educational level as factors influencing people's political views. Other critics have pointed out that Adorno and Horkheimer assumed that all authoritarian political movements are right-wing, whereas left-wing groups are also capable of authoritarian attitudes and behaviors.

Baumeister, Roy. *Evil: Inside Human Violence and Cruelty.* New York: W. H. Freeman & Company, 1999. Baumeister's book represents a social scientist's attempt to understand evil from the evidence of actual incidents. He does not draw his illustrations from literature or film but rather from real instances. His main purpose is "to understand the causal processes that produce evil actions." In order to do this, Baumeister calls attention to what he calls "the magnitude gap," that is, the vast difference between victims' and perpetrators' view of evil deeds. He maintains that understanding the causality of evil, one must begin with the perpetrator's perspective, which minimizes or trivializes the consequences of the act. The specific role of ideology or religion in motivating some perpetrators is discussed in chapter 6, "True Believers and Idealists." Baumeister essentially identifies the same process of "satanization" described by Mark Juergensmeyer and Aaron T. Beck in their respective books. He then links idealism specifically to terrorist acts, noting that one major difference between idealism and other motivations for evil acts is that "idealistic evil is nearly always fostered by groups, as opposed to individuals." The book is not easy reading because most of its examples are nightmarish, but it should be required reading for anyone seriously interested in the relationship between religion and violence.

Beck, Aaron T. *Prisoners of Hate: The Cognitive Basis of Anger, Hostility, and Violence.* New York: HarperCollins, 1999. Dr. Beck, well known for his development of cognitive-behavioral therapy as a treatment for depression, seeks to extend his clinical findings to the treatment of violence. Beck deals with group as well as individual disturbances, describing what he calls "collective illusions" in chapter 9. He maintains that groups are more likely than individuals to stereotype others to the point of creating massive misperceptions—the process that Mark Juergensmeyer calls "satanization." Beck uses Terry McVeigh and skinhead organizations as specific examples of right-wing group illusions leading to terrorism but is careful to cite the Weathermen of the late 1960s as an instance of a left-wing group that developed its own set of collective illusions. On the basis of his clinical experience with paranoid patients, Beck regards the outer display of hate and hostility in members of extremist groups as a cover for inner vulnerability. He recommends the training of a new generation of psychologists and psychiatrists to deal specifically with violence between ethnic or political groups.

Berger, Peter L. "The Worldview of the New Class: Secularity and Its Discontents." In B. Bruce-Briggs, ed. *The New Class?* New York: McGraw-Hill, 1979. Berger identified the so-called new class's attitude toward religion as one of its chief identifying features. He pointed out that it "is a highly secularized group" even though some of its members had entered the denominational bureaucracies of the mainstream churches. He also identified the dominant worldview—secular humanism—of the new class as in part the by-product of its employment patterns. Many of its members were employed in the fields of education or government planning and administration, "where power derives from the manipulation of symbols rather than things."

Bruce, Steve. *God Is Dead: Secularization in the West.* Malden, Mass.: Blackwell Publishing, 2002. Bruce is a British sociologist who has not been persuaded by the arguments of other scholars that secularization theory is outdated. His attempt to apply his analysis to the United States, however, is less convincing than his treatment of the European situation.

Fowler, James W. *Stages of Faith: The Psychology of Human Development and the Quest for Meaning.* San Francisco: Harper & Row, 1981. Fowler's book has been virtually required reading for courses in Christian education at the seminary level almost since its publication. The author outlines seven stages in faith development, from the "undifferentiated" faith of infancy to the "universalizing faith" of spiritually mature adults. Although Fowler never uses the word *fundamentalist,* he does refer to entire faith groups, as well as individuals, that remain at the stage 2 ("mythic-literal") and stage 3 ("synthetic-conventional") levels. In one telling aside, he lashes out at televangelists who try to address the "religious hungers" of adults who have not grown beyond stage 3. He attacks the "powerful electronic media, attractive personalities and sentimental 'God talk'" of the electronic churches as "a parody of authentic Christianity and an abomination against biblical faith." Many writers since Fowler have thus used his categories as a way to label fundamentalists as cases of retarded spiritual development.

Hood, Ralph W., Jr., Peter C. Hill, and W. Paul Williamson. *The Psychology of Religious Fundamentalism.* New York and London: Guilford Press, 2005. The three authors of this book include two former members of fundamentalist churches, one of whom had been a minister in the denomination he left. They are presently professors of psychology and approach fundamentalism from the standpoint of beliefs and knowledge processes. In particular, they are interested in how fundamentalists read their sacred texts: "Insofar as there is a fundamentalist search for meaning, it must be found within a sacred text." Unlike the contributors to the Fundamentalism Project, these authors do not emphasize opposition to the modern world as a defining characteristic of fundamentalism.

Lifton, Robert Jay. *Destroying the World to Save It: Aum Shinrikyō, Apocalyptic Violence, and the New Global Terrorism.* New York: Henry Holt, 2000. Dr. Lifton is a well-known professor of psychiatry who has written several books on the psychological problems of people in the modern era, including studies of Nazi doctors, survivors of Hiroshima, and Vietnam veterans. This book on the Aum Shinrikyō cult in Japan deals not only with the role of the guru in such a group but also with the group's fascination with death and apocalyptic violence, expressed as a collective "urge to kill the world." Lifton finds some parallels between Aum Shinrikyō and Christian Identity groups in the United States that are both thought provoking and disturbing.

Rapoport, David C. "Comparing Militant Fundamentalist Movements and Groups." In Martin E. Marty and R. Scott Appleby, eds. *Fundamentalisms and the State:*

Remaking Politics, Economies, and Militance. Chicago and London: University of Chicago Press, 1993. David Rapoport is an expert on international terrorism who teaches political science at the University of California at Los Angeles. He makes the point, in chapter 18, that fundamentalists can exploit any religion's potential for violence, even when that religion is generally regarded as relatively peaceful. As he sees it, the two chief sources for religious violence are the group's beliefs about its origins on the one hand and millenarian or apocalyptic expectations on the other.

Print Articles

Bolce, Louis, and Gerald DiMaio. "Religious Outlook, Culture War Politics, and Antipathy toward Christian Fundamentalists." *Public Opinion Quarterly* 63 (Spring 1999): 29–61. The authors of this article are professors of political science at New York University who specialize in studies of the changing patterns of political party affiliation in the United States. They discuss the attitudes of members of the "new class," to use Berger's term, toward religiously conservative people.

Correno, Thaddeus. "Fundamentalism as a Class Culture." *Sociology of Religion* 63 (Fall 2002): 335–360. Correno seeks to resolve the dispute between sociologists of religion who regard fundamentalism as a by-product of the class structure of American society and those who consider it a cultural response to the value conflicts of modernity. He suggests that fundamentalism is most adequately viewed as an intersection of structural and cultural factors. The first part of the article is a useful historical summary of American fundamentalism and an introduction to the scholarly debate for the general reader.

Jones, Marsha. "Fundamentalism Revisited." *Sociology Review* 10 (September 2000): 32–33. This article is a brief review of recent books about fundamentalism, combined with an explanation for the revival of interest in the subject.

Juergensmeyer, Mark. "Holy Orders: Opposition to Modern States." *Harvard International Review* 25 (Winter 2004): 34–38. A political scientist attempts to answer two questions: Why is religion so often the basis for opposition to the state? And why has this opposition turned violent in the early 2000s? He proposes that politics itself has become "religionized," and religious fundamentalism is as much a reaction to economic globalization and the loss of a sense of national identity as to modernization by itself.

Paloutzian, Ray F., J. T. Richardson, and L. R. Rambo. "Religious Conversion and Personality Change." *Journal of Personality* 67 (June 1999): 1,047–1,079. This article has won several awards for excellence in its field as well as being frequently cited by other writers in the social sciences. The authors conclude that religious conversion affects certain "mid-level" personality traits, such as feelings and attitudes, but not the more basic personality traits (defined as extroversion-introversion, adjustment to society, agreeableness, conscientiousness, and openness). These results were not affected by whether the conversion was a rapid or gradual occurrence or whether the person converted to an established religion or a new religious movement.

Stark, Rodney, and William S. Bainbridge. "Of Churches, Sects, and Cults: Preliminary Concepts for a Theory of Religious Movements." *Journal for the Scientific Study of Religion* 18 (1997): 117–131. This article is the source of the newer definitions of *sect* and *cult* that have gained general acceptance among religion scholars since the 1990s. The authors attempt to define these terms in a neutral way that avoids the negativity that the words acquired in the mass media.

Web Documents

Bolce, Louis, and Gerald DiMaio. "The Politics of Partisan Neutrality." *First Things* 143 (May 2004): 9–12. Available online. URL: http://www.firstthings.com/ftissues/ft0405/opinion/demaio.html. Accessed October 27, 2005. This article offers a historical outline of the changing composition of the Democratic and Republican Parties since 1972. The authors attribute many of the changes to the increasing secularism of the Democrats.

Federal Bureau of Investigation. *Project Megiddo.* Center for Studies on New Religions. Available online. URL: http://www.cesnur.org/testi/FBI_004.htm. Accessed December 12, 2005. *Project Megiddo* is the FBI's report that was sent to law enforcement officials around the United States in the fall of 1999 concerning the possibility of domestic terrorist attacks related to the new millennium. The report discusses *The Turner Diaries* as a blueprint for domestic terrorism, identifies Christian Identity groups as possible sources of trouble, and refers to doomsday cults and the significance of Jerusalem toward the end. The document observes, "In segments of the Islamic world, close political and cultural ties between Israel and the United States are often perceived as symbolic of anti-Islamic policies by the Western world. Attacks on Islamic holy sites in Jerusalem, particularly by Christian or Jewish extremists, are likely to be perceived by Islamic extremists as attacks on Islam itself."

Hudson, Rex A. *The Sociology and Psychology of Terrorism: Who Becomes a Terrorist and Why?* Federation of American Scientists. Available online. URL: http://www.fas.org/irp/threat/frd.html. Accessed November 29, 2005. This important document, published by the Federal Research Division of the Library of Congress in 1999, two years before 9/11, noted a change in the motivation as well as strategy of terrorist groups between the 1970s and the 1990s. "When the conventional terrorist groups and individuals of the early 1970s are compared with terrorists of the early 1990s, a trend can be seen: the emergence of religious fundamentalist and new religious groups espousing the rhetoric of mass-destruction terrorism. . . . These groups have a different attitude toward violence—one that . . . seeks to maximize violence against the perceived enemy, essentially anyone who is not a fundamentalist Muslim or an Aum Shinrikyo member." Among other features, the report contains detailed profiles of Osama bin Laden, Sheikh Ahmed Yassin, and Hamas—including an account of the recruiting and training of suicide bombers.

Huff, Peter A. "The Challenge of Fundamentalism for Interreligious Dialogue." *Cross Currents* 50 (Spring–Summer 2000). Available online. URL: http://www.crosscurrents

.org/Huff.htm. Accessed October 28, 2005. Written before the events of September 11, 2001, this article is a plea for including fundamentalists in ecumenical and interfaith conversations. Huff, a professor of historical theology at Saint Anselm College in New Hampshire, recounts his own history of growing up in a Southern Baptist household, becoming more liberal in his college and seminary years, and adopting an unreflective hostility toward fundamentalists. He remarks that his opinion was largely formed by popular stereotypes. He then became disillusioned with liberal Christianity and rediscovered some positive values that fundamentalism has to offer world religions. Huff concludes that "Interreligious dialogue will never fulfill its unique mission until it recognizes the fundamentalisms of the world as valued conversation partners."

Last, Jonathan V. "God on the Internet." *First Things* 158 (December 2005): 34–40. Available online. URL: http://www.firstthings.com/ftissues/ft0512/articles/last.html. Accessed December 2, 2005. An intriguing analysis of the potential effects of the Internet on fundamentalist and traditionalist groups as well as mainstream religious groups. The author cites a 2004 study by the Pew Foundation to the effect that "64 percent of Internet-using Americans—82 million people—say they use the web for religious purposes. They are more likely to be female, white, middle aged, and college educated. Catholics and Jews tend to use the Internet slightly more heavily than Protestants. Half of these users report that they attend church at least once a week." The Pew study also reported that the Internet seems to be accelerating the tendency toward emotional expressiveness and individualism in spiritual practices.

Minogue, Kenneth. "Fundamentalism Isn't the Problem." *New Criterion* 22 (June 2004): 1–6. Available online. URL: http://www.newcriterion.com/archive/22/june04/minogue.htm. Accessed December 16, 2005. The author, emeritus professor of political science at the London School of Economics, regards the contemporary tendency to use the term *fundamentalism* loosely as the fruit of political correctness combined with an unrealistic view of human nature and historical ignorance of the positive contributions of the nation-state.

Moyers, Jim. "Psychological Issues of Former Members of Restrictive Religious Groups." 1999. Available online. URL: http://home.earthlink.net/~jcmmsm/article/. Accessed December 17, 2005. The author is a former member of the Seventh-Day Adventist Church who presently works as a professional marriage and family therapist. In this brief article, he outlines some of the recurrent psychological difficulties experienced by many people who leave fundamentalist groups in any religion, not just former Seventh-Day Adventists. These difficulties include "shattered faith syndrome" (difficulty trusting new people or finding a new source of meaning and direction in life), intense feelings of shame for having once accepted a belief system now regarded as incredible, depression, fear of being betrayed by the psychotherapist, and feelings of isolation and rejection if other family members have remained within the group or sect. Moyers suggests that the person "should be encouraged to look at the positive as well as negative aspects of having belonged to a restrictive religious group. It may be helpful to think of the involvement as a developmental stage that was important, in ways both good and bad, in shaping one's life."

Young, Robert M. "Why? Psychotherapist Robert M. Young Examines the Motives for Religious Extremism." *New Internationalist* 370 (August 2004). Available online. URL: http://www.newint.org/issue370/why.htm. Accessed October 30, 2005. Young interprets religious fundamentalism as the end result of a psychological process known as regression. Regression is defined by the medical profession as a return or moving backward from one's present level of psychological maturity to a more primitive level when under stress. It is often characterized by what is known as splitting, namely a tendency to see everything as black or white, evil or good, with no middle ground between the two polar opposites: "They [then] act out. Where acting out is, thought is not. And terrorism is, of course, a very dramatic form of acting out. The religious fundamentalist who blows up a trainload of people going to work in the morning is operating at the extreme end of killing in 'a higher cause.' Their hatred enables them to act out unconscious fantasies."

ROMAN CATHOLIC TRADITIONALISM

Books and Book Chapters

Cuneo, Michael W. "Life Battles: The Rise of Catholic Militancy within the American Pro-Life Movement." In Mary Jo Weaver and R. Scott Appleby, eds. *Being Right: Conservative Catholics in America.* Bloomington: Indiana University Press, 1995. The author is a professor of sociology at Fordham University who has done extensive fieldwork among Catholic pro-life activists. The essay, chapter 11, traces the history of the Roman Catholic pro-life movement from its beginnings in 1970 in a meeting in Chicago that led to the foundation of the National Right to Life Committee (NRLC) through the crisis precipitated in 1973 by *Roe v. Wade* to the changes that took place in the 1980s, when Protestant evangelicals joined the pro-life movement in large numbers. Cuneo also examines the role of the Catholic bishops in the pro-life movement and the gradual exodus of Roman Catholics from the Democratic Party because of its position on abortion.

Davies, Michael. *Apologia pro Marcel Lefebvre.* 3 vols. Dickinson, Tex.: Angelus Press, 1979–85. Davies, a convert to Roman Catholicism who died in 2004, wrote these volumes in defense of traditionalist Catholicism as well as of the archbishop himself. The biographer does not attempt to hide the fact that he regards Lefebvre as a contemporary saint. The volumes do, however, offer English translations of a number of the archbishop's sermons, letters, and brief articles. Readers who are unfamiliar with the canon law and church-political aspects of Catholic extreme traditionalism may find that the sermons clarify the central issues in the dispute between Lefebvre and the papacy.

Dinges, William D. "'We Are What You Were:' Roman Catholic Traditionalism in America." In Mary Jo Weaver and R. Scott Appleby, eds. *Being Right: Conservative Catholics in America.* Bloomington: Indiana University Press, 1995. Chapter 11 is a good introduction to Lefebvre's movement and other features of extreme

Catholic traditionalism. Dinges divides the movement into three time periods: 1962–71, 1971–84, and 1984 to the mid-1990s. He then provides an overview of such organizations as the Society of St. Pius X, the Society of Saint Pius V, and the Society of Traditional Roman Catholics. Dinges identifies three motifs in extreme Catholic traditionalism that in his view have intensified since the 1980s: renewed efforts to legitimate dissent following Lefebvre's excommunication, increasingly hysterical denunciations of Pope John Paul II, and sharper critiques of the U.S. Constitution and democratic political ideals.

Dinges, William D., and James Hitchcock. "Roman Catholic Traditionalism and Activist Conservatism in the United States." In Martin E. Marty and R. Scott Appleby, eds., *Fundamentalisms Observed.* Chicago and London: University of Chicago Press, 1991. The coauthors of chapter 2 are recognized experts on American Catholicism. Dinges focuses on the Lefebvrist schism and other ultratraditionalist groups concerned with worship and devotion, while Hitchcock looks at Operation Rescue and other activist groups.

Ginsburg, Faye. "Saving America's Souls: Operation Rescue's Crusade against Abortion." In Martin E. Marty and R. Scott Appleby, eds. *Fundamentalisms and the State: Remaking Politics, Economies, and Militance.* Chicago and London: University of Chicago Press, 1993. Ginsburg, who is a professor of anthropology, examines the tactics and results of Operation Rescue as the organization existed in the early 1990s. In chapter 23, she points to two distinctive features of the movement: its confrontational stance and its success in joining Roman Catholics and evangelical Protestants. Most of the chapter is devoted to a history of the pro-life movement following *Roe v. Wade* (1973) and the emergence of Operation Rescue after the mainstream movement lost much of its energy in 1983. Ginsburg notes that Operation Rescue suffered some legal and financial setbacks in the early 1990s as the result of lawsuits brought by pro-choice groups. She also contrasts Randall Terry's apparent inability to work within the political system with Jerry Falwell's skills in that area.

Madrid, Patrick, and Pete Vere. *More Catholic Than the Pope: An Inside Look at Extreme Traditionalism.* Huntington, Ind.: Our Sunday Visitor, 2004. This book is essentially a historical explanation of the reasons for Archbishop Marcel Lefebvre's break with Rome, followed by a series of chapters attempting to answer traditionalists' objections to the Second Vatican Council. It is a helpful introduction for general readers as well as Roman Catholics who are seeking to understand the mindset of the archbishop's followers. It is particularly useful for readers without any background in Roman Catholic law, as it explains that aspect of the Lefebvre schism in a brief and straightforward fashion.

Sullivan, James A. "Catholics United for the Faith: Dissent and the Laity." In Mary Jo Weaver and R. Scott Appleby, eds. *Being Right: Conservative Catholics in America.* Bloomington: Indiana University Press, 1995. The author was vice president of Catholics United for the Faith (CUF) at the time he wrote chapter 5. He discusses the history of CUF as an example of lay activism within the church, of the very kind that the Second Vatican Council wished to encourage. Sullivan points out that one aspect of CUF that differentiates it from most other conservative Catholic organizations is its emphasis on understanding the role of the laity in the light of the Second Vatican Council and rethinking it theologically, whereas most conservative groups operate almost as branches of the ordained hierarchy. He has some interesting comments about the impact of the Lefebvre schism on CUF in terms of attacks from the far right.

Weigel, George. "The Church's Political Hopes for the World; or, Diognetus Revisited." In Carl E. Braaten and Robert W. Jenson, eds. *The Two Cities of God: The Church's Responsibility for the Earthly City.* Grand Rapids, Mich.: William B. Eerdmans Publishing, 1997. Weigel discusses the political role of Christianity in the modern world in terms of people's *indifference* to questions of faith rather than their opposition. He also discusses the impact of secular intellectuals in creating "a toxic social and cultural environment whose primary victims are . . . those on the margins of society, who have far less room for error in the conduct of their lives."

———. "Roman Catholicism in the Age of John Paul II." In Peter L. Berger, ed. *The Desecularization of the World: Resurgent Religion and World Politics.* Washington, D.C.: Ethics and Public Policy Center, 1999. The author, who is a senior fellow at the Ethics and Public Policy Center in Washington, D.C., interprets Pope John Paul II's emphasis on human rights and the importance of culture as a Roman Catholic answer to the crisis of modernity. Weigel regards the pope as having "greater intellectual significance for the Church and its address to the world than any other since the Reformation." As a result of John Paul II's development of a social doctrine for the church and a new commitment to moral action, Roman Catholicism is in a unique position "to foster an international public moral argument in which those who do not share Catholic theological convictions can participate fully."

Zimdars-Swartz, Sandra L. "The Marian Revival in American Catholicism: Focal Points and Features of the New Marian Enthusiasm." In Mary Jo Weaver and R. Scott Appleby, eds. *Being Right: Conservative Catholics in America.* Bloomington: Indiana University Press, 1995. This article, chapter 9, will be helpful to readers who have had little contact with this particular aspect of Roman Catholicism. Zindars-Swartz outlines the revival of devotion to the Virgin Mary within American Catholicism in the 1980s and 1990s, particularly the increase in the number of alleged apparitions of the Virgin during this time period. Apparitions were reported in two places in the United States—Conyers, Georgia, and Scottsdale, Arizona. One interesting new development is the link between Marian piety and the charismatic movement as well as Catholic traditionalism. In addition, the Marian movement is now largely led by the laity rather than by the clergy, as it was prior to the Second Vatican Council.

Print Articles

Allen, John L., Jr. "Pope Meets with Schismatic Leader." *National Catholic Reporter* 41 (September 9, 2005): 13. This article includes a short summary of the Vatican's attempts since 1999 to heal the schism between Rome and the Roman Catholic traditionalists identified with the Society of St. Pius X, as well as an account of Pope Benedict XVI's meeting in August 2005 with Bernard Fellay, the present superior of the society.

———. "Traditionalists Deny Rumors of Reconciliation." *National Catholic Reporter* 39 (May 2, 2003): 3. This is a brief article denying rumors that were circulating around Easter 2003 regarding a supposed reconciliation between the Vatican and three of the four bishops ordained in 1988 by Archbishop Marcel Lefebvre.

"Benedict XVI and the Lefebverites." *National Catholic Reporter* 41 (September 9, 2005): 28. This editorial praises the recently elected pope for making a gesture toward reconciliation with the Society of St. Pius X but also advises Benedict to "insist that any reconciliation with the Lefebverites not come at further diminshment of conciliar reforms." It describes the society as "a destructive force within the Catholic community."

"Buddhist Monks." *U.S. Catholic* 69 (April 2004): 11. A brief news article on the disruption of a demonstration of Buddhist prayers and chants by a group from the Society of St. Pius X. Some Buddhist monks had been invited to the Basilica of St. Adalbert in Grand Rapids, Michigan, in February 2004 to demonstrate their prayers and methods of chanting. The members of the society, including several children, sat near the front of the basilica and recited the rosary in loud voices, which prevented the monks from completing their presentation.

Dulles, Avery Cardinal. "Religious Freedom: Innovation and Development." *First Things* 118 (December 2001): 35–39. This article is basically an exposition of the Second Vatican Council's Declaration on Religious Freedom, known by its Latin title *"Dignitatis Humanae."* The author discusses Archbishop Marcel Lefebvre's conviction that the declaration was contrary to established Roman Catholic doctrine "and could not be adopted without violence to the Catholic faith," and proceeds to outline the ways in which the declaration appears to contradict the various statements of 19th-century popes on church-state relationships.

———. "True and False Reform." *First Things* 135 (August–September 2003): 14–19. Archbishop Marcel Lefebvre's movement is described as a "reactionary traditionalism" seeking "to undo the work of the [Second Vatican] Council itself." The author also notes the difference between the missionary activities of Mormons and fundamentalist Protestants and the relative indifference of most Roman Catholics to evangelization.

Kuehnelt-Leddihn, Erik von. "The Road Back to Rome." *National Review* 40 (October 14, 1988): 24. The author of this brief article, written a few months after Archbishop Marcel Lefebvre's excommunication, predicted that the members of the traditionalist movement would return to Rome rather quickly. History so far has not borne out the author's hopeful prediction.

Lefebvre, Marcel. "La déclaration du 21 novembre 1974, Itinéraires, no. 195." Translated in vol. 1 of *The Collected Works of His Excellency Archbishop Marcel Lefebvre.* Dickinson. Tex. Angelus Press, 1985. Angelus Press was founded in 1978 by Father Carl Pulvermacher as an apostolate (form of service) of the SSPX. The press moved to Kansas City in 1992 and presently carries more than 300 titles. Its three-volume edition of the letters, sermons, meditations, and other writings of Archbishop Lefebvre is the most accessible English translation of the archbishop's works.

O'Grady, Desmond. "A Tale of Two Prelates: An Ecumenist and a Schismatic." *Commonweal* 124 (January 31, 1997): 20–24. Written by a longtime Vatican correspondent for English-language periodicals, this article compares Archbishop Marcel Lefebvre with another 20th-century French churchman, Léon-Étienne Cardinal Duval. After World War II both men served Roman Catholic dioceses in Africa, Lefebvre in Senegal and Duval in Algeria.

Web Documents

Dikete, Fidele O., et al. "A Case Study in Catholic Fundamentalism: The Defenders of the Magisterium in the Archdiocese of San Antonio." Unpublished M.Div. thesis, Oblate School of Theology, 2001. Available online. URL: http://www.dotm.org/oblate-thesis.htm#Catholic%20Fundamentalism%20Defined. Accessed December 9, 2005. This paper is a study of a small fundamentalist group led by laypersons that appears to be limited to one Roman Catholic archdiocese in the Southwest. The Defenders of the Magisterium attend Mass and catechetical classes in various parishes to see whether orthodox doctrine is being taught and the Eucharist celebrated correctly. Anything that seems amiss is then reported in a newsletter and on the group's website (URL: http://www.dotm.org/). The group's criticisms focus on religious professionals and the architect responsible for ongoing cathedral renovations. The Defenders thus illustrate the characteristic features of Roman Catholic, as distinct from Protestant, fundamentalism: "Catholic fundamentalism . . . is an approach to the Catholic faith that minimizes historical consciousness, places authority almost exclusively in the papacy, interprets doctrine literally and acontextually, takes a strongly apocalyptic approach, and operates within a self-contained system of thought that leads to strong doubts about the good faith of others."

Mazza, Michael J. "In the Line of Fire: Fr. John Rizzo, Ex-SSPX." *Fidelity Magazine* 14 (May 1995). Available online. URL: http://sspx.agenda.tripod.com/id21.html. Accessed January 12, 2006. *Fidelity Magazine* was a monthly journal begun by conservative Roman Catholics in 1982; it ceased publication in 1996, when its title was changed to *Culture Wars.* The editors of and contributors to *Fidelity* were as concerned with the inadequacies of the ultratraditionalist reaction against modernity as they were with the Roman Catholic Church's failure to regain control over its own institutions, including its colleges and universities. For this reason, a number of articles published in *Fidelity* dealt with the Society of St. Pius X (SSPX) and various reports of cultlike attitudes and behaviors exhibited by some members of the SSPX. "In the Line of Fire" is an account of a priest who graduated from a seminary of the SSPX and became disillusioned with the society on the basis of the treatment he received from other members. According to the article, the SSPX made death threats against Father Rizzo after his departure from it and has continued to harass him with abusive telephone calls. The article is not terribly well written, and readers will want to make up their own minds about the events reported, but the overall picture presented of the SSPX agrees with reports from other former members.

Vere, Peter John. "A Canonical History of the Lefebvrite Schism." Available online at http://www.catholicculture.org/docs/doc_view.cfm?recnum=1392. Accessed October 10, 2006. Written in 1999 as a master's thesis for the Faculty of Canon Law of Saint Paul University in Ontario, Canada, this paper on the history of Archbishop Lefebvre's foundation of the SSPX and his break with the papacy is a useful supplement to the book that Vere co-authored with Patrick Madrid, *More Catholic Than the Pope.* It is, however, a highly technical study of the legal aspects of the ultratraditionalist controversy and may be of interest primarily to Roman Catholics rather than to general readers.

JUDAISM

Books and Book Chapters

Aran, Gideon. "Jewish Zionist Fundamentalism: The Bloc of the Faithful in Israel (Gush Emunim)." In Martin E. Marty and R. Scott Appleby, eds. *Fundamentalisms Observed.* Chicago and London: University of Chicago Press, 1991. Chapter 5 is an extremely detailed account of the evolution of Gush Emunim (GE) from its beginnings up through the early 1990s. The author spent several years in the mid-1970s traveling around Israel with the leaders of the movement and interviewing members of their families. The result is one of the most detailed treatments of the settlement movement available in English. Aran updated his work on GE in a 2005 interview, listed under "Web Documents."

Heilman, Samuel C., and Menachem Friedman. "Religious Fundamentalism and Religious Jews: The Case of the Haredim." In Martin E. Marty and R. Scott Appleby, eds. *Fundamentalisms Observed.* Chicago and London: University of Chicago Press, 1991. This essay, chapter 4, does not deal directly with the settler movement associated with Gush Emunim. It is, however, useful as background information for understanding Orthodox Jewish objections to the Israeli nation-state and for introducing the reader to a group that most Americans know little about.

Lawrence, Bruce B. "Fundamentalists in Defense of the Jewish Collectivity." In Bruce B. Lawrence, *Defenders of God: The Fundamentalist Revolt against the Modern Age.* San Francisco: Harper & Row, 1989. This account of Jewish fundamentalism, chapter 6, repeats one of Lawrence's basic beliefs about fundamentalism in general—that it is about group identity rather than individualism, and always places "the collective good above individual choice." Interestingly, Lawrence disagreed with other writers about identifying Meir Kahane, the founder of the Jewish Defense League and the Kach Party, as a fundamentalist. He considered Kahane an activist and right-wing ideologue best described as a "counterfeit fundamentalist." Lawrence saw Gush Emunim as unlikely to survive the recurrent power struggles within Israeli politics as well as being weakened by the death of its charismatic leader, Zvi Yehuda Kook.

Liebman, Charles S. "Jewish Fundamentalism and the Israeli Polity." In Martin E. Marty and R. Scott Appleby, eds. *Fundamentalisms and the State: Remaking Politics, Economies, and Militance.* Chicago and London: University of Chicago Press, 1993. In chapter 5, Liebman maintains that Jewish fundamentalism is not the sole cause of either the importance of religious symbols in Israeli society since 1967 or the new nationalist strain in Jewish piety. Moreover, he thinks that the political impact of Jewish fundamentalism in Israel has tended to moderate both the *haredim* and the religious nationalist movements. With regard to Gush Emunim, the movement seems to have become less religious and more nationalist.

Lustick, Ian S. *For the Land and the Lord: Jewish Fundamentalism in Israel.* New York: Council on Foreign Relations, 1988. Although this monograph was written before the events of 1994 and 1995 (Baruch Goldstein's act of mass murder and the assassination of Prime Minister Yitzhak Rabin), it is still one of the few book-length accounts of Gush Emunim (GE) in English. It has been updated by the work of Ehud Sprinzak and the coauthors of *Jewish Fundamentalism in Israel,* listed below. Lustick's work, however, is still a useful account of the early years of GE and the organizations that it helped to found, Amana and the Yesha Council (settlers' community organization).

Rosenak, Michael. "Jewish Fundamentalism in Israeli Education." In Martin E. Marty and R. Scott Appleby, eds. *Fundamentalisms and Society.* Chicago and London: University of Chicago Press, 1993. Rosenak's basic point in chapter 14 is that different Jewish fundamentalist groups emphasize different priorities and have different social ideals even though they all operate within the theological and educational traditions of Judaism. Rosenak maintains that it was a combination of the trauma of the Holocaust and the loss of the social idealism of the first generation of Israeli pioneers that led to the multiplication of fundamentalist schools in Israel. Haredi schools are generally closed off from the outside world, while the nationalistic-fundamentalist yeshivot such as Mercaz Harav, which produced the first generation of Gush Emunim leaders, saw their task as educating an elite within Israeli society as a whole. In summarizing the contributions of Jewish fundamentalist education to Israel, however, Rosenak concludes that its rigid approach "indoctrinates instead of educates." "Our religious traditions, in this age more than ever, need an education for both conviction and intelligence, for spontaneity and creativity as well as loyalty."

Sacks, Jonathan. "Judaism and Politics in the Modern World." In Peter L. Berger, ed. *The Desecularization of the World: Resurgent Religion and World Politics.* Washington, D.C.: Ethics and Public Policy Center, 1999. Sacks is Chief Rabbi of Britain and the Commonwealth and therefore contributes an account of Judaism in the modern world from a European rather than an American perspective. His chapter is clear, well organized, and informative about the unique difficulties that Jews have had to confront since the 19th century. Sacks is forthright about contemporary problems in defining Jewish identity and the possibility that Judaism may disappear altogether because of assimilation.

Shahak, Israel, and Norton Mezvinsky. *Jewish Fundamentalism in Israel.* London: Pluto Press, 1999. The authors of this book regard Jewish fundamentalism as a serious threat to the future of Israel as a united country. Writing from a left-wing political perspective, they trace the history of Gush Emunim and other nationalist fundamentalist movements. They have included a chapter on the roots of Jewish fundamentalism in medieval and early modern Judaism, which contains historical information that the reader is not likely to find elsewhere.

Sprinzak, Ehud. "Three Models of Religious Violence: The Case of Jewish Fundamentalism in Israel." In Martin E. Marty and R. Scott Appleby, eds. *Fundamentalisms and the State: Remaking Politics, Economies, and Militance.* Chicago and London: University of Chicago Press, 1993. In chapter 19, Sprinzak, a political scientist, distinguishes among the various Jewish fundamentalist groups in Israel on the basis of the form of violence that they resort to when threatened. He defines the sporadic violence of the *haredim,* or ultra-orthodox, as essentially defensive in nature. Their militancy, as he sees it, is characterized by a siege mentality and a sense of fighting an uphill battle against secularism. Gush Emunim (GE), by contrast, is a movement that is best described as settler vigilantism. Sprinzak maintains that GE members are not opposed to the power of the Israeli state; they are violent toward Arabs primarily because they see the state as failing in its duties to protect the settlements. The third type of violence is associated with the Kach movement founded by Meir Kahane. It is distinctive in that it is openly motivated by revenge. Sprinzak does not consider a fundamentalist takeover of the Israeli state to be a likely outcome, but he is concerned with the slow erosion of Israel's culture of democracy and the possibility of an institutional collapse.

Print Articles

Gorenberg, Gershom. "Burning Gush." *New Republic* 210 (April 18, 1994): 21–22. Gorenberg's article is a useful short summary of the evolution of Gush Emunim and its relationship to Kach, a much more militant fundamentalist group that could be considered an American import. Gorenberg maintains that secular Israeli politicians do not understand the religious emotion driving the settlement movement and so fail to perceive their capacity for violence. As the article was written before the assassination of Prime Minister Yitzhak Rabin, some of the author's comments make eerily prophetic reading in the early 2000s.

Heilman, Samuel C. "Jews and Fundamentalism." *Jewish Political Studies Review* 17 (Spring 2005): 1–7. Heilman is a well-respected expert on the *haredim* who has contributed a lengthy chapter to the first volume of the Fundamentalisms series. In this relatively brief article, he classifies Jewish fundamentalisms as either passive (the *haredim*) or active (groups such as Gush Emunim) and then proceeds to discuss the decline of non-fundamentalist Jewish Orthodoxy. Heilman sees American Orthodox Jews as likely to embrace fundamentalist models in order to preserve Jewish identity.

Mirsky, Yehudah. "The Inner Life of Religious Zionism." *New Leader* 78 (December 4, 1995): 10–14. In this article, Mirsky provides a concise history of the intellectual background of Gush Emunim (GE), beginning with the different intellectual currents within 19th-century European Judaism that helped to shape Abraham Isaac

Kook. He then attempts to summarize Kook's mystical teachings and their connections to the nationalistic fervor and interest in science that animated so many of his contemporaries. Mirsky thinks that Kook saw the Messiah not as a historical personage but rather as a historical process that would introduce the world to a redemptive combination of a holy law, benevolent nationalism, and socialism. Mirsky maintains, however, that the rapid growth of GE after 1967 had less to do with theology than with the "rush" or "high" that its members experienced from belonging to it.

"Settlement Sprouts on West Bank." *Los Angeles Times,* April 17, 1991, p. A6. This article is a brief news report about Gush Emunim's (GE) overnight construction of a settlement at Revava prior to the visit of the U.S. secretary of state. It is significant insofar as it illustrates the length to which GE was prepared to go to gain publicity for its cause.

Steinberg, Gerald M. "Interpretations of Jewish Tradition on Democracy, Land, and Peace." *Jerusalem Letter/Viewpoints* 439 (October 2, 2000): 6–7. This article is a discussion of the growing tensions in Israel between secular and religious perspectives on the peace process in the Middle East. Steinberg points out that security policy and issues of war and peace did not divide secular from religious Israelis for the first two decades of the nation's existence; it was the 1967 war that proved to be a turning point in this regard. He identifies the attitude of "illegalism" (violating Israeli law in the name of higher religious obligations) that characterizes Gush Emunim as basically antidemocratic. He also observes that some factors affecting Israel, including the process of peace negotiations with the Palestinians, are beyond the country's control.

Web Documents

Elazar, Daniel. "The Constitution of the State of Israel." Jerusalem Center for Public Affairs. Available online. URL: http://www.jcpa.org/dje/articles/const-intro-93.htm. Accessed November 16, 2005. Daniel Elazar was an eminent professor of political science who specialized in studies of federalism, the Jewish political tradition, Israeli politics, and Israel's relations with the world Jewish community. Although the Basic Law of Israel has been amended twice since Elazar wrote this article in 1993, it is still an illuminating introduction to the general issue of an Israeli constitution combined with a historical explanation of Israel's present lack of a single constitutional document. Elazar's outline of the various ways in which constitutions can be understood—as frames of government, as legal codes, as revolutionary manifestos, as expressions of a political ideal, and as modern adaptations of ancient constitutions—offers food for thought for readers interested in political science.

Flükiger, Jean-Marc. "Jewish Messianism and the Settler Movement after Gaza Withdrawal—Interview with Gideon Aran." *Religioscope* (November 26, 2005). Available online. URL: http://religion.info/english/interviews/article_212.shtml. Accessed January 31, 2006. This interview allows Aran to discuss the changes in Gush Emunim (GE) since his major paper on the movement was published in

1991. One major change that Aran sees is the loss of messianic fervor in Jewish fundamentalist groups: "The messianic impulse of Jewish religiosity has been knocked down." He predicts that messianism will either disappear from the movement altogether or be related "to some objectives different from the territorial ones, like social problems, poverty, poor education, ethnicity, absorbing new immigrants, etc." Another possibility that Aran considers is that the *haredim* and GE members may become more like each other.

Goldberg, Jeffrey. "A Reporter at Large: Among the Settlers." *The New Yorker* (May 31, 2004). Available online. URL: http://www.newyorker.com/fact/content/articles/040531fa_fact2_a. Accessed December 5, 2005. This lengthy article on the settler movement in Israel by an American reporter is divided into six segments, titled "The Zealots," "The Meaning of Zionism," "The Underground," "The Sheikh," "The General," and "Israel's Future." Each segment can be accessed separately by clicking on the menu to the right, just below the author's byline. Goldberg was able to interview both Abdel Aziz Rantisi and Sheikh Ahmed Yassin before they were killed by Israeli helicopter strikes in March and April 2004; those interviews are included in the third segment, "The Sheikh." The hate-filled quotations from both leaders of Hamas are chilling. Goldberg's conclusion in the sixth segment, however, is likely to provoke controversy: He argues that although the settlers have not endorsed the sort of systematic violence that the Palestinian extremists have advocated in targeting all Jews, "there are [still] similarities." "Like the theologians of Hamas, the ideologues of the settlement movement have stripped their religion of all love but self-love; they have placed themselves at the center of God's drama on earth; and they interpret their holy scriptures to prove that their enemies are supernaturally evil and undeserving of even small mercies."

Ha'aretz Flash News. "The 10 Who Made Israel What It Is." Available online. URL: http://www.haaretz.com/hasen/pages/Flash3.jhtml?itemNo=572826&contrassID=100subContrassID=4&sbSubContrassID=0. Accessed October 28, 2005. This brief news item documents the fact that Rabbi Zvi Yehuda Kook, the spiritual mentor of Gush Emunim, is still regarded as one of the most important figures in the history of the state of Israel.

Katz, Yaakov. "Extremists Boast They Cursed Sharon." *Jerusalem Post,* January 6, 2006. Available online. URL: http://www.jpost.com/servlet/Satellite?cid=1136361024759&pagename=JPost%2FJPArticle%2FShowFull. Accessed January 8, 2006. This news article describes the *pulsa denura,* a medieval Jewish ritual in which the participants call on "angels of destruction" to pursue an individual that they believe to be evil. A group of far-right fundamentalists associated with the Kach movement had conducted the ritual in July 2005, just prior to Israel's scheduled withdrawal from Gaza. "Upon hearing the news of Sharon's stroke [on January 5, 2006] . . . the group broke out in song and dance and celebrated the prime minister's fall throughout the night."

Mitnick, Joshua. "Jewish Extremists Back in Spotlight." *Jewish Week,* July 30, 2004. Available online. URL: http://www.thejewishweek.com/news/newscontent.php3?artid=9696. Accessed October 23, 2005. This article is an update on developments in the summer of 2004 regarding Ariel Sharon's proposal to evacuate the settlements in the West Bank and Gaza Strip. Activists affiliated with Kach were reported to be planning violent protests to derail the disengagement. One plot was said to involve crashing a plane into the Dome of the Rock on the Temple Mount in order to provoke a war with the Muslims. The Yesha Council kept its distance from the radical activists, leading one observer to note that the settler movement appeared to have split into two parts: "The settler movement is struggling with itself and grappling with the contrasting lessons of the last decade."

National Religious Party (Mafdal). "Mafdal." Available online. URL: http://www.mafdal.org.il/?sid=27. Accessed October 24, 2005. This is the English-language page of the NRP's Web site, offering a brief description of the distinctive features of the party and a statement of its political purposes and goals. It includes a link to a page listing the laws enacted by the NRP. The remainder of the Web site is in Hebrew.

Riley, Naomi Schaefer. "The Hard Sell: Jews Consider Proselytizing to Fight Assimilation." *OpinionJournal,* December 16, 2005. Available online. URL: http://www.opinionjournal.com/taste/?id=110007688. Accessed December 16, 2005. This article describes a growing trend among Reform as well as Conservative Jewish groups in the United States to abandon the traditional Jewish policy of not pressing the non-Jewish spouse in an interfaith marriage to convert. As of 2005, 47 percent of married Jews are married to non-Jewish partners, but only 8 percent of their children identify themselves as Jews. The author points out that the situation is a delicate one: "Many of the Christians, Buddhists and atheists [who have married Jews] may have agreed to raise their children as Jews with the understanding that no one would try to change their own religious beliefs. They may now feel as if an implicit contract has been broken."

Sicherman, Harvey. "The Sacred and the Profane: Judaism and International Relations." *Foreign Policy Research Institute Wire* 10 (January 2002). Available online. URL: http://www.fpri.org/fpriwire/1001.200291.sicherman.judaismintlrelations.html. Accessed November 23, 2005. This article was originally delivered as the sixth annual Templeton Lecture on Religion and World Affairs. Sicherman, a former aide to three secretaries of state, summarizes Jewish thought on international affairs as a combination of biblical narratives and concepts, the record of statecraft in ancient Israel, and the development of Jewish political thought since the establishment of the state of Israel. He outlines two radically opposed medieval interpretations of the concept of the messiah, one that identified the messianic age with a return to the land of Israel and one that maintained that the basic human condition had to undergo a radical change before the Messiah would come. Sicherman maintains that both secular and religious Zionism drew on both these streams of thought, often unwittingly. He then places such movements as Gush Emunim within the larger framework of this outline of Jewish thought.

Wurmser, Meyrav. "Zionism in Crisis." *Middle East Quarterly* 13 (Winter 2006). Available online. URL: http://www.meforum.org/article/875. Accessed January 4, 2006. Wurmser, who is the director of the Center for Middle East Policy at the Hudson

Institute, analyzes the splits within Israeli society that were exposed during the withdrawal from the occupied territories in August 2005. He maintains that these divisions "threaten to overpower that which still unifies the majority of Israelis." Wurmser not only recounts the history of the settler movement and its relationship to the two Rabbis Kook but also points to a newer dispute over who "owns" the Jewish state—the descendants of the secular pioneers who built Israel in the 1940s or the religious Zionist settlers who now bear the burden of defending it? More than 50 percent of the officer corps in the current Israeli army are Orthodox Jews. In addition, Wurmser notes that the settlement movement is internally divided between the mainstream and the radical Kach minority. He concludes that the disengagement from Gaza is a "defining moment for Israeli society" regarding the actual nature of the state and asks the question: Can Israel continue to exist as a Zionist state without some connection to Judaism?

ISLAM

Books and Book Chapters

Ahmad, Mumtaz. "Islamic Fundamentalism in South Asia: The Jamaat-i-Islami and the Tablighi Jamaat of South Asia." In Martin E. Marty and R. Scott Appleby, eds. *Fundamentalisms Observed.* Chicago and London: University of Chicago Press, 1991. This essay, chapter 8, offers an introduction to the work of Abul Ala Mawdudi, regarded as one of the most influential Islamic thinkers of the modern period. In describing the organization that Mawdudi founded, the Jamaat-e-Islami, Ahmad makes an important point: Fundamentalist movements in Islam are primarily political rather than intellectual. "They are not content to act as pressure groups, as are the ulama [teachers of the law] and the modernists. They want political power because they believe that Islam cannot be implemented without the power of the state."

Lawrence, Bruce B. "Fundamentalists in Pursuit of an Islamic State." In Bruce B. Lawrence. *Defenders of God: The Fundamentalist Revolt against the Modern Age.* San Francisco: Harper & Row, 1989. In chapter 8, Lawrence presents fundamentalism in Islam as the third of three phases, the first two being revivalism and reform. He does not, however, regard Muslim fundamentalism as a single entity, showing from four case studies (Iran, Indonesia, Pakistan, and Egypt) that fundamentalist movements within each country reflect local political and social conditions. Lawrence maintained at the time this book was written that Muslim fundamentalists were unlikely to succeed in any country outside Iran in imposing an Islamic order opposed to the West on their society.

Legrain, Jean-François. "A Defining Moment: Palestinian Islamic Fundamentalism." In James Piscatori, ed. *Islamic Fundamentalisms and the Gulf Crisis.* Chicago: Fundamentalism Project of the American Academy of Arts and Sciences, 1991. Legrain, in chapter 4, interprets the Gulf War of 1991 as a turning point for Hamas: The organization distanced itself from Saddam Hussein during the conflict, not least because the Palestine Liberation Organization (PLO) supported him. Legrain regards this decision as a gamble that Hamas considered worthwhile because it was "an opportunity to challenge the PLO for control of the Palestinian resistance movement." The outcome of the Gulf War did indeed bring Hamas new sources of popular support.

Lewis, Bernard. *What Went Wrong? The Clash between Islam and Modernity in the Middle East.* New York: HarperCollins, 2002. The hardcover edition of Lewis's book was at the page proof stage on September 11, 2001, which must have seemed like an ironic climax to the point he makes repeatedly throughout the book: Western dominance provokes anger and resentment in the Muslim world because it is felt to be unnatural. Lewis sets the stage in the first chapter by reminding the reader that prior to the Renaissance, the Islamic world was far more culturally advanced and militarily powerful than Europe. It was not until the late 17th century, however, that Muslims were compelled to recognize that the West had not only caught up with them but surpassed them. Lewis observes that one reason why the gap continued to widen was Muslim disdain for learning from infidels. At the present time, however, he sees the largest obstacle to positive change as Muslim attitudes of "grievance and victimhood."

Na'im, Abdullahi an. "Political Islam in National Politics and International Relations." In Peter L. Berger, ed. *The Desecularization of the World: Resurgent Religion and World Politics.* Washington, D.C.: Ethics and Public Policy Center, 1999. The author, a professor of law at Emory University, regards Islamic fundamentalism as the product of underlying social crises in Muslim countries. He suggests that one possibility for avoiding self-fulfilling prophecies in Islam's relations with the West is to redefine Islamic identity in a way that respects the rights of other citizens. An-Na'im is particularly opposed to Samuel Huntington's notion of an unavoidable "clash of civilizations." "No single theory can possibly account for all the complexities facing all societies."

Ramadan, Abdel Azim. "Fundamentalist Influence in Egypt: The Strategies of the Muslim Brotherhood and the Takfir Groups." In Martin E. Marty and R. Scott Appleby, eds. *Fundamentalisms and the State: Remaking Politics, Economies, and Militance.* Chicago and London: University of Chicago Press, 1993. In chapter 8, Ramadan observes that "fundamentalism" in Islam does not refer to a wish to return to earlier forms of religious life but rather to purify Islam, to make it into a blueprint for government, and to prepare it for life in the modern world without Westernizing it. This account of the Muslim Brotherhood is helpful background information for understanding the roots of Hamas as the Palestinian branch of this movement.

Voll, John O. "Fundamentalism in the Sunni Arab World: Egypt and the Sudan." In Martin E. Marty and R. Scott Appleby, eds. *Fundamentalisms Observed.* Chicago and London: University of Chicago Press, 1991. Voll's chapter provides a chronological account of the beginnings and development of the Muslim Brotherhood, the changing patterns of Muslim fundamentalism under Egyptian presidents Gamal Nasser, Anwar Sadat, and Hosni Mubarak, and the influence of the radical Sayyid Qutb.

Warraq, Ibn. *Why I Am Not a Muslim.* Amherst, N.Y.: Prometheus Books, 1995. Warraq's book is an angry attack on the faith into which he was born. It makes for some interesting comparisons with the two writers who have used a similar title for explaining their rejection of Hinduism. Warraq, who lives in England, was prompted to write his book in the aftermath of the Salman Rushdie affair of 1989. His disgust with the fatwa issued against Rushdie was compounded by what he regards as the West's criminal failure to defend Rushdie's freedom of speech. Although the book contains several long chapters analyzing the history of Islam and the literary history of the Qur'an, the reader will note long before the chapters on Islam's treatment of women and homosexuals, its imperialism, and its contempt for non-Muslims that the author's central reason for abandoning Islam is moral revulsion rather than intellectual disdain. The final chapter, "Islam in the West," is a warning—especially but not exclusively to Britons—to defend Western values and resist increasing Muslim pressure to impose Islamic beliefs and practices on the entire society.

Warraq, Ibn, ed. *Leaving Islam: Apostates Speak Out.* Amherst, N.Y.: Prometheus Books, 2003. Warraq compiled this book of testimonies written by apostates from Islam in part to raise the consciousness of the West about the consequences of apostasy in the Muslim world. His preface points out that the penalty for leaving Islam is still long prison sentences or even death in such countries as Iran or Pakistan; there is no recognition of religion as a private conviction that an individual is free to change, as there is in the West. The first part of the book is a historical overview of Muslim apostates, including an account of Muslims who were religious skeptics in their time. The second part of the book contains the testimonies of 26 individuals who contacted the Institute for the Secularisation of Islamic Societies, grouped into two categories: those who were born Muslims and Westerners who converted to Islam and then left it. Readers who are interested in the psychology of religion or the specific process of deconversion from fundamentalism will find these narratives poignant as well as intellectually absorbing.

Print Articles

Elegant, Simon. "Southern Front: Muslims Have Been Fighting for Decades for a Separate State in Thailand's South. Now, for Many, the Goal Is No Longer Independence but Jihad." *Time International* (Asia Edition) 164 (October 18, 2004): 35–37. This is a brief news report of clashes between fundamentalist Muslims and religious Buddhists in Thailand.

Lewis, Bernard. "The Roots of Muslim Rage." *Atlantic Monthly* (September 1990): 47–60. Lewis's article has been frequently cited by other scholars; among other things, it stimulated Samuel Huntington to write his well-known essay on the "Clash of Civilizations"—an expression that he borrowed from Lewis's article. Long before September 2001, Lewis maintained that the source of Muslim anger at the United States had little to do with either Israel or American support for corrupt rulers in the Middle East. Rather, he traced it to Muslim fundamentalism and its opposition to both secularism and modernity: "Islamic fundamentalism has given an aim and a form to the otherwise aimless and formless resentment and anger of the Muslim masses at the forces that have devalued their traditional values and loyalties."

Odone, Cristina. "The Power of Martyrdom: The Killing of the Hamas Spiritual Leader Gives Militant Islam Another Potent Image." *New Statesman* 133 (March 29, 2004): 8–9. This is a short news item about the death of Sheikh Ahmed Yassin that essentially underscores the point made by Avishai Margalit in the Web document listed below—namely, that the ideal of martyrdom is a larger factor in Muslim fundamentalist violence than economic deprivation.

Rotella, Sebastian. "Fundamentalism in French Workplace." *Los Angeles Times,* November 26, 2005, p. B-9. This article is a report on the problems confronting private employers in France in dealing with fundamentalist Muslim employees. Rotella comments that "a recent study by a think tank here [in Paris] paints a picture of rising fundamentalism in the workplace, ranging from proselytizing to pressure tactics to criminal activities."

Web Documents

Center for Religious Freedom. *Saudi Publications on Hate Ideology Invade American Mosques.* Freedom House. Available online. URL: http://www.freedomhouse.org/religion/pdfdocs/FINAL%20FINAL.pdf. Accessed November 17, 2005. This document is an 89-page report published in 2005 on the types of inflammatory materials circulated in Muslim mosques in the United States. It was compiled after a year-long study of more than 200 separate documents. Most of these publications are funded and published by the government of Saudi Arabia.

Chesler, Phyllis. "How Afghan Captivity Shaped My Feminism." *Middle East Quarterly* 13 (Winter 2006). Available online. URL: http://www.meforum.org/article/794. Accessed December 2, 2005. Chesler is better known for her books on feminism and psychotherapy than for her writings on religion. Since the early 2000s, however, she has added the condition of women under Islam to her list of concerns. In this article, she describes her own experience in the early 1960s as the Western bride of her college sweetheart, a Muslim from Afghanistan. Chesler's new husband changed overnight after the couple arrived in Kabul, and she discovered that his father had three wives. She then found that she was virtually under house arrest: "I had experienced gender apartheid long before the Taliban made it headline news." Chesler was finally able to escape because she fell ill and her father-in-law was afraid that she might die in his home. She presently refuses to accept multiculturalism in the sense of cultural relativism: "What I experienced in Afghanistan as a woman taught me the necessity of applying a single standard of human rights, not one tailored to each culture."

Cook, David. "America, the Second 'Ad: Prophecies about the Downfall of the United States." Center for Millennial Studies at Boston University. Available online. URL: http://www.mille.org/scholarship/papers/ADAM.html. Accessed January 4, 2006. Cook is an expert on Islam who originally presented this paper at the Center for Millennial Studies at Boston University. After noting that predictions about the collapse or divine punishment of the United States are quite common in recent Islamic fundamentalist literature, Cook observes that they present a problem for the Muslims who write these apocalyptic scenarios. The reason is that traditional Muslim apocalyptic writing is a strict literary form and is usually ascribed to Muhammad himself or his companions. Since there is no mention of the United States in the Qur'an or the hadith (traditions), contemporary Muslim writers are forced to identify America with an obscure group mentioned in the Qur'an—namely, the people of 'Ad, a "criminal people" who are otherwise unknown to history. The second half of Cook's paper shows in detail the ways in which different modern Muslims have combined this notion of the United States as a second 'Ad with other apocalyptic themes, such as the appearance of a Dajjal (an Antichrist figure) or the coming of the Mahdi, a messianic personage.

Eltahawy, Mona. "After London, Tough Questions for Muslims." *Washington Post,* July 24, 2005, p. B7. Available online. URL: http://www.washingtonpost.com/wp-dyn/content/article/2005/07/22/AR2005072201629.html. Accessed November 27, 2005. Eltahawy is a columnist for the pan-Arab newspaper *Asharq al-Awsat.* In this opinion column, she criticizes Muslim imams who condemned the London suicide bombings in July 2005 but refuse to condemn suicide attacks directed against Israelis. Eltahawy points out that Muslims living in the West have obligations to the societies in which they live, not just rights and privileges: "And what about assimilation? It is not bigoted to ask Muslims if they are integrating into the societies they are living in."

Fukuyama, Francis, and Nadav Samin. "Can Any Good Come of Radical Islam?" *OpinionJournal* (September 12, 2002). Available online. URL: http://www.opinionjournal.com/extra/?id=110002251. Accessed November 15, 2005. Fukuyama in this opinion column takes issue with the description of al-Qaeda as a "fundamentalist" organization on the grounds that it "is not a movement aimed at restoring some archaic or pristine form of Islamic practice . . . it is best understood not as a traditional movement but as a very modern one." He attributes the rise of radical Islam at least in part to the influence of Mawdudi, who was "perhaps the first to attach the adjective *Islamic* to such distinctively Western terms as *revolution, state,* and *ideology.*" He identifies the other major source as Sayyid Qutb, who advocated the use of violence to achieve the goal of an Islamic society. Although Fukuyama concludes that Islamism "has little to offer" the Muslim world, he suggests that it may yet have one positive side effect: By failing in its attempt to defeat the West, it "may yet help pave the way for long-overdue reform."

Kramer, Martin. "Coming to Terms: Fundamentalists or Islamists?" *Middle East Quarterly* 10 (Spring 2003). Available online. URL: http://www.martinkramer.org/pages/899528/index.htm. Accessed December 18, 2005. Kramer's article outlines the shifts in English usage in referring to fundamentalist Islam. Arnold Toynbee referred to "Islamic fundamentalists" as early as 1929, but *Islamic fundamentalism* did not come into widespread use until the Iranian revolution of 1979. Kramer discusses various writers' preferences and notes that *political Islam* and *militant Islam* are also often used in the early 2000s. His central point is that "it is impossible to predict which terms will prevail in the West's own struggle to come to terms with change in contemporary Islam. It will depend on what Muslims do—and on what the West desires."

———. "Fundamentalist Islam: The Drive for Power." *Middle East Quarterly* 3 (Summer 1996): 37–49. Available online. URL: http://www.martinkramer.org/pages/899528/index.htm. Accessed January 4, 2006. Instead of speaking of different varieties or types of Muslim fundamentalism, Kramer chooses to emphasize its uniformity: "What is remarkable about fundamentalist Islam is not its diversity. It is the fact that this idea of power for Islam appeals so effectively across such a wide range . . . creating a world of thought that crosses all frontiers." He then gives thumbnail biographies of men he considers forerunners: Hassan al-Banna, the Egyptian founder of the Muslim Brotherhood, and Navvab Safavi, an Iranian student who started a secret movement called the Devotees of Islam. The ideologues that he discusses include Abul Ala Mawdudi, Sayyid Qutb, and Ayatollah Ruhollah Khomeini.

Leavitt, Matthew A. "Hamas from Cradle to Grave. *Middle East Quarterly* 11 (Winter 2004). Available online. URL: http://www.meforum.org/article/582. Accessed January 3, 2006. The author is a former FBI counterterrorism intelligence analyst. In this article, he discusses the internal organizational structure of Hamas in order to refute the common opinion that the charitable side of Hamas has no connection with its military wing. He offers evidence from various sources ranging from Human Rights Watch and the U.S. Treasury Department to Israeli intelligence that the social services of Hamas are closely integrated with terrorism. In some cases, Hamas military operatives hold day jobs in its social service organizations. In other instances, they recruit suicide bombers from the ranks of the students in their primary and secondary schools. The author concludes, "Islamic social welfare groups must not be given a free pass simply because they provide humanitarian support alongside their support role for terrorism."

Lewis, Bernard. "Annals of Religion: The Revolt of Islam." *The New Yorker* (November 19, 2001). Available online. URL: http://www.newyorker.com/fact/content/?011119fa_FACT2. Accessed December 8, 2005. Lewis draws an important contrast in this article between the West, which regards the nation as the "basic unit of human organization," and the Muslim mindset, which tends "to see not a nation subdivided into religious groups but a religion subdivided into nations." He also points out that one reason for the failure of so many Americans to understand certain Muslim grievances is that they overlook the intense seriousness with which Muslims take history. Lewis interprets the recent development of Islamic terrorism as media driven: "Their primary purpose is not to defeat or even to weaken the enemy militarily but to gain publicity—a psychological victory."

Margalit, Avishai. "The Suicide Bombers." *New York Review of Books* 50 (January 16, 2003). Available online. URL: http://www.nybooks.com/articles/15979. Accessed December 7, 2005. Margalit, an Israeli, is presently a research fellow at the Law School of New York University. His analysis of Palestinian suicide bombers begins by noting that they are part of a general erosion of the long-standing taboo against targeting civilians in wartime. He traces the origins of Palestinian suicide bombing to the actions of Hezbollah in Lebanon and the Tamil Black Tigers in Sri Lanka in the 1980s. Margalit regards the desire to be a martyr (*shahid*) as more important in the minds of the individuals who volunteer to be suicide bombers, while the notion of jihad is uppermost to the organizations that train and employ them. He points out that there is no common psychological profile that can be used to identify potential bombers, nor are most of them economically deprived. He concludes that "the main motivating force for the suicide bombers seems to be the desire for spectacular revenge; what is important as well is the knowledge that the revenge will be recognized and celebrated by the community to which the suicide bomber belongs."

Ottolenghi, Emanuele. "Hamas without Veils." *National Review,* January 26, 2006. Available online. URL: http://www.nationalreview.com/comment/ottolenghi 200601261002.asp. Accessed January 26, 2006. The author, a political scientist and research fellow in Israeli studies at Oxford University, argues that Hamas's victory in the Palestinian parliamentary election in January 2006 is a positive development. He maintains that its majority in the government will mean that the party will have to govern, not just form a coalition, and thus it will have to show its true face: "What Hamas does is what the PA [Palestinian Authority] will stand for."

Pipes, Daniel. "The Mystical Menace of Mahmoud Ahmadinejad." *New York Sun,* January 10, 2006. Available online. URL: http://www.meforum.org/article/pipes/3258. Accessed January 11, 2006. This article describes the current president of Iran's belief in the coming of the Mahdi, explains this belief for Westerners unfamiliar with it, and explores what this conviction might imply for future political developments.

HINDUISM

Books and Book Chapters

Center for Religious Freedom. *The Rise of Hindu Extremism and the Repression of Christian and Muslim Minorities in India.* Washington, D.C.: Freedom House Publications, 2003. This book is a study of the Sangh Parivar and its effects on turning India's tradition of relative tolerance into a campaign to drive out or eliminate religious minorities. It traces the use of violence and acts of terrorism by the Rashtriya Swayamsevak Sangh (RSS), the Vishwa Hindu Parishad (VHP), and the Bajrang Dal, all organizations belonging to the Sangh Parivar. The Bharatiya Janata Party encourages attacks on Christians and Muslims by accusing the former of "forcing Hindus to convert" and the latter of being traitors to India. The international president of the VHP was quoted as saying that the Gujarat mass killing of Muslims in 2002 was a "successful experiment" that should be repeated throughout India. The book recommended that the State Department place India on its list of "countries of particular concern" (CPCs) in regard to religious freedom.

Elst, Koenraad. *Ayodhya and After: Issues before Hindu Society.* New Delhi: Voice of India, 1991. The author is a Belgian who has lived in India for a number of years. This book is a study of the aftermath of the 1982 destruction of the Babri Masjid, a mosque in Ayodhya, and the increased violence between the Hindu and Muslim communities.

Frykenberg, Robert Eric. "Hindu Fundamentalism and the Structural Stability of India." In Martin E. Marty and R. Scott Appleby, eds. *Fundamentalisms and the State: Remaking Politics, Economies, and Militance.* Chicago and London: University of Chicago Press, 1993. In chapter 11, Frykenberg provides an outline of India's history that is clear and well organized for readers new to the subject. He is then able to explain exactly why Hindutva (Hindu nationalist fundamentalism) is a threat to the unity of India as a nation. He regards Hindu fundamentalism as responsible for triggering counter-fundamentalist movements among other faith groups in different parts of the country: the Sikhs in the Punjab, the Muslims in Kashmir, and the Christians in southern India. Frykenberg predicts that if the Dalits (untouchables) are ever unified by a single fundamentalist movement, the result might well pull apart the country.

Gold, Daniel. "Organized Hinduisms: From Vedic Truth to Hindu Nation." In Martin E. Marty and R. Scott Appleby, eds. *Fundamentalisms Observed.* Chicago and London: University of Chicago Press, 1991. Gold's chapter 9 is a good overview of two major Hindu nationalist organizations, the Arya Samaj and the Rashtriya Swayamsevak Sangh. He compares and contrasts the two groups throughout the chapter with regard to their history, membership, growth, internal structure, relationships with Indian political parties, and ideology.

Hartung, Jan-Peter, Gillian Hawkes, and Anuradha Bhattacharjee. *Ayodhya 1992–2003: The Assertion of Cultural and Religious Hegemony.* University of Leicester, South Asian History Academic Papers 9. Leicester, U.K.: Centre for the History of Religious and Political Pluralism, 2003. This set of articles is an academic study of the destruction of the mosque in Ayodhya and the spread of Hindutva ideology in the years since. The first section focuses on the role of the Indian government in failing to prevent the tearing down of the mosque and the riots that followed.

Ilaiah, Kancha. *Why I Am Not a Hindu.* Bombay: Bhatkal Books International, 1996. The author is presently a professor of political science at Osmania University in Hyderabad, India, and has been active in the civil rights movement for Dalits. *Why I Am Not a Hindu* is essentially a critique of Hindutva from the perspective of a Dalit. He maintains that Hindu nationalism is essentially a class-based movement: "Hindutva is nothing but Brahminism." Ilaiah thinks that conversion to Christianity or Islam is an option for "educated Dalit-Bahujans . . . as a major alternative means of mobilization and protest" and that Hindutva adherents are basically demonizing Muslims and Christians as a way of displacing the anger of the oppressed classes.

Thapar, Romila. *Early India: From the Origins to AD 1300.* Berkeley: University of California Press, 2004. This book is a complete revision of Thapar's first book on the history of India, published in the early 1970s; thus, it takes into account the archaeological findings and other additions to scholarly understanding of Indian history of the past three decades. It is a good introduction for students interested in understanding Hindutva, as the author takes apart the historical myths and fabrications that underlie Hindu fundamentalism in the early 2000s.

Print Articles

Agnavesh, Swami, and Rev. Valson Thampu. "Are We Creating an Anarchic Society?" *Hindu Sunday Magazine* 124 (March 31, 2002). This article is a reflection on the growing instability of India as a nation. Coauthored by a religious Hindu and a Christian minister, the piece was published about a month after the 2002 riots in Gujarat.

Demerath, N. J., III. "The Pitfalls of Pluralism: Talibanization and Saffronization in India." *Harvard International Review* 25 (Winter 2004): 16–19. The author interprets the Gujarat riots of 2002 as evidence that India is "a civilization that is coming apart." He regards violence between Hindus and Muslims as having both a "bottom-up" and a "top-down" explanation; that is, some of it comes from a kind of mob psychology while some of the violence is triggered or manipulated by political leaders who hope to gain from it.

Singh, Manpreet. "Hindu Radical Redux: Church Leaders Report More Than 200 New Incidents of Persecution." *Christianity Today* 49 (May 2005): 19. This is a brief news report of incidents of violence against Christians that have occurred since the Bharatiya Janata Party was voted out of power in spring 2004.

Web Documents

Chatterji, Angana. "Orissa: A Gujarat in the Making." *Dissident Voice* (November 1, 2003). Available online. URL: http://www.dissidentvoice.org/Articles9/Chatterji_Orissa.htm. Accessed October 17, 2005. This is an online article about the attempts of the Sangh Parivar to repeat its 2002 "experiment" in Gujarat, Orissa, a state on the eastern coast of India where the murder of Graham Staines and his two sons took place in 1999. The article recounts the forced conversion of Christians to Hinduism as well as militant attacks on Muslims.

Datta, Pradeep K. "Hindutva and Its 'Mhystory.'" *Seminar* 522 (February 2003). Available online. URL: http://www.india-seminar.com/2003/522/522%20pradip%20kumar%20datta.htm. Accessed January 10, 2006. This article, by a political scientist at Delhi University, offers an analysis of Hindutva's peculiar notion of history, namely, that it should be combined with myth. The result is, first, that "the hypothetical nature of historical evidence is replaced by assertions." The second element is "that of willed forgetting. Any detail that disturbs the positive self-image of Hindus must be jettisoned." Datta sees Hindutva's rewriting of history as essentially a way to protect the self-image of Hindus at the expense of other groups: "Hindutva's narrative of the past revolves around two basic elements: the glory of ancient India and the humiliation and oppression of Hindus in the medieval and colonial periods. The project for self-recognition draws on both."

Kumar, Krishna. "Religious Fundamentalism in India and Beyond." *Parameters, U.S. Army War College Quarterly* (Autumn, 2002). Available online. URL: http://carlisle-www.army.mil/usawc/Parameters/02autumn/kumar.htm. Accessed December 21, 2005. Kumar maintains that the way to solve conflicts between two fundamentalist communities, such as Muslims and Hindus in India, is to work toward better communal relations. He opts for a nonreligious approach: "Our collective survival lies in recognizing that religion is not the solution. We have but one choice, the path of secular humanism, based on the principles of logic and reason." With regard to Indian Muslims in particular, Kumar recommends an internal reformation: "In India, what Muslims need is the preservation and strengthening of their religiocultural identity. The only solution to the problem faced by the Indian Muslims is to look inward to their own weaknesses, rectify the moral lapses in their personal behavior and realize their potential as bearers of the universal message of Islam."

Marshall, Paul. "Hinduism and Terror." *First Things* 144 (June–July 2004): 10–13. Available online. URL: http://www.firstthings.com/ftissues/ft0406/opinion/marshall.htm. Accessed December 10, 2005. Marshall's article has also been republished by the Center for Religious Freedom associated with Freedom House. He begins by noting that religious violence in India is often ignored in the United States because Muslim terrorism tends to grab the headlines and because India is an ally of the United States. He then offers an overview of Hindutva's ideology and the organizations that make up the Sangh Parivar. Marshall traces the involvement of the Bharatiya Janata Party (BJP) in the increasingly violent attacks on Muslims and Christians since 2002. In one instance a Hindu mob was able to identify Muslim-owned homes and businesses because the attackers had address lists supplied to them by the BJP. Marshall also describes the BJP's selective appointment of school officials who carry out the saffronization of textbooks and curricula.

Nath, Ramendra. "Why I Am Not a Hindu." Available online. URL: http://www.infidels.org/library/modern/ramendra_nath/hindu.html. Accessed January 4, 2006. This was originally published as a pamphlet by the Bihar Rationalist Society in India in 1993. Nath begins by stating his dislike of the use of *Hindu* as a synonym for "Indian." This is a direct criticism of Hindutva, which maintains that Hindu religion and Indian nationality describe the same group of people. Nath then goes on to state why he is not a Hindu in the sense in which Mohandas Gandhi claimed to be one. He rejects Gandhi's belief in the authority of the Vedas as holy texts. Nath clearly objects to the Vedas on moral as well as "scientific" grounds. He sees them as the foundation of an unjust social system in their establishment of the caste system, their disregard for women, and their restricting children to the occupations of their parents. At the end of the pamphlet, he attacks belief in reincarnation, karma, and the existence of the soul in general as contrary to reason.

Sarkar, Tanika. "Historical Pedagogy of the Sangh Parivar." *Seminar* 522 (February 2003). Available online. URL: http://www.india-seminar.com/2003/522/522%20tanika%20sarkar.htm. Accessed December 30, 2005. The author is a professor of history at Jawaharlal Nehru University in Delhi, India. This article examines the class composition of the Rashtriya Swayamsevak Sangh (RSS), the paramilitary group founded by Keshav Baliram Hedgewar, and finds it to be mostly highly educated upper-class Brahman. It then proceeds to note that contemporary methods of studying and writing history are problematic to this leadership cadre: "The Sangh's relationship with history is therefore particularly fraught. It needs to possess the past, yet the accepted methods of representation are anathema to it." One tactic that the RSS has used is the construction of its own schools. In the second part of the article, the author describes a typical saffronized textbook: "The silences are resounding. There is no analysis of caste, poverty, gender abuses, no mention of what Hindus have done to Hindus. . . . Power, historically, seems to generate from Muslims as a homogeneous bloc directed at a seamless mass of Hindus. So students are not insulated from violence; rather they are flooded with a surfeit of violent tales, demanding violent reflexes in response."

Thapar, Romila. "Hindutva and History." *Frontline* 17 (September 30–October 13, 2000). Available online. URL: http://www.flonnet.com/fl1720/17200150.htm. Accessed January 8, 2006. Thapar is a highly regarded historian of ancient India, the period in the country's history that Hindutva ideologues ransack for proof that Hinduism is indigenous to India. Thapar maintains that Hindu nationalists ignore the evidence of archaeology and linguistic studies in order to prove that present-day Hindus are direct descendants of the earliest inhabitants of what is now India and are therefore entitled to possess the land. Thapar remarks, "The Hindutva obsession with identity is not a problem related to the early history of India but arises out of an attempt to manipulate identities in contemporary politics." She also notes that the Indian media cooperate with Hindutva distortions of historical evidence. "Engineers, computer experts, journalists-turned-politicians . . . assume infallibility, and pronounce on archaeology and history. And the media accord them the status."

Chronology

This chapter presents a list of significant events and dates related to religious fundamentalisms. It begins with major events in ancient and medieval history that are important in understanding contemporary political and religious institutions.

13 B.C.E.

- Augustus Caesar, the first Roman ruler to take the title of emperor (*imperator*), asks the Senate to decree the building of the Ara Pacis, or altar of peace, for the offering of annual sacrifices for Rome's prosperity. Augustus is depicted on the altar wearing religious attire. The next year, 12 B.C.E., he takes the title of *pontifex maximus,* the highest office in the Roman state religion. This attachment of Roman civil religion to imperial authority sets a precedent for later church-state relationships after the empire becomes Christian.

311 C.E.

- ***April 30:*** Emperor Galerius issues the Edict of Toleration, which ends the Roman government's persecution of Christianity. In return for this benefit, he asks Christians "to pray to their God for our safety, for that of the republic, and for their own, that the republic may continue uninjured on every side, and that they may be able to live securely in their homes."

330

- ***May 11:*** Emperor Constantine I refounds the city of Byzantium as Nova Roma, or New Rome. It becomes the capital of the eastern half of the Roman Empire and is known as "Constantine's City," or Constantinople.

391

- Emperor Theodosius I establishes Christianity as the official religion of the Roman Empire. He forbids sacrifices to the pagan gods, disbands the Vestal Virgins, and ends state subsidies to the remnants of Roman civil religion. After the end of the Olympic Games in 393, Theodosius cancels future games. The Olympics are not held again until 1896.

590

- Pope Gregory I (Gregory the Great) becomes the first bishop of Rome to borrow the title of *pontifex maximus* from the old Roman civil religion.

632

- ***June 8:*** Muhammad dies in the city of Medina in Arabia. He is followed by the first caliph ("successor" or "deputy"), Abu Bakr.

732

- ***October 10:*** Charles Martel, leader of the Franks, defeats a massive Muslim army four times the size of his own led by Emir Abd al-Rahman near the city of Tours in west-central France. Charles is given the nickname Martel (hammer) for the way he "smashed" the enemy army at Tours.

1215

- ***June 15:*** Under pressure from the barons of England, King John I signs the Magna Carta, guaranteeing certain English political liberties and providing for the church's freedom from domination by the monarch. Some of the provisions in the Bill of Rights added to the United States Constitution can be traced back to the Magna Carta.

1258

- ***February 10:*** The Mongol leader Hulagu Khan sacks Baghdad, ending the Abbasid caliphate. One descendant flees to Egypt, where the caliphate continues as a shadow institution.

1453

- ***May 29:*** Constantinople falls to the Ottoman Turks under Sultan Mehmet II after a siege lasting seven weeks. The loss of the city causes the western European monarchies to look toward the Atlantic as the sea route to the East. Mehmet adopts the title of caliph to justify his conquest of other Muslim countries.

1492

- ***January 2:*** The city of Granada falls to the troops of Ferdinand and Isabella, thus ending 800 years of Islamic rule over southern Spain.
- ***August 3–October 12:*** Christopher Columbus leaves the port of Palos de la Frontera in Spain and makes his first voyage across the Atlantic. The voyage ends when a sailor sights the island of San Salvador at 2 A.M. on October 12.

1529

- ***September 29–October 14:*** The Ottoman Turks under Sultan Suleiman I (Suleiman the Magnificent) besiege Vienna. They are finally driven away by the defenders led by Nicholas, Graf von Salm. The failure of the siege marks the high point of Ottoman power in Europe.

1534

- The English Parliament enacts the Act of Supremacy, which makes King Henry VIII "the only supreme head in earth of the Church of England." The Anglican Church thus becomes the first European state church that is neither Roman Catholic nor Eastern Orthodox.

1559

- ***April:*** Queen Elizabeth I reinstates the 1534 Act of Supremacy, which had been repealed by her sister, Queen Mary.

1571

- ***October 7:*** The Battle of Lepanto, the last naval battle to be conducted with galleys powered by human rowers, results in a crushing defeat for the Ottoman navy by a combined Christian fleet representing the Papal States, Venice, Genoa, Spain, Naples, and the Knights of Malta. Although the Turks rebuild their navy, they no longer control the Mediterranean Sea.

1582

- Publication of the Douai-Rheims Version of the New Testament, translated by Roman Catholic exiles from England living in France. The translation of the Old Testament is held up until 1609 owing to lack of funds. The Douai-Rheims translation becomes the standard Bible of English-speaking Roman Catholics until the 20th century; it is still favored by ultratraditionalists.

1611

- The printer Robert Barker offers the first printing of the King James Version of the Bible for 10 shillings in a loose-leaf form, or 12 shillings for a bound copy. The so-called Authorized Version becomes the standard translation read in English-speaking countries after the restoration of the Stuart monarchy in 1660.

1620

- ***November 21:*** The Pilgrims who crossed the Atlantic on the *Mayflower* sign a compact that becomes the first governing document of Plymouth Colony. The Mayflower Compact is considered the first written American constitution.

Chronology

1636

- Foundation of Harvard College, the first institution of higher education in the English-speaking colonies of North America.

1649

- ***September 12:*** The Ottoman Turks under Kara Mustafa Pasha are defeated at the gates of Vienna by a combined army led by the duke of Lorraine and Jan Sobieski, the king of Poland. Mustafa Pasha is executed in December.
- ***September 21:*** Cecilius Calvert, Lord Baltimore, the proprietary governor of Maryland, issues the Act of Toleration mandating acceptance of all Christian denominations in the colony. The act is considered a forerunner of the First Amendment of the U.S. Constitution.

1699

- ***January 26:*** The Treaty of Carlowitz is signed, ending the Austro-Ottoman War (1683–97). The Ottoman Empire agrees to give up various territories in Europe to Austria, Poland, and Venice. The treaty indicates that the balance of power between an Islamic empire and the West is shifting in favor of the West. The Ottoman Empire enters on a long period of gradual decline.

1730s–1740s

- The Great Awakening stirs the churches of New England.

1737

- Jonathan Edwards publishes *A Faithful Narrative of the Surprising Work of God in the Conversion of Many Hundred Souls in Northampton.*

1738

- The English evangelist George Whitefield arrives in Savannah, Georgia, and makes his first preaching tour of the American colonies.

1750

- Jonathan Edwards moves to Stockbridge, Massachusetts, where he serves as a missionary to the local Native American tribe as well as pastor of the town's Congregational church.

1757

- ***June 23:*** Colonel Robert Clive defeats the nawab of Bengal at the Battle of Plassey, thus beginning British expansion into India.

1770

- ***September 30:*** George Whitefield dies in Newburyport, Massachusetts, on his last preaching tour of the colonies. He is buried under the pulpit of the Old South Presbyterian Church.

1787

- ***September 17:*** The draft of the United States Constitution is completed at the Constitutional Convention in Philadelphia.

1789

- ***April 30:*** George Washington delivers his first inaugural address after taking the oath of office in New York City as the first president of the United States.
- ***September 25:*** Congress passes James Madison's draft of the Bill of Rights, which is then to be ratified by the states.

1791

- ***December 15:*** Virginia becomes the last state to ratify the Bill of Rights.

1807

- Andover Seminary is founded, the first American institution for theological study at the graduate level.

1816

- ***December 22:*** The United States signs a peace treaty with the dey of Algiers ending the Second Barbary War. The dey is compelled to agree to stop enslaving Christians.

1823

- ***September 22:*** Joseph Smith claims that God has directed him through the angel Moroni to a hillside near Palmyra, New York, where a stone box containing gold plates is hidden. He is not allowed to remove the plates for translation until 1827. Smith's manuscript is published as the *Book of Mormon* in 1830.

1833

- Massachusetts formally disestablishes the Congregational Church, the last state in the Union to do so.

1835

- David Friedrich Strauss, a German biblical scholar, publishes the *Life of Jesus Critically Examined.* The book is translated into English in 1846 by George Eliot (Mary Ann Evans).

Chronology

1844

- ***June 27:*** Joseph Smith, the founder of Mormonism, is murdered in jail in Carthage, Illinois. His death creates a leadership crisis for the new faith.
- ***October 22:*** The 50,000 followers of William Miller, an American Baptist minister who has predicted Christ's Second Coming on this date, experience what has come to be known as the Great Disappointment. Miller's movement eventually leads to the foundation of the Seventh-Day Adventist Church in 1863 and the Jehovah's Witnesses in 1881.

1847

- ***July 24:*** Brigham Young and the first group of Mormon pioneers enter the Salt Lake Valley of Utah and decide to build a permanent settlement there.

1857

- ***September 11:*** A wagon train of farming families from Arkansas is attacked by a group of Paiute Indians and Mormon militia near Mountain Meadows, Utah. About 120 unarmed men, women, and adolescents are killed; 17 younger children are rescued by the U.S. Army and returned to relatives in Arkansas. The motive for the massacre is thought to be a rumor that the wagon train included some men who had been part of the mob that killed Joseph Smith.

1859

- ***November 24:*** First publication of Charles Darwin's *On the Origin of Species by Means of Natural Selection.*

1864

- ***December 8:*** Pope Pius IX issues the controversial *Syllabus of Errors.* Among other matters, the pope condemns freedom of religion and separation of church and state. The condemnations shock many Roman Catholics as well as Protestants; Catholics in the United States generally ignore the *Syllabus.* It will become one of the papal pronouncements that leads Marcel Lefebvre to decide that the decrees of the Second Vatican Council cannot be reconciled with previous church tradition.

1869

- ***December 8:*** Opening of the First Vatican Council, which officially defines papal infallibility (that the pope is preserved from error when he makes a formal statement regarding faith or morals), a dogma of the Catholic Church. The council is interrupted by the outbreak of the Franco-Prussian War in 1870 and does not close formally until 1960.

1875

- ***April 7:*** Swami Dayananda Sarasvati founds the Arya Samaj, a religious society intended to reform Hinduism by returning to the Vedas and purifying worship rituals, in Bombay (Mumbai), India.

1881

- A team of British biblical scholars publishes the Revised Version of the New Testament, which is essentially an adaptation of the King James Version to late 19th-century English. The revision of the Old Testament is published in 1885. The project offends a number of American fundamentalists, who start the King James Only movement to prevent the Revised Version from being adopted by their churches.

1889

- ***September 26:*** After several years of growth and transition from meeting in tents and private houses, the Chicago Evangelization Society acquires a permanent building, changes its name to Moody Bible Institute, and opens its doors to its first full-time students.

1890

- ***May 6:*** The Church of Jesus Christ of Latter-day Saints officially renounces polygamy in order to gain statehood for the Utah Territory. Utah is finally admitted to the Union as the 45th state in 1896; it is one of the few in which women have the right to vote.

1893

- ***September 11:*** First meeting of the World Parliament of Religions in Chicago. The conference marks the beginning of American interest in Buddhism and Hinduism. Buddhist missionaries from Japan arrive in California, and a Hindu yogi makes a tour of the United States.

1899

- ***November:*** Sigmund Freud, a Viennese neurologist, publishes the first German edition of *Die Traumdeutung,* translated into English as *The Interpretation of Dreams.*

1906

- ***April 18:*** Beginning of the Azusa Street revival in Los Angeles, led by an African-American evangelist, William J. Seymour; it becomes the first phase of a worldwide Pentecostal movement.

Chronology

1907

- ***July 3:*** Pope Pius X issues "Lamentabili sane exitu," in which he condemns 65 theological errors associated with modernism. It is followed on September 8 by an encyclical, "Pascendi Dominici gregis" (Of feeding the Lords flock), in which the pope describes the modernists as "thoroughly imbued with the poisonous doctrines taught by the enemies of the Church" and removes them from teaching positions in Catholic seminaries and universities.

1909

- ***January:*** Cyrus I. Scofield publishes the first edition of the Scofield Reference Bible through Oxford University Press. This annotated version of the King James translation becomes the handbook of fundamentalists committed to dispensational premillennialism.
- ***September 7–11:*** Sigmund Freud delivers five lectures on "The Origin and Development of Psychoanalysis" at Clark University in Worcester, Massachusetts. Given in German, the lectures are translated by a graduate student and published in the *American Journal of Psychology* in April 1910. The lectures establish Freud's reputation in the English-speaking world.
- ***November 5:*** First meeting of the editorial committee that publishes *The Fundamentals*. The first volume of the 12-volume set appears in February 1910. The Bible Institute of Los Angeles republishes the original volumes in a four-volume format in 1917.

1915

- Formation of the All-India Hindu Mahasabha, or great council, to counter the growing political power of Muslims and secularists in India.

1917

- ***April 1:*** The evangelist Billy Sunday begins his last major preaching campaign in New York City.
- ***May 13–October 13:*** Three shepherd children from a village near Fátima, in Portugal, have visions of the Virgin Mary on the 13th day of each month. Conservative and traditionalist Roman Catholics take very seriously the anticommunist messages given to Lúcia dos Santos, the only one of the three children to survive to adulthood. The visions lead to the foundation of the Blue Army of Our Lady, a worldwide society of lay Catholics who meet for weekly prayer and other devotions.

1919

- ***January 16:*** The Eighteenth Amendment to the Constitution is passed, making prohibition of beverage alcohol the law of the United States. The amendment is the last major social victory of Protestant fundamentalism. Prohibition is later repealed on December 5, 1933, with the passage of the Twenty-first Amendment.

1920

- ***April:*** Conservative members of the Northern Baptist Convention hold a preconvention conference to discuss the problem of false teaching in Baptist schools. By 1921, the group begins to call itself the Fundamentalist Fellowship.
- ***September 16:*** A TNT bomb placed on a horse-drawn cart explodes in front of the New York Stock Exchange during lunch hour, killing 33 people and injuring another 400. The bomber, suspected to be a member of a left-wing anarchist group, is never found.

1921

- ***May 2:*** Vinayak Damodar Savarkar, an Indian nationalist imprisoned on the Andaman Islands, is moved to a jail at Ratnagiri on the western coast of India. While in prison at Ratnagiri, he writes *Hindutva,* his best-known work on Hindu nationalism.

1922

- ***May 21:*** Harry Emerson Fosdick, a liberal Baptist clergyman, stirs controversy when he preaches a sermon titled "Shall the Fundamentalists Win?" He is answered by "Shall Unbelief Win?" a sermon delivered by Clarence Macartney of the Arch Street Presbyterian Church in Philadelphia.
- ***November 1:*** The National Assembly of Turkey formally abolishes the Ottoman sultanate. The last sultan, Mehmet VI, goes into exile on the Italian Riviera. His cousin becomes a ceremonial caliph for the next 16 months.

1924

- ***March 3:*** Turkey's new republican government under Mustafa Kemal Atatürk abolishes the caliphate. This decision is interpreted by Muslim fundamentalists in the 1990s as a profound humiliation for Islam.

1925

- ***July 10:*** Opening day of the Scopes "monkey trial" in Dayton, Tennessee. John T. Scopes, a high school biology teacher, had agreed to allow his use of a textbook teaching Darwin's theory of evolution to serve as a test case for the constitutionality of a state anti-evolution law. The outcome of the trial is a public-relations disaster for American fundamentalists.
- ***September:*** The Rashtriya Swayamsevak Sangh, a Hindu nationalist society based on the principles of Hindutva, is founded by K. B. Hedgewar in Nagpur, India.

Chronology

1927

- Bob Jones, Sr., an evangelist and revival preacher, founds Bob Jones University in College Point, Florida. The school moves to Greenville, South Carolina, in 1947.
- Sinclair Lewis publishes *Elmer Gantry,* a satirical novel about a hypocritical and loose-living fundamentalist evangelist. The book is banned in Boston and publicly burned in several smaller cities. Lewis is awarded the Nobel Prize in literature in 1930.

1928

- ***March:*** Hassan al-Banna, a schoolteacher in Cairo, founds the Egyptian Muslim Brotherhood, an organization dedicated to the Islamicization of Egyptian society.

1929

- ***September 25:*** J. Gresham Machen, a conservative Presbyterian professor who left Princeton Seminary because of its liberal tendencies, presides at the opening convocation of Westminster Theological Seminary, the new institution he founded in Philadelphia.

1936

- ***June 11:*** Formal constitution of the Orthodox Presbyterian Church. The new denomination suffers a severe blow within months when J. Gresham Machen dies in January 1937.

1937

- ***June 4:*** Carl McIntire and several other ministers leave the Orthodox Presbyterian Church to found the Bible Presbyterian Church, a strict fundamentalist group.

1941

- ***January 6:*** President Franklin D. Roosevelt delivers the State of the Union address to the 77th Congress. In it, he enunciates the famous Four Freedoms, the second of which is "freedom of every person to worship God in his own way—everywhere in the world."
- ***August:*** Abul Ala Mawdudi, a journalist and Islamic scholar, founds the Jamaat-e-Islami, an Islamic fundamentalist movement dedicated to reconstructing Pakistani society in accordance with the teachings of Islam.
- ***September 6:*** Carl McIntire founds the fundamentalist American Council of Christian Churches in opposition to the mainstream Federal Council of Churches (forerunner of the National Council of Churches).

1942

- ***April 7–9:*** More than 140 church leaders gather in St. Louis, Missouri, to form the National Association of Evangelicals, a coalition of conservative but nonseparatist Protestant churches.

1947

- ***February:*** Bedouin shepherds searching for a lost sheep in the Judean desert near the Dead Sea discover some scrolls in a cave. Between 1949 and 1956, archaeologists discover 10 more caves in the area containing similar scrolls, all belonging to the period between 200 B.C.E. and 68 C.E. The 800 texts and manuscripts turn out to be early copies of biblical books as well as some previously unknown works by a separatist Jewish community similar to the Essenes. In addition to shedding light on the history of early Christianity and first-century Judaism, the scrolls influence newer translations of the Bible. This development leads to conspiracy theories among some fundamentalists, such as the notion that the scrolls were later forgeries or that they were planted by space aliens.
- ***May:*** Six evangelical scholars meet in Chicago to plan the location and construction of Fuller Theological Seminary.
- ***August 15:*** India and Pakistan become self-governing members of the British Commonwealth following the partition of India.

1948

- ***January 30:*** Mohandas Gandhi is assassinated by Nathuram Godse, a radical linked to right-wing Hindu organizations. Vinayak Damodar Savarkar, the founder of Hindutva, is accused of involvement in the murder conspiracy but acquitted for lack of evidence.
- ***May 14:*** Official establishment of the state of Israel as a secular parliamentary democracy.
- ***December 10:*** The United Nations General Assembly issues the Universal Declaration of Human Rights, which defines freedom of religion as a basic human right. Eleanor Roosevelt is one of the drafters of the declaration.

1952

- ***November:*** Publication of the Revised Standard Version (RSV) of the Bible. The new translation offends Protestant evangelicals, who begin to work on their own versions. It also revives the King James Only movement among fundamentalists, who maintain that the RSV is based on corrupt Greek and Hebrew manuscripts, including the "forged" Dead Sea scrolls.

Chronology

1953

- ***February 5:*** First presidential prayer breakfast. It is held during the first term of President Dwight D. Eisenhower, with Billy Graham participating.

1954

- ***May 29:*** Pope Pius XII declares Pope Pius X a saint. The canonization Mass draws 800,000 worshippers.
- ***October 26:*** Mahmoud Abd al-Latif, a member of the Muslim Brotherhood, fires eight bullets at Gamal Abdel Nasser, the president of Egypt. The assassination attempt fails because the gunman is a poor shot even at close range. Al-Latif and five leaders of the Brotherhood are hanged on December 9.

1955

- ***December 10:*** Billy Graham's decision to accept the sponsorship of the New York City Council of Churches for his 1957 crusade in Madison Square Garden leads to an open break between evangelical and fundamentalist Protestants.

1957

- ***May 15–September 1:*** Billy Graham's crusade in New York City. On July 18, Martin Luther King, Jr., gives the opening prayer at the crusade service in Madison Square Garden. On July 20, Vice President Richard Nixon is a speaker at the service in Yankee Stadium; 100,000 people attend, with another 20,000 turned away for lack of space.

1962

- ***October 11:*** Pope John XXIII opens the Second Vatican Council.

1965

- ***December 7:*** Pope Paul VI issues "Dignitatis humanae," the Second Vatican Council's Declaration on Religious Freedom. Its full title is "On the Right of the Person and of Communities to Social and Civil Freedom in Matters Religious." The declaration is one of several documents of the council that lead Archbishop Marcel Lefebvre to believe that the Council Fathers have strayed from the tradition of the church.

1966

- ***August 29:*** Sayyid Qutb, an Egyptian intellectual and radical Muslim fundamentalist, is hanged for plotting to overthrow the Egyptian government.

1967

- ***May:*** Rabbi Zvi Yehuda Kook delivers an impassioned speech about the holiness of the land of Israel at Mercaz Harav, the yeshiva his father, Abraham Isaac Kook, founded in Jerusalem.

- ***June 5–10:*** Six-Day War. Israel wins a surprising victory over Egypt, Syria, and Jordan. On June 7, Israeli paratroopers enter the Old City of Jerusalem. Religious Zionists interpret these events as proof that history is on their side.

1969

- ***August 21:*** Michael Dennis Rohan, an Australian, tries to burn down the al-Aqsa Mosque on the Temple Mount in Jerusalem. He claims to be acting on instructions from God to destroy the mosque so that the Jews could rebuild their temple on the Temple Mount and thus prepare the world for the second coming of the Messiah. Rohan is arrested and tried, committed to a mental hospital, and eventually deported from Israel.

1972

- ***January 26:*** A bomb explodes in the New York office of well-known performing arts manager Sol Hurok, killing his receptionist and injuring Hurok and 12 bystanders. A member of the Jewish Defense League is suspected; the suspect moves to Israel and is later reported to be living in the West Bank among a group of militant settlers.
- ***September 5:*** The Palestinian terrorist group Black September enters the Israeli athletes' living quarters at the summer Olympics in Munich, Germany, taking nine hostages. The hostages and one police officer are killed during a botched rescue attempt late at night.

1973

- ***January 22:*** The United States Supreme Court hands down a controversial decision in *Roe v. Wade,* thus opening the way for several decades of public debate and protests over abortion.
- ***October 6–24:*** Yom Kippur War. Although the tide has turned in favor of Israel by the time the United Nations imposes a cease-fire, the shock of the initial attack and Israeli losses during the first week prove to be a severe psychological blow to the country.
- ***December:*** Carl McIntire claims that the first sightings of the comet Kahoutek are signs of the Second Coming of Christ.

1974

- ***February 19:*** Students and faculty at Concordia Theological Seminary in St. Louis, Missouri, form a procession and walk off the seminary campus in protest of the suspension of the school's president by officials of the Lutheran Church–Missouri Synod. They set up a seminary in exile, or Seminex, in midtown St. Louis.
- ***March:*** Founding of Gush Emunim at a meeting in the settlement of Kfar Etzion; about 200 people participate.

- ***September:*** Richard G. Butler forms Aryan Nations, a Christian Identity group, as the political wing of Wesley Swift's Church of Jesus Christ–Christian. A 20-acre compound is built at Hayden Lake, Idaho.

1978

- ***September 28:*** Pope John Paul I dies after a pontificate lasting only 33 days, thus providing material for a number of conspiracy theories circulating among ultratraditionalist Roman Catholics.
- ***November 18:*** More than 900 of Jim Jones's followers die at the Peoples Temple settlement called Jonestown in the jungles of Guyana after drinking fruit punch mixed with cyanide. A visiting U.S. congressman and members of a United Press International film crew are killed in an ambush when they try to leave from a nearby airstrip at the end of their visit.

1979

- ***June 1:*** Jerry Falwell, the pastor of a large independent Baptist congregation in Virginia, founds the Moral Majority, a conservative political lobbying group. The formation of the group is the result of a struggle for control of Christian Voice, an evangelical advocacy group that began in 1978.
- ***November 4:*** A group of 66 Americans working at the U.S. embassy in Tehran, Iran, are taken as hostages by a mob of fundamentalist Muslim university students.

1980

- ***April 5:*** Formation of the Bharatiya Janata Party, a Hindu nationalist political party influenced by the fundamentalist ideology of Hindutva.
- ***June 2:*** Members of Gush Emunim booby-trap the cars of three West Bank Palestinian mayors with bombs. Two of the mayors are injured.
- ***August 10:*** About 300 members of Gush Emunim try to force their way onto the Temple Mount but are stopped by the Jerusalem police.

1981

- ***January 20:*** The American hostages in Iran are released into U.S. custody minutes after U.S. president Ronald Reagan's inaugural address.
- ***May 13:*** Mehmet Ali Agca, a Turkish nationalist militant who had previously murdered a newspaper editor, fires two shots at Pope John Paul II. Agca is captured by the crowd in St. Peter's Square before he can escape. During his years in prison, Agca tells police a variety of contradictory stories about political groups with which he claims involvement; his lawyer concludes that he is lying. During his 1981 trial, he claims to be the Second Coming of Jesus Christ.

- ***June 24–25:*** Six young people from the village of Medjugorje in Herzegovina, Yugoslavia, report having visions of the Virgin Mary on two successive days. The local bishops condemn the vision as a false apparition, while the Vatican withholds judgment.
- ***October 6:*** Anwar Sadat, the president of Egypt, is assassinated by Muslim fundamentalists belonging to a group called Jamaat al-Jihad.

1982

- ***April 11:*** Alan Harry Goodman, an American who joined the Israeli army, goes on a shooting rampage on the Temple Mount, killing one Muslim and wounding three. At his trial, Goodman tells the judge that by "liberating the spot holy to the Jews," he expected to become king of the Jews.
- ***July 25:*** Yoel Lerner, a member of Meir Kahane's Kach Party, is arrested for plotting to blow up the al-Aqsa Mosque on the Temple Mount.

1983

- ***July 25:*** A group of gunmen associated with Gush Emunim open fire on the Islamic college in Hebron, Israel. Three students are killed, and 30 more are wounded.
- ***October 23:*** A suicide bomber drives a truck loaded with explosives into the U.S. Marine barracks in Beirut, Lebanon, killing 241 servicemen and injuring 60 others. The attack remains the deadliest assault on Americans overseas since the end of World War II.

1984

- ***June 18:*** Robert Jay Mathews and three other members of The Order, an offshoot of Aryan Nations, kill Alan Berg, a controversial radio talk show host, in Denver, Colorado.
- ***July 24:*** Ronald and Dan Lafferty, Mormon fundamentalists, murder their brother Allen's wife, Brenda, and 15-month-old daughter as punishment for refusing to accept the principles of Mormon fundamentalism.
- ***October 31:*** Indira Gandhi, the prime minister of India, is assassinated by her Sikh bodyguards in retaliation for her ordering the Indian army to storm a Sikh holy place (the Golden Temple) in June 1984.

1985

- ***June 23:*** A bomb explodes in the baggage handling area of Narita Airport in Japan, killing two workers and injuring four others. An hour later, a second bomb goes off in the forward cargo compartment of Air India flight 182, at that point off the western coast of Ireland headed for London. All 329 persons on board, most of them Canadian citizens, are killed. It is the worst single terrorist attack before September 11, 2001, and remains the largest mass murder in Canadian history. The bombs are eventually traced to a cell of Sikh fundamentalists in Vancouver seeking revenge for India's raid on the Golden Temple in 1984.

- ***October 11:*** Alex Odeh, the regional director of the American-Arab Anti-Discrimination Committee (ADC) in Santa Ana, California, is killed by a bomb planted in his office. The Jewish Defense League praises the attack but denies involvement in the murder.
- ***October 15:*** Kathy Sheets and Steven Christensen are killed in Salt Lake City, Utah, by two package bombs delivered to Sheets's home and Christensen's office by Mark Hofmann. Hofmann, a dealer in rare Mormon documents, has resorted to murder in order to buy time to get out of financial difficulties and to prevent being exposed as a forger.
- ***December 27:*** Four terrorists from the Abu Nidal Organization attack the El Al and TWA ticket counters at Rome's Leonardo da Vinci Airport with grenades and automatic rifles. Thirteen persons are killed and 75 wounded before Italian police and Israeli security guards kill three of the gunmen and capture the fourth. Three more gunmen from the same group attack the El Al ticket counter at Vienna's Schwechat Airport, killing three persons and wounding 30. Austrian police kill one terrorist and capture the others.

1986

- ***September 17:*** Televangelist Pat Robertson announces his intention of running for the U.S. presidency in 1988 if he can gather 3 million supporters by the following year. He opens his campaign in September 1987.

1987

- ***March:*** Hamas is founded by Sheikh Ahmed Yassin and Abdel Aziz Rantisi as the Palestinian wing of the Muslim Brotherhood.
- ***July 5:*** The Tamil Tigers, a guerrilla organization seeking to establish an independent Tamil state within Sri Lanka, carries out its first suicide bombing. An operative named "Captain Miller" detonates a truck bomb at an army camp in Nelliady, killing 40 Sri Lankan soldiers. The Tigers are responsible for 168 suicide bombings between 1987 and 2005, using more than 240 of their members. The technique of suicide bombing will be adopted by Hamas in the 1990s.
- ***November 28:*** Randall Terry leads 350 protesters from Operation Rescue in blocking the entrances of an abortion clinic in Cherry Hill, New Jersey.
- ***December 8:*** Beginning of the Intifada, or Palestinian uprising. It is sparked when an Israeli tank runs over four children who had been throwing stones at the tank.

1988

- ***June 30:*** Archbishop Marcel Lefebvre, founder of the Society of St. Pius X, consecrates four bishops in Ecône, Switzerland, in defiance of a warning from Pope John Paul II. Lefebvre is excommunicated the next day, along with the four new bishops.
- ***August 18:*** Hamas issues its charter (or covenant), describing itself as a wing of the Muslim Brotherhood in Palestine, and commits itself to jihad for the liberation of Palestine.
- ***December 21:*** Pan American flight 103 is blown up over Lockerbie, Scotland, by a charge of plastic explosive hidden inside a radio in the forward cargo hold. All 243 passengers and 16 crew members are killed, along with 11 Lockerbie residents on the ground. Two Libyans are put on trial, and the government of Libya eventually accepts responsibility for the bombing.

1989

- ***February 14:*** Ayatollah Ruhollah Khomeini, the leader of Iran, issues a fatwa against the novelist Salman Rushdie for apostasy and blasphemy for his novel *The Satanic Verses.* Khomeini calls on all "zealous Muslims" to execute the author as well as his publishers. Rushdie's Japanese translator is killed in Tokyo in 1991, and, also in 1991, his Italian translator is stabbed in Milan. In 1993, his Norwegian publisher is shot and severely injured in Oslo.
- ***July 10:*** Jerry Falwell officially disbands the Moral Majority, claiming that its mission is accomplished. The organization is succeeded by the Christian Coalition, which is funded by money left over from Pat Robertson's failed presidential campaign.
- ***December 6:*** Marc Lépine (born Gamil Gharbi), the son of an Algerian immigrant to Canada who changed his name out of contempt for his alcoholic father, kills 13 female students and one female administrator at the École Polytechnique de Montréal while screaming "I hate feminists." Four men and eight more women are wounded before Lépine shoots himself. He leaves behind a letter saying that feminists had ruined his life, and a list of 19 prominent Quebec women he had intended to kill.

1990

- ***November 5:*** Rabbi Meir Kahane, the founder of the Jewish Defense League and the radical right-wing Kach Party in Israel, is shot and killed in downtown Manhattan by an Egyptian immigrant.

1991

- ***April 17:*** Members of Gush Emunim construct a settlement at Revava overnight, prior to the visit of U.S. secretary of state James Baker.

- ***May 21:*** Rajiv Gandhi, former prime minister of India and the older son of Indira Gandhi, is assassinated by a 17-year-old female suicide bomber while campaigning in Sriperumbudur, India. The assassin, Thenmuli Rajaratnam, was associated with the Tamil Tigers. The bomb kills 16 bystanders in addition to Gandhi and Rajaratnam. Following the assassination, seven suspected Tamil Tigers commit suicide after being surrounded by police.

1992

- ***July 13:*** Abortion protester Robert Schenck, a convert to fundamentalist Protestantism from Reform Judaism, is arrested for pushing a dead fetus in Bill Clinton's face at the 1992 Democratic Convention.
- ***December 6:*** A mob of angry Hindus tears down the Babri Masjid, a mosque in the town of Ayodhya in northern India. At least 2,000 people are killed in the riots that follow the destruction. The Vishwa Hindu Parishad, a religious-cultural organization associated with the Bharatiya Janata Party and Hindutva ideology, is banned for two years for inciting mob violence.

1993

- ***February 26:*** A car bomb planted by Islamist terrorists in the underground parking garage of the World Trade Center explodes, killing six and injuring 1,040 other persons. Six conspirators are convicted of the crime in 1997 and 1998.
- ***February 28:*** Agents from the Bureau of Alcohol, Tobacco, and Firearms attempt to arrest David Koresh at the Branch Davidian compound in Waco, Texas. Four agents and six Branch Davidians are killed in the shootout, which is followed by a 51-day siege.
- ***March 10:*** Michael Griffin shoots Dr. David Gunn, an abortion provider, in Pensacola, Florida. Gunn dies instantly.
- ***April 19:*** End of the siege of the Branch Davidian compound in Waco, Texas. The resulting fire kills 80 members of the group. The disaster will provide Timothy McVeigh with a motive for mass murder in 1995.
- ***September:*** The Church of Jesus Christ of Latter-day Saints excommunicates and disfellowships the "September Six," a group of leading Mormon historians, lawyers, and writers, for expressing feminist and other liberal ideas. The church's action sends a shock through the intellectual Mormon community.
- ***September 13:*** Public signing of the Oslo Accords in Washington, D.C. The agreement was negotiated between the Palestine Liberation Organization and the state of Israel as a step toward eventual resolution of the Palestinian-Israeli conflict.
- ***October 19:*** Clarence Kelly, the superior of a group of priests that has broken away from the Society of St. Pius X, is consecrated a bishop by Alfredo José Méndez-González, the retired bishop of Arecibo in Puerto Rico.

1994

- ***February 25:*** Baruch Goldstein, a physician in the Israeli army, kills 29 Muslims in the Cave of the Patriarchs in Hebron, Israel. He is beaten to death by the survivors. Two Israeli army guards testify at the inquiry that Goldstein had an accomplice, but the inquiry commission finds that Goldstein acted on his own.
- ***April 6:*** The first Hamas suicide bomber drives a car with a bomb into a bus in Afula, Israel, killing eight people.
- ***July 29:*** Paul Jennings Hill kills Dr. John Britton, an abortion provider, and his bodyguard outside a clinic in Pensacola, Florida.
- ***October 5:*** Members of the Order of the Solar Temple are killed or commit mass suicide in a settlement outside the town of Chiery, Switzerland. Another group commits mass suicide in Quebec.

1995

- ***March 20:*** Five members of Japan's Aum Shinrikyō cult release sarin, a nerve gas, in the Tokyo subway system during the morning rush hour, killing 12 passengers and injuring 5,500 more.
- ***April 19:*** Timothy McVeigh sets off a fertilizer bomb in a rented truck in front of the Alfred P. Murrah Federal Building in Oklahoma City, Oklahoma. The worst domestic terrorist attack in the United States up to that time, it results in the death of 168 people.
- ***September 19:*** The *New York Times* and the *Washington Post* agree to print the Unabomber's 35,000-word manifesto. Theodore Kaczynski's brother David recognizes the writing style and notifies federal authorities.
- ***November 4:*** Yitzhak Rabin, the prime minister of Israel, is assassinated by Yigal Amir, a former combat soldier and right-wing student from Tel Aviv's Bar-Ilan University. Amir becomes a hero to the radical religious right in Israel.

1996

- ***April 3:*** Theodore Kaczynski is arrested outside his cabin near Lincoln, Montana. He is eventually sentenced to life imprisonment without the possibility of parole.

1998

- ***October 9:*** U.S. Congress passes the International Religious Freedom Act of 1998; it is signed into law by President Bill Clinton. The act mandates an annual report to Congress on the status of religious freedom in 197 countries around the world.
- ***October 23:*** Dr. Barnett Slepian, an abortion provider, is shot and killed in the kitchen of his home in Amherst, New York, by James Charles Kopp. Kopp flees abroad and is arrested in France in 2001.

Chronology

1999

- ***January 22:*** Graham Staines, an Australian missionary in Orissa, India, is burned to death in his station wagon along with his two young sons by a crowd of Hindu extremists.
- ***August 10:*** Buford Furrow, Jr., a fringe member of Aryan Nations, attacks a Jewish day-care center in Los Angeles, injuring five people, and kills a Filipino-American letter carrier an hour later.
- ***September 15:*** The Federal Research Division of the Library of Congress releases a report on "The Sociology and Psychology of Terrorism," warning that terrorists in the 1990s have a different motivation from those of the 1970s, namely religious fundamentalism. In addition, the report states that the new terrorists are willing to use weapons of mass destruction to inflict maximum civilian casualties rather than targeting only political leaders or small groups of people.
- ***October 20:*** The Federal Bureau of Investigation issues *Project Megiddo* to American law enforcement officials. The report is the result of nine months of investigation into domestic terrorist groups who might commit violence intended to bring about the end of the world at the turn of the new millennium. The title of the report refers to a hill in northern Israel associated with apocalyptic speculations about the final battle between good and evil.
- ***October 31:*** EgyptAir flight 990 crashes into the Atlantic Ocean off the island of Nantucket, killing 217 people. The National Transportation Safety Board determines in 2002 that the first officer (copilot) intentionally caused the plane to dive into the ocean but offers no explanation of his motives.

2000

- ***September 28:*** Beginning of the Second Intifada, which is sometimes called the al-Aqsa Intifada. The riots that begin on September 29 are blamed on Ariel Sharon's visit to the Temple Mount.
- ***October 12:*** Two al-Qaeda suicide bombers on a small fishing boat loaded with explosives attack the USS *Cole,* a U.S. Navy destroyer making a fuel stop in the harbor of Aden, Yemen. The explosion kills 17 sailors and wounds another 39.
- ***December 31:*** Rabbi Binyamin Kahane, the son of Meir Kahane, is machine-gunned together with his wife by Palestinians as they are returning from Jerusalem to their home in the West Bank.

2001

- ***January 6:*** The Hayden Lake, Idaho, headquarters of Aryan Nations is put up for auction when the group is forced to declare bankruptcy following a civil lawsuit against it.

- ***February 15:*** Mayor Rudolph Giuliani of New York City, a Roman Catholic, is called a "theocratic fundamentalist" by a group of left-wing artists for criticizing the use of public money to fund a photographic exhibit depicting Jesus at the Last Supper as a naked black woman. Giuliani had been similarly attacked in 1999 for his opposition to a painting displayed at the Brooklyn Museum that showed the Virgin Mary smeared with elephant dung.
- ***March 6:*** The Taliban of Afghanistan begin the demolition of two giant statues of Buddha carved into the side of a cliff at Bamiyan some time in the fifth or sixth century C.E. The cliff had been listed as a UNESCO World Heritage site. The images are considered idolatrous and therefore "unislamic." A cleric associated with the Taliban remarks, "Muslims should be proud of smashing idols. It has given praise to God that we have destroyed them."
- ***July 23:*** The government of Israel makes an official decision to construct a security fence as a defense against Palestinian suicide bombers. The first stage of the fence becomes operational in July 2003.
- ***September 11:*** Islamist terrorists hijack four commercial airliners, crash two into the World Trade Center towers in New York City and a third into the Pentagon outside Washington, D.C. The fourth plane crashes near Shenksville, Pennsylvania, apparently as a result of passengers attempting to take control of the aircraft.
- ***December 22:*** Richard Reid, a British convert to Islam, tries to blow up American Airlines flight 63 with a bomb hidden in his shoe. He is subdued after a struggle with two flight attendants and a group of passengers. During his trial, he states openly that he is an Islamic fundamentalist and an enemy of the United States.

2002

- ***February 27:*** Beginning of anti-Muslim violence in Gujarat, India, which is triggered when Muslims set fire to a train carrying Hindu worshippers returning from a pilgrimage to Ayodhya, killing 59 persons. The riots that follow are estimated to cost the lives of 2,000 Muslims.
- ***July 4:*** Hesham Hadayet, an Egyptian national living in the United States, opens fire while standing in line at the El Al ticket counter at Los Angeles International Airport. Hadayet kills two people and wounds four others before he is shot and killed by a security guard. American and Israeli officials disagree as to whether Hadayet was a terrorist or had other criminal motives.
- ***July 22:*** An Israeli air strike kills Salah Shehada, the head of Hamas's Izz al-Din al-Qassam Brigades, by dropping an aircraft bomb on his house in Gaza.
- ***October 2–24:*** John Allen Muhammad and Lee Boyd Malvo kill 10 people and injure three others during a three-week spree of sniper attacks in the Baltimore–Washington, D.C., metropolitan area. Muhammad, who had joined the Nation

of Islam and had changed his name in 2001, is sentenced to death at the end of his trial in 2003 on the grounds that the murders were acts of terrorism.

- *October 12:* Islamic militants set off two bombs in Kuta, a resort on the Indonesian island of Bali. The final death toll is 202, most of them young tourists, with another 209 seriously injured.

2003

- *March 20:* Beginning of Operation Iraqi Freedom.
- *December 13:* Iraqi leader Saddam Hussein is captured near his hometown of Tikrit, in Iraq.

2004

- *January 5:* Angry Hindu nationalists ransack the Bhandarkar Oriental Research Institute, protesting an American scholar's publication of a book on Shivaji, a 17th-century Hindu king in Islamic India. The book was not a biography of Shivaji but a study of the way records of his life have been used in folk stories. The mob destroys 18,000 books and 30,000 manuscripts in a half-hour rampage. The Indian government compels Oxford University Press to withdraw the book from sale in India.
- *March 11:* Four commuter trains entering Madrid, Spain, during the morning rush hour are blown up by bombs concealed in backpacks or duffel bags. The attacks kill 191 people and injure another 1,460. Two Islamic extremists who blew themselves up during a police raid on their apartment on April 2 are thought to have been responsible for the train bombing.
- *March 22:* Sheikh Ahmed Yassin, the founder and first leader of Hamas, is killed by Hellfire missiles fired by an Israeli helicopter gunship.
- *April 14:* Abdel Aziz Rantisi, a pediatrician who assumes the leadership of Hamas following the death of Sheikh Ahmed Yassin, is killed in an Israeli raid.
- *April–May:* The Bharatiya Janata Party is voted out of power in India in a stunning electoral upset. The party's loss is attributed to backlash from the Gujarat riots of 2002.
- *September 1–3:* Chechen terrorist Shamil Basayev, a convert to fundamentalist Islam, leads a group of 27 men and five women in taking hundreds of schoolchildren and adults hostage in a school in Beslan, Russia. The siege ends on the third day when the captors set off explosions inside the school and Russian security forces storm the building. According to the Russian government, the death toll is 331 civilians, including 186 children, and 11 soldiers, with hundreds more injured. One surviving hostage commits suicide after returning home.
- *November 2:* Theo van Gogh, a controversial Dutch filmmaker and journalist, is murdered in Amsterdam in broad daylight by Mohammed Bouyeri for

criticizing Islam, particularly in his 2003 book, *Allah weet het beter* (Allah knows best). Bouyeri claims to have killed van Gogh in order to fulfill his religious duties as a Muslim.

- ***November 11:*** Yasser Arafat, the leader of the Palestine Liberation Organization (PLO), dies of unknown causes in a Paris hospital.

2005

- ***January 19:*** Norma McCorvey, the "Jane Roe" of *Roe v. Wade,* having become a Roman Catholic and a pro-life activist, petitions the Supreme Court to overturn its 1973 decision.
- ***April 19:*** Josef Cardinal Ratzinger is elected to the papacy as the successor to John Paul II. He takes the name Benedict XVI. He is the oldest person to be elected pope since Clement XII in 1730 and the first German pope since Adrian VI in 1522.
- ***July 5:*** Six Muslim militants disguised as Hindus storm the makeshift Hindu temple at Ayodhya by driving a jeep loaded with explosives into a security wall. The men are killed by security guards inside the temple.
- ***July 7:*** Four suicide bombers associated with an Islamist paramilitary organization detonate their bombs in the London public transportation system, three on subway trains and the fourth on a bus. The attacks kill 56 people and injure another 700 persons. It is the first suicide bombing attack to be carried out in western Europe.
- ***July 21:*** Twenty extreme right-wing Jewish fundamentalists gather around a grave in northern Israel to conduct a *pulsa denura* (Aramaic for "lashes of fire") ceremony against Prime Minister Ariel Sharon for his plan to evacuate the Jewish settlements in the occupied territories. The ceremony is supposed to release "angels of destruction" to kill Sharon within a month.
- ***August 11:*** Salman Rushdie writes a guest column for the *Times* (London) urging the importance of reforming Islam.
- ***August 15:*** Israel begins the withdrawal from the settlements in the Gaza Strip.
- ***August 29:*** Pope Benedict XVI meets for 35 minutes with Bishop Bernard Fellay, superior general of the Society of St. Pius X, in an effort to heal the ultratraditionalist schism.
- ***September 17:*** Addressing the General Assembly of the United Nations, Iranian president Mahmoud Ahmadinejad concludes his speech with a prayer for the appearance of the Mahdi, a "rightly-guided one" or apocalyptic savior figure who is supposed to rule before the end of the world. Ahmadinejad's remarks after returning to Iran suggest that he sees himself as the Mahdi.
- ***October 22:*** Fundamentalist Muslims threaten to bomb the offices of the Danish newspaper *Jyllands-Posten* for publishing cartoons of Muhammad. They

also threaten to track down and kill the artists responsible for the cartoons. Prime Minister Anders Fogh Rasmussen defends the newspaper on the basis of Denmark's tradition of freedom of speech.

- ***October 27–November 15:*** Civil unrest in France, marked by the burning of cars, attacks on police and passersby, and destruction of schools, shops, and post offices. The riots are attributed to France's failure to assimilate its growing Muslim population.

2006

- ***January 4:*** Prime Minister Ariel Sharon of Israel is hospitalized after a severe stroke, throwing the country's political process into turmoil. Right-wing extremists claim the next day that their *pulsa denura* ceremony worked. Ehud Olmert becomes acting prime minister.
- ***January 4:*** Robert Schenck and two other fundamentalist clergy enter the hearing room of the Senate Judiciary Committee and put holy oil on the chairs where Judge Samuel Alito and the members of the committee will sit for the judge's Supreme Court confirmation hearings.
- ***January 26:*** Hamas wins a parliamentary majority in the Palestinian elections.
- ***March 3:*** Mohammed Reza Taheri-azar, a 22-year-old Iranian immigrant, drives a rented sport utility vehicle into a crowd of students on the campus of the University of North Carolina (UNC), striking nine and injuring six. He later tells police that he had planned the attack more than two years earlier, while he was a student at UNC, to "avenge the deaths of Muslims around the world."
- ***April 14:*** Ehud Olmert becomes prime minister of Israel, according to the Basic Law of Israel, 100 days after Ariel Sharon's incapacitation.
- ***April 24:*** Three bombs explode in a supermarket and two cafeterias in the Egyptian resort town of Dahab, killing 23 persons and wounding 62 others.
- ***May 4:*** Zacarias Moussaoui is sentenced to life in prison without possibility of parole for his role in the terrorist attacks of September 11, 2001. Moussaoui, who had boasted of his participation in the attacks, told Judge Leonie Brinkema after she pronounced the sentence, "I fight for my beliefs."
- ***June 2 and 3:*** Canadian police and security agents arrest a group of 17 men alleged to be members of an Islamic terrorist cell in the Toronto area. One of the men had ordered 6,600 pounds of ammonium nitrate fertilizer, or three times the amount that Timothy McVeigh had used to make his truck bomb in 1995.
- ***June 7:*** Abu Musab al-Zarqawi, considered the mastermind behind hundreds of terrorist acts in Iraq, is killed by a U.S. airstrike on his hideout near Baqubah, north of Baghdad.

- ***June 23:*** Seven men are arrested in Florida on charges of involvement in a terrorist plot to blow up the Sears Tower in Chicago and government buildings in Miami.
- ***July 12:*** War breaks out between Israel and Lebanon following Hezbollah rocket attacks on Israel and the kidnapping of two Israeli soldiers. The conflict is known as the July War in Lebanon and the Second Lebanon War in Israel.
- ***August 10:*** British police arrest 25 men of Pakistani origin affiliated with a radical Muslim group. The men are suspected of plotting to destroy as many as 10 aircraft flying from the United Kingdom to the United States. Their peroxide-based liquid explosives were to be carried on board in containers, disguising the liquids as sports drinks or toiletries.
- ***August 14:*** Armed conflict between Israel and Lebanon is ended by a ceasefire brokered by the United Nations. Post-ceasefire incidents of rocket firing, rock throwing, and other hostile acts continue through mid-October.
- ***September 12:*** Pope Benedict XVI delivers a lecture on the role of faith in the university at the University of Regensburg, Germany, where he served as a professor and vice rector between 1969 and 1971. The lecture is misunderstood and misquoted by radical Muslims to generate angry demonstrations around the world as well as threats to kill the pope.
- ***September 17:*** Sister Leonella Sgorbati, an Italian nun working as a nurse in Mogadishu, Somalia, is shot to death hours after a local imam called for violent retribution against the pope.
- ***October 1:*** The Israeli army completes its withdrawal from Lebanon.
- ***October 13:*** Three French police officers are ambushed and severely injured in a Paris suburb by a group of more than 50 Muslim youths—the fourth in a series of gang beatings of police since September 2006.
- ***October 24:*** Jeffrey Don Lundgren, the founder of a breakaway sect of fundamentalist Mormons, is executed in Ohio for the murders of five of his followers in 1989.
- ***October 26:*** A Muslim imam in Sydney provokes a furor in the Australian press by comparing non-Muslim women to "uncovered meat" that attracts cats and maintaining that such women deserve to be raped. He also stated that women in general are "weapons" used by Satan to control men.
- ***December 30:*** Saddam Hussein is executed by hanging in Baghdad after being convicted by an Iraqi court of crimes against humanity.

2007

- ***January 15:*** The Danish newspaper *Jyllands-Posten* publishes an article to quell a rumor that one of the Danish cartoonists involved in the cartoon controversy of October 2005 had been murdered by a fundamentalist Muslim.

Glossary

This chapter presents terms that often arise in discussions of fundamentalist groups within the major religions of the world.

aliyah ***(plural, aliyot)*** The immigration of Jews to Israel. The term may also refer to the honor of being called to the reading desk in a synagogue to recite the blessings over the Torah.

American exceptionalism The belief that the United States has a special role to play in human history. The term, which originated with Alexis de Tocqueville in the 1830s, may refer to a secular notion of patriotism, as well as to explicitly religious beliefs about a divine purpose for the nation.

apocalyptic Of or relating to a genre of Jewish or Christian writings, mostly produced between 200 B.C.E. and 350 C.E., that were thought to be prophetic revelations of the divine purpose. Many writings of this type describe the end of history as a cataclysm in which the forces of good do battle with and eventually triumph over the forces of evil.

apologetics The branch of theology devoted to defending or proving the truth of one's religion or denomination. A treatise offering such a defense or proof is called an *apologia*.

apostasy Renunciation or abandonment of one's previous religious faith or loyalty. In Islam, apostasy is considered worse than unbelief; the traditional penalty for it is death.

apostolate A Roman Catholic term for mission. *Apostolate of the laity* refers to a task or mission assigned to laypeople.

Ashkenazi ***(plural, Ashkenazim)*** A Jew of central or eastern European ancestry.

biblical inerrancy The belief that the Bible is the inspired Word of God, is infallible in every detail, and contains no errors in the original autographs. This view was expressed in the 1978 Chicago Statement on Biblical Inerrancy, formulated and signed by a group of more than 300 scholars from a variety of evangelical denominations.

blasphemy An impious or irreverent utterance or action against God or sacred things; an act of cursing or reviling God.

blood atonement A controversial Mormon doctrine that originated with Brigham Young around 1856 to the effect that there are some sins that are unpardonable unless the offender's blood is "spilt upon the ground." The Church of Jesus Christ of Latter-day Saints officially repudiated this teaching in 1978; however, some conservative Mormons still use it to justify capital punishment, particularly execution by firing squad.

born-again A term used in some American Protestant churches to refer to an intense personal experience of religious awakening or recommitment, as in *born-again Christian.*

caliphate The institution of a unified Islamic state. Prior to its abolition in 1924 by the secular government of Turkey, the caliphate represented a succession of rulers who were descended from Muhammad and held spiritual as well as temporal authority. After 1517, the Ottoman rulers took the title of *caliph* as well as *sultan.* Some Muslim fundamentalists are presently seeking to reestablish the caliphate.

canon law The codified internal legal system of the Roman Catholic Church, governing such matters as the disposition of church property and qualifications for high office in the church as well as regulations governing the clergy, religious orders, and forms of worship. The term *canon* is derived from the Greek word for "rule" or "practical law." The last major revision of canon law was carried out in 1982 and took effect in 1983.

charismatic movement An interdenominational movement among Christians that is characterized by ecstatic religious experiences that may include speaking in tongues or instantaneous healing.

Christian Identity A blanket term applied to an assortment of groups, some of which call themselves churches, that are characterized by anti-Semitism and a white supremacist ideology. Most, though not all, groups in this category were influenced by British Israelism, a 19th-century belief that white Europeans are descended from the 10 lost tribes of Israel. Christian Identity groups are most numerous in the western United States and in South Africa, where they are known as "Israel Identity" groups.

Christian Zionism The beliefs held by some fundamentalist and other conservative Christians that the foundation of the state of Israel and the subsequent return of many Jews to the Holy Land are fulfillments of biblical prophecy (specifically the book of Ezekiel) and that the building of the Third Temple is the necessary precondition for the Second Coming of Christ. Most Christian Zionists also accept DISPENSATIONALISM.

civil religion A term that is variously used to refer either to a religious element in the common culture of a nation, as in the belief that the United States has a special God-given mission to fulfill, or to ritual expressions of patriotism (such as singing the national anthem at baseball games), whether or not these rituals have an explicitly religious dimension. The earliest forms of civil religion developed in the ancient Greek city-states, but the first government to have a civil religion in the full sense of the word was the Roman Empire under Augustus Caesar (63 B.C.E.–14 C.E.). The phrase itself was coined by the French philosopher Jean-Jacques Rousseau (1712–78).

communalism A term that is used in contemporary India to describe favoritism toward certain religious communities at the expense of others. The Hindu nationalist Bharatiya Janata Party (BJP) accuses the secular Congress Party of communalism in favor of minority religions in India, while leaders of the Congress Party accuse the BJP of communalism in favoring the Hindu majority.

confessional A term used to refer to churches defined by subscription to a formal profession of faith, such as the Augsburg or Westminster Confessions. In Germany, the various Christian churches are still referred to as *Konfessionen.* Confessional churches in the United States are one subcategory of conservative churches.

conversion The adoption of a new religion or set of religious beliefs. The term can also refer to a change from a state of indifference or rejection of religion to strong conviction and a new sense of enthusiasm or fervor. *Conversion experience* refers to an identifiable spiritual awakening or similar event in a person's life, which some groups consider necessary to full membership.

cult A sect or small group considered to be unorthodox or extremist; a deviant religious organization with novel beliefs and practices. Some scholars of religion prefer not to use the term because it has acquired so many negative connotations from its association with groups that have practiced mass suicide or terrorism.

encyclical A papal letter intended for general circulation among the bishops of the Roman Catholic Church. The English word is derived from the Greek word for "circular."

extreme traditionalism A term that is sometimes used as a synonym for *ultratraditionalism* in the Roman Catholic Church. Extreme traditionalists are opposed to the reforms of the Second Vatican Council, particularly the revisions of the Mass, greater openness to non–Roman Catholic Christians, and a more democratic view of the distinction between clergy and laity.

Dajjal In Islamic apocalyptic writings, an evil figure resembling the Antichrist of Christian eschatology. The Arabic word means "deceiver."

Dalit In the Indian caste system, a person outside the four castes and considered below them. Dalits were formerly called outcasts or untouchables. The word *dalit* in Hindi means "stepped on" or "crushed."

deism Belief in the existence of God on the basis of human reason and the natural order, usually combined with the rejection of a supernatural source of revelation. Deism in the West is largely a product of the late 17th and 18th centuries.

denomination In the United States, an organized subgroup that has existed within a major religion for many years and that usually has some form of authority over local congregations. It is used appropriately to refer to the Eastern Orthodox, Roman Catholic, and Protestant Churches as well as the four major organized branches of Judaism. Some writers also use the term for the major branches of Hinduism and Islam, but other scholars do not consider it the best usage for these religions.

dispensationalism A conceptual scheme for understanding biblical history by dividing it into periods, or dispensations. The pattern accepted by most Christian fundamentalists posits seven dispensational periods: innocence (before humanity fell into sin), conscience (the period between Adam and Noah), government (the period between Noah and Abraham), patriarchal rule (from Abraham to Moses), Mosaic law (from Moses until the coming of Christ), grace (the present age of the church), and the coming millennial kingdom of Jesus Christ. The Scofield Reference Bible, first published in 1909 by Cyrus Scofield, a minister and theologian, helped to popularize dispensationalism in the United States.

doctrine A church or religion's body or system of teachings. It may refer either to the entire system or to a portion of it, as in Calvin's doctrine of predestination. A doctrine is less authoritative and binding than DOGMA.

dogma ***(plural, dogmata or dogmas)*** A specific religious doctrine regarded as central and authoritative that must be held by all followers of that religion. In Christianity, the core dogmata are the statements of faith contained in the Nicene Creed (fourth century C.E.). Eastern Orthodoxy adds the decrees of the first seven ecumenical councils. The Roman Catholic Church declared the Assumption and Immaculate Conception of the Virgin Mary, along with papal infallibility, to be dogmata in the 19th century. In Islam, there are six dogmata: belief in God, in angels, in all the prophets and messengers sent by God, in the Scriptures, in the day of judgment, and in destiny or fate.

ecumenism A movement within Christianity to promote reunion of the separated churches. It should not be confused with denominational or religious pluralism, which is intended to foster improved relationships and mutual goodwill among the various branches of Christianity or among members of different religions.

eschatology The set of doctrines in Christianity, Judaism, and Islam referring to the last things—death, the end of the world, the end of history, a final judgment, an afterlife, heaven, and hell.

evangelical A term that originally meant "derived from or in keeping with the Gospels." In the U.S. context, it usually refers to churches that emphasize the authority of the Scriptures over that of a church hierarchy and stress the importance of personal conversion. Since the 1970s, however, it is sometimes used more broadly to refer to Protestant bodies that are conservative in their teaching but not fundamentalist. In Europe, particularly Germany, it is often simply a synonym for the Lutheran Church.

fatwa *(plural, fatawa)* In Islam, a legal opinion issued by a member of the ULEMA regarding a specific question. Because Islam has no central religious or legal hierarchy, however, it is not completely clear as to who can issue valid fatawa and which individuals are bound by them. Most fatawa concern ordinary matters, not death sentences or declarations of war, which typically draw media attention. Fatwa should not be used as a slang term for papal decrees or statements by secular leaders.

fundamentalist Originally, a term that referred to a movement within some American Protestant churches in the late 19th and early 20th centuries to return to the foundational or core beliefs of Christianity through emphasizing the authority of the Bible. It is sometimes used more broadly to refer to recent movements in other religions that try to preserve certain aspects of their traditions from being overwhelmed by modern, particularly Western, culture.

hadith The traditions about the life and sayings of Muhammad and his companions that are not recorded in the Qur'an. They serve together with the Qur'an as the basis of Islamic law, SHARIA. The most reliable hadith are the collections by al-Bukhari (c. 870 C.E.) and al-Muslim (c. 875 C.E.). Al-Bukhari's collection contains 7,275 hadith, and al-Muslim's, 9,200 hadith.

halacha *(halakha)* The collective body of Jewish rabbinic law, custom, and tradition; it covers the practical application of the commandments in the Torah. The word may also refer to an individual law or tradition established by the halacha.

***haredi* (plural, *haredim*)** A Jew who belongs to the most conservative form of Orthodox Judaism, Haredi, sometimes called ultra-orthodox. The word *haredi* means "to tremble" in Hebrew and is taken from a passage in Isaiah that describes the pious as those "who tremble at God's word." Both *ultra-orthodox* and *haredi* are terms used more often for this group by outsiders rather than by the members themselves.

heresy A religious opinion or doctrine at variance with orthodox teaching. It can also refer to the willful and obstinate maintaining of such a doctrine or the refusal to accept a dogma.

hijab A veil or head covering worn by Muslim women. It has become a controversial symbol of Muslim separatism as well as of the subordination of women in several European countries.

Hindutva A fundamentalist ideology that identifies Hinduism with Indian nationalism and use of the Hindi language. It regards the land and rivers of India as sacred soil and urges the purging, forced conversion, or expulsion of Muslims, Christians, and other "foreign elements." The name means "Hinduness" and is taken from the title of a book published by V. Savarkar in 1923. The ideology of Hindutva is reflected in the organizations that make up the Sangh Parivar and in the SAFFRONIZATION of school materials.

imam A term for a Muslim religious leader that carries different meanings in different branches of Islam. For Sunni Muslims, the imam leads the faithful in prayer and is not necessarily a cleric. Sunnis also use the term to refer to the founders of major schools of religious law. For Shiites, an imam is a leader of the community appointed by God, almost a messianic figure. Different Shiite groups recognize five, six, or 12 imams. *Imam* is also occasionally given as an honorific title to theocratic Shiite rulers.

integralism A conservative movement within 19th- and early 20th-century Roman Catholicism that believed that every single element of Catholic teaching had to be upheld as "integral" to the "seamless garment" of the church's doctrine.

jihad An Islamic term derived from a root that means "to strive" or "to struggle." It has a range of meanings, from inward spiritual struggle to perfect one's faith to political movements or war regarded as divinely ordained.

kabbalah ***(kabbala, cabala)*** A mystical religious tradition within Judaism that emphasizes esoteric knowledge of God and the nature of the universe, and the path that devout adult Jews must follow to learn these secrets. It teaches that every letter, word, number, and punctuation mark in the Hebrew Bible contains a hidden meaning and offers methods of interpretation for uncovering these meanings. Rabbi Isaac Luria (1534–72) is the most important figure in the development of kabbalah in the modern period. The Hebrew word means "something received" or "handed down."

karma In classical Hinduism, a term that refers to the law of cause and effect in human actions. All human acts, whether positive or negative, have consequences that will determine a person's position in the next cycle of birth and death.

kippah (plural, kippot) Also called a *yarmulke*; a thin, slightly rounded cloth or knitted skullcap worn by observant Jewish men during prayer or while studying sacred texts, although some traditionalist men may wear a *kippah* all day. Some Jewish feminists also wear *kippot* as a sign of the equality of the sexes in Jewish practice.

liturgy A formal or highly ritualized order of public worship, especially the celebration of the Eucharist, or Holy Communion. The *liturgical churches* are those Christian bodies (Anglican, Eastern Orthodox, Lutheran, and Roman Catholic) that use such an order of worship at the main Sunday service.

magisterium In the Roman Catholic Church, the authority to teach and interpret doctrine vested in the pope and the bishops by virtue of their office.

Mahdi In Muslim apocalyptic writing, a messianic figure sent by God in the end times to wage war against the enemies of Islam and establish a kingdom on earth before the last judgment. There have been several false Mahdis in Islamic history. The current president of Iran is reported to consider himself the Mahdi.

mainline churches A term used to refer to a group of Protestant bodies in the United States that are moderate—neither liberal not fundamentalist—in belief. Some observers refer to the following "seven sisters" as the mainline churches: the American Baptist Churches USA, the Disciples of Christ, the Episcopal Church, the Evangelical Lutheran Church in America, the Presbyterian Church USA, the United Church of Christ, and the United Methodist Church.

millenarian Relating to speculation about the millennium, or period of a thousand years. Among Christian fundamentalists, the millennium is usually understood as a thousand-year reign of Christ as promised in Revelation 20:4–6.

mitzvah ***(plural, mitzvot)*** In Judaism, the commandments given by God, specifically the 613 commandments contained in the Torah. The term is sometimes extended to include any Jewish law or any act of human kindness (such as burying the body of an unknown person), since all moral laws are regarded as derivations of God's commandments.

modernism A late 19th- and early 20th-century intellectual movement within the Roman Catholic Church that sought to reinterpret the church's teachings in the light of contemporary philosophical and scientific thought. It was formally condemned by Pope Pius X in 1907. In the Protestant churches, modernism usually refers to acceptance of literary and historical criticism of the Bible and an emphasis on ORTHOPRAXIS rather than ORTHODOXY.

orthodoxy Correct teaching or doctrine.

orthopraxis Correct practice or conduct, as distinct from doctrine or belief.

parachurch organizations A collective term for interdenominational groups that began in evangelical Protestant churches in Britain, Australia, and the United States and presently devote themselves to social welfare, education, and evangelism. In the United States, the best-known parachurch organizations are InterVarsity Christian Fellowship, the Navigators, and Campus Crusade, which form Bible study and fellowship groups at colleges and universities. Other parachurch organizations have opened homeless shelters, food pantries, disaster relief programs, and study centers. The term *para-church* is derived from the Greek and means "alongside the church."

Pentecostalism A movement within Protestant Christianity characterized by an emphasis on the gifts (charisms) and present activity of the Holy Spirit in the church, on holiness of life, and on emotional expressions of faith, including speaking in tongues.

pluralism In religion, pluralism usually means the acceptance of the reality of religious diversity in society and the need for an attitude of tolerance and mutual respect. It is also sometimes used to refer to the belief that society benefits from diversity and that it should be promoted. Pluralism should not, however, be used as a synonym for ECUMENISM.

polity A specific form or system of church government. The three main types of polity in the Christian churches are episcopal, presbyterian, and congregational.

postmodernism A general term referring to a group of developments in art, architecture, literary theory, philosophy, and other fields that emerged in the late 20th century in reaction to modernism. It is also sometimes used to refer to a rejection of the modern acceptance of reason as the measure of all things that developed during the Enlightenment or to a rejection of any absolute value system.

proselytizing The act of seeking to convert a person of another religion (or of no religion) to one's own. Christianity and Islam are proselytizing religions, whereas Judaism is not. The word *proselytizing* often carries negative overtones, and it is not always easy to draw the line between evangelizing or bearing witness to one's faith and intrusive proselytizing.

Rapture When capitalized, the word refers to the belief of some Christian groups that God will take some believers up into heaven before the Second Coming of Christ, while nonbelievers will remain on earth before the end time. The New Testament verse usually cited as the basis for believing in the Rapture is 1 Thessalonians 4:17.

reconstructionism ***(Christian reconstructionism)*** A theological and political movement within one strand of Calvinism in the United States that urges Christians to put their faith into action in all areas of life, including civil government and cultural productions. It envisions bringing civil law into line with the moral standards of the Old Testament as summarized in the Ten Commandments.

religious Zionism An ideology that bases Zionist beliefs about the importance of Israel for the Jewish people on religious tradition rather than secular nationalism. Rabbi Abraham Isaac Kook is generally regarded as the founder of the religious Zionist movement, which took political form in Gush Emunim.

restorationism A belief held by some dispensationalist Christians who reject *supersessionism*. Restorationism is the belief that at the end of time, God will visit the Jewish nation, and there will be a large-scale conversion of Jews to Christianity. It should not be confused with the belief that the present-day church is the replacement of the Jews as God's chosen people.

saffronization A term used to describe the rewriting of Indian history to fit the assumptions or preconceptions of HINDUTVA supporters and other extreme Hindu nationalists.

schism A split or division within a group. In religion, it is used most often to describe splits within Christian denominations, although it can also be used to refer to the division between Sunni and Shiite Muslims. Schisms may result from a variety of political, ethnic, linguistic, liturgical, and other factors; they are not always caused by disagreements over religious doctrine. A person who initiates a schism or belongs to a split-off group is called a *schismatic*.

sect A deviant religious organization with traditional beliefs and practices. Most sects are offshoots or subgroups of major religions and are held together by charismatic leaders.

sedevacantism The belief, held by an extreme group of Roman Catholic ultra-traditionalists, that Pius XII was the last valid pope, that his successors were either excommunicated or improperly elected, and that the Roman See is therefore empty. The term comes from the Latin phrase *sede vacante*, which means "vacant see."

Sephardi *(plural, Sephardim)* A Jew of Spanish, Portuguese, or North African ancestry.

sharia The Arabic word for Islamic law, which is held to regulate all of life; thus, sharia covers business contracts and social matters as well as religious rituals and obligations. The main sources of the law are the Qur'an, the HADITH, applications of previous rulings to new situations, and the consensus of the ULEMA.

supersessionism The belief that the Christian church is the replacement or fulfillment of God's promises to Israel and that, therefore, Jews who reject Jesus as the Messiah have failed their calling as God's chosen people. The Roman Catholic Church and most mainstream Protestant bodies have renounced supersessionism; many fundamentalists, however, still hold the doctrine.

theocracy In its literal meaning, a system of government in which God is the head of state. The term was first used by Flavius Josephus (c. 37–101 C.E.), a Jewish historian, in order to explain ancient Israel's government to non-Jews. *Theocracy* is also used as a description of government by officials who are regarded as divinely guided. The term should not be used to refer to a state church or as a synonym for civil religion.

Third Temple A holy building not yet constructed that is the focus of the religious hopes of some fundamentalist Jews and Christians. Several organizations in Israel are making preparations for its eventual construction on the Temple Mount in Jerusalem. The First Temple, sometimes called Solomon's Temple, was built by King Solomon around 950 B.C.E. and destroyed by the Babylonians around 586 B.C.E. The Second Temple was built on the same site around 515 B.C.E. and stood until 70 C.E., when it was destroyed by the Roman army sent to put down the Jewish revolt that had begun four years earlier.

Torah The Hebrew term for "teaching" or "law." It refers most often to the first five books of the Hebrew Bible (Old Testament): Genesis, Exodus, Leviticus, Numbers, and Deuteronomy, sometimes called the five books of Moses, or the Pentateuch. *Torah* may also be used to refer to the scroll on which the five books are written, used in synagogue services, or to the entire body of Jewish law.

ulema ***(ulama)*** In Islam, the body of trained clerics or teachers of Islamic law, SHARIA. Members of the ulema are not priests in the sense of having special sacramental powers or spiritual status.

voluntarism ***(voluntaryism)*** The principle or practice of supporting churches and other religious institutions by voluntary contributions from their members rather than by state subsidies derived from taxation of the general population.

yeshiva ***(plural, yeshivot)*** An Orthodox Jewish academy or school of higher instruction in Jewish learning. It may enroll older students from all walks of life who wish to learn more about Judaism as well as prepare some for the rabbinate.

Index

Page numbers in **boldface** indicate major treatment of a subject. Page numbers followed by *f* indicate figures. Page numbers followed by *b* indicate biographical entries. Page numbers followed by *c* indicate chronology entries. Page numbers followed by *g* indicate glossary entries.

Index

Index

Index

Index

Index

V

W

Y

Z